This is for my mom and dad, who set my compass for this journey.

TABLE OF CONTENTS

VERY
FINE
FINE
FINE
FINE
PEOPLE

VERY FINE FINE FINE PEOPLE

Confessions of an American Fool

A.R. MOXON

ESSAYS, 2016-2023

VERY FINE PEOPLE

Confessions of an American Fool

Collected Essays: 2016-2023

Copyright © Andrew Moxon, 2024

All Rights Reserved

1st J. Goat Press Printing: June 2024

Grand Rapids MI

The Reframe

armoxon.com

ISBN: [979-8-9899949-0-8]

ISBN [979-8-9899949-1-5] (eBook)

Library of Congress Control Number: 2024907684

Designed by Marina Drukman

10 9 8 7 6 5 4 3 2 1

A catalog record for this book is available

from the Library of Congress

VERY FINE PEOPLE

(April 2023)

This is not the proclamation of an expert. This is the confession of a fool.

Maybe I should explain.

◆ ◆ ◆

I WROTE all the words you'll find between these covers sometime between December 2016 and early 2023. Most were written after August 2017, which was a key date in my rapidly dawning awareness of the true nature of my country. August 2017 is when tiki-torch waving Nazis invaded Charlottesville, Virginia, in defense of treasonous confederate slaveholders and their own perceived supremacy. We know they were Nazis because they were chanting "Jews will not replace us," and "blood and soil," and all the other Nazi hits, and because they believed in Nazi causes and utilized Nazi symbology, and so on.

August 2017 was also when the White Christian president defended those who marched with the Nazis as "very fine people." I call him "the White Christian president" because the people who support him are overwhelmingly understood to be a specific thing known as "white," and overwhelmingly identify as a specific thing known as "Christian," and the White Christian president made quite a show over the years of representing U.S. citizens exclusively based on whether or not they support him.

And, no doubt, there were white Christians who marched in the Nazi invasion of Charlottesville (titled "Unite the Right" by its organizers) and these were the "very fine people" toward whom the White Christian president gestured, to make the case that the pro-Confederate cause—which celebrates traitors who murdered their fellow citizens in order to preserve the institution of chattel slavery—shouldn't have the rightness of their position questioned, simply because of the apparently coincidental direct allyship of overt Nazis.

And there were those who noticed that the White Christian president's words amounted to a defense of the Nazis, and this act of noticing this observable and obvious truth offended his mostly white Christian supporters to no end. The presidential defenders drew a distinction they found important: he was very clearly not defending *the Nazis* who were there, he was defending all the *other people* there, who were *not* Nazis. The very fine people didn't chant the Nazi slogans, I suppose; they just marched in the same crowd, and for the same basic cause. They must have heard the chants, but one must assume they had invented different reasons to march, and different causes. This was the distinction. We are meant to find this distinction meaningful.

But I knew better then, and I imagine you did, too. The White Christian president's words were clearly meant as a defense of the Nazis, because the presence of the very fine people did what it always does whenever very fine people find common cause with Nazis. Nazis and Confederates and Christian nationalists and other authoritarian supremacists only ever rise on the permissive shoulders of masses of very fine people willing to lend their moral authority to a monstrous cause— yes, and their energy, too, and their normalcy and niceness and well-scrubbed politeness, and their deliberate unawareness as regards the methods and intentions of those with whom they march, and yes, their Christianity, too—because how could a *religious* person ever support atrocity if they did so out of a *religious* conviction? Their very fine presence in solidarity with monsters defends and enables the monstrousness.

I find myself thinking a lot about them—the very fine people.

They're *my* people. I am somebody deemed "white." I was raised Evangelical Christian. When the White Christian president made a show of representing white Christians exclusively, it is people exactly like me that he meant. In August 2017, the White Christian president, like all cheap hucksters, knew quite well which lies people would believe, knew quite well what lies his people wanted to hear, and knew quite well the lies they depended on for fortune and identity.

So he told the lie of the very fine people.

It's a popular lie. It's a traditional lie.

For most of my life, to one extent or another, I believed it.

And so I am a fool.

◆ ◆ ◆

Once upon a time, and for most of my life, I believed in the very fine people of America—by which I mean I recognized that there were people who disagreed with me about politics, but I also believed that what most mattered was what we all had in common, without considering who was excluded when *we* said "we." And it must be admitted, we're all mostly very *nice* people. Meet us, you'll see. Most are nicer than me, I'd say. Very capable. Friendly. Volunteer in our churches, many of us. Give to charity. Some of us *form* charities, and some of those charities do really wonderful things, whose effects can be shown on a flowchart. We mow our lawns. We pay our taxes. We work hard. We love our kids. If you have a flat tire on the side of the road, we'll help you out. For example, take me. I am *a pretty nice person*, most of the time, and if I see you have a flat tire by the side of the road, I will be happy to hold the hub cap level and not spill the lug nuts while a more capable person than me actually helps you, while making vague affirming sounds and hoping you don't notice my lack of basic mechanical ability. I want to be sure you know, in case you didn't grow up among white Christian evangelical conservative Americans, as I did, that most of us aren't pretending. We really are very nice, very kind, very generous. We are, by these and other measures, very fine people.

This made me think that fascism would be unpopular, particularly with people such as us.

It made me believe that white supremacy was defeated, specifically *by* people such as us.

And so I am a fool.

My parents were Christian missionaries, so I grew up in another country. It had been called the Belgian Congo for years and years. It was called Zaire when I was there. It is called the Democratic Republic of the Congo now. It was pillaged for a century by Belgians, and when the Belgians were kicked out, the people of Zaire elected a man named Patrice Lumumba, and the rumor was he had socialist leanings, which means that he wanted the wealth of the country he led to benefit the people in that country, and this made my country very uncomfortable, so we sent the CIA there to stage what David Robarge called in his 2014 paper *CIA's Covert Operations in the Congo, 1960–1968: Insights from Newly Declassified Documents,* "a series of fast-paced, multifaceted covert action operations" which represented "the largest in the CIA's history up until then" and "comprised activities dealing with regime change, political action, propaganda, [and] air and marine operations . . . ." And somewhere in there Lumumba was murdered by somebody for some reason, and was replaced somehow by a kleptocratic monster named Mobutu Sese Seko who *did* continue to pillage the country, but who did *not* have rumored socialist leanings, and who was *not* murdered by somebody for some reason. Perhaps it was coincidence that a rapacious dictatorial pillager of resources avoided a (rumored) socialist's fate, and was not overthrown and tortured and killed like Lumumba. Instead of experiencing all that, Mobutu ruled for decades, as he robbed all the riches for himself and his country fell into further ruin, but remained, as Robarge puts it, "a reliable and staunchly anticommunist ally of Washington's until his overthrow in 1997," and so my country—which is the United States of America—was comfortable once again. Anyway, that's where I grew up: in one of the most naturally rich and unnaturally impoverished places in the world. My father was a doctor. My mother is an educator and a nutritionist. They were there to try to make a dire situation somewhat less dire for the people nearby, and I think they and their colleagues did, and I'm glad about that, and it cost them a lot, and I'm less glad about that, but that is perhaps a story for another day.

When my family returned to the United States, the contrast in wealth and resources and infrastructure and ease and overall stability and available opportunity was stark. Somewhere in there my parents appear to have instilled in me some basic sense of the truth of the matter, but certainly most other available sources explained to me—both in words and in millions of silent assumptions—that this disparity existed not because a rapacious dictator had been placed in charge of Zaire through the self-serving actions of my country, but because we were uniquely blessed by God, and/or because our country is, was, and always has been The Greatest Country In The World. This made sense to me, by which I mean there was no real challenge to the narrative, and nothing much transpired as I grew up to shake my confidence in these received assumptions. My parents and my experiences did furnish me with a compelling sense that a society ought to care for those in need, and that all people deserved equal representation, and that inequalities in society ought to be corrected. And these weren't controversial things to believe back then.

Yet there was still some room for disagreement. In my orbit were those who held that our society was already perfectly and unimprovably equal, and so anyone who now suffered, or experienced need or lack, did so not because of inequality, but only because of the regrettable but natural results of their own poor choices—and therefore any attempt to further improve our already perfected society represented unnecessary governmental overreach, and any attempt by the government to care for those in need represented dangerously destabilizing and unjust theft, and any talk of a collective duty to care for anyone who had been overlooked or to support the demands for justice of anyone who was still marginalized represented divisive and polarizing rhetoric. I debated these people, because I disagreed with this somewhat . . . but our political differences didn't concern me much. We might argue, but we certainly wouldn't think any worse about one another or assume bad intentions or a fouled moral compass, over what was really just a *political* difference. And anyway, though I could clearly see that some inequalities existed, I assumed they would be eventually and automatically corrected, like racism had been corrected, back in the far distant past—in the late 1960s, seven years before I was born, when the CIA was active in the Belgian Congo.

Some people were conservative. I was liberal.

Some people were Bulls fans. I was a Pistons fan.

Those were about equal values to me.

I spent the summer after my freshman year of college working for my mom's co-worker's husband, who owned and operated a roofing business. This meant I mostly worked with my mom's co-worker's husband's brother, whose name might have been Tim, so let's call him "Tim." Every day, Tim listened to that famous rodeo clown of the airwaves, Rush Limbaugh, who had been gifted with a big bellicose voice that commanded attention, and who used that gift to call feminists Nazis, and Hillary Clinton a baby-eater, and Clinton's 12-year old daughter an ugly dog. Rush—who we eventually learned was a drug addict—liked to proclaim that drug addicts were all criminals who should be punished severely, and that impoverished people were all lazy and should be punished severely, and that people who believed that it was a society's responsibility to care for those in need were all fools who hated America and wanted to destroy it, because they were evil people who wanted evil things and could not bear the sight of goodness. Every day Rush treated us to these and other comedy bits, and he was paid millions and millions of dollars for using his gift that way, and so the hours passed easily on various rooftops around my hometown. I thought Rush was nuts and his jokes were cruel, but I also considered him mostly harmless, because who would actually take such a person seriously? Maybe Tim thought that way, too. We never talked about Rush or the things Rush said. Tim sure did want to listen, though, and I sensed it was going to be easier and more comfortable to just listen along than to argue with Tim about Rush, so that's what I did. I assume Tim kept listening in the years after that summer I spent roofing. It's not clear to me when people stopped laughing at Rush and just started nodding, or if they were all nodding from the beginning, because I wasn't paying attention, and all the people I knew were very fine people, and we were the greatest country in the world, and I had faith in that.

This faith was shaken in the aftermath of September 11, 2001, as I watched our frightened country get lied into a disastrous and criminal multipronged opportunistic war, and I couldn't help but wonder at how effortlessly so many of us were able to metabolize the steady flow of damning information about the lies that had fueled those wars, how seamlessly they welded the contradictory available information onto their previous belief structures, leaving their support for the damned liars at our nation's steering wheel completely unaffected. I had to wonder how it was that they hadn't noticed certain things that were becoming unignorable even to coddled little me about the bigotries in our country and how many people clearly supported them, and about the way inequalities did their harm whether or not you supported them or even acknowledged them. And I had to wonder at how many fringe bigots were positioning themselves as Republican and Evangelical Christian leaders, and were met with—if they were met with anything at all—only the politest of remonstrations, the merest 'ahem' bookended by calls for unity in the church despite our *political* differences. I began to suspect the day was coming when the Republican Party, and the Christian church that supported it, who had for so long played wink-and nod politics with authoritarianism and white nationalism, would find that their ability to play both sides against the middle was no longer tenable, that they would be forced, by the preferences of the very voting base they had been cultivating, to run somebody who was an open white supremacist and fascist.

I was right about that.

I also saw very clearly that this would at last be a bridge too far for all my very fine people. I was certain that they would finally see the truth of what they had supported, would finally turn away, that the Republican Party would be lost in the wilderness for an age, until it was finally willing, after decades of pushing an anti-human worldview, to change and grow and rejoin humanity.

I was wrong about that.

The white supremacist arrived, and he couldn't have been a bigger cartoon farce: Donald Biggestbest Trump himself, rodeo clown of all rodeo clowns, a man you wouldn't trust to feed a soft-serve ice cream cone to a stray badger, much less lead a country. And the very fine people—*my* very fine people—went for him. I watched some of them posture at opposing him— an opposition that mostly focused on their discomfort with his grotesque tone and crude behavior—but that was in the early days, when they still thought, as I did, that the idea of such a man actually becoming president was preposterous. As soon as it became clear that he was indeed to be the Republican standard-bearer, I watched them each, one by one, with only a handful of exceptions, drop their diaphanous hankies of performative opposition and stand before all of us exposed, proudly wearing their new emperor's clothes, willingly bowing before their gobby golden calf. Willingly? Enthusiastically. It was a growing enthusiasm. It was almost as if people who had been waiting for permission to embrace authoritarianism had finally been given it. I watched as the white evangelical Christian church in the United States—the tradition that raised me—revealed itself as the enthusiastic, sustaining, energetic, rapturous force powering a successful, openly white supremacist, authoritarian, fascist political movement, led by a pig of a man, an incurious narcissistic fool without a single redeeming quality. And I watched, as those within that religious tradition who were uncomfortable with this reality set themselves to the work of keeping comfortable relationship with those who had embraced fascism, even if it came at the expense of their relationship with those who were menaced by it.

This was the rapidly dawning horror for me as 2015 bled into 2016: the understanding that this—*this*—was not only what my very fine people were willing to go along with, it's *what they had wanted all along*. This was the anointed one they'd been waiting for, the pain messiah they'd finally summoned to hurt the people they wanted to see hurt, to control the people they believed it was their natural right to control, and to protect themselves from their growing fear that they and their comfort would no longer be treated by American power as supreme. The answer to the question "what outrages against humanity will white evangelical Christians in the United States tolerate?" proved the same as the answer to the question "what proofs of its own inhumanity will white Christians in the United States look the other way to avoid knowing?"—which is to say, anything and everything. What I learned was this: the moment of falling away won't ever come, not because very fine people don't see the disastrous and unsustainable course we've set, but because they perceive some advantage within it for themselves, and so have decided to decide that the course is good.

Not just good, but *goodness*.

Not just right, but *righteousness*.

Not just a way of living, but "our way of living"—a phrase in which the most interesting word to ponder is "our."

What is *our* meaning when *we* say *our?*

Who do *we* mean when *we* say *we?*

We sure don't mean everyone.

And then Trump won the election, and my already-crumbling world broke. I sat that night in the dark, watching the results come in, not knowing what to do, feeling menaced and nauseous, and understanding that a lot of people were feeling far more menaced than me; because unlike me, they had never been considered *we*; because unlike me, they were going to be under an even more direct and targeted threat, now and for the foreseeable future. The overwhelming thought I had was this: "A lot of people are going to suffer and die because of this, and the people who voted for this know it, and knowing it makes them feel happy and safe." And also came the inescapable gnawing recognition that this had always been the case, and it was only now, with this shock to my comfortable system, that I was finally seeing it.

And I was right about that.

That election night, I didn't know what to do. Eventually, I began to do what I could. You bring what gifts you have to the moments you find yourself in. If I am anything, I am a writer. My skill, humble though it may be, is to present ideas that other people already know but cannot name, using language that names it for them. I'm told this is encouraging, to know that somebody else feels that way too, and helpful, enabling a more constructive way to think about those ideas. Sometimes I'm not bad at doing this, so that is what I did, and I published some of it online, where it found an audience. You'll find some of it in here, a bit cleaned up from the original publication, along with some previously unpublished additions.

More specifically, here's what you'll find between these covers:

In the months after the 2016 election, while still reeling from the permanent demolition of the reality I'd known, and the betrayal of every fine principle I'd thought our nation represented by institutions and people I'd thought trustworthy—I wrote an essay called **Sky**. It was my lament. It ended with as much hope as I could muster, along with a call to my fellow very fine people, a call to those who I had believed were better than they had proved themselves to be. It was a call to work to prove that they could be as good as they insisted they already were. Six years later, that invitation is still open, but it has to be admitted that *we* have collectively proved *ourselves* to be even worse—more gleeful in ignorance and cruelty, more toxic in intent, more destructive in action, far more willing to construct vast moats of unawareness between ourselves and the inconveniences of caring about other human beings—than even the most jaded newly awakened fool would have dared believe.

Near the end of the first year, in 2017, I posted a series of essays called **Bubbles**, naming what I perceived to be the terrible lies our nation has been founded upon and concluding with what I perceived as our role in the world, which is to live as good stories, as works of art. And I still believe this today...though after witnessing the response of our institutional structures to the atrocities of the ensuing years, I wonder what else might be required of us, if we are to defend human art from those who seek to destroy it.

More recently, I wrote a series called **Streets**. It was begun in the year before the 2020 election, continued through that election and the violent (and still ongoing) attempt to overturn it, and finished while the outcome of that election was still in hazard, in the aftermath of a still-impending insurrection, with

Trump out of office but at his liberty, his party entirely in his thrall, his fascist vision being pushed with all tools at their disposal. It was my attempt to answer the question *how did we get here?*

Most recently of all, I published a series of essays in my weekly newsletter, The Reframe, which represent most closely where I am now. I'm collecting them here in an edited and restructured form, in a series called **Spirit**. They're about where we've arrived, and how we got here, and where I think we should go from here if we're interested in survival as a nation and a species—an open question, I realize. It's my attempt to answer the question *what do we do now?*

The things printed between these covers are things I've learned recently, but they aren't things recently true. Only my awareness is new. Maybe yours is, too. There are others who've known all these things, and more besides, for a long time. How long? Their whole lives. They've been telling us about it all along, and *we* haven't heard until recently. I have to conclude *we* haven't wanted to know.

We? I.

I haven't heard until recently. *I* have to conclude *I* haven't wanted to know.

These things were always obvious to many people in this country.

So please remember, this is a fool's confession.

If you're one who has been wise to these matters your whole life, I hope my words honor your experiences, and I sincerely apologize for all the ways they will fail. This book represents my progressing awareness, my ongoing attempt to contend with the country I'd failed to see, and figure out what sort of person I want to become, as I reconstruct myself and my shattered worldview. Perhaps you will find my progression interesting, too, in the manner of watching a baby deer learn to walk.

And if you're a fool like me, still reeling even years later from new knowledge of old truths long known, my hope is that this will help you. My hope is that my story is familiar, and that these essays will put words to *your* story, and that having words to put to your story will help you tell it. My hope is to demonstrate how my frame has moved over the years and put words to my slow discovery—about what is broken, and how repair might occur, and what sort of person to try to become in the aftermath of painful new awareness—and then to give an idea of how we might create unlikely but necessary change, how the frame might be moved for others, too, for more and more, in our nation and in our world.

So here goes.

SKY

(December 2016)

PERHAPS this will be hard to read. Laments often are. It may bring you comfort, or it may make you angry. It may make you think more of me, or less. It may offend you. Rest assured it offends me.

So be it.

Once upon a time, there was a man who spoke of torture as a good in itself, to be pursued whether it was effective or not. Who promised to use the power of the state to enact violence upon scapegoated religious and ethnic minorities. Who praised himself for nursing petty grudges, for treating revenge as justice. Who threatened the press with retaliation for reporting certain truths about him. Who bragged about sexual assault. Who mocked people braver than himself, and called their bravery weakness. Who lied seemingly without strategy, as if lies were good to tell only for the telling. Who showed a shocking indifference to the very concept of truth. Who praised brutal dictators for their brutal methods. Who seemed (and seems) to be receiving shadowy support from one of the brutal dictators he admires. Who claimed (and claims) dictatorial power for himself.

He appeared entirely confused about the basic facts of geopolitical reality, or of how our government works, or even of the function within our government of the office he proposed to hold. He had a clear and obvious history of fraud and hucksterism, of enriching himself at the benefit of others with less leverage, and was even engaged in a lawsuit for defrauding college students, which he settled for $25 million. He speculated with frightening casualness about destabilizing actions: proliferation and even use of nuclear weapons, defaulting on our debts and our treaties, backing out of our most long-standing alliances. He whipped his crowds into frenzies, then directed their ire toward journalists reporting the events—many of whom he threatened to prosecute once in power. He threatened to imprison his chief political adversary, to the delight of his chanting crowds, who wore t-shirts decorated with vulgar and threatening slogans of hatred and violence and rage. He promised to steer us directly into the deadly heart of oncoming climate catastrophe. He sneered at the very idea of sustainable and renewable energy sources. That's a short list, and incomplete. It's a hell of a short list.

But wait, listen: Tens of millions of people went for it.

Tens of millions of people voted to make him the most powerful man in the world. He will soon have the ability to blast the planet to an irradiated cinder, if he sees fit. He will continue to run his business, which appears to involve sitting in a golden throne and putting his name on things. He's given every indication, despite some laughably thin feints toward divestment, that he will run that business from the Oval Office. Maybe he'll even put his name on new things, like laws. Laws: a whole new product line, and a potentially lucrative one. He owes the banks of foreign powers millions and millions of dollars. One wonders what laws they'll want passed.

His party is in control, too. Its members don't seem bothered by any of this. They're a bit more focused on enforcing checks upon ethics watchdogs who have pointed out their party leader's multifarious and historically unprecedented infractions. They'd rather ignore those, so they can immediately—*immediately*—

get down to the serious business of divesting millions and millions of the most vulnerable people in our society from the only chance they have at affordable health coverage. They plan to replace this program with something...someday. The musings we've heard so far suggest they will be replacing it with the opportunity to save up hundreds of thousands of dollars to pay for medical bills if you need them someday, or, if you don't have hundreds of thousands of spare dollars, to maybe go screw yourself. So, a lot of people are going to die in the coming years, who would otherwise have lived, and the party is rushing to make it happen, and their mood is exceedingly celebratory. Meanwhile, they're ignoring as peccadilloes the caricatured infractions of a man who expounds provable lies, and then when exposed simply doubles down on the lie, a man who is considering throwing the press out of the White House and other maneuvers straight out of the dictator handbook. It's really something to see.

It's hard to understand what people hoped for from him other than this. It's hard not to assume they were responding to the shockingly frank bigotry, his promises to return to an earlier time, the knowing use of slogans employed by racists and fascists of days past. These certainly seemed to generate the most applause. But I don't want to think that of my country or my fellow citizens. I really want it to be something else.

Let us consider other possibilities.

Many seem to think that a great thing about him is his frankness. They liked that he "tells it the way it is." Then again, a lot of the most popular examples of "telling it like it is" are things that aren't true at all, and the same people who seem most likely to believe his appeal lies in his frankness also seem most likely to believe that he doesn't really *mean* his more shocking proposals. It's a bit confusing, then, parsing what is meant by "telling it like it is," since it appears to rely on selective trust in his insincerity, and a belief that "the way it is" involves many things that *aren't*. Many voters, excited by

promises to "drain the swamp," but now disappointed by signals the new president has given suggesting an eagerness to
rob us all (like recent declarations that the president-elect
will nominate a Goldman Sachs foreclosure kingpin to Trea-
sury and a Putin-connected oil executive to State), have been
admonished for taking his words so literally. For what it's
worth, the alt-right, the neo-Nazis, and the KKK are very
excited about his more shocking proposals, and they remain
confident our new leader meant every word.

Some people thought he would be less likely to make them
pay more in taxes, I suppose. So perhaps at last now we know the
answer to the old hypothetical about whether we'd be willing
to travel through time and sacrifice our lives to prevent the rise
of a self-professing tyrant. Answer: We wouldn't even suffer a
hypothetical increase in our income taxes.

I'm told folks voted for him because they were tired of being
called racist. I imagine that *was* hard for them—who wants to
be considered racist? If this complaint is yours, I imagine reading this is also hard. I sympathize; it's not particularly easy to
write. But then again, voting for an open racist seems an odd
response to the complaint. And, perhaps, if it is painful to be
considered racist, consider this: it may be even more painful to
live under racist oppression.

Many seem to have mainly enjoyed that he wasn't Hillary
Clinton, and it's certainly true to say many concerns and crit-
icisms could be levied against her. But the man they voted for
as an alternative already stood actualized as the cartoon parody
of any potential danger she may have hypothetically posed. Bad
judgment? Corruption? Fraud? A proclivity to violent retaliation? A worry about temperament? Untrustworthiness? Lack
of transparency? Hard to believe this list of concerns would be
yours, but your acceptable alternative would be this man.

Or maybe they believed the more lurid stories, the debunked,
the ridiculous. Hillary murdered 80 people close to her. She

invented cancer and put it in your cell phone battery. She is secretly seven tiny demons all stacked up in a pantsuit and glued together with the blood of aborted fetuses. She controls the Yosemite super-volcano, along with a cabal comprised of George Soros and 17 other Jewish industrialists. I don't know what all. I know there are people like this, who have seceded from objective reality into a dystopian alternate dimension, where they can perhaps supplement the powerlessness they feel in their lives with the comfort of false control, of being one of the few with the secret knowledge unavailable to the masses. I don't know what to do with them, because they live in an alternate dimension.

Anyway, here we are. In grave moral and physical danger. All of us. And for what?

I've heard the same line again and again since the election: "America isn't a different country today than it was before the election." Jon Stewart trotted it out. I think I heard it from President Obama. I fear I agree with the statement. I'm puzzled, though, because I think it is meant to be reassuring, to think we've always been the country capable of such a choice.

To me, this statement doesn't imply that we're still great.

It implies that we were never good.

It has to be admitted, people responded to him for what he is. Which means we are left with the statements and proposals by which he distinguished himself. And millions of us—*tens* of millions—*preferred* him specifically for those points of difference, either excited by his promises to return us to a time when our system existed only for the benefit of certain people, or at least willing to overlook those promises, in favor of some material or policy advantage. And ultimately, the reason is immaterial. A man ran for president promising to use the power of the state to bring violence to scapegoated religious and ethnic minorities, to make America torture again, to make it easier for an already-militarized police force to employ violence, who praised dictators, who bragged about sexual assault, who praised vengeance as good, who promoted debunked conspiracy as fact, who stated his determination to ignore as conspiracy what the data overwhelmingly indicates is an oncoming global catastrophe. There was some other reason to vote for him, that allowed you to overlook these facts?

Save it, please. The reason really doesn't matter. It was a bad reason. We've seen this before. History has a word for Germans who joined the Nazi party, not because they hated Jews, but out of a hope for restored patriotism, or a sense of economic anxiety, or a hope to preserve their religious values, or dislike of their opponents, or raw political opportunism, or convenience, or ignorance, or greed. That word is "Nazi." Historians study and learn from their motives, but there is a broad understanding: their motives aren't exonerative. They joined what they joined. They lent their support and their moral approval. And, in so doing, they bound themselves to what came after. Who cares any more what particular knot they used in the binding?

What am I saying here? Am I saying we are Nazis? The answer, I suppose, has to be "no." Nazis are Nazis. We are Americans. But what that will mean in decades to come—"American"—has been thrown into hazard. I had thought I lived in the sort of place that doesn't allow Donald Trumps to happen. That seems an impossibly naïve thing to believe now, as does any sort of trust the world once had in us. Democracy, like history, reveals our intentions by our choices and our actions, not our claims.

We are what we are. And Donald Trump will be president.

As a result, I'm bereft. Bereft of the country I thought I was living in. Bereft of the people I thought I lived among. Bereft of what I believed was a shared direction, despite divergent opinions. Bereft of a belief in the possibility of a common dialogue or even a common reality. Bereft of the spiritual heritage I was born into, because of *course* Trump's most enthusiastic supporters are white Evangelical Christians. Christians voting for a new Herod to hold the power of a Caesar is a pretty good joke for the universe to tell, I suppose. He's even promised to go after the (anchor) babies.

My translation of the Bible is full of all this toff about loving your enemy, about how love of money is the root of evil, about showing hospitality to the widow and orphan and the immigrant, and admonishments against drawing the sword lest you die on it. My copy of the Bible tells me not to worry about money; it doesn't ask "but who's going to *pay* for that?"—it tells us the cost is paid already. My copy of the Bible tells me that if you wish to pretend to care about babies unborn, maybe you shouldn't be so hostile to the idea of making sure they're cared for once they are born and inconveniently and expensively needy, and perhaps you shouldn't make so many of their mothers into the welfare-queen antagonists of your narratives, and perhaps you shouldn't make weaponry a right more important than health and food. Maybe healing and wholeness and liberty is something that should be available to even the pagan. Maybe the door should be open for the undocumented immigrant. Maybe I got a trash translation. Maybe the other Bibles are all about the joys of using political power for your own aggrandizement instead of the call to self-sacrifice for the benefit of others; maybe they're about the dangers of anchor babies and welfare mothers, about how paying tax money toward a shared life is tyranny, about how with terrorists you have to kill the families, folks, believe me, kill the women and children, you've got to go after the families, and we're gonna torture again, folks, we're gonna torture, believe me . . . .

You know what?

I do believe him.

◆ ◆ ◆

You wake up and the sky is gone. At times that's how it seems. You wonder at it: How could there not be a sky? What will become of us now, in this world without a sky? Was it ever there, or did we just imagine it there, as an exercise of collective will? And then you talk to other people who insist the sky is there. They say: It's not gone, it's just red now. Don't be a sore loser, just because you didn't want it red. Accept that we *did* want it red. It'll be *fine* if it's red. Move on with your life and suck it up, butter-cup. But the sky isn't red. It's not anything. It's just . . . *not*. It is a not-ness. An un-sky. A nothing.

And then you start talking to people who laugh, not without compassion, that you ever fell for the idea there was a sky. They say: That big vast emptiness? Oh, yes. That's always been there for us. Is it there for you now? How . . . interesting. We can tell you a thing or two about that emptiness, if you'd listen. We've been watching it an awfully long time.

The sky is the future. Or it was the future. That's how it seems, at times. How odd, to speak of the future in the past tense. But the past tense presents us with further troubles. It seems the past is gone, too.

Growing up, we were taught that we were a kind and good and just country. The story we were given was of a nation born of a righteous cause, not quite made perfect by the godlike men who forged it, but honed to apotheosis over the decades that fol-lowed. The destruction of the Native nations and their people, ah, tsk, a shame, we'd change it if we could, but unfortunately that's all in the unrecoverable past. Slavery, a dark stain, but by now expunged entirely. Jim Crow, slavery's shameful cousin, absorbed by a saint named King, who led a boycott (a pleasant and polite and non-disruptive one, it seems, in our memories), then stood on some stairs to give a universally admired speech about his dream of inclusion, and then, his work seemingly ac-complished, having seemingly changed minds forever, ascend-ed harmlessly into the clouds.

Somehow we are never culpable. It was always a long time ago. Mistakes were made, but we'd never make them ourselves. It was always somebody else holding the gun, the whip. We ar-

rived here *after* that, you see, born blameless, without any af-
terbirth or shock, into the greatest country in the world. Our
genocides we absolved ourselves of, because they served to illus-
trate not the evil we'd done, but how far we'd come from it. We
stood on the prow of the ship, looking forward as we cut new
water, not aft looking back at whatever may have been churned
up in the wake. Not big on the rearview mirror, us, not fans of
the over-the-shoulder glance, unless it was to imagine ourselves
into those stories set in those times, making ourselves the protagonists. We would have been the ones to build false walls in
our home to hide slaves. We would have marched with King. We
would have spoken out against the Japanese camps. We would
have stood at Stonewall. Our moral arc bends ever toward justice; an inevitable thing. That was the story. America was already
great, because it was always good. Sometimes you'd hear stories
about a random injustice or brutality. A policeman who had
become a little too enthusiastic—a bad apple, and surely justice
was served, because you'd have heard about it in the papers if
it hadn't been served. A gay teen beaten to death in a cornfield.
A car displaying a banner celebrating a war to preserve human
slavery on its bumper sticker. The KKK marching again, how
quaint. Ah, you'd think (if you were like me), we still have some
minor work to do. Cleanup on aisle seven.

Technology has changed some of that. We see with new eyes
now, unless we choose not to. We see videos, dozens and dozens
of them, new ones each week it seems, of police shooting unarmed Black people again and again and again and again. Can
you remember all the names? I can't anymore, or maybe more
accurate to say I don't. And I ask myself: why can't I? It seems an
ignorance I have chosen, but also the choice feels like one that I
was optimized to make: as if the sheer number of names created
is in effort to convert the names to numbers, to turn people into
a trend. We see the speed with which so many seem willing to
seek and find the nearest handy reason the victim deserved his

or her fate. We see the news organizations find a Sunday School photo to represent the shooter and a mugshot to represent the victim. We see acquittal and acquittal and acquittal. We see failure to prosecute.

And, perhaps, we begin to wonder.

We see the people protesting, unarmed, asking only that their lives be thought to matter as much as another's, and we see the stormtroopers with their massive guns and their tanks, arrayed against a civilian population almost reflexively, like defenses in an organism's bloodstream mustering against a disease. And we wonder, perhaps: why do they look so much—so exactly, if we're honest—like an occupying force?

We see the white ranchers seize government land, pointing their guns directly at law enforcement officials, speaking openly of armed insurrection against the government, of revolution, of war. We see them, later, seizing a government building. They aren't protesting after centuries seeing their children and brothers and sisters killed without consequence by authority. Rather, they don't want to have to pay a grazing fee. Is it with surprise that we notice it: law enforcement is seemingly less frightened of these white men and their guns than they had been of an unarmed black woman in a sundress, or a 12-year-old boy playing in a park? Were we surprised to see police so level-headed in this far more dangerous situation, so much less likely to escalate, so reluctant to respond with immediate lethal force? Why, those fellows with their arsenal didn't even get convicted. They were less threatening to the system, apparently, than a man, arms up, lying on the ground next to his autistic ward begging not to be shot. (He was shot.) We might contrast all of this to the treatment of the Native protesters at Standing Rock, and wonder . . . is the genocide against Native people relegated only to the past? Would we change it, if we could? We might wonder: Are we seeing the system breaking down, unable to cope with new challenges? Or are we seeing a system working exactly as always intended? Do we as a collective of white people actually secretly want the police to control brown people by force? Are we quietly hoping that force will prove lethal, sporadically enough to soothe our consciences, but frequently enough to promote an order less immediately costly than the pain of culpability or the justice of restitution? Or is it not so secret, not so quiet, and thinking it was so is merely the product of listening selectively?

If not, why are prosecutions so rare, and convictions even less so?

If not, why aren't we protesting these killings? Why aren't we in the streets?

Do all lives matter? If so, why wouldn't we act like it?

Why don't I remember all the names?

These are things we might wonder.

◆ ◆ ◆

White Christian America reveres Dr. Martin Luther King Jr. almost as much as it reveres Donald Trump, it should be noted. You remember him—the peaceful universally admired guy who gave the speech that ended racism. If Facebook and newspaper op-eds are any measure, we white Christians can't stop bringing him up, almost as a cudgel, an admonishment to those today who would dare demand their own human dignity, for not issuing their demands as antiseptically as *we* remember it being done by Dr. King. And perhaps a Christian like myself, deemed "white," might begin to wonder: Why was King enshrined as the peaceful one only once he was peacefully dead? Is King's being safely dead *our* favorite thing about him? These days, we white Christians can claim to have brought his dream to reality, and Dr. Martin Luther King Jr. will not protest—and we white Christians don't like protest. Heavens, no—it's so *divisive*. Dr. Martin Luther King Jr., he wouldn't have approved of *this* protest, nor *that* one, and certainly not *that* one, and now that he is dead, we can establish ourselves as proxies for his disapproval. His protests were so polite! Why, nobody had any problem with them at all! Dr. King agrees with all of us in white Christian America so much, these days. Oh my, he never stops agreeing with us. Just ask us; *we'll* tell you. Yes, and what ever happened to Dr. King, anyway, after he gave that speech that ended all inequality forever? We white Christians, opposed to justice's demands, don't seem to ask that one as much.

No matter, I told myself. That's a dying strain, it's not who we are these days. That's just a few bad apples. We've made so much progress. They'll exhaust themselves in a final futile sputter. We're just about to turn the corner. Sure, there are racists, bigots, white supremacists, lost-causers, and they're loud, but they're dying out, and they know it. They'll eventually run somebody on an overtly racist platform, and they'll lose huge—I disagree with Republicans, but most of them won't stand for stark white supremacy, surely, and *obviously* Christians won't be able to align themselves with it—and we'll show them it's no use, and they'll retreat, retrench to positions even more compromised, less fortified, further back, smaller, diminished. We're a better country than that.

But then Donald Trump, a half-rate and transparently obvious bullshit artist, a greasy reality TV star most skilled at demonstrating his manifest ignorance, promising mostly the goodness of violence and the strength of vengeance, offering to return America to an earlier time, railing against the inconvenience of practicing sensitivity toward the perspectives of others, received 63 million geographically convenient votes to become the most powerful person in the world. Perhaps, if you're like me, you took a moment then to ponder that statement about bad apples and what they do to the whole barrel. And, perhaps, if you come from a Christian background, you remembered another saying, about recognizing a tree by its fruit. And, it must be said, though we refuse to face it: In America, our trees have long borne a strange fruit.

Here's what we've lost, or at least what I've lost: The assumption of goodness' inevitability. The assumption of the goodness of those around me. The assumption of good intent in their hearts. Here's what I've lost: The wool from my eyes—the one favor Donald Trump may ever do for me. An illusion, particularly a pretty and a convincing one, can be a painful thing to lose. I've gained a vision of tens of millions of people desperate to bend history's arc back toward an injustice that unnaturally favored them, and willing to fight for that regression, willing even to risk species-wide extinction rather than suffer the pain of facing the consequences of their own mountainous indifference. The moral arc of the universe may bend toward justice, but the gears of history grind the weak. There are people now who are giddy, almost with the air of a teenager behind the wheel of a sweet-sixteen hot rod, to test out their perceived new warrant to deliver retributive and violent indifference to the people they deem unlovely. A headscarf yanked off here. A slur shouted in public there. A swastika scrawled on a wall here. A Nazi propagandist advising the president of the United States in the corridors of power there. A crowd of sieg heils in a government building, in praise of our new leader here. A few million children stripped of health insurance with no serious attempt at a replacement there.

They think this is allowed now: the Nazis, the white supremacists, the Christian nationalists. Sixty-three million people, complacently or enthusiastically or ignorantly aligned with white supremacy, gave them the idea it is.

It's going to be our job to show them otherwise. We *must* show them otherwise.

And.

Even if you voted for Trump—*especially* if you voted for Trump—the door is wide open for you to join in that struggle.

You show them otherwise, too. All you have to do to join...is join. Your intentions were good? Excellent. I believe you. I've badly misunderstood you? Excellent. I believe you. Now, show it. Show your good intention by your good actions.

You, like all of us, possess tremendous moral authority. Don't lend it any longer to those who have promised to squander it on atrocity. They seem intent on doing as they say. If you wait too long, they will leave you with none left to withdraw. Use it instead to protect those different than you. Use it against your own advantage, for the advantage of those who have none.

And.

If you, like me, did not vote for Trump, there is the great danger of complicity. You will be offered, if you, like me, are "white" and straight and employed and well-off and cis-gendered and able-bodied and healthy and property-owning, the opportunity to be indifferent. Resist that current. If the universe bends toward justice, the engine it has chosen for this good work is the hard and sacrificial struggle of good people willing to acknowledge the basic humanity of all other people. People who don't think profitability is the foundational metric of goodness. People who don't think life holds a value that begins at conception but ends the moment it enters poverty. People bold and willing to become pebbles in the gears of oppression. To give time and money. To link arms with a married (or unmarried) gay couple. To take sides in a cafeteria skirmish with a trans teen. To take a truncheon in the head for a Muslim. To paraphrase Jesus (another favorite who those of us in white Christian America appear by our words and deeds to consider as safely dead as Dr. King): to live, first you must die. Or, as another poet says, love's the only engine of survival.

So, what's next?

First, we lament. We acknowledge the un-sky, the void. We listen to those who've been staring at it far longer than us. We name the challenge with clear eyes. And then we get to work.

Let us hope our leaders will prove other than they promise to be. Let us not be so naive to think it likely. Let us oppose in a fierce and broken love. Let us meet with friends, and eat good meals with them. Let us consider people before money, and notice where our society fails to do so. Let us make art, and try to make it well. Let us refuse to allow a comfortable silence to enfold a hateful or ignorant statement. Let us stand up against hate, bodily if necessary. Let us learn our system, and work within it. Let us call our leaders, and advocate for those who suffer. Let us practice generosity without care for the merit of the beneficiary, but only for their need. Let us investigate before we publish. Let us loudly proclaim the humanity others try to diminish. Let us loudly proclaim the humanity of those who do not share our values, even as we oppose them. Let us never celebrate the suffering of those who oppose us, for they suffer, too. Let us seek to divest ourselves of unearned cultural advantage. Let us enter spaces where our voices are not primary, and listen without thinking to speak. Let us create space to speak, in places where our voices are primary, for those who have had no voice. Let us reject false optimism. Let us embrace a reckless hope.

Let us work.

Let us work.

Let us work.

We are a people who have dreamed of the sky. I'd like to see if we can make it real.

FRAME

BUBBLES
(August 2017)

1. ART

I find it useful to begin with art.

When we think of art, we think of something holding value, not first for its utility, or its economic or military worth, or its ability to facilitate commerce or to drive profit, or even its aesthetic beauty (though art may possess these qualities), but simply from its being; a value springing from the mere fact that it is an expression of something that would not otherwise exist.

Art is valuable simply because it *is*.

So, too, with human beings. Every human being is a unique and irreplaceable work of art, carrying intrinsic and unsurpassable worth.

That's worth repeating.

Every human being is a unique and irreplaceable work of art, carrying intrinsic and unsurpassable worth.

Suppose ethics were an exercise in determining the most important priorities between competing values. If that were true, it seems to me that whatever value was prioritized highest would define that culture in ways both visible and invisible, in ways that would be immediately observable if somebody were to encounter that culture, in ways that would be endlessly uncovered if that culture were scrutinized. Suppose we decided that, for any ethic to be truly moral, it must take as its primary priority the life and dignity of every human being, because we understood that any ethic taking any other value as its top priority would, inevitably, arrive at barbarism. That's where I choose to set my compass. The life and dignity of every human being should be the top priority of our ethics, and the bedrock of our assumptions about what is important and good. It should be the foundation of our politics. It should inform our economics. It should guide our rhetoric. Any other tool, quality, value, or principal that comes into conflict with this priority, no matter how good it might be, must be subordinate to this primary one—because every human being is a unique and irreplaceable work of art carrying intrinsic and unsurpassable worth—which I've noticed is a popular thing to *say* you believe, but it's an unpopular thing to *truly* believe. Human beings who ascribe to this idea tend to practice it only conditionally—both about others, and about themselves. I've known this. I've *done* this.

But I've also known this: There have always been those who openly reject this idea, those who have chosen to place themselves above art, who act as ruthless curators, who insist that only *some* people are unique and irreplaceable work of art carrying intrinsic and unsurpassable worth, and then only if they exist within certain expected parameters. Humans falling outside this narrow range of preference present themselves to these curators as problems to be solved, or as raw material to be used, and these curators understand exactly where best to stow unworthy human material so that it will no longer offend them; they've become expert in systems that will use human beings as if they were a resource.

Those curators—white supremacists, predatory capitalists, religious hucksters, nationalists—were always distressing to me; they gained their advantages where they could, and enacted their unfortunate intentions on their targets, but it was my belief that their advantage was slowly decreasing. Now, however, the curators are moving ruthlessly, and quickly, without subterfuge. Their intention is to harm those already harmed, to marginalize those already marginalized, to reclaim their birthright of being not just the *most*, but the *only*. These people, who intend to replace others with a vacancy they think will leave more of everything for themselves, do not want to be replaced, and they'll tell you so. They use the language and tactics of white supremacy, of Jim Crow. They appropriate the signals and slogans of Nazism. They don't see much value in the arts—which perhaps helps explain their attitude toward the art that each human being represents, and perhaps explains why the art they most wish to preserve are totems publicly honoring traitors who fought a war to expand and preserve mass human enslavement, and why they refer to this art as their history and their heritage. They have exposed themselves for what they are, these curators of human worth, and their supporters have not abandoned them. Their supporters think they are just fine. They're supportive, enthusiastic, even delighted. The fear and dismay of the rest of us energizes them.

As a result, I'm not all right these days.

I'm frequently enraged. I store a lot of my rage in discrete 280-character buckets on social media, but sometimes it overwhelms me, and I pace my house, delivering devastating rejoinders to imagined adversaries. I'm frequently filled with joy at the simplest things. Basic kindnesses. A story of a person helping another person. A story of bravery. A story of sacrifice. A reminder of what human beings are—which is art. Some tiny affirmation of our unsurpassable worth will spring up and startle me with its immediacy. Each moment seems more precious these days, each person I meet seems more beautiful. The art of human beings can be ignored or denied, but its quality will inevitably show. I cry at movies more now. I cry at concerts. I never used to do that before. I go on long runs through adjacent neighborhoods. Everywhere I go, I see yard signs that hadn't been there last summer. IMMIGRANTS ARE A BLESSING, they tell me, and SCIENCE IS REAL, and HATE HAS NO HOME HERE and WHEREVER YOU'RE FROM, WE'RE GLAD YOU'RE HERE and BLACK LIVES MATTER and KINDNESS IS EVERYTHING. It seems many of us feel compelled to say these things, which we'd previously thought to be assumed. These signs are everywhere, everywhere.

Except...they're not *everywhere.*

It's understandable they aren't in every yard—everyone expresses themselves in their own way—but, very evidently, these sentiments are not in every heart. I know now for a fact there are millions of others who believe very much the opposite. Who will fight against those things, and who very much resent being scolded or even reminded about them. The signs don't remind me so much of what we all think, as they remind me of what we all apparently disagree about—and they are the most basic possible statements of decency and awareness, so obvious as to seem childish, almost puerile. I find myself increasingly uncomfortable in crowds, particularly crowds that skew demographically in favor of our political lurch toward white supremacy and kakocracy. We seem to be at a tipping point, where our politicians feel safe in their jobs even while telling lies for which contrary video evidence exists, in order to pass legislation that will bring about the inevitable bankruptcy and suffering and death of thousands, of tens of thousands, of millions. We seem to be at a tipping point, where the idea that objective knowledge is desirable, or even exists, may be called into question, and the best minds of history and science might be scorned in favor of badly spelled memes from sweaty conspiracists. We seem to be at a tipping point, where those who would like to speak the language of mass extermination feel free to test these ideas outside the laboratories of their own twisted imaginations. We seem to be at a tipping point, where people will either decide that these things are unacceptable and must be fought, or else are the acceptable new state of things. Polling evidence suggests that white people, especially white Christians, are undiminished in their enthusiasm for all this barbarism, undiminished in their hopefulness that it might pass into general acceptance.

I go to church. My church is a large one, full of white Christians. I know many of them well, and many of them sort of well, and I recognize even more. They're good people, committed to bringing measurable change to marginalized and oppressed people. I'm sure of it. I'm positive. In the parking lot, I see a bumper sticker.

The sticker says TRUMP.

You can say a whole lot of different things to a whole lot of different people with a single printed word these days, in a world of ICE raids and shredded environmental regulations and militarized police forces and proposed Muslim bans and trans bathroom bills and racial voter suppression and military bans and eager proposals to strip health care from special needs kids and the elderly and . . . well. The list, as they say, goes on. You can really get a lot done with a single word. I'm not in a single one of the groups targeted, so if I feel as if I'm falling down an endless hole when I see that TRUMPer bumper, I ask myself . . . how does it strike someone who *is?* I find myself wondering: who else feels increasingly uncomfortable in crowds? Who else has *always* felt uncomfortable in crowds?

I spend time wondering what I believe about basic things. When so many seem so intent on the warehousing and destruction of so much priceless human art, disorientation seems inevitable. When the story you told yourself about your society's innate momentum toward decency turns out to be a comfortable myth, uncertainty seems the one certainty. I used to trust my country, and the people in it. I don't trust either anymore, or my own judgment, either. And then, there's this: The people who want to effect these rough changes, and the people who seem comfortable with them if they are enacted— they are human beings too. And every human being is a unique and irreplaceable work of art carrying intrinsic and unsurpassable worth. Even if they themselves fail to recognize this, I must honor this truth about them.

I wonder what to do with that. I think about it all the time. How to confront this? How to win this debate humanity is having over its own soul? How to effect a change in the other direction? How to practically oppose? How to persuade? How even to communicate in a basic way to others who have accepted for their own ethic a grounding reality I find unacceptable?

How, anymore, to *be*?

My conclusion is this: It is not going to work to win the current debate. It is rather going to be necessary to reframe the terms of the debate—to insist on a great reframing—until we are having a different conversation entirely. In fact, I suspect we need to decline most debate as an instrument of change. A debate won does not appear to change a heart or a mind. It's not even a debate *won*, really: In an age when people choose their own facts based on their existing assumptions, people choose a debate's winner ahead of time, too, based on those same assumptions. And debate has never really been a tool for changing hearts or minds. A tool for conversation, perhaps; education and edification, maybe; not change. Debate is at best a tool for sharpening the mind, for organizing thoughts. It's the whetstone, but it isn't the knife. When used to persuade, it is at best a bludgeon.

What changes minds, I think, is story.

A story well-told is good. Even better is a story well-lived. It seems to me many of our old stories don't work anymore. Maybe they did once, and to the extent that they did, it is appropriate to honor them for that, but I don't think it's going to be appropriate to go on telling the old stories in the old ways. We put too many lies into the telling, and the truths in our stories have not been ones we've been frequently willing to live. We need to go to work on telling a new story, or, perhaps, exhuming an even older and forgotten one which insists that human beings are art—not to defeat the old story point-by-point, but to simply refuse the old story on the merits, and to compel human spirits with the new. Once we've become good at telling it to ourselves, we need to start telling it to others. Who knows? It might even work.

It's 2017. I am trying to find a new way to exist in the world, with my new understanding of what my country is, and what so many of the people who live here seem to believe. This represents my attempt, such as it is, to do that.

It has been useful for me to have written it.

I dare hope it will be useful for you to read it.

So: first frame, then spirit.

2. DIVIDE

I read a fair bit, over this long warm winter, over this crisp clear summer, about what the meaning of the election really was. I read that it represented the end of "identity politics," and I learned that "identity politics" is a term which seems to mean "voting for somebody who is not a white man," while "voting for a white man" is apparently an act that has nothing to do with identity. I read that it was time for us all to unite behind our new president, but little of what that unity would entail. I read that if he succeeded, we would all succeed, a sentiment that seemed unconcerned with the question of what, exactly, he considered success, or at what, precisely, he intended to succeed. I read that it meant we all need to spend a lot of time thinking uncritically about the fears and needs and desires of specific demographics of voters, and stop focusing so much on the fears and needs and desires of all other people from all other demographics, because our divisive focus on all those other demographics is what had driven that one specific demographic—aggrieved white voters—to such an extreme course.

Our news outlets—who got their election coverage wrong—are scrambling all over themselves to teach us, their presumed liberal audiences, what we all got so wrong about the election. They're huddled up in rural diners all over the country, talking to people who voted for Donald Trump, and in so doing they're managing to teach the rest of us many valuable lessons. From all this important journalism, I have learned that I am in a bubble, and that it is part of my job to get out of that bubble—a very important task, apparently. I've learned that there are people who are "regular" and "hard-working" and "working-class," and I've learned that these terms exclusively indicate aggrieved white voters, and that understanding this fact will be part of getting out of my bubble. I've learned there are many reasons these regular hard-working working-class people voted for Donald Trump, reasons having little to do with the many and varied fascist and hateful and violent things he promised to en-act and that they cheered for, which he continues to promise to enact and which they continue to cheer for, and that it is now my task to discover what those things are, and support those things, and exonerate all the Trump voters without asking them to change in the slightest, and that these acts of understanding and exoneration are part of getting out of my bubble. I've been given to understand that the tone of rhetoric among those who oppose fascism has become much too sharp and hectoring. I am now tasked with finding a tone much more conducive to comity with people who seem to have no interest in comity, and that this work is also part of getting out of my bubble. I've heard there are two sides to everything, and that it's very important to consider and respect and understand and publish both sides, by only ever considering or respecting or understanding or pub-lishing one of those sides, and this is part of getting out of my bubble. Most of all, I've read a lot about how *divided* we are as a nation—the most divided we've been in over a hundred years. I've learned there has been far too much *scolding* about inclusivity and fairness and equality and kindness, and resentment over this scolding has fueled this political seismic activity, has created and exacerbated these fault lines, and prised apart the tectonic plates of our political body. I've learned it is my job now to reach out and mend this divide, and doing this is part of getting out of my bubble.

What I *haven't* heard is anything about how all the people who Donald Trump and his party threatened and attacked and continue to threaten and attack are going to stop being threatened or attacked if I do any of that.

I haven't heard anything about how, if I choose to move on, those who continue to live under the constant dread of promised menace and violence and bigotry are going to be able to move on. Moving on doesn't seem to be an option for them. Compliance with newly proposed laws appears to be more the order of the day for them. Getting press-ganged out of the country appears to be their new role; that, or else being barred from entering it, or else facing imprisonment for crimes disproportionately enforced in their neighborhoods, or being vilified for protests against brutality, or facing cruel retaliation for standing up against injustice, or living in fear that their skin or their dress or their customs will lead to either threats of violence or else the genuine article. Nor have I heard how my reaching out to mend the divide is going to protect millions of people— including those who voted for Donald Trump and his Republican Congress—who rely on access (often only recently acquired) to health insurance and health care, who now face the very real possibility of losing that access, and suffering or even dying from a treatable malady. I haven't heard anything about how all these people are going to be protected from the effects of the intended Republican strip mining of load-bearing girders of our social infrastructure, which provide relief to many who might otherwise have suffered, and allow many who might otherwise have died to live, whose funds will now be used to further enrich the already wealthy. I haven't heard anything about how any of us expect our grandchildren to live on a planet that is swiftly tilting toward uninhabitability. All the healing and mending and understanding, it seems, now needs to be performed by marginalized and threatened people, on behalf of powerful and comfortable people who continue to threaten them. And doing this, it seems, is how we get out of our bubbles.

I can't help but wonder why that should be.

It's worth pondering why every call for civility is issued for the benefit of those who have dedicated their lives to incivility. It's worth pondering why every call for healing centers on those who have done the harming. It's worth pondering why the people who cry the loudest about our divisiveness and political incivility never direct their laments at the people who elected a corrupt and mean racist bully. So I'm thinking about bubbles, and about our nation's great divide. But before progressing, let's move the frame a bit. Let us think about justice and order. And let's think about priorities.

◆ ◆ ◆

Some people talk about **justice** as a primary value.

Others talk about **order**.

We could define these two terms any number of ways, and arguments between those definitions could make their own essay. Best to settle on some definitions, then. For these purposes, let's take *order* to mean **"a system which, to the best of its ability, maintains itself with consistency through any attempted disruption."** This is the quality that allows us to assume that tomorrow will follow the same rules as today. It supports the sort of predictability that allows both society and individuals to make and enact projections and plans. It is the soil from which can spring innovation, growth, wealth, stability, and comfort.

It's good. Order is *very* good.

Now, let's take *justice* to mean **"the extent to which a system recognizes and ensures, to the best of its ability, the essential dignity, equal standing under the law, and basic physical and spiritual needs, of all human beings."** This is the underlying bedrock upon which the soil of order rests, which, when perfected, is smooth and level, with none afforded systemic advantage over another and none systemically robbed. Thus, justice defines the shape of order—that is, if order is just.

It's good. Justice is *very* good.

It's worth repeating that both order and justice are good and necessary things. I personally am not a fan of disorder. I dare hope we can all get behind justice.

The question is: which is most important?

It's an important question.

I'd observe that human urges that we might traditionally call "evil" aren't usually a product of creativity or innovation. Indeed, in my own religious tradition, "evil" is often understood to involve not brand new things that are evil, but rather corruption of existing things that are good, by degrading them down or elevating them up out of their proper places. Take prosperity, for example. To prosper is good. It can be *very* good. But when prosperity becomes more important than questions of whether your prosperity will cause people to die who might otherwise have lived, then prosperity—a good thing—has become badly corrupted.

It's putting the second thing ahead of the first thing.

It's letting order define the shape of justice.

I think it's good to think of things like *evil* in this way, if we believe people are art. We choose our priorities, and as our priorities inform our beliefs, we can take on the corrupted and inartful shapes of our bad assumptions. We might later in moments of clarity glimpse the forms our bad assumptions have caused us to take and fail even to recognize ourselves anymore, and in such moments, we may pause to wonder how we arrived there, and attempt to change; or else we might deny the truth of what we have become, might become resentful, might wonder how other people could possibly understand us to be something we have through our actions manifestly proven ourselves to be. That's what makes this all so insidious. Human art corrupted by bad priorities and assumptions will remain art, and some measure of innate goodness inherent to their humanity will still be observable. Those who intend great injustice can always retreat to some island of inherent human goodness from which to defend themselves.

Here is the defining frame I propose: The chief priority among all competing good things is recognizing and ensuring the inherent dignity, legal equality, and basic human needs, of all human beings. Justice, in other words. This is a justice founded on the idea that every person is a unique and irreplaceable work of art, carrying an intrinsic and unsurpassable worth. It is, crucially, a justice with its foundation in love. I submit that a casual observer can tell a lot about a society by observing how, when, and why it prioritizes justice over order, or order over justice. If a society is unjust, an insistence on a more perfect justice is not going to view the natural disruption to order that restoring justice will bring as a bad thing. Not because the society hates order, but because it has determined that order must first demand justice—otherwise it is going to be an ordered injustice, a terrible order not worth the cost it will levy upon the soul and conscience. But if a society prefers order above justice, it's going to focus on the particulars of the existing rules that support that order, with little consideration as to whether or not those rules establish justice; and those who prioritize order are going to ignore and suppress and dismantle any rules that do not support that unjust order. Not necessarily because they hate justice (though some clearly do), but because they recognize that establishing a more perfect justice will necessarily require a great disruption to their desired order, a terrible price they deem to not be worth the cost to stability and prosperity.

And so some will prefer *equality and justice for all.*

And some will prefer *law and order.*

And the difference matters. It matters a lot.

In a perfected system, law and order would be exactly the same thing as justice. A peaceful order resting upon a system that is completely just is a great aspiration, if an unattained one. This sort of perfected justice and order would mean nobody is being assaulted, or robbed, or starved, or sleeping without shelter, or exposed to tainted water, or made unwelcome in public spaces or public life, or harassed, or barred from equal treatment under the law, or expected to accept less pay for equal work, or forced to accept pay that does not allow them enough upon which to live, or otherwise abused in any other way. It would mean that any rules or actions making such abuses likely or inevitable would be ended, with consequences enforced for infractions—consequences which restore essential human dignity and provide basic human needs to the victim, while still maintaining and protecting human dignity for the perpetrators.

This sort of justice would require a great deal of honesty and deliberation and probity and intention and hard work and willingness to change. When such a society found injustice within itself, it would need to be willing to submit itself to the hard and costly work of correction. Cost is something we would all prefer to avoid, but avoiding cost, while important in its right place, is not more important than justice. Thus, a society preferring justice to order would be willing to pay the price to do the good work necessary to dig up the soil of order, so it might repair the fault lines in justice's underlying bedrock.

But a society preferring order to justice would greatly resent any finding of fault.

And in an order-preferring society, one might ask: Why point fingers? Why create "us versus them" narratives? Why not just accommodate the people already being accommodated?

Pointing out fault lines of inequality is so polarizing... it's so *divisive*.

A preference for order over justice represents a preference to cover over fault lines with new soil, rather than to address the underlying imbalance. It is a desire that insists order and justice are already the same, without doing the hard and costly work to make it so; meanwhile, it allows a favored elect to continue reaping massive advantage from the unjust order, and even— provided they are ruthless enough—to strip away the covering soil, to work at adjusting the fault lines to restore injustices already ameliorated, to Make Past Injustices Great Again. Let us not forget, there are categories other than those who prefer justice to order, or order to justice.

For example: There are those who prefer *injustice* to either justice *or* order.

Abuse still does exist, and so does cruelty, and so does corruption.

We're not *always* dealing with a competition between two good things.

Allow me to suggest that, when there is a great divide between those who prefer order, and those who prefer justice, the resulting divide is a clear indicator that the undergirding system over which these people contend is deeply, fundamentally, abusive and unjust. Allow me to suggest that the greater the divide between those who prefer order and those who prefer justice, the more abusive and unjust the existing order of that system is likely to be, and the more likely that the actual preference is not for the order, but for the injustice. This suggests to me that these calls for civility may not truly be motivated by a desire to see ideological bubbles popped, but preserved. Is the person who is confronted with an uncomfortable truth about themselves and responds by changing the one in the bubble? Is it the person who responds with resentment and retaliation the one who *isn't* in a bubble? Really?

If I am one who prefers order to justice, it may seem to me that those who demand justice are saying that order is bad and should be destroyed. But even if I fail to understand what they are saying, I will notice that they are opposing me. I will become aware of the divide. It may well be that the great contentions of our great divide are the only indication complacent people will ever perceive that the order they support is unjust, and that their support of it makes further injustice not only likely, but inevitable—that their support of an abusive order is what enables abuse. It may well be that the great contentions of our great divide are the only thing separating an abusive system from those people the system is designed to abuse. It may be that unity, while a good thing, is not more important than justice. It may be that before we decide if unity is appropriate, we must ask what it is we intend to unify around. And it may well be that our present great divide, rather than being the problem we must solve, is actually a very, very, very good thing.

I must confess, I've lost my patience for those who save their first tears for the divide rather than its causes.

3. SPIRIT

So let's ponder bubbles.

Here is what I think a bubble is: a mirror that won't let you see yourself; an invitation to perceive the world through a distorted and self-reinforcing lens, which hides from view a belief you'd rather not admit you hold. I think this is what was meant in all the newspapers, too, in those articles reporting from rural diners, the ones that told me I'm trapped in a liberal bubble. What I gather from the overall tenor of these articles is that I didn't realize that people *really like* Trump, or that these people who like Trump really exist, or that the reason they like Trump usually involves resentment at a world that they believe doesn't care about them. I find these conclusions odd, though, because I, like pretty much everyone else, actually knows all those things. Maybe those were the things that the people who wrote the articles didn't know, and now they—still not letting themselves know that they were the only ones who didn't know—are telling us that their bubble is ours, while reporting on people in middle America as if they are a novel new species they've just discovered.

But they're not *all* wrong about me; I expect I *am* still trapped inside many bubbles, as I'd daresay is most everyone else in my orbit. The luckier you are in life, the more illusions you can afford to give yourself, so my guess is I don't even recognize the bubbles I'm still in. But there's one bubble I'm aware of, even if I'm not always entirely free of it. I'd even call it a "liberal" bubble, which should please those journalists out on safari in local diners. What *I* mean by a "liberal" bubble is a belief that the system is fundamentally sound and self-repairing; that all those who operate within it might be misguided but are fundamentally well-meaning; that sins of the past have no bearing on the reality of the present; that justice is a thing that will happen inevitably, automatically, and incrementally, simply by defending our existing order. I suspect a "liberal" bubble popped late last year for thousands or millions of us. When it popped, many self-professed liberals took a look around, and saw, clearly, and perhaps for the first time, that there is a malignant spirit alive in our country, which has captured the hearts of a large and growing portion of our population.

Every spirit I've ever observed wants something—whether it's for the team to win the game or for the mission to be a success, or to make sure that nobody who is hungry gets food without establishing that they've earned it. I've been pondering our malignant spirit for some time, and I think I understand what it wants.

What the malignant spirit that has captured us wants is this: genocide and slavery.

Literally. Genocide and slavery.

◆ ◆ ◆

Wait.

Did I just say people literally want *genocide and slavery?*

Not exactly.

I think we've all learned by now that there exist some deeply twisted people who actually do want these things, and that they appear to be far more numerous than we thought, but no, I don't believe most people literally want genocide and slavery. However, we are captured by a *spirit* that encourages people to accept propositions that make slavery and genocide inevitable, a *spirit* that entices people to find reasons to accept and flatter those who truly want those things, a *spirit* that convinces people to protect order while cultivating a deliberate and practiced incuriosity about what malicious effects that order creates, a *spirit* that harbors active hostility against any inquiry into those effects, against any voice speaking of harm done, against anyone listening to such voices, a *spirit* that literally wants genocide and slavery.

Genocide and slavery. That's quite a claim.

Stick with me; I'll try to show you what I mean.

Let's start with what I mean when I say *spirit.*

I find it useful to think about these struggles in terms of spirit—a term I think is widely misunderstood, because its use by specific religious traditions and dogmas frequently leads people to believe that talking about *spirit* means engaging in those traditions, even believing in supernatural events and beings. No. My background is a religious one, but you don't need a religious grounding to understand what spirit is, and you don't have to believe in supernatural beings, either. I'd actually argue that "spirit" is something that is widely understood and widely observed. Here's how I would define it: **Spirit is what happens when groups of people create a collective belief and translate that collective belief into systemic action.** Through spirit, humans create what is possible and not possible—create, in other words, the endlessly mutable form of reality that we might refer to as "the way the world is."

We talk about the *spirit of the law* as something distinct from *the letter of the law*—the way a law can be written to do one thing, but is often used, because of applied collective human will, to do a different thing. There's what the law *says* (or even what the people who wrote it intended) and then there's what it actually *does*, which reveals the deeper intentions of those who carry it out and perhaps benefit from that enforcement.

That's spirit. Completely apart from religious context, we call it spirit.

And we talk about *team spirit*—the way that a group of people can come together to achieve goals beyond what might have been expected of them given their experience or talent...or the way a team can fall apart and fail to achieve objectives that seem as if they ought to have been easily within their grasp.

That's spirit. Completely apart from religious context, we call it spirit.

Or we talk about how something is done *in a certain spirit*— a spirit of joy, a spirit of generosity, a spirit of anger, a spirit of violence. It's a way of saying that different people can do the exact same thing while making it clear they're doing it for very different reasons.

It might help to think of spirit as atmospheric, because like spirit atmosphere is invisible but observable, and also inevitable. If something's in the air, you're going to breathe it. If you want to stop breathing it, you have to change the atmosphere. It's also non-optional. Pull the atmosphere away, and something else will take its place. Take atmosphere away entirely, and human beings won't survive. That's what I think of when I say human beings are *spiritual.*

Spirit is the thing we're all in, all the time.

So, if you need unlikely change to happen, spirit is the thing to change.

◆ ◆ ◆

One reason I find "spirit" such a useful frame is that it helps us understand that we are, at the core, fighting against malicious *ideas*, not malicious *people*—which is not to say that there are no malicious people, or to deny that some people have made themselves contemptable through their adherence to malicious ideas; nor to say that the fight against malicious ideas will not mean setting ourselves in opposition to those contemptable people, and in solidarity with people harmed by those malicious ideas. It's only to say that at the core, the issue is not a matter of individual people, but a matter of atmospheric spirit. People gather, and they join their belief to something, and that belief leads to collective and individual actions, and those actions start exerting actual real-life effects, and eventually create a context for what is and is not permitted, worthy, valued, or even possible. Spirit creates something more powerful than individual belief or individual intent, and while it might seem mysterious, it's very real and observable. Spirit is, quite simply, how human beings make things happen at a societal scale, which has a direct impact on what your options as an individual even are. Think: What can you do independent of the context of what humans do collectively? Try. Try reacting to this essay completely individually, without using any of the systems and developments and philosophies that human beings have made together over the centuries. Try to imagine the humans who made those systems and developments doing so without the use of previous developments advanced by those who came before, or without acting against those developments to change them. It's a silly suggestion. You can't do it. I know, because I wrote these words within that context, and they were delivered to you within that context, and you learned to read within that context, and also how to think, and also what an "essay" is.

Again, I use "spirit" because I think our problem is a matter of spirit. People who have committed themselves to inhabiting false alternate realities have created their own complicated logics to support the realities they have chosen, and have access to their own informational superstructures that will reinforce those choices in perpetuity. So, while the cause of justice is logical and reasonable, I doubt it is logic or reason that will save us. I've learned that the opportunity to explain clearly observable things to people demonstrating a persistent and ongoing determination to not observe those things is not a particularly effective use of energy. What is needed are changes in the core beliefs of millions, new answers to fundamental questions of what is good and what is true and what is most important.

And that's an atmospheric change—a *spiritual* change.

Spirit it is, then.

This spirit gripping our nation is... bubbly. It creates many bubbles. It offers many temptations to not know things we'd rather not know. One of our great temptations now is to think that this spirit of fascist supremacy we see manifest in Donald Trump and his movement is a new spirit, rather than one of the animating forces of our national character, burrowed deep into our history, nestled near the heart, tendrils threaded throughout the body politic, contracting, expanding, regressing here, invading there. Another of our great temptations is to imagine that this spirit has exclusively captured *them*. It *has* captured a lot of "them," this spirit. That has become clear to thousands and millions of "us." It's also clear to us that most of "them" don't know it. "They" are in bubbles, and want us to rejoin "them" there again. And that's the greatest temptation of all.

If you're like me, you often *want* to rejoin them. It's comfortable in there. It's not nearly as troubling. And then, sometimes, if you're like me, just when you think we're free of our bubble, there comes another "pop," and people once again look around to learn that once again, we have been joined with "them" all along, captured by our nation's malignant spirits, believing that justice is a thing that's delivered to the doorstep without any effort on our part, gazing into mirrors that don't let us see ourselves. And perhaps "we" express our shock at this realization in clumsy and angry and hostile ways that "they" find deeply offensive. But "they" also find that the simple fact that "we" see it this way is itself deeply offensive. "They" don't see it that way at all. And "they" are angry and offended, and complain of uncompromising attitudes, even as "they" refuse to compromise on anything. And "we" mourn, because "they" are still our friends and family.

They're not bad people, we tell ourselves. They're not evil. We *know* them. They're often integral parts of our lives. When we need them, they're there. They care about us. We care about them. And the truth is: They *aren't* evil, mostly—not as evil as commonly presented and understood. They might even have friends—real, actual friendships—with people who fall into categories they propose to harm or neglect as a matter of spirit. They might even be willing, given proper criteria and circumstances, to sacrifice time and resources to help people within these categories.

All of this is both important to remember and entirely beside the point.

The reason it's important to remember is that it's true, and we're hopefully committed to truth. The reason it's beside the point is this: They joined with a spirit that wants genocide and slavery, and we are fighting that spirit. And foundationally, we're fighting the spirit, not them.

The question, I think, is one of alignment. Are we aligned

toward a justice with its foundation in love? Or are we aligned toward preserving an order that has selected some other thing—likely some other good but less vital thing—as its primary guiding priority?

I think of a compass.

The compass determines the direction. The direction determines the navigation. The navigation determines the course. The course determines the path. The path arrives at the destination. That's the order—but it starts with the compass; the directional imperative. To set the compass wrong means that even if you arrive at your destination, it will be a bad destination.

Let's think of the law.

Law, conceptually speaking, is a good thing, I think. It would be difficult to imagine that any sort of justice could be achieved without application of just law. We might think it wise, then, to make the law our compass. But if law is our compass, we will only be as just as our laws can be—and we won't meet the challenge of changing them when they fail. In fact, we won't even recognize them as having failed, because they, being our compass, will be the realized end, and a purpose in and of themselves, and it's terrifying to consider what atrocities law-oriented people will permit, provided the atrocities have the proper permits. It's a generally understood thing that an action can be deeply unjust, even if it is lawful, while breaking the law can be fundamentally and heroically just. Martin Luther King was thrown in jail for demanding justice in ways deemed illegal. Joe Arpaio was legally pardoned for running unlawful concentration camps in Arizona. If we petition solely to the law for questions of morality, it seems clear we will fail to arrive at justice.

Or, let's think about something in the news in recent years, something that is very popular with liberals. Let's think about *means testing.* Means testing is a way of constraining some public aid to make sure that only those who need it receive it...which seems eminently sensible, but there's a spiritual problem. Making sure that everyone hungry is fed is an urge that springs from a spirit of generosity, of plenty, of care; a spirit that believes that every person has intrinsic worth and dignity that must be honored. Making sure that only those who *deserve* food receive food, or that those who haven't *earned* food should receive less food, or food of a diminished quality, springs from a spirit of lack, of control; a spirit that believes that life must be earned, and that receiving basic needs is a matter of deserving them. This can seem counterintuitive, because the purpose of means testing *seems* to be to prevent people of means from improperly accessing resources meant for those without means. But when we means test, we create administrative and structural hurdles that wealthy people can easily overcome; hurdles that force people without means—the very people meant to receive the aide—to spend time and energy and maybe even money they can ill afford proving their need is a deserved one. By trying to make sure that a public good—free lunch for the students in our community, say—is mediated through the question of who deserves it, we make it harder to do thing we're ostensibly trying to do. Worse, we take money we could spend on feeding people, and spend it making sure only the *right* people are fed, because we are approaching the question "should everyone be fed?" from a spirit of lack—which means that, spiritually speaking, we're aligned *with* abusive wealth, not against it. And that's a problem of spirit.

People aligned with a spirit of greed very much want people to be aligned with a spirit of lack, because people aligned with a spirit of greed intend to horde wealth, which will naturally create a great deal of lack. If one intends to create a great deal of lack, it is all for the best that as many people as possible come to see lack as part of the natural moral order, and so in order to convince people to see lack as part of the natural moral order, people aligned with greed are willing to pay. In fact, they're willing to pay more—*much* more—than the cost of a lunch, provided it prevents hungry children from receiving a free lunch, because hungry people getting food simply for the fact of their humanity creates a spirit of plenty, while figuring out whether or not it is deserved helps reinforce the spirit of lack upon which greed depends.

And means testing helps a greedy spirit do that.

Means testing seems designed to keep greedy people of means away from good things they can afford. But at a far deeper level, means testing is spiritually aligned *with* greed.

Yet so many of us desire means testing anyway. Why? Spirit. We're not primarily worried about hungry people. We're worried about what's *deserved*. We believe there isn't enough. We believe in lack. And we'll pay for lack. We'll pay more for lack than what plenty costs, because our compasses aren't set to caring for everyone's needs; they are set to making sure that anyone who gets also first deserves. Which means that deep down we believe that life is something some people deserve, and others don't.

We're talking about free school lunch. We could be talking about many things. We could be talking about affordable college, or affordable housing, or access to medical care. We could be talking about many things.

It's a bad compass setting.

It's a problem of spirit.

Here's what I think: any compass that does not use as true north a justice founded in love (that is, a justice that ensures the inherent dignity, legal equality, and basic physical and spiritual need of all human beings) will inevitably fail to recognize that people are art. It will arrive at one barbarism or another, in a way that confounds intention, because even a well-intentioned navigator will go to a terrible place if that's where the compass points. Navigation can be corrected. A course can be adjusted. New paths can be devised to arrive at the correct destination. But if the compass is wrong, the corrections and adjustments will be incorrect, the new path just as wrong as the one before, and the destination will remain a foul one.

We are primarily fighting the lies, not the people who believe them. Our primary focus is on establishing correct priorities between competing good things—not on a battle between good things and evil things, but a battle against the spirit that has captured us, which tells us the lie that there are priorities higher than human dignity and life. Justice grounded in love is our priority, and we must insist on it. Any other priority is based on a lie; and many very fine people can believe a lie, and participate in a spirit that wants genocide and slavery.

Maybe we had heard it before. Maybe we even "knew" it. But now we *know* it.

The bubble is popped. For thousands and millions of us, there's no going back.

But how can we possibly go forward?

4. RELATED

What the malignant spirit that has captured us wants is this: genocide and slavery.

I made the claim, so let me lay it out.

If you want to enact genocide and slavery, it doesn't seem to me that you need to convince a population to consciously *want* genocide and slavery. I suspect no society that has ever committed genocide or enacted slavery has ever let themselves see themselves for what they were. It seems to me the more effective method is to convince large groups of people to accept a series of propositions that will lead them there, that make such an end first possible, then likely, and finally inevitable, even normal, and then to convince them that their own perceived normalcy makes what they are doing normal, and their own innate goodness makes what they are doing good.

What you need are bubbles.

Example: most U.S. citizens who consider themselves "white," if asked, probably don't think the United States is responsible for multiple genocides. We might, if pressed, admit that these genocides occurred, and even that they were very sad, perhaps even bad. But in my experience, most of us white citizens in the United States reject the notion that the United States is responsible for multiple genocides. Yet the U.S. *is* responsible for multiple genocides.

We've forgiven ourselves—by *we* I mean we white U.S. citizens.

It was a long time ago—that's what we say.

The past has no bearing on today—that's what we say.

Yet somehow, even though the past has no bearing on today, we still tend to revere our founding fathers. We put them on our currency, resist any attempt to deconstruct the mythologies we've built around them, propose to follow their every intention to the letter. These facts from the past must hold a guiding and overriding bearing upon the present, it seems. And it's a matter of historical fact that many of our founders owned slaves and built extraordinary wealth from their labor, and the rest, who may have opposed slavery, were nevertheless willing to compromise with them on the matter. All of them participated in some way in our genocide of the many and various native cultures who lived in this land for millennia before our country's founding. And now *we* live on that land. That wealth shaped the country in which *we* live. And yet, these are the facts about our founding which we insist must have no bearing upon the present. So it seems our insistence is that the past must have no bearing upon the present, except in those cases when we insist the past must have a guiding and overriding bearing upon the present. It appears that in my country *we* propose to only inherit wealth, not responsibility.

And our unwillingness to look back centuries equips us well, it seems to me, to also not notice what we as a country did decades ago, or years ago, or last year, or yesterday.

This all makes sense to me, in a way. No society thinks of itself as evil. In fact, it seems to me that many of the most harmful and abusive societies in history have thought of themselves as exceptionally good, even the pinnacles of humanity. We might be able to think of examples from recent human history, nations guided by regimes now widely understood to be evil, who thought of themselves as uniquely good, predestined for triumph, humanity's natural masters. Nor do individuals think of themselves as evil, any more than societies do. We tend to mediate our understanding of our actions through our goodness, not our badness; our strengths, not our weakness; our successes, not our failings. It seems to me likely that every society that has ever committed genocide and enslaved others has been full of good people—brave people, intelligent, well-read, who loved their children, and helped one another with good will, and gave to charity, and so on and so on and so on, people of many good qualities and actions and habits—so many, it must have seemed impossible—wicked, even, or divisive, or foolish, or harmful—to believe something bad might be true of them; perhaps even people like those you'll find in my country today, who prefer order to justice, rather than justice to order, which is all that is needed to introduce propositions and arguments that end, either implicitly or explicitly, with phrases like "and that's why a lot of people unfortunately will have to die." You wouldn't hear people express these propositions out loud in blunt terms—not at first. You'd have to watch for actions taken and statements made, to see what logical assumptions hide behind such actions and statements—because anyone who wants to unravel great foundational truths is going to need to create great foundational lies.

I think the spirit that desires genocide and slavery rests on three great foundational lies.

◆ ◆ ◆

The first lie is this: we aren't related to one another.

Genocide is the utter repudiation of the great truth, which

is that all human beings are art, and of other truths which rest upon this great truth. If I am somebody who actively wants to move people to join with a spirit of genocide, first I'm going to have to work on dissolving the truth of interconnectivity, the idea that we all belong to each other. Not "belong" in the sense of property, but rather in the sense of shared responsibility and accountability and relationship; the great truth of human reality, which is that we all belong to an interrelated human ecosystem from which we are fundamentally inextricable—that we are all related.

If I want genocide, I'm going to have to dispatch this idea right away. I'll want to foster the notion that each of us is a self-created being, and our successes and our failures arise exclusively from our own effort and choices. I'll want to encourage people to believe that the suffering of another person is entirely the business of that person, and nothing to do with anyone else. It may be necessary for me to expand the definition of "self" to include one's family and friends, perhaps one's neighborhood, or ethnicity, but eventually there will come some boundary, some delineation, that I will find useful to create, and then entrench, and then exploit, to ensure that those I have set on the other side from me will be the ones who will pay for the crime of existing, will pay whatever penalty I choose, for whatever reason I choose. There are questions that come naturally, when we aren't related to one another. They are "I" questions—an "I" that will always include certain preferred people who I include whenever I say "I," and that will always, crucially, exclude the rest.

Why should I pay for education when I don't have children?

Why should I pay to see the hungry fed when I buy my own food?

Why should I pay to shelter the homeless when I worked hard to own my home?

Why should I pay to clean the lead from *their* water when my pipes run clean?

Why should I pay for the sick to receive care when I am healthy?

Why should I have to pay for prenatal care when I'm not a woman?

Why would my money go to provide relief to a country I don't live in?

Why would I let that family fleeing danger into my country when I am already safe?

These are the questions people ask, in a society that no longer believes that we are all related. In a country that has believed this lie, there will soon be few to ask:

What is the price to be paid for an uneducated population?

What is the price to be paid for a nation that won't care for those in need?

What is the price to be paid for potential ungrasped?

What is the price to be paid for a nation of desperate people?

What bill will come eventually due because a country has been destabilized by invasion and occupation and warfare, what bill will come due if a population is made desperate by need?

When we aren't related, these questions don't need to be asked. Failure and success are hermetically sealed at the individual level. The only price to be paid for a society that fails to see to everybody's education, health, shelter, food, water, and other basic physical and spiritual needs will be paid by the specific individual who suffers, not society. Freedom becomes a very specific and compartmentalized concept, customized to one's own particular preferences.

The only education that affects me is my own education.

The only health that affects me is my own.

The only shelter that affects me is my own.

The only water and food that affect me are my own.

The only prosperity and the only safety that matter are my own.

How will I know when I've successfully convinced people of the lie that we aren't related? Well. . . . If we were a society that believed in this way, we would likely find many people who had started to believe that their ability to survive and thrive and prosper was entirely the product of their own effort and talent and ingenuity. We'd begin to see people who equated their moral virtue with their own ability to survive. We'd begin to see that prosperity was taken to be indicative of a moral virtue greater than that of those who merely subsist, and the greater the prosperity, the greater the moral virtue that it would imply. We'd likely find many people who began equating wealth itself as interchangeable with moral virtue, an equation that would result in more and more people becoming obsessed with accumulating more and more wealth—much more than they could ever spend, because at a very basic level, they seemed to believe it literally made them more virtuous and worthy of life. We might find others, not wealthy, who nevertheless began to believe this lie, who ascribed virtue to the wealthy simply for the fact of their wealth—a belief that would, as it grew in popularity, facilitate an ever-increasing disparity in wealth. We might find that anyone criticizing any injustices endemic to such a divide was declared to be enacting some sort of "class warfare," while those who sought to increase the disparity would be thought to be doing so specifically in terms of increasing virtuousness. In fact, the disparity itself would be defended as virtuous, while those calling for remedies to disparity would be thought of as divisive.

◆ ◆ ◆

In a society captured by this first genocidal lie, protection of humans who had property would become a more important function of law than protection of humans without property, and protection of property would be seen as more important than protection of propertyless humans. Eventually, protection of property and wealth would become, as a practical matter, the primary goal of law, with protection of humans held as a nominal aspiration, and a distant secondary function. The ability of incorporated organizations to efficiently gather wealth might afford them greater protections and consideration under the law than that offered individual people. In time, those organizations might begin to be worshipped in subtle ways, their logos adorning the chests and backs and feet of people loyal to their specific values, their leaders elevated to positions as high priests of our thoughts and beliefs and virtues. In time, the idea that these organizations should be honored with greater protections and considerations under the law than human beings simply for their outsized ability to generate wealth (which would be, after all, proof of virtue) might become enshrined as received wisdom. The more the government of such a society became dedicated to protecting and providing for property rather than people, the more the idea of community would be met with hostility.

Public good would become the necessary enemy of private good.

Public services would become the necessary enemy of private purchases.

If property happened to be destroyed during a demonstration protesting the destruction of a human life, the destruction of the property would be treated as the more shocking matter by far, and would be used to justify negation of the protesting organization's cause, no how matter how just their demand, no matter the reality of whether or not that organization's members were responsible for the destruction or merely adjacent to it.

The idea of government being a mechanism by which humans choose to organize their shared life for common good would be replaced by ideas like this one: "The most frightening words in the English language are 'I'm from the government and I'm here to help.'"

The idea of tax collected for public values such as education or health would be framed as monstrous, while the idea of large and powerful individuals and entities seeking relief from any responsibility to contribute to the societies within which they

operate might be seen as pragmatic and necessary and even virtuous. After all, if wealth is the same as virtuousness, then tax
is not how a shared life together is funded, nor is it a price paid
for the continuance of health and thriving within the society
that has fostered your own health and thriving; rather, it is the
theft of your moral virtue, taken from you and given to unvirtuous people who, being unvirtuous, will surely waste it, and
upon whom (given their unvirtuousness), any investment must
be considered either a beneficent gift or an immoral waste.

You might begin to hear people expressing the opinion that
a society that taxes its citizens to ensure basic physical needs
for all people is engaged in slavery of those taxed, while people
toiling at jobs that do not provide wages enough to sustain life
should stop their immoral complaining and work harder. You
might even begin to hear catchphrases like "tax is theft." The
idea of tax collected upon an estate might begin to be held as
not only undesirable but evil. The idea that the public should
have some claim upon one's virtue, rather than passing the full
measure of virtue down to one's own personal line of heredity,
would seem like the gravest injustice. Meanwhile, the idea of
inherited accountability would seem as foolish as the idea of
inherited wealth would seem wise. *Of course* money should be
handed down with absolute fidelity from parent to child. *Of
course* the beneficiary should be absolutely free from questions
of how their parent acquired that wealth. *Naturally,* no account
should be made of past injustices—not when we aren't related to
each other, not when our only meaningful societal relationship
is our individual relationship to our perfectly virtuous wealth.
Naturally, time should be allowed to launder our guilt, make
our fiduciary sheets as white as snow. We might see all these
sorts of things, in a society guided by a spirit that wants genocide. We might even start to suspect, as we tracked the ways
this lie naturally led to wealth disparity, that those who wanted

genocide wanted it precisely for the ways it facilitates the gathering of wealth and power to fewer and fewer people.

If this were a deeply ironic universe, people might even fully believe all these propositions while worshiping within a religious tradition that taught there exists no greater danger to the soul than the love of money, that there exists no harder way to enter heaven than to make the attempt while encumbered with wealth. If we were a society that believed we were not all related, all these might be exactly the sort of things we see and hear.

This is the final conclusion of the first foundational lie: **Other people do not matter.**

And, of course, every lie will levy a penalty upon those who believe it, even as it endangers those who believe it and those who do not alike—because a lie fails to recognize reality, and reality will not be denied forever.

Here is the penalty inherent in believing this lie: **dissatisfaction.**

A growing sense that I have not been given my due. A gnawing sense that I should have more than I have. A sneaking suspicion that any good thing that comes to another might better have come to me. A life lived not in appreciation for the good that has come to me, but in discontented grasping after the more I could theoretically get. A deliberate choice to live in a world not of abundance and relationship but of isolation and lack.

And here is the danger: **vulnerability.**

Living in a world in which we aren't related means living in a world in which others, resentful of their lost advantage, seeking for the phantom limb of it, will inevitably seek some scapegoat, and will eventually land upon me. Living in a world where we aren't related means living in a world where those who have best learned how to press a mean advantage will eventually consume their easiest victims, and then, filled with greed's hunger, engorged with the virtues of wealth and power, will turn at last to feast upon me.

When I choose to live in world in which other people do not matter, I choose to live in a world in which I will not matter, either.

5. EARNED

OK—we've destroyed the idea that we are all related to one another. What's next?

Next we need to demolish the fundamental truth that human worth is intrinsic. To do this, we'll have to tell the second foundational lie: that **life must be earned.** After all, if we don't think life is something that is earned, we can't make two buckets—and it takes two buckets to enact genocide. One bucket is for the right people, who have earned life. And the second bucket is for the wrong people, who have not. (Here's where an astute reader might sense some potential hypocrisy, realizing that I've been putting people into buckets labeled "Prefers Justice" and "Prefers Order"... and perhaps so. But hold on, astute reader; we'll get there.)

I want to be clear, we don't put the wrong people in their bucket to *kill* them—it's too early for that. It's not that they deserve death. They just haven't earned life. As a result, they don't deserve sympathy when they die, or empathy when they suffer, or assistance when they struggle. In fact, to provide them these things when they haven't earned them is immoral, because... well, because they haven't *earned* them. Why should they get the basic necessities of life, and why should I have to pay for them with my own wealth—which is, let's not forget, my moral virtue?

This is why a spirit that wants genocide begins with the idea of separation—the notion that we aren't all related. With that accomplished, it's going to be very easy to convince people that life is something you earn, to convert other human beings from perceived art to a presumed infraction, an undeserving existence, a life unearned.

But *how* does one earn life?

We have to use some metric, so we can figure out who goes into what bucket. We can make the metric for earning life anything you like—or we could make it about many things. For ease, we might want to marry it up with unjust beliefs that already exist within a society. So, for example, in a culture that equates wealth with moral virtue, we could make it about wealth.

If wealth were interchangeable with morality, then the lack of wealth would naturally become interchangeable with immorality. When life is something earned, after all, it stands to reason that those who die and suffer are those who have failed to earn life. If they failed, then they must have deserved to fail. In fact, it becomes essential to believe that they deserved to fail, because if they didn't fail to earn life, then something else failed them, which would suggest that society is relational—which it is *not*. They *have* to be at fault, because if they aren't to blame for their own suffering . . . well. If they aren't at fault, then the fact that I am healthy and well wouldn't be entirely a result of my own virtue. If they aren't to blame for their own suffering, I wouldn't be a totally unconnected free actor in the world, entirely responsible for my own success, entirely free of responsibility for all others. If they aren't to blame for their own suffering, someone else might be to blame, and worse, that someone else might even be me. And I do not want to be at blame, because being at blame means you haven't earned life.

And life *must* be earned.

And that's how it works.

An abusive system seeks to perfect itself by invoicing the costs of its own injustice to those suffering its abuses. Thus, injustice will deny its own existence, or convert itself to justice by converting the suffering it causes into blame, and then delivering the blame to those who suffer as an act of righteousness.

Who is at fault for the social woes caused by poverty? Why the lazy poor, of course, who'd rather suckle the government teat than work hard like good people. Who is at fault for the collapse of the housing market? The greedy poor, of course, who chose to take the predatory loans Wall Street sold, after Wall Street lobbied to make them legal. Who is at fault for the threat of terrorism? Immigrants, fleeing countries our country destabilized, families on the run from the unrest our economic and foreign policies have caused. Who is at fault for the national debt? Welfare mothers, of course, having babies they can't afford, who I now have to pay for. Why are there abortions? Irresponsible women just don't want to have to take care of babies that have been made unaffordable by policies I support, because they can't control their bodies, bodies I insist on controlling myself. Did you get sick? You must have lived an unhealthy lifestyle. I don't smoke and I run 20 miles every week. I'm not sick. You should have done what I did.

Drug addicted? You should have had a stronger will, like me. I'm not addicted.

Depressed? Cheer up. Be more grateful, like me. I'm grateful.

Kids go to a bad school? You should have sent them to a better one. That's what I did.

Uneducated? You should have studied harder. I studied harder.

Get raped? What were you wearing? I'd have dressed differently.

Cops shot you? Should have obeyed them. I'd have obeyed.

Drowned in a flood? Why didn't you evacuate like I would have? Better still, why did you choose to live there in the first place? I chose to live someplace that is not currently underwater. Do people of color struggle in generational poverty? They really should have focused more on the family unit. My family eats dinner together every night and we read the Bible. And where are their fathers? In prison? Shouldn't have sold marijuana. I didn't sell marijuana. It never even occurred to me to do that. I had no reason to do that, and because I had no reason to do that, it therefore follows there is no reason for anyone to do that.

I deserve life because I have it. Others have failed to earn it and therefore don't deserve it. The reason they failed? Who knows? Who *cares?*

These aren't questions people who have earned life need to ask.

◆ ◆ ◆

In a society captured by the idea that life is earned, we might find that hard work creates profit for those who have already earned life, so hard work is held to be interchangeable with virtue. And virtue is already interchangeable with wealth, so hard work and wealth will become similarly entangled, to the point that, if I am wealthy, I don't have to work hard to be considered hard-working. I might not even need to work at all. My money and other people might do all the work for me. I don't even need to actually earn life by my own standards in order to earn it. Because of my wealth I *become* hard work. I *become* moral virtue. It is through my possession of these outward signs of having earned life that my society deems I have earned my life. And it is through the lack of those outward signs in others that my society deems that those others have not. So yes, we could use wealth to make two buckets. But wealth is just the metric. Once we have the metric, it can be used many ways, to harm whoever society deems unfit.

Suppose, for example, that you live in a society that believes all the things I just mentioned. And then suppose that, for centuries of its history, this society's laws considered certain people to be property of other people. Suppose that during those centuries the dividing line between people who *were* property and people who could *own* property was whether or not they were considered "white."

Next, suppose that for millennia some women were given to men by other men, in financial transactions called "marriages," while other women were owned by men as concubines or kept as mistresses or purchased as prostitutes, and any women not entangled in one of these ownership-based arrangements were marginalized in other ways, suspected of malign oddity or strange defect, persecuted, prosecuted, and worse.

In such a society, whiteness and maleness would become interchangeable with property, and therefore interchangeable with wealth, and therefore with virtue. Whiteness and maleness would themselves become *assumed* moral virtues. They would be *implied* hard work. They would be *implied* wealth. They would be *implied* ownership of property. And, therefore, they would carry an implication of having earned life. Conversely, to be not-white or not-male without agreeing to become property would make your existence interchangeable with theft. Not *being* a thief, but being *theft itself*—in other words, possession of a body that should be the property of another person. Non-whiteness and non-maleness would themselves be *assumed* laziness and poverty. They would make you *implied* poverty. They would make you *implied* property. And, therefore, they would carry implications of having not earned life.

Living without the mantels of assumed morality conferred by whiteness and maleness would be the difference between experiencing a society to which you are assumed to *belong* and experiencing a society to which you are assumed to be a *belonging*. After centuries, this society wouldn't even think about it. These would be habitual beliefs. They would be the reflexes of our systems of law and power. They would be tradition. They would be our spirit, our atmosphere. They would be the settings of our compasses. They might even appear in this society in the actions and words of people who claimed they believed no such thing. They would be bubbles; mirrors that didn't let us see ourselves.

So if men tended to make more money than women for the same work, they would be considered naturally more virtuous and hard-working, by the very fact of their advantage. A society that believed foundational lies would invent any number of reasons why this gap did not *really* exist, or was in fact natural or good, or was the fault of women. And if white people tended to have more wealth than Black people, they would be considered naturally more virtuous and hard-working, by the very fact of their advantage. A society captured by foundational lies would invent any number of reasons why this discrepancy didn't *really* exist, or was in fact natural or good, or was the fault of Black people. In such a society, phrases like "regular, hard-working people," might be used interchangeably in public discourse with white people, with an implied corollary about those not deemed "white."

In such a society, women might have a common shared experience, in which they found themselves observed in public spaces by men, who seemed to feel a general right of ownership over women's bodies. In such a society, we might regularly find that any report of sexual abuse would be met with a general response primarily concerned with considering the adverse effect of the accusation upon the accused, rather than a concern over the effect of the abuse on the victim. In such a society, we might find that when women are raped or assaulted, the particulars of her activities would be closely parsed to discover what she might have done to earn such rough treatment, as if the investigation were not about discovering the facts around the crime done to her, but about satisfying in our minds the reasons the raped woman *deserved* her rape, and in what particular way the assaulted woman actually already belonged to her assailant. We might find that when a young white rapist is sentenced, the judge publicly frets about what damage the sentence might wreak upon his promising future and what damage it might do to his implied moral virtue, as if there were no resource more precious than a young white man's potential. We might discover that a wealthy white man can brag about sexual assault and still win the presidency, if he is wealthy enough (or at least famous enough for being purportedly wealthy). We might find men who come to the defense of an abused woman framing their willingness to do so along the strangely specific contexts of transitive empathy on behalf of the women they "have" in their own lives—*as the father of three daughters ... as a husband . . . .* We might find comments, jokes, even elaborate ceremonies premised on the assumption that the relationship of a father to his daughter is best understood as an obsessive and faithful stewardship, on behalf of some future beneficiary, of a perfectly unsullied vagina.

And in such a society, we would discover Black people who know they walk the streets observed by people considered "white" who treat the presence of Black bodies and lives as if they carry a general sense of danger and theft. We might find that, when a Black person is killed by police, the particulars of the victim's past are closely examined for infractions, to be breathlessly presented as an obvious part of a story that seems to be not about why an unarmed human being was shot dead, but about why the dead person might *deserve* to be dead. And, should the victim prove particularly virtuous, the story might become about how this particular death was tragic, in comparison to all the others. We might find an increasingly militarized law enforcement, who views any calls for consequence arising from abuses of power upon Black bodies and lives as a direct attack upon their ability to do their jobs, and even an attack upon their own lives. We might discover that charges for violent crimes committed by police are very rarely pressed, no matter how voluminous the pool of evidence of shocking police corruption and brutality and murder becomes. We might find, in rare instances when charges are pressed against police, that acquittals are the norm. We might find that a grassroots movement which exists to proclaim that Black lives actually matter (despite the contrary assessment of the justice system), and also to demand that public servants hired to protect them stop murdering them, is spoken of on mainstream media platforms as equivalent to terrorist organizations or hate groups. We might find powerful people calling for laws to be passed making it legal to run such protesters over with cars. We might discover that a political party can come to power while actively working to strip Black people of the right to participate in society as equal voters. We might find them nominating as their leader a man who took out a full-page ad in the paper of record to demand the execution of five innocent Black kids, a man who declared Mexicans rapists, a man who proposed a Muslim ban and a border wall, a man whose solution to the problem of police brutality was to relax existing standards in order to make the police even less hesitant to employ violence and harassment against people whom our society deems to have not earned life. We might find that this man referred to such unfettered injustice as "law and order," and we might find that when he did, millions nodded and clapped and cheered.

If this were a deeply ironic universe, we might even find that people aligned with all these ideas worshipped in a religious tradition that spoke of a deity who fed and healed without price, taught that he was a shepherd who would search for every lost sheep, and that in his kingdom there was no wealth, or race, or religion, or gender.

Those are the sorts of things we might find, in a society dedicated to the idea that life is something you earn.

This is the conclusion of our second lie: **Other people do not matter, and it's their own fault that they do not.** And, of course, every lie will levy a penalty upon those who believe it even as it endangers those who believe it and those who do not alike—because a lie fails to recognize reality, and reality will not be denied forever.

Here is the penalty for believing this lie: **insecurity.**

When I believe this lie, others with greater leverage can compel me to twist myself into discomfiting and violent shapes, just to prove that I have earned the right to live. I might spend my life focused not on the living, but on the desperate attempt to prove my right to be alive.

Here is the danger of believing it: **abandonment**.

When I believe life is something that is earned, then eventually I, being human, being finite, with a body that ages and dies, will fail. No matter how strong, or smart, or successful, I will fail. And, having demanded a world where life is earned, I will have no longer earned life. I may even believe this lie of myself. It will certainly be believed of me, who has taught the lie for so long.

When I choose to live in world in which life must be earned, I choose to live in a world in which I will inevitably earn death.

6. REDEEMS

We've convinced our society that we aren't related to one another.

We've convinced our society that life is something you have to earn.

We're close to making genocide inevitable now.

What's next?

Next, we must convince our society of the third foundational lie: that **violence redeems**.

This is not particularly hard to do. We humans are good at violence. It's hardwired right into our amygdalae. It's the distillation of the plot of many of our most popular movies. If you hit me, I hit you harder. If you hit back harder still, I hit you back hardest of all. Eventually I will hit you so hard you can't hit anymore, and then the problem of *you* will be solved. If they bring a knife, you bring a gun. They send one of yours to the hospital, you send one of theirs to the morgue. That's the Chicago way, and that's how you get Capone, yipee ki yay, motherfucker. Roll credits. This is order's narrative: There are villains. You kill villains, and order is restored. You kill the boss villain at the end of video games after killing all the sub-villains. The hero kills the boss villain at the end of movies after killing all the sub-villains. Order is restored.

One important part of order's narrative is that the hero doesn't just show up and start violencing all over the place until the place is full of violence. The hero ends the violence that somebody else started, with redeeming violence of their own, which escalates until at last it has cleansed the narrative of all sources of bad violence. So we see that violence can't merely be the solution in order's narrative; it also has to be the problem. Violence can't merely be very very good, it also must be very very bad. This is why we must first determine that we aren't all related, and that life must be earned. You need only look at who is doing the violence to know if it is good violence or bad violence. People who haven't earned life do bad violence that could never be good, and people who have earned life do good violence that could never be bad.

"They" do bad violence to us. "We" do good violence to end it.

Certain conclusions present themselves.

If they keep doing bad violence after our good violence, it is because we didn't do enough good violence previously. The solution becomes obvious: we must do more good violence at them—harder violence, or more-widely applied, or more brutal, or all three. The violence isn't just good; it redeems. It is the perfected instrument for restoring bad things to goodness. We know our violence is good, because *we* do it. We revere it. We have parades and whatnot. Their violence is bad violence. We know it is bad, because they do it. We hate it. We will eradicate it from the face of the planet, like we did in World War I, which ended all war, and World War II, in which we stopped evil in its tracks forever, and the Cold War, in which we permanently stabilized the world through proxy violence in countries other than that of our primary adversary, and also the War on Drugs, which stopped the drug epidemic, and the War on Terror, which has stopped terrorism forever . . . .

Let me push back against myself on behalf of those of you who might imagine I am losing my marbles. What the hell am

I suggesting, exactly? That we *shouldn't* have fought Hitler in WWII? That violence is *never* appropriate? That we *oughtn't* to revere those who served and suffered and even died in our armed conflicts? That we should just let terrorists go on with their heinous deeds, consequence-free? What if we were all speaking German right now, huh, what then? Or, how about this: What if there were some maniac in my house ready to kill my kids? What if my wife were attacked? What if I was being beheaded by terrorists? I'd feel a bit differently then, wouldn't I?

Well . . . yes.

I suppose I would feel differently about violence, if that were happening. Those things sound horrific. So let me say, right here and now, that if some maniac were getting ready to murder my children, I would welcome a weapon for the chance to stop that maniac, or the sudden appearance of somebody armed with both a weapon and the intention to stop that maniac. That would be just the ticket in that situation. I would not turn it down. I would also like to take this opportunity to express my opinion that Hitler was bad. It is good that we stopped him, and it is to the credit of our country and our allies and those who bravely served that we did stop him. Glad to finally get that off my chest. I'll say it again: Hitler was really bad. Good that we stopped him. Let me also say that people who put their physical well-being and their very lives at risk in service of others exhibit a bravery that I believe deserves our wonder and our respect.

I would also observe that bravery isn't what receives our first respect, as a society.

We seem to be more into the redemptive power of violence.

It's worth remembering that we rarely set ourselves in opposition to things that are evil in and of themselves; rather we find ourselves dealing with some good thing that has been elevated above its proper place. The key question, usually, is one of priority between good things. For example, order and prosperity and hard work are not bad, but they become corrupted when they are made more important than the unsurpassable worth inherent to human beings, who are art. Is it like this with violence? Can we imagine times when violence becomes necessary to prevent some terrible abuse from taking place?

I think we can. At least we might name something that can be good, within certain contexts where violence has been made inevitable by abusive intent.

Let's talk about physical bravery.

Physical bravery can be very good.

◆ ◆ ◆

It's 2017 now. Recently in the news there was a story about a man, captured by our foundational lies, who boarded a train with a knife. There he saw a woman with whom he knew he shared no relation, because her outfit marked her as a Muslim. Because she was a Muslim, he believed she represented bad violence, and had therefore not earned life. He set about to make her understand, at the foundational level of terror, that she had not earned life. He made it clear to everyone nearby that he intended to relieve her of the life he had decided she had not earned. The man with the knife had decided to make violence inevitable. Three brave men stepped in to stop him, and this act created a violent altercation between them and him, instead of between her and him. Ricky John Best, 53, died in the train car. Taliesin Myrddin Namkai Meche, 23, succumbed to his wounds in the hospital. A third man, Micah David-Cole Fletcher, 21, was injured and hospitalized but survived. I think it was good that those men acted to protect that woman. I think it was *very* good. I think it is appropriate to honor such acts of physical bravery, and the sacrifice that frequently accompanies them.

The question is not whether physical bravery is good. It very obviously can be very good, and even heroic. And certain acts of physical bravery will engage with violent intent, which will create an inevitable violent outcome, in order to try to change the nature of the violence, and the outcome. I don't know a non-violent way to stop a hypothetical maniac from hypothetically killing my children once he's in my house with murderous intent, and I very much do not want my children to be killed, hypothetically or otherwise. So it seems violence has a very specific appropriate scope when properly applied within an orientation aligned toward justice. It addresses a specific and immediate problem, which is frequently if not always unexpected. It has a temporary duration and a clear goal with a clear end point. It is most frequently done on the behalf of others. It is not instigated. And, crucially, it is done because without the application of violence, some other violence will inevitably occur, and no power better than violence is available in the immediate moment to counter it. But violence always strikes me as a tragedy or at least the result of a lack of imagination. Despite previous hypotheticals involving home-invasion maniacs, some other solution is almost always available.

Even to the extent that it is necessary, violence is only ever a fix. It is never a solution. It is the weakest power. If any other power is available to fix the immediate problem, that power is the better power. But the compass decides the navigation, and the navigation sets the course, the course decides the path, and the path determines the destination. And if our compass tells us that we are not related, it will also tell us that other people do not matter. If it tells us life is something that some people have not earned, it will also tell us it is their own fault that they do not matter. Little wonder, then, with such a compass, that our course becomes a preemptively violent one. Little wonder, then, that violence is so often our first solution, or even our only solution.

When violence is posited as a natural solution, it has been inappropriately elevated. When it becomes the preferred solution, then the society that prefers it has oriented itself to violence, a compass setting that states "we will use violence as a first choice to achieve our objectives." It is an orientation toward violence that says that violence is the strongest power, not the weakest, the first resort, not the last. It's an orientation toward violence that believes violence redeems, that creates a *preference* for violence as the prime mover of justice, or even a conflation of violence and justice as being interchangeable. It's an orientation that can make a non-violent response seem fearfully foolish. It's an orientation that makes violence not only likely, not only preferred, but inevitable.

As I mentioned earlier, those who demonstrate physical bravery on behalf of others deserve our wonder and our respect. I also think they deserve more: a deep examination, on our parts, prior to any decision that requires them to exhibit that bravery; and after, an interrogation of our motives and objectives behind decisions—such as the decision to go to war, such as the decision to create a world that permits people to live in abject poverty—that made this violence so apparently necessary; and a thorough inquiry after the fact, as to whether those motives were honored and those objectives achieved. Exactly why did we put brave people into a desperate risk? Did we honor their astounding selflessness by setting our goals to appropriate ends? Did we secure those ends? Are we willing now to sacrifice and pay the price to provide for those brave people who acted on our behalf, and ensure those ends are maintained? In what way was the violence they were compelled to enact, however admirably brave it might have been, a sign of some turn we missed on our road, some collective failure to select justice at some earlier point? What cost might we now have to bear, what changes might we make to our foundational beliefs and institutions, to honor their brave sacrifice by reorganizing our society in such a way as to make such sacrifices unnecessary in the future?

When violence is my orientation, I no longer have to ask those questions. I don't have to worry about motive or objective—the violence itself represents purity of motive and objective in and of itself. And I no longer have to concern myself with the aftermath, because if I believe that violence redeems, then the aftermath to violence will always be more violence, until we at last come to the end of violence, an end we will only reach when those who have not earned life no longer exist. I think this, incidentally, is why so many who claim to revere the military also support policies that abandon veterans. If I am a violence-oriented person, then honor was never the point: violence was. When dealers of violence no longer can provide the violence I need them to enact in order to make me feel safe, they will have reached the end of my reverence for them, and can be discarded. I might point to their neglect as a rationale for not taking care of other neglected people who aren't veterans when we haven't yet taken care of the veterans, but I certainly won't support actually caring for them. Taking care of our veterans isn't profitable, after all, and life is something you must earn.

My orientation toward violence advises me that the way to stop the threat of maniacs entering my house to kill my children is to identify all the maniacs and kill them before they ever enter my house—or, failing that, to always be ready at a moment's notice to kill any hypothetical maniac—to assume that it is my job to be constantly watchful for maniacs and ready to deal my perfected violence upon them at any sudden adrenalized moment. This is an orientation toward violence that puts my family in greater danger, not less, because the presence of firearms is strongly correlated with firearm-related death, and the person most likely to kill you is a family member, but I will still prepare myself for violence that endangers my family in the name of keeping my family safe, because I am oriented toward violence, which means that I believe violence is the only thing that could ever save my family from violence.

The way to end crime is to lock up or kill all the criminals, by my definition of criminal.

And the way to end terrorism is to kill all the terrorists, by my definition of terrorist.

And the answer to those who have not earned life is that they have earned death.

And somebody ought to deliver that death.

And I am somebody.

So, hey, let's kill all the Muslim extremist terrorists. Right? So we attack a place where some of the terrorists are. We also attack a place where the terrorists *aren't*, but which seems like the sort of place terrorists might go. The terrorists see that we are now there. They meet us there and begin to attack. We attack back. We attack with the largest and most expensive and powerful military the world has ever seen. We dig in. They kill us. We kill back harder. Homes are reduced to rubble. Hundreds of thousands of unaffiliated people—spouses, children, parents, siblings, neighbors, friends—die in all this carnage.

They keep killing us.

We decide our mistake was not killing hard enough. We surge.

At some point, it becomes natural for us to be at war.

We start to praise our bombs on television for their beauty and size and sophistication. We build remote-controlled airplanes that can deliver death from heights undetectable to the naked eye, and they deliver death and destruction until normal people on the other side of the planet begin to live in terror of a clear blue sky, and the flag that is painted on those aircraft—red, white, and blue—becomes for them a symbol of terror.

There is not less violence now than when we started. There is more.

There are not fewer terrorists now than when we started. There are more.

We have eagerly joined with the terrorist in bringing terror to the innocent. And still we, captured in our belief of violence's redeeming strength, think the answer is that we have not yet been fierce enough in our prosecution of good violence—obviously so,

because bad violence still exists. Many of us think the problem
is that we haven't yet cast a wide enough net of violence. Perhaps
we need to kill different people, in some new countries. Perhaps
we need to suspect more people abroad to see if they need death.
Perhaps we need to start suspecting more people here at home.
Perhaps we need to start rounding those people up.

We begin to see suspicion of such people as common sense.

We begin to see the existence of such people as a grave danger.

We begin to think that something should be done about
those people.

We begin to think that *we* should be the person to take those
actions.

We begin to carry knives on trains.

You see?

We are no longer addressing a specific and immediate problem. We are no longer engaged in something of temporary duration with a clear goal and a clear end. We are no longer engaged
on behalf of others. We are no longer checking to see if some
other, stronger, braver, better power might be available to us. And
we are instigating, using our fear of potential violence we imagine
might come tomorrow as the only justification we need to deliver
actual violence today. We are *oriented* toward violence. It is not
a fix; it is a solution. Moreover, it is *the* solution—the only one.
We think it will redeem the evil we see. And when the violence
grows, we conclude violence has not yet redeemed the conflict
only because there has not yet been violence enough.

The suggestion that we do something other than violence begins to seem dangerously weak. In fact, it seems like a moral failing, even a betrayal of the memory of physical bravery enacted
on our behalf. It seems like siding with the enemy. *I suppose you
want to invite the terrorists over for tea, do you? Have you forgotten those who sacrificed for your freedom?*

Rules preventing us from enacting any sort of "good" violence begin to seem ridiculously naïve. *Suppose there's a bomb*

set to go off in one hour and you have in your custody the only man who knows its location . . . .

◆ ◆ ◆

If you found a society that had been captured by the idea that violence redeems, you would likely find a society that advocates torture. You'd probably find a society that spends an inordinate amount on weapons and armies—as much, perhaps, as the rest of the world combined. You'd probably discover a society that considers the unfettered ability to personally own weapons to be a more important human right than the right to health care or food or clean water or education. You'd probably find a society that believes strongly in the death penalty, and thinks brutality in prisons is a well-deserved and necessary part of any punishment, and thinks any victim of police brutality probably deserved it. You'd probably find a police force that looked more and more like a military, and you might discover that this force is oriented toward violence as a first response, particularly toward those people that this society has already decided represents presumed moral deficiency and theft and failure to earn life.

You might find that the concept of diplomacy is scoffed at in such a country. You might find a country that invades a country that has not attacked it, and frames this action as a *defensive* strategy. You might find presidential candidates in such a society suggesting that we murder the civilian populations of our enemies. You might find it's an applause line. You might find presidents who boast, as evidence of their moral strength, that when they are hit, they hit back a hundred times as hard. You might find a country that believes any atrocity is allowable, provided only that some enemy might potentially do something that can be framed as similarly atrocious.

If you wanted to know which people such a society considered an enemy, you'd probably look for the people whose acts of aggression were never permitted, and for whom even the hint of potential aggression justified a hugely aggressive response—if *response* is the correct word to a hypothetical preemptive act. You might look for the people against whom acts of violence were rarely prosecuted. Or, to put it another way, you'd probably want to look for which people the police stood in front of to protect, and which people the police faced to oppose.

If this were a deeply ironic universe, you might even find that the people most aligned with all these violent ideas worshipped a deity who admonished his disciples to put their swords away lest they die on them, who presented an example of a God who would sacrifice Themself even to death rather than utilizing any of their infinite power to harmful purpose.

This is the conclusion: **Other people not only do not matter, but it is their fault they do not matter, and it is good if, as a consequence for their failing, they are harmed. But it is even better if they are killed.**

And, of course, every lie will levy a penalty upon those who believe it even as it endangers those who believe it and those who do not alike—because a lie fails to recognize reality, and reality will not be denied forever.

Here is the penalty for believing this lie: **cowardice.**

If the only best solution is violence, then I will be ready to enact it with less and less qualm from an ever-increasingly comfortable position. If I live in a world where violence redeems, then I will become more and more ready to allow it to be delivered to more and more people, even while the threat I perceive grows nearly as quickly as my fear of the world around me, grows nearly as quickly as the every-increasing proliferation of violence that I insist be enacted on my behalf to redeem my fear of that threat. And I will increasingly feel safer the more this violence is done on my behalf, by power structures who will make the violence happen automatically, without my even having to think about it, while I cower with my personal arsenal, hiding from everything that makes me afraid, which increasingly will be a list of everything that exists.

And here is the danger of believing it: **harm.**

The threat that I fear will inevitably grow, because, oriented toward violence, I am creating a world of violence to live in. If I insist on a world where violence redeems, eventually those I threaten will agree to meet me on the deadly battlefield upon which I have insisted, will attack me not from their strength but from their weakness, will try to redeem the problem of me using the very sword I have drawn.

A world in which violence redeems is a world that will inevitably kill me, maybe once, but more probably a thousand times.

◆ ◆ ◆

So those are three foundational lies that any genocidal spirit seeks to establish: First, that we are not related; second, that life must be earned; and third, that violence redeems.

Once these lies are established, genocide becomes inevitable.

The tracks are laid. Now we can focus on efficiency.

You just need a little push. A little blame. An undue focus on crimes committed by a specific group. Build the largest industrialized prison system and the largest military ever known. Take police forces already trained to view specific neighborhoods as war zones, their residents as foreign hostiles, and themselves as an occupying force, and empower them to greater boldness.

Start testing certain concepts, speaking aloud ideas that have hidden for generations behind cover of euphemism.

Start saying we need law and order, by which you mean stopping people randomly on the streets and frisking them.

Start suggesting that our problem is an unbecoming timidity when it comes to violence.

Start saying that we need to bomb them until the sand glows.

Start saying we need to go after the women and children.

Start suggesting that an entire desperate population is a poisoned handful of candy.

Return to a policy of enforcing draconian drug laws in minority populations. Start praising dictators who murder suspected drug users in their own countries.

Propose a travel ban. Fight to enact it in court.

Start rounding people up. Split up some families. Get people used to that idea.

Conflate a vulnerable group with rape. Call them animals. Then go after the most productive and openly integrated and cooperative members of that vulnerable group, to make sure the totality of the dehumanization across the entire group is made clear.

When we feel threatened, suggest the answer is to kill all the people in a country.

All of these things are things I've heard in recent months from the White Christian president, accompanied by the cheers of some very fine people.

7. PROFIT

So that's genocide accounted for. Now for slavery.

For slavery you take genocide, and make it profitable.

As we are nothing if not a hyper-capitalist society, it seems to me slavery has always been our favorite flavor of genocide. Wealthy men, addicted to the high of free labor and all the attendant benefits, founded our nation. Not fans of taxes, those guys. Also not huge fans of paying for labor—so they baked slavery right into our national cookies. Some of them had reservations about slavery, I hear. I've been told this means that they were actually pretty good dudes. Anyway, those good dudes got over those reservations, and so, we eventually fought a war to end slavery. That's the story I learned—and it's a true story, to an extent. We did fight a war. And slavery ended—in the form it had been taking, anyway. So perhaps it's correct to say *we* fought a war to end slavery. But *we* also fought *us*. Therefore, there's another story that also has to be true for that statement—"we fought a war to end slavery"—to be true. *We* also fought a war to *preserve* slavery. Those who preferred the order of slavery more than they preferred the order of a unified country lost their war. Those who preferred the order of a unified country more than they preferred the order of slavery won. And now we are all inheritors of the victor's preference: a restoration of unified order, which as a practical matter happened to bring about the great justice of emancipation. Yet many of *us* still living today think the lost cause of the vanquished should not have been lost, and long to restore that order, to let rise again to greatness that which has been laid low. There are still those of *us* who fly the flag of that cause, and erect statues to honor those who lit the flames of that war, and who are hostile to any suggestion that these practices be discontinued. *We* consider it a moral outrage when anyone observes that *our* ancestors fought a war to preserve slavery, and *we* frame such an observation as an intolerant attack upon *our* heritage. That's not what that flag means to us, *we* proclaim, as if only we get to choose the meaning of symbols once those symbols have been put to violent uses against others, as if we can divorce that meaning from history's memory (any more than Germans could fly the swastika and proclaim that it has nothing to do with Nazis, without also admitting that the perspective of Jewish people and all other groups the Nazis murdered means nothing to them).

One can find in this country reenactments of plantation life on actual former plantations, presenting a narrative that actually slavers were mostly kind, and slaves were mostly well-treated, and many of them were almost family members. You can find history books that say the same. You can find school boards that insist these books be used in schools to the exclusion of others. You can find people who will tell you Black people had it better when they were bought and sold and owned and used like livestock. If you want to meet any of them, I would direct you to right-wing cable news, or to your nearest social media outlet, where these unlovely souls feel free, under hoods of anonymity, to unburden themselves of their horrid thoughts by unleashing them upon the rest of us. And these days, sometimes they don't even bother with the hoods.

The Union won the war, it's true. But they seem to have ceded to the slavers the victor's perquisite to write the history books. We might conclude it is because the Union, even in victory, still preferred order to justice. We might wonder, if we happen to prefer justice to order: Did the Union, having secured the order of unity, comfortable with their own flavor of injustice, feel little need to quibble about the morality of the slavers' taste for slavery? We might even wonder if the Union didn't have a taste for free labor as well. We might wonder if it's *our* favorite flavor, the true North of our nation's moral compass.

Or, perhaps, if we don't have to, we don't wonder.

◆ ◆ ◆

I think of our foundational lies. I see the evidence that we believe them everywhere. It seems to me that if we have already determined that we are not related to each other, and that life must be earned, and that violence redeems those who have not earned life, and that the buckets we use to divide the people who have earned life from the people who haven't are labeled PROFITABLE and NOT PROFITABLE, then slavery seems the natural and intended destination of our national spirit. It is, in other words, the expected and preferred outcome of that series of beliefs. Once wealth becomes self-evidently fungible with moral justice, anything that creates a greater profit will eventually be taken to be moral and just. And cheaper labor creates greater profit. But free labor creates even more profit. And so, in certain expanding circles, free labor starts to be understood to be very, very good. In such a society, the desire for slavery would never be far from power. You'd need to be in a bubble to miss it.

I think about corporations. Maybe you work for one. No big deal if you do; a lot of people do. It's very beneficial for many to do so. A corporation is an entity that ensures profits for a small group of shareholders, assisted by others they pay (often quite handsomely) only as long as they demonstrate skill enough to assist in the continual strategic growth of that profitability, by using that skill to create more value than they are paid, with the surplus going to the shareholders. A corporation is an excellent tool for accomplishing these things, by which I mean that at those things it is extremely effective. And many corporations achieve this value by creating products that people want, which enhance the lives of people who use some of the value they have earned (often from other corporations) to purchase those products. I think many of us have benefitted from this tool we call "corporation" in some way or another, particularly if we are the kinds of people who have figured out how to provide more value to a corporation than the corporation provides to us, which is what makes us profitable to them.

I want to acknowledge all this, because I think for some people reading what comes next, there will perhaps be a tendency to believe that I am demonizing corporations, or that I am saying profits are bad, or that work is bad—this because the general framework we are given is that we are dealing with things that are only good and only bad, rather than with things that, while they can be good in their place, have been improperly elevated above greater goods. You'll read what I have to say about corporations and slavery and tell me that no no no, corporations do not *create* slavery, they actually can be seen, anywhere you look, working to *prevent* slavery. Within a certain framework, this is quite true. Corporations *don't* want slavery. To the extent that corporations *want* anything, they want to maximize profit, in the same way that a chainsaw might be thought to *want* to cut. My point is that the chainsaw doesn't care what it cuts. And, if regulations and public opinion are arranged in such a way that association with slavery creates massive financial and reputational penalties, and the cost of the penalty is sufficiently greater than the cost of compliance, and then most corporations will probably take the steps necessary to avoid being associated with slavery and to be seen taking these steps—not because a corporation cares about the plight of enslaved people (people within the corporation might care very much indeed, but a corporation is a tool, not a person, and does not care) but because such penalties, if effectively structured and enforced, harm profit. But even if they do not take this step (and even as I notice that this step requires regulation by an outside force), I agree: corporations do not *create* slavery. Corporations are only a tool, an instrument for generating profit—and profit can, I think, be a good thing. No, it is a human spirit desirous of slavery that creates slavery, and such a spirit is going to naturally reach for the most effective possible tool, and is going to oppose any regulation to the use of its tools. And perhaps, if we are extremely sharp-eyed, we will notice a national current moving to deregulate corporate industry.

Corporations make a very effective tool for delivering certain types of value and driving certain results. However, they make a terrifyingly poor tool for pondering the essential dignity of human beings or providing for basic human needs, particularly the needs of humans lacking either the wealth to afford the benefits the corporation provides, or the skill to assist in the growth of the corporation's profits. And it would be as unfair to blame a corporation for failing to do so as it would be unfair to blame a chainsaw for being an ineffective syringe; no, we should save our critique for those forcing us to use a chainsaw for injecting medicine, when a syringe is both available and cheaper. Corporations as a matter of their design view the people that labor for them as assets, as resources, and routinely evaluate those resources to make sure they remain strategically relevant and valuable toward the execution of their mission, which is the continual growth of their profit for the benefit of their private owners or public shareholders. If it is determined that these resources (humans) are no longer strategically relevant and valuable toward their mission, they are jettisoned. Since the mission of most corporations is to create profit for their shareholders, this is a very appropriate thing for corporations to do, within the context of the *private* policies of a corporation.

But.

If we believe the primary mission of a just society is not to create profit (which is a different thing than saying that we are *against* profit), but rather to provide for the basic needs and equality under the law of all human beings, then the view that corporations take toward people is an extremely inappropriate and harmful orientation for a society to take toward people from a context of that society's *public* policy. And it is *extremely* corrosive to organize a society of human beings so that corporations, more and more, are the *only* realistically available method of survival or justice for human beings. And it is *hugely* corrosive to any society of human beings to create a society that exists *primarily* for the benefit of corporations—that is to say, for the growth of profit to benefit only a few.

Nevertheless, in a society captured by the idea that profit is moral virtue, captured by the assumption that unprofitable people have not earned life, the idea might arise that our government—which is the mechanism by which we organize our shared life together—might be better run as a corporation, to capture all of a society's plenty as if it were profit, and this idea might begin to seem very reasonable and wise and moral. In a society that has been captured by foundational lies, you might find that the larger a corporation gets, and the more powerful, and the more influential, the better its size and power and influence are deemed to be. The reason is simple: A corporation is the most effective tool yet devised for capturing and growing profit. If profit is your goal, a corporation is absolutely the thing to do it. If profit is your greatest moral value, then a corporation becomes the most moral thing imaginable. And, in such a society, being unprofitable becomes a kind of original sin.

◆ ◆ ◆

You might find that heath care is allowed to become a product in such a society. A product like health care is literally life where there would have been death, healing where there might have been suffering, a product which has by its very nature a market value approaching infinity. So this product might be allowed to reach such near-infinite valuations on an open market in a society that is oriented toward profit as a first priority. This, in turn, might create a massive market for health insurance—itself barely affordable for individuals—the acquisition of which can only be realistically secured through a corporation, requiring individuals to sedulously maintain their profitability so as to continue, quite literally, to earn life.

You might even find that health care corporations produce drugs and market them in such a way that it brings not healing and life and easing of pain, but addiction and death. You might find that these corporations are allowed to continue in this manner for decades, that the family that owns such a company might be permitted to go largely unpunished for doing so, simply because doing so was so gloriously and morally profitable.

In such a society, you might see a bill proposed to deny health care coverage to millions, for failing the most important moral test—for failing, through illness, to be sufficiently profitable. Any consideration for the humanity of chronically ill people would be held as irrelevant beside the sin of their unprofitability, because we believe we aren't related to one another, and that life is something you earn, not something you're born with. In such a society, the idea that health care might be a right afforded to all humans by the simple fact of their humanity might strike many as a deeply offensive idea.

And we've only been talking about health care. We could be talking about many things.

The idea that access to clean drinking water should be a right might seem offensive, or at least impractical, precisely because its lack of market value will devalue it—an argument that presupposes that the only value that can exist is money. The idea that a person has a natural right to move across a border from an area that threatens their life to an area that doesn't might be framed as dangerous and offensive, precisely because the inflow of human beings will be expensive and disruptive. The idea that a labor force can organize might begin to seem deeply offensive and immoral, precisely because the human advantages to be gained would cut into the existing and outsized corporate advantages, which are driven by profit and result in profit. The idea that corporations might enact countervailing measures against organized labor, however draconian those measures might be, might be seen by many as desirable and moral. If the struggle that comes because of the resulting strife between labor and corporations causes disruption, the fault for the disruption will rarely be laid upon corporations for protecting the ultimate morality of their profits, but upon the laborers whose labor created the value, for the crime of demanding to share in the profit they created. In such a society, the idea that there might be restrictions upon how a corporation uses natural resources, on the grounds that those uses endanger human well-being, might begin to seem fatuous, short-sighted, onerous, even offensive. The idea that there should be restrictions placed on corporations to prevent them from using their outsized resources to influence government might seem outdated and foolish and strange. The idea that corporations might be allowed to maximize profits by consolidating, so that industries are controlled by fewer and fewer corporations of larger and larger size, providing more and more benefit to fewer and fewer people, might start to seem wiser and wiser. If we lived in such a society, it might begin to seem to us that everything should be incorporated, that even the justice system should be made profitable, that our prison systems should be incorporated, that crime and punishment should become a growth industry, that human imprisonment should become a product. The idea that prisoners could be used for pennies an hour at hard and dangerous labor might seem very reasonable and wise and moral to us, and the idea that we should make human imprisonment subject to the continual strategic profit growth demanded by private industry might not trouble us at all; and even if we reached a point where we imprisoned more of our population than any other country, we might go on proclaiming ourselves The Land of the Free, without a trace of irony—because what could possibly create more freedom than maximizing profit?

It might even begin to seem to us that war should become a growth industry, maximized for profit. You might even hear this idea suggested by the brother of the Secretary of Education, Betsy DeVos, herself working to make another public good—education—profitable. It might begin to seem wise to us that *everything* should be made profitable and, if it cannot be made profitable, that it (or they) should be jettisoned. It might seem as if real and proven future threats to human life should be ignored, if the solutions to these threats might threaten present profits.

If we lived in such a society, it might begin to seem to us that unemployment relief was deemed theft. It might seem to us that a free lunch given to a hungry child was a moral sin. It might begin to seem to us that citizens of a country should be considered at-will employees of the national corporation, their existence to be determined by what monetary value they are able to deliver in the coming fiscal year. At that point, equating a human being's profitability with their worth—with even their right to go on living—would become an almost unspoken conclusion.

And then, if we lived in such a society, we might start thinking that corporations are people, and that people—certain people, at least—are not. And we might decide to run our government—which is, again, the way human beings organize their shared life together—as if it were a corporation. And then we might hire a businessman to run it. And, if it turned out this entire premise was based upon a set of horrendous lies, you might find that the businessman we hire to run it would himself be the most horrendous sort of fraud, like some sort of basic-cable steak salesman who plays a billionaire on television, dabbles in real estate, and makes his money by not paying his bills.

The natural endpoint of a corporate country will always—by design and destination—be profit, and maximizing profit will always require jettisoning unprofitable people. And, since we are talking not about a single corporate endeavor, but a society, "jettisoning" will not mean firing people no longer deemed profitable so they can go find another job, but abandoning them to death, or incarceration, or a subsistence existence at the mercy of the demand to be profitable. And, should someone want to manufacture death for some group of people or another, they would merely need to arrange power to make it less likely for that group to be able to generate wealth. And so it seems to me that any country that chooses to become a business can only eventually have one product, which will be murder and theft for profit—which is not a judgment against the institution of business, but rather against the improper elevation of business as a higher moral priority than human art.

Here is the great and final conclusion of foundational lies built around profit: **There are people who do not matter, and it is their own fault. It is good if they suffer and better if they die, but it is best if, before they die, they can first be used.**

And, if this were a deeply ironic universe, we might see a

society believing all these lies while belonging to a religious tradition that worships a deity who taught followers that God would be found among the hungry, the thirsty, the prisoner, the stranger, the destitute; who taught that no one can serve both God and money; who taught that humans were to live like the birds of the air, not chasing after tomorrow, but rather coming to eat, freely, without price.

The penalty and the danger for believing this lie is this: **worthlessness.**

When I live in a world where my only value is the profit I can deliver, then I'll live my life trying to deliver it, and when I can no longer deliver it, I'll no longer feel my own worth. I'll become a person who can be used by whoever will value me, and, having so devalued myself, I'll never see the unsurpassable value of others. I'll wear the chains. I'll put them on myself, right after I've made them.

A world in which profitability is the prime measure of human moral virtue is a world in which I am no longer art, but product.

◆ ◆ ◆

Let's wrap up.

There are some who literally want genocide and slavery— true believers. And then there are the rest of *us*, very fine people who prefer order to justice, and the true believers wield that preference of ours with precision to achieve their rough ends.

Put together, this creates a human spirit that wants genocide and slavery.

Most of us who participate in this spirit don't *want* genocide and slavery. We've just been convinced of a set of proposals that will make them inevitable outcomes, and we've been convinced that these proposals are themselves inevitable truths, are in fact the only way a society can be organized.

We conservatives and libertarians don't exactly *want* genocide

and slavery, maybe. We just don't want the hassle of the disorder it's going to require to *not* have genocide and slavery.
This isn't how we think of it, because we've furnished ourselves
with bubbles, surrounded ourselves with mirrors that don't
allow us to see ourselves. We have architectures of justification we've constructed for our support of what may seem like
heartless propositions; we've sought and found proofs of their
efficacy and hidden morality, of their status as necessary and
pragmatic measures, not capitulations to evil.

We can send you links and memes. We have them at the ready.

We leftists and liberals and moderates are not so removed
from this, either. We're willing to go so far as to vote against
the greatest accelerants of the genocidal spirit, but if we win,
we aren't very interested in improving the national spirit further. And if we lose, we're pragmatic. After all, we tell ourselves,
there's not really much difference between the parties. Or
maybe we just think *both* sides are bad and so outcomes don't
matter, conceding badness as a given to which we've reconciled
ourselves. It's comfortable to reconcile. It makes us feel reasonable and open-minded or maybe above it all and untouchable in
our inability to be surprised. And, we think, whatever the other
party does, we can always say "I told you so." We can't say we
didn't know. But we can always say we never voted for it. It's a
thin blanket, but it gives us something at which to clutch. We have
architectures of justification we've constructed. We have furnished ourselves with mirrors that don't allow us to see ourselves.

We can send you links and memes. We have them at the ready.

There are some who talk about justice and equality for all.
But talk is easy; there are only a few of that number—a precious
few—who truly enact it. There are many others of us who talk
of law and order. And in the United States today, the order of
genocide and slavery is the order *we* fight to protect. If you don't
care for the term "genocide and slavery," try this one:

Death of the unprofitable, for profit.

That's our country right now. That's the spirit that has captured us.

That is our frame, defined.

We should change it.

Engaging in a debate set within this framework seems a futile occupation, for even if we "win" the debate, we still occupy a slightly less unjust space within an unjust frame. A debate within an unjust framework benefits the unjust position, by accepting injustice as a foundational premise. As long as you're in the wrong frame, you're still in the wrong picture.

The frame itself is the problem.

Lose the debate. Not in the sense of defeat. In the sense of casting it off.

Lose the debate. Move the frame.

Moving the frame of human perception moves human spirit.

It changes the atmosphere. It tells a new story.

We can resift order's soil if we like, and it looks like we should. But I think we'd do better to fix justice's bedrock. Fixing the bedrock is, it seems to me, more a matter of spirit than law. It's more a matter of desire than ideas. It's the heart, not the mind; the vision, not the spreadsheet; the compass, not the navigation.

It's a matter of alignment.

We move the frame by telling a better story than the one being told.

The best way for us to tell the story is to *be* the story.

So: let's go be good stories—let's go be *art*.

May we burst every bubble.

STREETS
(October 2020)

1. THE FIRST QUESTION

Three years ago, I wrote about our foundational lies, and concluded that our frame was wrong, that the answer to the bad stories we'd been telling ourselves was to tell a better story—to *be* a better story.

It was a good answer. Not very practical, but uplifting for sure. Very positive.

I still believe it's true.

It's not good enough.

It's not *wrong*, but it leaves me somewhat stranded, like I'm hanging from a branch on the side of a mountain and being advised that my problem is that I am in a bad place, and the answer is to climb to a better place.

OK. Great. Thanks!

Climb to a better place *how?* Be a better story *how?*

What story?

Three years ago, I also concluded that you don't move frameworks of belief by changing minds through debate, but by changing spirit through stories.

I still believe that, too.

So, let me tell you two stories.

◆ ◆ ◆

Story one: let's pretend, for the sake of argument, that there's a virus.

Let's pretend it's deadly. Let's say it's a novel new strain of an old structure that we've known about for a long time. In this story, the virus appears quickly, and it spreads quickly, and rapidly becomes a global pandemic. It harms a lot of people, and many of those it harms, it kills. In some places, people are better prepared for a virus, and fewer people get infected, and fewer people die as a result. In other places, people are less prepared for a virus, and more people get infected, and more people die.

Let's imagine that one reason this virus spreads so effectively is because a large number of people who get it are asymptomatic. Unaffected, they transmit it freely. They aren't in danger themselves, but they'll put other people in danger if they don't take the trouble to become aware. Some people will be harmed, and some will suffer permanent damage, and some will die, because of these asymptomatic super-spreaders, who will never even know that they were the cause.

Next, let's pretend it's discovered that the best way of containing such a virus is for everybody to agree, for the sake of those who are most vulnerable, to do some things that are inconvenient. Let's make up some random examples. . . . Let's say they'd need to wear something slightly uncomfortable on their faces, and avoid travel and social contact as much as possible at times of high infection, and perhaps spread out during necessary human interactions. Maybe they'd need to get a vaccine and then boost it every so often, perhaps annually. And let's say that the best way of defeating such a virus was for governments to invest heavily: providing meaningful and sustained financial relief for people whose livelihoods had been compromised either by the spread of the virus or by the measures needed to prevent the spread, and also providing a vigorous, nationally coordinated testing and tracing regime led by expert epidemiologists to learn as much as possible about the virus, and then spending whatever it costs to combat it.

We might dare hope that in time the virus in our story would be defeated. The virus would then seem, for all intents and purposes, to be gone. It wouldn't be gone, of course, but it would be contained, like smallpox is, like measles used to be. So even though the virus would seem to be gone, it would invariably, if we didn't stay mindful of it, come back in ways that would affect us all once again—because viruses mutate, grow, change, and eventually evolve into new strains.

I hope this totally hypothetical scenario isn't too divorced from everyone's recent experiences to be relatable.

In this story, any society that was wise and knowledgeable would invest in vigilant systems to monitor and guard against outbreaks—would commit, in other words, to knowing as much as possible about viruses in general, and then on spending what it costs to combat and contain them. Let's pretend that, in our story, some countries decide to do exactly this. But, in our story, there's a particular country that, though it has more resources than any other, decides instead to *ignore* the virus. Can you imagine this? A society containing millions of people who absolutely refuse to participate in the minor discomforts needed to contain the virus, who oppose the remedy on the basis of cost, or who choose ignorance about remedy rather than remedy itself? Can you imagine millions of people, all framing their decision about a systemic virus exclusively along lines of personal individual risk and intention and freedom, demanding proofs of things already known, then refusing the proofs when they are given? Verbally (sometimes even physically) attacking anyone who dares ask them to honor minimal social considerations and observe basic practices of public health? Try. Stretch your imaginations and pretend that there were people who became very angry even when confronted with the sight of other people engaging in the minor inconveniences that would contain a deadly virus.

Let's pretend that in this society there exists a well-funded corporate media infrastructure fully committed to validating the choices of these deliberately ignorant people, and increasing their ignorance by broadcasting further disinformation, false equivalencies, and outright lies. Imagine such an apparatus, wearing the trappings of authority and trustworthiness, but aligned to delivering to their viewers reinforcements of their ignorance, fully dedicated to framing that ignorance as wisdom, and urging their audiences toward increasingly extreme and aggressive acts in defense of that ignorance. Before long you might decide that such a society was committed, as a first priority, to ignorance of things already known, in order to satisfy the temporary indulgence of their own convenience. Before long you might even have to conclude such people had *aligned* themselves with the spread of the virus, no matter their stated intents. In our story, these people didn't align themselves with the spread of the virus primarily by actively and deliberately spreading it. They aligned themselves with it by simply refusing to know things that are already known, because they didn't want to accept the responsibility that came with knowledge, because they were intent on avoiding any inconvenience that might come with that responsibility.

Or, try this: Imagine a government that decided only to fight the virus to the extent that corporate profit was protected, and, outside of those bounds, would simply exercise a practiced ignorance that the virus existed, or else claim the virus had been contained and now was over, or that it was simply a new part of the immutable unchangeable way things now were. Imagine the leader of such a government who decided to suppress testing, because the report of infection was politically damaging.

Imagine a government that decided to not invest in monitoring or guarding against the next virus, that even dismantled existing apparatuses and safeguards in order to save a relative pittance. Before long, you might decide that such a government was not committed to the health of its citizens. Before long, you'd have to conclude that such a government had deliberately chosen ignorance of things already known, in order to satisfy the temporary benefit of other interests. Before long one might even have to conclude such a government had *aligned* itself with the spread of the virus, no matter its stated intents. Members of the government would say that they were against viruses—of course. But any perceptive observer would know better. In our story, this government didn't align itself with the spread of the virus by actively spreading it. It aligned itself by simply refusing to acknowledge things that were already known, because it didn't want to accept the responsibility that came with knowledge, because it was intent on avoiding any cost that might come with that responsibility.

End of story one.

◆ ◆ ◆

Story two: let's pretend there's a disease called "cancer," and that there's a person who has it. Let's say it's been growing in this person's body, stealthy and invisible, for long months and years. Let's say it's only made certain localized parts of the body less comfortable as it grew—twinges and aches that in retrospect might have been considered warnings to heed. Now let's say that for the first time there is an unignorable visible sign; a tumor grown so large it distends the belly. Let's imagine a doctor who runs some tests. She prescribes immediate surgery to remove all affected tissue, an aggressive campaign of medication and treatment, frequent testing, and a radical change to diet, exercise, and environment.

Now: Let's imagine a patient who ignores all symptoms and refuses all the tests. You'd have to assume that—for whatever reason—they don't want to know the frightening truth. Right?

Or imagine our patient refuses the treatment, because in their estimation the treatment is too *radical.* You'd have to assume the patient had decided, for whatever reason, that the treatment was no longer worth the pain or the cost; that they'd decided instead (as some do, as they progress to end-of-life care) to let matters progress on the established course, with all the fatal consequences that choice entails.

Correct?

But now imagine our patient accepts the initial surgery, but refuses the lifestyle changes. You'd have to assume they'd decided that the likelihood of a recurrence wasn't worth the effort to prevent it, or that the decrease of enjoyment in their life wasn't worth a decreased likelihood of recurrence of a deadly condition.

Yes?

But…imagine our patient makes these decisions *without* facing the reality of what those decisions mean, refuses all diagnosis and treatment and measures meant to prevent recurrence, not from a difficult-but-clear decision that the fight is not worth the pain of treatment or the cost of change, but because they imagine—despite any evidence—that the fight can be won without any cost. Imagine our patient insists that diet and environment don't affect risk factors for recurrence of cancer, or insists that their body isn't a system—that what's happening in one organ in the abdomen can't possibly affect any other part of the body. Imagine our patient decides, despite all available evidence and the exhortations of multiple oncologists, that the tumor is the only problem, that the cancer from which it grew doesn't exist, that the clearly proven environmental factors that fostered it are actually unproven. Imagine our patient makes their only priority a return to the familiar comfort of their life exactly as it was before they received the knowledge of the diagnosis, and expects health to be the result.

Before long, you'd have to understand our patient as somebody committed, as a first priority, to not knowing things that are already known, in order to try to return to a previous state that is no longer attainable. Before long, you'd understand that our patient is putting their entire body in grave danger, not because they've made a measured, aware, and purposeful decision about their physical being, but simply because they don't want to acknowledge the reality in which they now find themselves. Before long, you'd have to conclude that this patient is *aligned* with the spread of the cancer, whether or not they claim that as their intent.

Our patient in this story doesn't align themselves with the spread of the cancer by actively spreading it. They align themselves with it by simply deciding to not know things that are already known, and by not taking active steps to oppose it.

Or, try this: Imagine our patient exists within a healthcare system that makes their ability to pay for treatment and prevention a higher priority than the treatment and prevention itself. Imagine this system commands doctors and hospitals to refuse to allow the tests or treatments, unless that first priority can be satisfied. Imagine a healthcare system that lets people die if treating them isn't profitable, and which commits itself to maximizing those profits. Imagine a system structured so that the patient having an already-existing sickness—a pre-existing condition—actually makes it *less likely* for that person to receive health care.

Before long you'd understand that such a system was not committed to health as a first priority. Before long you'd have to conclude that such a system had deliberately chosen ignorance of things already known, in order to satisfy the temporary benefit of other interests. Before long you might even have to conclude such a system had *aligned* itself with cancer and every other type of disease, no matter the intents of well-meaning people within such a system who diligently and earnestly labored for, and often achieved, the healing and health of others. Those who control and defend such a system will tell you that they are against cancers—of course they are. But any perceptive observer will understand their deeper intentions. Such a system doesn't align itself with the spread of cancer by actively spreading it, but simply by refusing to acknowledge things that are already known, because it doesn't want to accept the responsibility that comes with knowledge, because it is intent on avoiding any cost that might come with that responsibility, and on reaping the benefits that come from the existence of the problem.

End of story two.

◆ ◆ ◆

It seems to me that viruses and cancers have a number of clear similarities and intersections. Both are opportunistic, both committed only to their own growth. Both are systemic, in that what they consume are healthy systems—first destabilizing them, and then, if left untreated, compromising them to the point of failure. Both ought to be prevented and treated no matter the cost, if the patient desires treatment. Surely we all agree on that point, right?

Right?

In both cases, effective treatment involves: first, knowledge that they exist; then a short-term change—often radical, often targeted—to eliminate the threat; then a remedy—a permanent, holistic, watchful, strategic, systemic restructuring of priorities and behaviors—to monitor for and prevent recurrence. In both cases, aligning *against* the spread requires active, persistent, determined, informed, and transformative action. In both cases, aligning *with* the spread requires only passivity, which will prevent the needed transformative action.

Virus and cancer: all either needs to devour a healthy system is for you do nothing.

They'll do the rest.

The differences between viruses and cancers are also instructive.

A deadly virus has no place whatsoever in a healthy system. A virus spreads by mutating a new form for which a healthy system has not yet developed a defense. The treatment for such a virus is systemic eradication. The ongoing remedy against a virus involves monitoring for new strains to detect them, containing them as they're detected, and eliminating them once contained. A perfectly healthy system will contain zero deadly viruses.

A cancer typically grows when a system improperly prioritizes a part of itself that would otherwise be healthy and natural: bone, breast, lymph, lung, liver. Treatment for a cancer is meant to, hopefully, restore the tissue to a right balance within the system, removing the cells committed to an unhealthy growth while saving the cells that the system requires to function properly. After treatment for liver cancer, for example, a person in remission will still have some part of a liver, just one that (hopefully) remains free of cancer. And, though liver cancer springs from the liver, the existence of liver cancer doesn't mean that livers in general are bad, and the suggestion that somebody working to eradicate liver cancer is in some way *anti-liver* would be a foolish notion indeed.

With a virus, the challenge is keeping it out of the system entirely. You defeat the viral attack on the body's systems, then keep vigilant against the next mutation, because if you don't, it will grow, and spread, infecting more and more, taxing our response systems, and making us more vulnerable, especially those of us who were vulnerable already, including those of us with . . . cancer. With a cancer, the challenge itself is systemic. The ongoing remedy for a cancer often involves testing and monitoring not just of the affected area, but of the entire system, to ensure all of it is working in a way that is healthy and sustainable. A tumor is often merely the most unignorable symptom of a systemic vulnerability, demanding radical changes to the configuration of body and lifestyle. In many cases, in order to preserve the body, things cannot go on as they have previously, because to return to such a state makes disaster inevitable, and failing to make radical changes compromises the entire body, making it susceptible both to recurrence of tumors and even external factors, like . . . viruses.

When we find our systems compromised by either cancer or virus, we should not avoid radical and transformative change, if we would align with health. We should *seek* radical remedy and transformational change. We should *desire* them as if they were survival itself—which they are. And, if we would align against recurrence, we should never avoid a systemic restructuring, no matter the expense. We should seek it. We should *desire* it as if it were survival itself—which it is. If we care about health, we must never refuse to know what we know. The cost of ignorance is, eventually, everything. The cost of knowledge, however painful, can never exceed it.

So now that we have that out of the way, it's time to talk about the United States and the world.

◆ ◆ ◆

These days, talking about the United States and the world means talking about the person who is currently, as I write this, the Republican White Christian president of the United States, who actually is—and I still cannot believe I am saying this—Donald Trump.

So: he's a liar.

So: he's a fascist.

So: he's an authoritarian.

So, he's using his office to enrich the businesses he still owns and from which he still profits. So, he encourages and celebrates police violence, and advocates the use of military force against peaceful protest. So, he's using the exact language and phrases of white supremacy and neo-Nazis and fascists, and pursuing their exact desired policies. So, he's deliberately demolishing all norms and standards of a functional democracy, in service of demolishing democracy, in service of himself. So, he's working to put himself entirely above the law, and, even more, positioning himself *as* the law, as someone whose authority must not be questioned, to whom loyalty is irreducible from patriotism, for whom criticism must be understood as not just criticism of the country but as an attack on it. So, he used the power of his office transactionally, first to try to destabilize the coming elections, then to try to punish political enemies by imposing medical sanctions on his own citizens during a pandemic—premeditated manslaughter at best, genocide at worst.

Also: His entire party has rallied around these efforts in support of them—almost as if somebody doing what he is doing was their plan all along. Also: his followers, his true believers, millions and millions strong, all cheer for him, and the worse he gets, the more that he perfectly embodies all of the worst things any of us warned he might become, the more they seem to love him. They cheer and cheer and cheer, and they tell us to get over it, and they say "fuck your feelings," and then they tell us they love the way he makes us weep, because they love to drink our tears. And they take to the streets and government buildings with massacre weapons to win back their never-lost right to honor a murderous movement to preserve chattel slavery, or to establish their right to spread a virus to the satisfaction of their own convenience. And they laugh and laugh and cheer and cheer and yet they never seem to get happy. They cheer for a system that is optimized for the abuse of the marginalized by the powerful, not because they are powerful, but because seeing the abuse of those more marginalized than them comforts them that they are not so marginalized as that.

Also: comfortable masses, tens of million strong, seem not to worry about any of this, as long as it doesn't touch them personally. If you think this list of quite-obvious truths seems hysterical, overwrought, scolding, divisive... then be even more comforted than you have already made yourself! You have a lot of company. You speak the language of comfortable masses, for whom the report of abuse is seen as the real abuse, who save their ears for the resentments of the attackers, not the screams of their victims—because the screams of the victims carry a moral duty to respond, while the attackers ask only for an easy silence. I know this, because, if I'm honest with myself, I know it's a silence I've given many times before—and so, if you are a comfortable person, have you. Still, there are those among us who are now, in this rough authoritarian age, coming to these inescapable realizations of truths which are only new to us. The tumor at last distends the belly, and now we know.

Also: there are those of us—not white enough, wealthy enough, male enough, abled enough, cis enough, straight enough—for whom this is no revelation, because this authoritarian abusive country is the only one we've known.

So. Here we are. And the question is: what next?

Next? Well, either he wins, or he loses. Either he gets what he wants, and his party gets what they want, and his cheering hordes get what they want, or else they don't.

If he wins, it's a grim matter but at least it's a simple matter. We have enough of a trendline to see exactly where we're headed. We'll see the full-throttle victory of all our old worst historical traditions and the death of all our best aspirational dreams for ourselves. We'll see the final death rattle of whatever shreds remain of our tattered global reputation, and the irrevocable end of our oldest alliances. We'll fully commit to being an authoritarian kleptocracy, a theocratic genocidal white ethno-state. There will be some semblance of something they'll call "elections." There will be some semblance of something they'll call "the news." There will be something they call "the law." And many things we already see will be escalated: troops whose ostensible purpose is to protect our borders, ranging far from the border; other troops called "police" whose ostensible purpose is to protect our citizens, occupying neighborhoods full of citizens, all of them acting as they see fit to create the sort of general and specific terrors that comprise their true missions; locations that will be called something less overt than "concentration camps"; people dying on the street because they no longer have what's needed to survive in a country that has been architected in such a way to digest and destroy unprofitable people.

Yes, I think that's what they'll do. If not, why are they already doing it more and more, as much as they're able, as quickly as they're able, everywhere they're able? It's not comfortable to know, but those not knowing it reveal a willful effort to not know things already known.

And if he and his party lose? If we actually manage to temporarily halt their advance?

That's a somewhat more hopeful matter, but not so simple. Because we've learned things about ourselves, and our country, and our friends and neighbors, and our systems of administration and authority, that we can never un-know. We now know who will look the other way, and what they'll look the other way for. We know who will find reasons to accept unacceptable things, or become confused about obvious truths and obvious lies. We know now what people will stand for. We know now what people will *cheer* for. When the chips are down, you find out what people are like when the chips are down. And then you know.

We've watched the message of an openly fascist, openly corrupt, openly white supremacist president grow, and spread, a new strain of an old virus against which we'd stopped being vigilant, mutated for a world of international television and internet media, a sensationalized version of our country's oldest sins. We've heard those who would cheer this spiritual infection of hate, who would gather in red-capped throngs to spread this soul-rot between each other. We've seen the enthusiasm of some—the eagerness, even the joy—at the thought that they might once again become great; that in a nation that was beginning to tentatively seek redemption, they might consider themselves already absolved; that in a nation that was listening to more and more voices, they might become the only voice once more; that in a nation that was seeking diversity, they might once again become not just the default consideration but the only one; that in a nation that was imperfectly seeking equality, they might again become the sole priority. We've seen the quick acclimation of others to this new reality, as they opened themselves to this new infection of old lies, seeking some advantage they might press, as the most vulnerable populations first felt the effects. We've heard all the excuses they give themselves for all this. And we've heard all the threats they've offered, the retribution they've promised to deliver, if they don't get their way. We've seen the sunglasses-hat-goatee warriors on the steps of government buildings toting their privately owned massacre weapons, and we've noticed that our police show far more deference to them than to others who present far less threat to a peaceful order, whose cause is justice rather than supremacy. We've seen the cops rioting, brutalizing crowds every night with military equipment and thuggish tactics, for the crime of challenging their state-sanctioned license to murder with impunity. They aren't going to stop cheering for it, even if voters depose their beloved hate goblin. They're not going to stop expecting it, or demanding it, or fighting for it. They've seen the white supremacist authoritarian anti-democratic state that Donald Trump would bring, and they very much want it. They think it's *great*.

But there's more.

We now know that, even though Trump is a disruption to the

status quo in some ways, he isn't *only* a disruption to the status quo. In many ways, he is a part of that status quo's inevitable progression. He's the result you can expect to see, in a society which believes that we have no shared society beyond individual desire, that life must be earned, that profit is how you earn it, and that violence redeems. We can see that Trump isn't a disruption to business as usual, but rather a purified concentrate of that business. In other words, even though he spread a virus, Trump isn't a virus. He's the first unignorable tumor—for those of us comfortable enough to have ignored the previous symptoms. Yes, he'll have to be removed completely, but afterward things are going to have to be different. If they aren't, then we'll find ourselves here again.

And we may well find ourselves here again.

Even many opposed to the spiritual virus of MAGA America aren't interested in quarantining it, or vaccinating against it. Some still remain opposed to radical transformations of our ways of living. Some want only to remove the tumor of Trump, then return to the exact situation that allowed it to grow. We've heard all the justifications for this, because we *know* them. We often *are* them. These complacent masses aren't strangers, any more than the cheering red-capped throngs are strangers. For many of us—probably most of us—they're the people we grew up with and live around. They're *us*. Happy, smiling, friendly, many of them. They love their kids. They go to church. They work hard. They pay their taxes. They walk their dogs. They love us, some of them. Yes, and we love them, many of them—and if we seem so angry, perhaps the reason is that the anger we feel toward these friends and family and neighbors, while appropriate and honest, is easier than the deep sorrow and mourning, that those we love would so willingly, eagerly, or complacently align with a man who has no redeeming characteristics, align with a spirit that pursues atrocity, energizes hate, demolishes democracy, and promotes an empty promise of tawdry glory that's as chintzy and false and ignorant as everything else about its grotesque leader. We share our lives with these people, whether they (or we) will admit it or not. We share families and neighborhoods and associations and workplaces and nations.

I see two questions we have to face, in the teeth of this new knowledge. These questions sound simple, but aren't. They will be the same questions after the election as before, no matter the result—and so will the answers.

I'll get to the second question eventually.

The first question is about awakening, conviction, and confession.

It's this: *How did we get here?*

I'll tell you how I think we got here.

I think we drove, on streets we built.

2. STREET

Here's my situation: There's a street in front of the place where I live.

Perhaps you can relate.

Let me describe this street. It's rather hard, mostly smooth, mostly flat, made of some sort of composite material, beveled slightly downward at the edges to accommodate rain runoff, pocked here and there with lids covering access points to sewer and water infrastructure. We call these access points "manholes," though I assume women will also fit down them. The street is connected to the houses lining it by a series of umbilicals we residents call our "driveways." This street is connected to some other streets, which connect to still other streets, which connect to yet even more streets, some of which arrive at other locations within the city, others of which lead out of the city, to other destinations. I'm given to understand this is a common setup. Maybe this is a shared experience between us.

It's the street where I live, this street I've described to you. This makes it *my* street, even though other people drive on it, walk on it, jog down it, bike down it.

Once somebody ran by in a giant inflatable tyrannosaurus rex costume. Fun times!

I drive and walk on the other streets, too, many of them lined with houses and apartments. People live there is my assumption. I suppose the people in those houses and apartments think of these streets as *their* streets, even though I drive on them. Yes, I drive and walk on *their* streets. I don't ask first. I don't even think about it; I just do it. Everyone is very cool about it. Nobody complains. And I pay this hospitality forward, too; as I believe I've mentioned, other people drive and walk down *my* street every day, and they don't ask permission either, and I'm extremely cool about it, though my dogs are not cool about it.

They bark.

I use my street every day. It's how I go places. If my street was gone, I'd miss it. I'd have to hunt for parking somewhere a block away, and trudge out to my car whenever I wanted to drive. If everyone else's streets were gone, I'd miss them, too. Interestingly enough, if all the streets disappeared, I'd miss everybody else's streets more than I'd miss my own. Moreover, if all of *their* streets were gone, it wouldn't really matter if my street were still there. I'd have to walk everywhere, or get a vehicle that could handle cross-country driving, like for example a sturdy wagon and a brace of oxen.

The value of *my* street depends, intrinsically, on all of *their* streets. And the value of *their* streets depends, in a miniscule part, on *mine*. And, it seems, the collective aggregation of *other people's* streets provides me more value—*much* more, in fact—than my own specific street provides me. It seems that in easily observable ways, collective value is far more useful to each individual than any individual value can be—even the value each individual gives themselves. Also: The value and benefit of our streets are inextricably entangled with each other. You can't take one away without diminishing the rest. Each one by itself would be a bizarre curiosity. Together, they connect a community. Which leads me to a set of conclusions that might surprise some people: (1) there is a society; (2) it exists; and (3) we're all part of it.

None of this happened because any of us—me, my neighbors, you, your neighbors, or anyone in between—actively intended to do it. It just happened. It's happening now—right now, as I type this—with literally zero effort from me. It would happen even if I focused all my effort on trying to make it not happen. It happens pretty much exactly the same way for me and my neighbors even if we disagree with each other on literally everything—if fact, what we believe or intend or think has no impact on the benefit we receive from our street, or upon any inconvenience we would receive if our street were demolished. All that really matters, from a practical purpose, is that we are where we are, all together at this point in time.

We *are*, and so it just *happens*.

Everyone I know has a street, in some manner of speaking.

I don't know anybody who constructed their own street.

How interesting.

◆ ◆ ◆

Question: Who put my street there, in front of the place where I live?

Who put *your* street there, in front of the place where *you* live? Have you ever wondered?

◆ ◆ ◆

Literally, I mean. Who did it? We're an individualistic society. So who's the individual responsible for my street? It's not a confusing question, but I don't find the answer immediately obvious. Do you know who put *your* street there? I mean, I presume at some point there was a construction crew, a group of people who did the actual labor of clearing the ground and digging the trenches for water and gas and sewer and electrical hookups to the various plots, then tamping it smooth, and grading it, and then maybe laying down gravel, and then a layer of boroscite, and maybe then five layers of muscelinated grist of various elasticities and torsions, and then the final layer of toprock before planating the asphalt surface.

Now I would like to be clear: I don't know how it's done at all. I am utterly clueless. In fact, I just made up most of those words I used. But . . . the road crew knew, I assume. After all, they did it. But I wonder: did any one of them know exactly every step of it? Is there any one person among them who could, all by themselves, build the street?

Maybe so.

After all, I assume they had a foreman of some kind, who had the plan for the street, and understood each piece of it, and directed the operation from start to finish. But could the foreman have operated each machine used in the construction? Did the foreman have the actual physical knowledge of each of the steps and how to practically enact them? Put another way: Had the foreman been left alone, could the street have still been built, however slowly, and, if so, would it have been as skillfully done? And even if the answer is "yes," can you say the foreman put the street there? Did the foreman decide on putting my street *there* instead of somewhere else?

What about the plan the foreman followed? Did the foreman make the plan? Probably not. Probably there was some sort of city planner, a highly trained civil engineer, perhaps an urban architect, who understood the proper way to build the street, who drew up the plan, and the methods, specifications, and regulations. Perhaps the same city planner was even the one who coordinated the efforts, who assigned the foreman and the road crew, who organized supplies.

But even in the unlikely scenario under which the city planner

did every bit of this work, could it be said the city planner *built* the street? First of all, could the city planner have done
all of the labor? Would the city planner have been in possession
of all the same tactical practical physical knowledge as the foreman and crew? Even if so, of course, you have all the industries
that made the materials and tools and equipment that came in
from elsewhere, which the crew used to build the street, and of
course all of that has to be purchased, and if it was purchased by
the city, it was purchased using tax revenue that came . . . from
all of *us*. But even if you take all *that* away . . . why did the city
planner decide to put the street *there?* Who put the guidelines
and rules and restrictions in place long before she was assigned,
which governed where and how the street could be designed,
placed, and constructed?

I assume the city planner decided to do that because she
was assigned to do it. And she was probably assigned to do
it because there were going to be houses put there. So there
was zoning and registration and parceling and decalogueing
and interdicting (again I cannot stress enough I have absolutely no idea of the actual procedure and may be making
some words up) and all of the administrative and legal activity that's necessary to have construction crews come out and
build houses to which a street might be connected, to connect
to other streets, without which the houses would add little
value to the city.

I presume all this happened because the city decided there
needed to be a street there.

Wait.

The *city* decided?

The city? Decided?

A city is a collection of buildings, isn't it?

How does a collection of buildings decide anything?

Who put my street there?

◆ ◆ ◆

I'm being coy, of course.

We know what is meant by "the city," when it comes to zoning decisions, and it isn't a collection of buildings. We all know—even if some of us find it psychologically convenient or comforting to pretend we don't—that society isn't property, but people.

We know why the street is there.

My street is there because somebody decided to build houses there, because cities need people, and people need houses, and houses need streets because people in houses need streets. Someone decided to build houses there because somebody decided they wanted a house there, either to live in, or to sell to someone to live in. But they wouldn't have wanted to do that, I presume, if there hadn't already been streets and houses nearby—would they? I mean, conceivably, the construction crews that put the houses on my street could have put those same houses in the middle of the deepest darkest part of one of my state's many forests, but they didn't. Why?

I'm only speculating here, but perhaps it's because it is very challenging and expensive to connect a house in the middle of the deepest darkest part of the wilderness to the rest of society, and unless a house can be connected to society, that house will hold very little value to most potential homeowners. Likely nobody would have come to live in them. And no city would agree to build a street for them or to them. Got that? The exact same houses which, if placed in my city, might be in high demand, would, if divorced from the communal force of society, hold almost no value. They'd rot away, unlived in, unknown, a bizarre and eerie curiosity for a hiker to find, or maybe a wolverine. The city agreed to build a street for those houses because *the city decided* there would be value to adding houses to the city, because they knew that if the city held more people, the city would gain more value. And people need houses. And people in houses, of course, need streets. And so my street was decided upon.

But we know it wasn't the *city*. It was the people in the city. *They* decided. But we know it wasn't *all* the people. It was the people appointed to the task of making those determinations. *They* decided. When we say *the city* decided, we actually mean them. Those people, in that moment . . . they *were* the city; a brief and targeted manifestation of our collective will to be a city of people with housing connected to streets.

Our collective will? Of course. All of us. *We* appointed *them* to *be* "the city," on our behalf, which reflects an almost holy amount of public trust. At least, those of us that participated in the process of appointing them did—those of us who bothered, or those of us who were allowed to, or those of us for whom the right to participate hadn't been made too dangerous or systemically difficult, appointed people to be "the city." And then there were others of us, who perhaps were too busy or disinterested or disaffected or disenfranchised to participate directly, but who nevertheless held a certain set of opinions about what is good and desirable—a general and shared knowledge set, which we might call "common knowledge," which would inform our appointed decision-makers' decisions in many ways, some of which they probably wouldn't even consciously think about. And then, the decision makers decided— probably not about every street and every house, but on a series of guidelines and rules that would govern the way such things would and would not be permitted, and the methodologies and restrictions around securing such permissions and executing plans based on those permissions. And if the common knowledge was based on deep fundamental truths, then all the people would be able to participate equally in appointing decision-makers, and their collective desire would be to provide for the life and dignity and thriving of all. And, if these representatives we had appointed were good at *being the city*, then they listened to what the "common knowledge" thought of that decision, and also remembered previous similar decisions, and tried to replicate what had worked for or benefitted the most people from those previous decisions, and tried to avoid what hadn't worked for or harmed people from those same decisions.

And in that way, as best they could, they used our public trust to represent our collective will. That's the idea, anyway.

And it occurs to me that streets are a delivery mechanism— one of many—for that collective will. Streets are how the collective will decides to deliver transportation, among other things. And then the city planner, drawing out the plans for *my* street, became a brief targeted manifestation of our collective will. And then the foreman, and the workers. And then, finally, me.

Because, look: Our collective will decided that my street should be there, for people to live in houses there. And they were right. There are people living in those houses. I'm one of them, and my neighbors are the rest. We live in the houses, connected to the street, and we drive on the streets, and we give value to the city. We don't live there *in order* to give the city value, but we give it value all the same. Nor can we *not* give the city this value, unless we choose to move away, in which case we only give our value to some other city or township or village or wide place in the road.

But of course, there was a time before any streets were built, when people decided to live *here* instead of *there*. It wasn't a random decision. Some natural confluence occurred that people recognized as providing some sort of natural value. In my city's case, as with so many cities, that confluence was something human beings naturally need: water. Water sustains life. It allows agriculture. It allows easy transportation to other settlements downriver, settlements comprised of people whose forebears made the decision to settle *there* for many of the same reasons as the forebears of my city decided to settle *here*. For my city, as with so many cities, our first street was one we had no hand in building at all—a river.

Nobody did anything to get the river. The river was there, delivering its value, and so people came to it, and from that natural delivery system, we built more systems of our own to deliver value to those living there—things like barges, docks, locks, fish ladders. And houses. And streets. So, in a very literal sense, my street can be seen as a tributary of a river.

My street...at its very origins, it wasn't something purchased or earned.

It was a *natural* thing. You might think of it as a natural gift. Natural.

But, if I and my neighbors weren't there, the houses would have no value and meaning, nor would the street—unless others came and lived there. If there were no people living in any of the houses, the city would have no value, no meaning. It would be a bizarre and eerie curiosity. For there to be value, we need there to be a community. And for it to exist, a community needs there to be us. And so it comes to be. The street is there on my behalf, because it was decided that somebody, to the incremental minuscule benefit of everybody else, should be where I now am, and *that* somebody turned out to be me. If it hadn't been me, it would have been somebody else, unless nobody else came, in which case the house, unlived in, would eventually cease to exist, and if this happened with all houses on the street, then so would the street.

We need there to be a community. A community needs there to be us. And so it comes to be. And so we come to be. Because we are *human*.

Human.

A street is a part of a *natural human system*. And I am a human. Thus, I exist, in a very observable way, within a natural system. To perceive it I just have to walk out to my mailbox and look both ways.

How interesting.

Who put my street there?

I did.

3. VALUE

So, then: The street in front of my house is a part of a system of streets—a part of a *natural human* system, a delivery mechanism for values naturally provided by human community. One significant use of streets is literal delivery—which make streets a particularly apt synecdoche for the ways natural human systems deliver value. Almost any system I can think of has observable qualities, and, if one is curious about a system, it might be useful to observe and catalogue that system's qualities.

So I think I'll do that.

◆ ◆ ◆

Remember, this system in which I take part is *natural*. If you trace it back far enough, it's established upon natural resources providing value that nobody made. Wide river or vast reservoir or shoreline, rich topsoil, natural minerals, teeming forest—you name it, humans are where humans are for natural reasons. And thus, on the location of what is now my city, a natural system of humans sprang up, which eventually developed to the point where it believed it would need a human where my house is, and I became that human. By being that human, I enrich my house and my street with value and meaning, and enrich my neighbors' houses with value and meaning, and they similarly enrich mine. There is a community, and I share in it. And that community has a collective will, and I share in that, too.

This value the streets provide: it's *shared*.

Shared.

My street is there now. I could go look at it, right now, if I wanted to.

Your street is there now, too, ready to offer its gifts of transportation and interconnectivity from your house to the very borders of your country, and beyond. Do this: Close your eyes and picture your street. Now picture the potential for transportation it provides. What does that potential look like? I mean the physical thing. Does it have physical form? If so, is the form you chose a metaphor? If you've ever actually *seen* the potential for transportation that all the interconnected streets provide, let me know. I never have.

My street is a delivery mechanism for the value a community provides. It does this so effortlessly that, in the manner of water to fish, or sky to birds, it's practically undetectable to me and all those who receive it. Until I started writing this, I rarely thought about my street. You could almost say I didn't see it. I have never seen the potential for transportation it provides.

This shared value the streets provide: it's *invisible*.

Invisible.

However invisible it is, it's the context from which everything else springs. Any trip I take, no matter how far I go, begins with my street, and only continues as it does because of the existence of other streets. If the streets weren't there, I'd be far less likely to arrive at my destination, or to even know the destination exists. It strikes me that this is another way streets resemble the whole of a natural human system, because natural human systems provide all the context for all my potential action: almost every possibility available to me, no matter how smart I am, no matter how innovative, no matter how successful—none of it would be possible if there weren't a community from which it springs, or a community to share in it. I may know more than anyone else, but who taught me? I may provide many thousands of jobs, but who provided the labor to fill those jobs that generated the profit that allowed me to provide more jobs? My innovations may provide incredible value, but who is there to appreciate them, and remunerate me for my contributions? No matter how skillful, or intelligent, or hard-working, or diligent, or innovative I am, this value that we all naturally share is *why* I'm able to apply those skills to anything more than myself and my own rugged and isolated subsistence.

This shared, invisible value the streets provide: it's *foundational.*
Foundational.

And: Imagine my neighbors weren't there. Imagine mine was the only occupied house on the block. My residence on an otherwise-deserted street would start to seem like a bizarre curiosity, or at least the emptiness of all the other houses would seem to me an ominous sign. It would be difficult for me to sell such a house—far more difficult than it would be for me to sell the exact same house in a fully occupied neighborhood. This leads me to an odd conclusion: my neighbors lend *more* value to my house than I do, even though they don't live in it. And even as we all lend our street meaning, all the other people in the city lend *more* meaning to our street than we lend to it, even though none of them live on our street. And this favorable unbalance exists in the relationship between each of those other people and their own streets, and all the other streets—including mine—that are not *theirs.*

And, in fact, the more I'm able to grow from this foundational soil of shared value, the more I owe to it. The more success I'm able to create for myself, the more I was able to create only because this foundation exists, which generates more potential and opportunity for an individual than that individual would ever be able to generate for themselves. A city of a million can do more than a town of a hundred—and *does* do more. The more people, the more opportunity, potential, and resource; and the more people there are to share in this generative value, the more the system generates to be shared.

This shared, invisible, foundational value I derive from my street—it's *generative.*
Generative.

There is no procedure set for collecting and distributing this value. There's no account into which this value will be deposited, no wait time for the receipt. It's just there. We can't *not* get this value. The system can't *stop* giving it. How could you live in a city and not live around its streets, or benefit from their existence? But the people who live in the city don't live there *in order* to give our street value. This value isn't generated and delivered through any intentional act on our part. As long as we live here instead of somewhere else, the streets will go on delivering to us the value of living here. And if we go somewhere else, then the streets *there* will deliver similar value in the same way. We seem to have a shared life in some mysterious way, which finds its center-point simply by existing *here*, instead of *there*. The value we give to each other is connected in ways from which we cannot separate ourselves.

This shared, invisible, foundational, generative value I derive from my street—it's *automatic* and *inextricable.*

Automatic. Inextricable.

How interesting.

◆ ◆ ◆

Remember, this natural system in which I take part is *human.* It involves humans. Humans have taken something that naturally occurs, and they built something around it. In so doing, they've taken what was natural and made it something else.

My street was built sometime in the 70s or the 80s. I know, because my house was built in 1990, and because I happened upon a map of my city drawn up from the late 60s and my street wasn't on it, though some surrounding streets were. It's new, my street. When the construction crew showed up, they put a street where no street had previously been.

However, my city was founded around 1840 or so, long before construction crews knew how to pave streets for cars—long before cars, in fact. Many streets in my city—the very streets that lend my street more value than my street lends them back—have been there for quite a while, and were, at some point, modernized. From this example I surmise that existing streets require maintenance and improvement, or they lose value. And—since streets give a city value, and the city returns a small portion of that value to the streets, which makes the streets more valuable, which allows the city to receive more value—I further surmise that a city that chooses not to maintain and improve its streets makes a foolish choice; chooses to slowly become less and less able to produce and deliver value in a changing world. My city was wiser than that. My city maintained and improved its streets, and so became a modern city.

The shared, foundational, generative, automatic, inextricable value that comes to me from all my city's streets, delivered all the way down to my street . . . it can be changed, enhanced. It's *configurable*.

Configurable.

My street wouldn't ever have been built, if the older streets, modernized and improved, hadn't been there to suggest the possibility of my street. The people who put those oldest streets there didn't do it for me to come enjoy them, yet I am here. There was no intentional act at the time to enrich me specifically, yet I am enriched. In some way, without intending to, I've inherited the value of those streets, laid down 150 years ago. And there's literally nothing I can do to divest myself of such an inheritance. It comes to me in *my* city as naturally as the rain that falls on the roof—*my* roof. Is it *my* rain? I suppose you could look at it that way. Some do.

The shared, foundational, generative, automatic, inextricable, configurable value of *my* street . . . it's *inherited*.

Inherited.

Now, here's something interesting. I don't make specific decisions about my street. The alterations made to this natural human system of streets are made based on what people appointed to make decisions about streets think the streets should be like, not on what I think the streets should be like. If *the city decides* that my street should receive only the best, I will receive only the best. And, if *the city decides* that my street is worthless and deserves nothing at all, I will receive nothing. If *the city decides* to appoint people knowledgeable about streets, knowledgeable decisions will likely be made. If *the city decides* to appoint corrupt dipshits, then corrupt decisions rationalized by dipshittery will likely be made. And my neighbors and I will all share in this configured inheritance in the same way we share in everything else in our natural human system—that is: foundationally, generatively, automatically, inextricably.

This leads me to some fascinating and uncomfortable realizations: it would seem that a natural human system can deliver not only positive value, but *negative* value—and that this inheritance has nothing to do with intention. I receive it even if it accrued years, decades, centuries before I was born. Nor is the value I gather from that inheritance something I can separate from myself. I receive it so effortlessly, it would be possible for me to receive it without even being aware of it, as one might imagine a tree receiving nutrients from its roots without a thought to the fungi connecting it to its forest, the way its leaves receive rain without a thought to anything like a cloud. My street is part of a natural human system in which I partake, established by a will in which I partake, to deliver value that is shared, invisible, foundational, generative, automatic, inextricable, configurable, and inherited; completely separate from my daily individual intentions; delivered to me not because of anything I did; delivered all because there was a general societal expectation of a *me*, and I have become that *me*.

How interesting.

And I wonder: how have we configured our streets?

How *are* we configuring them?

How will we configure them in the future?

What are our intentions, and how do they align with those configurations?

How do they align with our inheritances?

And I wonder: what else might I have inherited through this

configuration? And what have others inherited so that I might enjoy such an inheritance?

What other good? What other *harm*?

What I like about the street metaphor is, it's not a metaphor.

4. CONFIGURE

I will now say some obvious things about streets.

A street has *direction*. What I mean is, it leads from one place to another. It leads from and to the same places today as it did yesterday, with the same stops along the way. Where our streets start and where they lead reflect our community's historical priorities about which places were deemed important for people to be able to easily travel, and which were not. We didn't decide on these priorities, you and I, but if those configurations benefit us, then we benefit. If they disadvantage us, then we are disadvantaged. You might say we've inherited this configuration. If we want to make a street longer, we can extend it, but it will still lead out further in the same direction. If we realize the destination is no longer useful, or even harmful, we'd abandon the street, and build new streets to new locations. I'd conclude from all of this that a street's direction and destinations represent a series of decisions with easily observable priorities and intentions.

Put it this way: Streets are built. No street ever reached its destination by accident.

Like I said: obvious.

Here are some more obvious things to say about streets:

People made them. Other people, who inherited them, can change them.

People who build new streets or modify existing ones can set them upon a foundation that is even, or uneven. They can use materials that are sturdy, or shoddy. If they're uneven or decrepit or outdated, people can make them better.

Or . . . they can make them *worse*.

They? We.

We can configure streets to generate opportunity and value and health equally for all. Or we can configure them to generate ease for some and hardship for others, to capture opportunity and value and health away from some and give it to others. And the natural qualities of a natural human system mean that the theft and harm will be delivered to those it victimizes in the same way that the opportunity and health is delivered to those it favors: in a way that is shared, invisible, foundational, generative, automatic and inextricable.

If a street isn't maintained, it will fall into disrepair. If the disrepair isn't remedied, it will get worse, not better. A city that won't maintain its streets will eventually become a city incapable of creating or receiving the value of transportation. So, if we're wise, we maintain our streets. And so, simply by observing the conditions of our streets, we can make determinations, not only about which places are important for people to be able to access, but which places and which people are deemed *more* important. And which places and people are deemed less important.

If we no longer cared about a location that we previously deemed important, we might stop maintaining the street, and allow it to fall into disrepair. A casual observer would easily be able to detect the underlying priorities; about a place the community once valued, which it values no longer—and, if there are people still living on that street, about those people, too. And the people living there would also understand, of course. They, too, would understand at a glance what message was being delivered by their neglected and decaying street.

You might say that our streets are a tool—one of many— whereby a community reveals its priorities—its *real* priorities, the ones that can't be denied, because they are what's really happening. And, if we were to chart the full history of changes to our streets—of enhancement, creation, modification, construction, and of neglect, abandonment, and demolition, too—we could conceivably create a map of our community's historical and ongoing priorities and intentions regarding human access to transportation, and of which humans are valued.

Here are some more obvious things to say about streets:

Configuring streets—updating existing ones, building new ones—requires work. The steps involved might be thought of as the work of configuration.

If we wish to maintain our streets, or extend them, or modify them, or build new ones to serve new needs, we will have to . . . do it.

But first, right at the start, we'll have to realize that there's a need to do it.

And some time after that, but still before we do it, we'll have to accept that doing it is our collective responsibility. And some time after *that*, but still before we do it, we'll have to determine to actually do it, and make the necessary plans. And some time after *that*, but still before we do it, we'll have to agree to pay what it costs. And some time after *that*, the cost—in labor, in inconvenience and disruption, in actual money—will actually have to be paid. And only once all those steps have taken place will the street actually be changed or maintained.

If these steps don't take place, then the change won't happen. The street will degrade. And if somebody doesn't want to pay to fix the streets, they'll likely try to disrupt those steps that lead to repair. As I said: obvious—but I've learned that this is an age in which it has become useful and necessary, even powerful, to state plain and obvious things.

◆ ◆ ◆

I write speculative fiction sometimes, which can get weird. It's OK with me. I like weird.

Let's try a speculative scenario, something super weird.

Let's imagine that in a society just like ours, some foundational aspect of the streets was found to be harmful in a way that threatened everyone. Let's say for example that they had been built for individual personal vehicular transportation rather than highly scalable public transportation, and that this configuration created congestion and isolation and hazard, and made life increasingly difficult and dangerous for increasing numbers of people, and made ownership of individualized private vehicles a prerequisite for participating in society, which made cities far less livable and more difficult and dangerous to walk around in—and beyond that, the strain on non-renewable resources and the impacts on the environment that attended the consumption of those resources by these vehicles created effects that endangered the stability of all societies and the lives of everyone in those societies.

I warned you, I do sometimes come up with *very* weird fictional premises. Maybe that one is too far out there, too speculative. What if we made it something simpler, then: what if some part of all the streets, some chemical in their composition, were radioactive and deadly?

What then?

Well... if we valued the lives of people in our system, we'd need to replace the streets.

How many? All of them.

How far? To the furthest extent of the problem. To the very boundaries of the city. To the very foundations that create the hazard. In other words, the solution would require active, persistent, determined, informed, and transformative action.

At what cost? At whatever cost it took.

Otherwise, we'd have to accept that the streets would kill us, because we valued the money we would save by neglecting the streets rather than paying the cost to repair and enhance them more than we valued the lives of the human beings harmed by our harmful streets.

Right?

Like I said: obvious.

But hey, listen to this: What if we only fixed *some* of the streets? What if we only fixed the streets where most of the residents were deemed to be "white?" Or what if we—"unable to see color," but having inherited a system whereby those deemed "white" were more likely to own generational wealth, homes, and other property—only fixed the streets lined by houses of greater value?

That would work out, I suppose, provided you are someone wealthy enough to afford a valuable house, and provided the thought of your neighbors dying while you live is acceptable to your conscience.

But suppose human intentions are like streets. Suppose human intentions have a direction, too, and that living in a murderous system that is designed to see human life as disposable to financial convenience may become a problem for you tomorrow, if you are a human. Remember, every street has a destination. And no street ever reached its destination by accident. And a system that eats people will eat people.

But hey, listen to *this* wrinkle: Imagine in our scenario that most of the people *want* to fix the streets, but the city still refuses. What then?

I think we'd have to conclude that some portion of *us* are no longer what is meant when we say "the city decides." I think we'd have to conclude that the controls over our natural human system have been unnaturally stolen. We'd have to conclude that the problem of our radioactive streets is only the *immediate* problem, and that the larger undergirding problem is this: The way that our city makes decisions has been unnaturally misaligned, intentionally stolen.

We might call this theft "injustice."

Before we could reconfigure the streets, we'd have to reconfigure the means of configuration itself—the way *the city decides*. How far? To the furthest extent of the problem, to the very boundaries of the injustice, at whatever cost necessary.

The solution would require active, persistent, determined, in-formed, and transformative action, aligned to a compass that views as its true north a justice founded in love—that is, a justice that ensures the inherent dignity, legal equality, and pro-vision for basic human need, of all human beings, even those aligned against that compass setting. Or we'd have to accept that our unnaturally corrupted human system, designed to kill people for financial convenience, would kill us, if it ever became financially convenient for it to do so.

Right?

If the way *the city decides* has become as broken or useless or harmful as our hypothetically fatal streets, then our natural human system becomes potentially unable to solve problems—any problems. Our natural human system might even start to configure itself around a principle such as "government *is* the problem"—the idea that solving problems of people isn't a suit-able matter for cities to engage in. If our city is organized in such a way that it is unwilling to save people from death unless they are deemed worthy of life, then we are all vulnerable, not only to the problem of the streets, but to any danger that makes us unprofitable. This suggests that if we are people who wish to live, we will have to be willing to perform radical transforma-tive structural reconfiguration, not only on our city, not only on the ways in which *the city decides*, but on our spirit itself—our foundational beliefs and assumptions—and not just in any di-rection, but in a direction that leads us toward inclusiveness, completeness, plurality, and equality. This suggests that, should I discover that the natural value delivery system in which I exist has been unnaturally stolen and corrupted, the greater danger is not in radical structural reconfiguration, but in *refusing* to pursue radical structural reconfiguration.

Remember, cancer and virus require only your silence. They'll do the rest.

What happens when a system that eats unvaluable people

runs out of unvaluable people to eat? What happens when something changes dramatically, and you are suddenly less valuable?

If human intention is like a street, it will eventually reach its destination.

Eventually it will find you and me.

◆ ◆ ◆

Let's try another speculative scenario.

Imagine a city dependent on precipitation, where a few people decided to capture all the rain. Imagine they built a series of gutters and downspouts and barrels and cisterns, so that when the rain fell on all the houses, they could divert most of it away from some of the people and bestow it to a select few others. Imagine a city comprised of islands of perfect lush green, swimming in a vast sea of blasted and parched and unnatural desert. Imagine a city that manufactured drought during a rainy season, and horded water in times of manufactured drought.

Imagine a city that recognized the intrinsic value that a collection of people naturally generates—inextricable, automatic, inherited, shared, invisible—where a few people decided to configure it to capture all that value for themselves, and then expected to be praised as the givers of water when they allowed a bit of it to trickle down. Imagine, if you can, a society founded on a series of unjust lies—an *unnatural* human configuration of our natural human system.

Suppose the founders of some hypothetical society had learned that they could maximize for themselves the foundational, generative value that is the natural output of human society, by stealing it away from millions of other humans, and giving it all to themselves. Suppose they did this by utilizing the idea that it was not only possible but desirable, not only desirable but righteous, for human beings to own other human beings as possessions; that ownership of property was the only valid channel for determining who should provide value to society, and who should receive it. Suppose they founded their society on the proposition that the Owners should be the only people within the society allowed to partake in the collective will of the human system the Owned had built, and to control all the value delivered, and to parcel value out to the Owned only to the exact extent to which such an allowance would profit the Owner.

I would suppose that such a society, founded on human enslavement, would always turn themselves, whatever their stated intentions, back toward slavery. I would suppose that people in such a society would believe, at the bedrock level of their assumptions, that some people have more value and others have less, or even none, or even a negative value. I would suppose that such a society would behave as if a person's value is a matter of power and wealth, and to lack power and wealth is to lack any value. I would suppose that such a society would conclude that for those who lack value, life must be earned by providing profit to those whose lives matter. I would suppose that such a society would conclude that for a valueless person to receive some value that diminished the profit they could provide an Owner would be considered a grotesque and offensive theft; and would eventually conclude that a person who could not be used for profit had not earned life, represented theft, and had therefore earned death. I would suppose that such a society would believe the violence of neglect or the violence of brutality to be an acceptable way to redeem such a debt against such a valueless thief.

And then that society would configure itself to control and harm valueless people. You'd know this was the configuration of this society, no matter what individuals within that society said their individual intentions were, because this society would control and harm people, and justify it on a metric of cost and profit. And those with access to the power to change this configuration would not do the work of reconfiguration, which would reveal their deepest intentions.

And they might even configure their streets and roads so that the value of transportation was maximally available to those who could afford increasingly expensive personal vehicles, and almost non-existent for those who couldn't. And they might defend and expand this configuration, even when it became clear that this configuration made cities and towns far more inhospitable and dangerous to people, even once it became clear that the operation of these personal vehicles was a major factor in a global threat to all of their lives.

Oh man. I'm back to the same extremely unbelievable scenario as before. My friends will tell you I do that sometimes. Maybe this all seems too far-fetched to you. As I said, I write speculative fiction, which often requires a real stretch of the imagination.

◆ ◆ ◆

At an earlier time, I named a series of foundational lies, which I believed created a spirit that desires genocide and slavery. I still believe that.

You might think of a foundational lie as a virus—a thing that exists only to promote itself, which has no place whatsoever within a healthy system, which will eventually consume that system if left unchecked. You might think of a natural human priority configured around a foundational lie as a cancer—a corruption of something that under optimal circumstances would exist in a healthy system, but now exists only to grow itself unsustainably.

Imagine the most extreme example of my earlier picture: a system so unfair that every bit of value the city generates—every wage, every increase to property value, every bit of food, all permission to drive on the street or walk on the sidewalk, all permission to access shelter, every drop of rain—goes only to one person.

Let's make that person me. Hey, it's *my* example.

All value in my city—everything needed for a person to live—

now goes to me, and to me alone, which means my neighbors receive none. The only destination this configuration could ever arrive at would be one in which all my neighbors were crushed in the gears of my intentions, unable to provide our natural human system with value; leaving me alone, receiving only the value I can manage to deliver to myself, for however long that lasts. In time, I would become a bizarre and unsustainable curiosity. Having cut every other human out of my natural human system, I would have made an *unnatural* human system; a viral system that no longer generates the value that a community of humans naturally makes. Eventually I, too, would fail—not *despite* the fact that I have hoarded all the value, but *because*.

These lies contain their own deaths within them, you know. Unsustainable things don't sustain. A cancer dies with the body. A virus will die, once it runs out of bodies.

Any foundational lie left untreated will—like a virus, like a cancer—inevitably collapse the system. It will take institutions that, in a healthy system, would be vital to continued health, and transform them into something grotesque and malicious; will make these institutions susceptible to practices, ideas, and intentions that have no place in healthy society. Inevitably these foundational injustices, built on foundational lies, will devolve into social unrest and internal war until either they capture the system entirely, or else they are defeated.

Any society founded on many foundational lies would likely face a series of such collapses.

For example: such a society might find itself locked into an observable historical cycle, whereby all resources and power to make decisions would always inevitably become unnaturally allocated to fewer and fewer people, until most people struggled to find what they needed to survive even though resources were plentiful; until most people found themselves without recourse to effect any change, while a very few ruthless people managed to capture for themselves more resources than they could ever possibly use, which they would credit back to themselves as proof of their right to own it, and would use that wealth to capture even more power to decide what happens, which they would credit back to themselves as proof of their right to wield it.

If such a society managed, through some combination of luck or effort, to push back these unsustainable practices, it would be necessary for that society to engage in the same practices any survivor of cancer or virus finds it necessary to engage in, if they would align with ongoing health. There would need to be a diagnosis—acknowledgement that the unjust lies and their unjust practices existed; then there would need to be a short-term change—often radical, often targeted—to eliminate the threat; and then a long-term remedy—a permanent, holistic, watchful, strategic, systemic restructuring—to monitor for and prevent recurrence.

But what if our hypothetical society refused to do the work?

We'd have to assume that on the level of true intention they didn't want the cure.

Can you imagine it? A land that had a cure to a deadly disease, but the people *refused the cure?* Such a land would, I think, inevitably begin to collapse. Imagine a land that has become an *unnatural* human system, optimized for injustice. Imagine a land whose streets were built on a bad foundation, whose people decided to let them collapse rather than do the work of fixing them. Can you imagine it?

Society is created by the human priorities that configure it, priorities which begin as an idea, and become, through the work of configuration, *the way things are*—an inheritable state. So, human priorities configured for a sustainable system will move toward sustainability, while human priorities based upon an unsustainable lie will inevitably move toward the unsustainability of that lie, which will inevitably destroy that system in favor of the promotion of itself.

A system based on lies is an unjust system.

An unjust system is an unnatural system.

An unnatural system is an unsustainable system.

I'd suggest that one defining quality of an unsustainable system is, it won't sustain.

If I live in a system that eats my neighbors, I live in a system that will eat me in the end—even if I'm the one the system currently feeds.

This suggests that—even if I am entirely free of morality or empathy or basic decency, driven only by self-interest—I would do well to watch for dangers to my neighbors.

Which leads me to another question.

Who is my neighbor?

5. NEIGHBOR

Who is my neighbor? It's an ancient question. There must be an answer by now.

Well, there are the people to either side of my house. No question about them. You'd probably want to include the people directly across from me. After that, it can get fuzzy. When does the neighborhood reach its boundary? Two houses down? Three? Probably not. The people further down the street still feel like my neighbors. The next street over? Two streets over? Three? What do I mean by "neighbor" when I ask *who is my neighbor?*

I could look to the legally defined boundaries. Just go to Google maps and you can see the name of your neighborhood—"Godwin Heights" or "Flushing Meadows" or "Velociraptor Park" or whatever—and click on that name to see the exact boundary. To me, that way of defining the neighborhood seems precise but still somehow arbitrary. I'd propose that instead we look to our natural human system—the one that delivers value (and harm) as naturally as rain falls on roofs, or fungus unites a forest's roots, or streets connect houses to other houses. How far does *that* neighborhood stretch?

To rephrase: What are the outermost boundaries of our natural human system?

I think about all the steps necessary to maintain or modify or improve such a system, which begins with knowledge—awareness of the need and an acceptance of responsibility to act—and then ends with resolve—a decision to act and an agreement to pay the cost. Here's a suggestion for a workable definition of the boundaries of the neighborhood: The outermost boundaries are definable by the extent to which knowledge of connectivity can be achieved, and the extent to which our actions deliver value (or harm) to other people.

I feel like I still haven't gotten at what I mean.

Let me tell you a story.

◆ ◆ ◆

A hundred billion light years from our planet, on another planet, there exists a civilization, living much as we do. The people on our planet don't know about this planet. We have no knowledge of it, nor of any effect of our actions upon it. Thus, we feel no responsibility for it, because we could never maintain or modify or improve or harm it. This faraway civilization is not within the boundaries of our "neighborhood." Its denizens are not our neighbors.

But suppose something were to change. Suppose we were to develop a quantum telescope—a device that allows us to observe this faraway civilization in real time. Rather than detecting the report of light that escaped its source millions of years ago, the quantum telescope utilizes relativistic technologies, allowing us to see all intelligent civilizations across the entirety of their time; to look at how they live in their present, or peer into their past or their future. By observing the development of this civilization—including discoveries they will eventually make—we gain huge benefits, taking giant leaps forward in medicine, transportation, agriculture. We experience an unimaginable leap forward in our knowledge and abilities, made possible by a change in our technology—an innovation.

But suppose something further. Suppose when we train our telescope back to societies we'd previously observed, we discover something disturbing. The pasts of these far civilizations, their presents, their futures . . . are tragically changed now. The courses of their histories have now taken terrible turns, and reach tragic ends and early extinctions. We run tests. The results are conclusive: Use of quantum energy has led to effects we'd not anticipated. The fact that we have observed these civilizations has benefited our reality, but has changed their course for the worse. It seems impossible, but in some way that we don't understand, we seem, through quantum effects of observation, to have stolen their potential. More disturbing still, the very weft of reality, starting at the edges of the observable universe, moving inward, is beginning to warp and skew. We've drawn upon something necessary and vital, used it as a resource, and there is nearly unanimous consensus among our foremost experts that to draw upon it further—either by making further quantum observation or continuing to use the advancements gained thereby, which have become embedded into our daily lives—will speed the degrading effects. There is a growing understanding among us that to go on living as we have risks creating paradoxes that threaten existence itself.

We're conflicted.

We say: But we didn't intend to do it.

We say: I wasn't even alive when it was decided to do it.

We say: There's nothing we can do about it anyway.

We say: Yes, we could change. But why should we, when nobody else is going to?

We say: What does this have to do with me?

These are the things we say. They're the things we always say, when awareness dawns.

But the fact remains that we hadn't known, and now we do know.

Innovation has changed us. A global society has suddenly become universal.

We train our quantum telescope once again to the skies, and we see something new: civilization after civilization, all building quantum telescopes.

Suddenly an empty universe is filled with neighbors.

◆ ◆ ◆

It's a science fiction premise, I know. I put it forward for the same reason that most science fiction premises are put forward, which is to demonstrate something true about our present reality. Innovation—new technology, new concepts, new ideas—often expands our knowledge, which expands our potential, and has effects far beyond our intent, effects against which (or for which) we will have to decide how to align ourselves, regardless of intent.

Innovation, by the way, is itself a natural human system. "Human" because humans can discover it, use it, and configure it, then inherit the effects of those configurations. "Natural" because innovation isn't something created out of nothing; rather, it's the discovery of something that had previously been unknown, but which was always true, always there, always ready for humans to discover and configure.

In the story, we learned through innovation.

The innovation changed things in ways that couldn't be reversed.

And what we learned was always true. We just hadn't known before.

Innovation expands our awareness of the scope of the neighborhood, but it doesn't expand the neighborhood. Nor does innovation change our priorities or intentions; it just expands their effects, which provides us new opportunities to identify what those priorities are—the real priorities, the ones that are reflected in what actually happens. In the story, we discovered we lived in an entangled universe, and we always did. Learning that truth didn't make it true; it just made us aware in ways that forced us to reveal our priorities. Learning about the danger didn't change our priorities, which always favored securing the benefits to be gained from others far more than understanding the effects of the gaining. And ignoring the truth won't make it stop being true; it will just make us deliberately ignorant in ways that endanger our future existence. But that truth of our entanglement was always there, waiting for us to know it. Our knowledge and ability are what changed, and as that knowledge and ability changed, so did the scope of what we could maintain, modify, improve . . . or harm.

This suggests that the answer to the question *who is my neighbor?* is also subject to constant reassessment. We learn that people we hadn't thought were neighbors were actually neighbors all along. Do you see it? To our perspective, our "neighborhood" is getting bigger, and our count of neighbors is increasing. But in truth, *the neighborhood was always this size.*

Yesterday our awareness was one thing. Today it is something different.

What will it be tomorrow?

I think we could use another story.

◆ ◆ ◆

A long time ago, in a galaxy far, far away, there was a distant planet called "Earth," and when it had become a very old planet indeed, there lived upon it for a very brief time creatures called "humans," who—impressively—could stand upright and run for dozens of miles without taking rest, and who—less impressively, but more pertinent to this story—had enormous brains that allowed them to make marvelous connections between themselves and each other, and between disparate concepts, and between themselves and those concepts and other parts of the world. Because of these brains, they could make configurations, both intentional and unintentional, to their natural systems.

Let's say there was a time in this story, early in the history of these humans, when the outer limits of human connection were defined only by the biological family. These ties provided the mutual interconnectivity that allowed for shared values, which allowed for trust, which allowed for cohesion, safety, and survival.

This familial arrangement provided each human with a collectively generated value that was automatic, inextricable, invisible, natural, and inherited, and available only within the boundaries of the family. It was well understood in these human families that each person would act within their self-interest, but it would have been seen as a dangerous and destructive corruption of the very bedrock of familial society to put one's self-interest above the family interest in matters pertaining to the family. And it was clearly understood in human families that to harm one was to harm all, in a way that simply wouldn't be relevant if applied to anybody outside of the family.

For a brief while in the early history of human families, no knowledge of outside families even existed, but once that awareness was gained, there still didn't seem to exist any need for deeper knowledge of outside families, other than this awareness—they are not *us*. They are rivals for the resources we need. They are not to be trusted.

What sat at the bottom of this false belief was the great foundational lie: the people who are *us* matter, and the people who are *not us* do not matter at all.

These humans were *families*. They were *familial*.

Families were natural human systems.

Conflicts and abuses would arise when some member of the family decided that more of the natural benefits of their human system should come to them than they needed, at the expense of another who would receive less than they needed, especially if the beneficiary then managed to configure the family to reflect those unbalanced priorities, and solidify those imbalances into tradition. What sat at the bottom of all these imbalances was an expression of the same great foundational lie: *some people in our family matter more than others.*

Still, despite its shortcomings, the family was good. It was useful. It was generative.

But our story doesn't end there.

What happened next was that, over time, some families realized something that had always been true but hadn't yet been known. They learned that what they did affected the families nearby, and what families nearby did also affected them, and that any conflicts between families over the resources that all families need actually represented a waste of both energy and resource, and could even risk the destruction of the resources upon which all the families depended. What sort of resources? Oh, things like the water supply. The food supply. In other words, the future of human existence in the area.

These families learned there were actually enough resources for all the families nearby, and that families that joined together over their commonalities of need and proximity could create a human system that generated much more influence and value than single families acting apart.

This was an innovation.

Here was the name of this innovation: Tribe.

The humans had been familial. They became *tribal.*

Tribes were natural human systems.

Let's pretend that in our story, some familial humans saw the innovation of the tribe as a danger that threatened to put an end to families, and fought against the concept of "tribes" as a result. But they couldn't stop the knowledge of the innovation of tribe, and they couldn't choose to not live in a world where tribes generated more influence and value than families, and so, no matter how hard they tried, they increasingly had to live in a tribal world.

They were wrong, anyway. The tribe didn't put an end to families, any more than the family ended the individual—but it did put an end to the idea of the family as the outermost boundary of human connection. A tribe was simply a more effective natural human system than a family in many crucial ways, and it always had been. What the innovation of tribe *did* do was expand the possibilities of what a family could be, and offer *more* choices in matters of forming families. And so, the family remained a vital and important and honored structure within most human tribes. So, over time, it was understood that while everyone would have more responsibility for and loyalty toward their family members than other tribal members, anyone who put their family's interests over the interests of tribal cohesion would be creating a dangerous and destructive corruption of the very bedrock of tribal society, because the tribe was a natural human system which, as a practical matter, created *more* value than the family—in fact, it provided the context within which families existed.

The family had been the boundary of the neighborhood.

Now it was the tribe.

The problem with being familial wasn't that the biological family was *bad*—it was uniquely good, in many ways that remained and continued. The innovation of "tribe" simply went further into the truth of human connection, and so to try to make the family the outermost boundary of human connection meant living in a dangerous and unsustainable lie that would eventually fall to a greater truth. The humans had innovated, and learned, and now there were *more* neighbors. The tribal humans learned that more neighbors meant *more* resources and opportunity, not fewer. A tribe created new ties providing the mutual interconnectivity that allowed for shared values, which allowed for trust, which allowed for cooperation, which allowed for cohesion, safety, and survival. This arrangement provided each human with collective value available only through the innovative creation of the tribe, while allowing them to continue enjoying *expanded* benefits of being familial.

But this innovation of "tribe" didn't put an end to conflict or abuse among the humans. In truth, the creation of tribes involved more conflict, and new abuses, as the bad priorities already configured within families inherited to tribal systems. For example: Some families, less effective than others because of accidents of chance, were captured or conquered or absorbed, or isolated and starved of resources, by tribal humans who had no interest in the humanity of tribes to which they did not belong; meanwhile, families who most benefitted within the tribe still tried to use their influence to configure this new human system to unnaturally seize more influence, and to solidify these imbalances as traditions. What sat at the bottom of all these imbalances was an expression of the great foundational lie: *some families in our tribe matter more than others.*

Logic demands there would be more conflict, and more danger of abuse—this was, after all, a more efficient human system. It would naturally be more efficient at delivering its corruptions and harms in the same way it delivered its benefits—and there would grow among tribal humans the awareness that the harm this new and efficient system could deliver might, if unchecked, compromise their entire territory. So, among tribal humans there grew an awareness, prohibitions, taboos: that to harm one was to harm all, in a way that simply wouldn't be relevant if applied to anybody outside of the tribe. However, no common understanding with outside tribes existed, other than this awareness—they are not *us*. They are rivals for our resources. They are not to be trusted. What sat at the bottom of this false belief was the great foundational lie: the people who are *us* matter, and the people who are *not us* do not matter at all.

And so, the tribe was good. It was useful.

But our story doesn't end there.

What happened next was that some tribes realized something

that had always been true but hadn't yet been known. They learned that what they did affected the tribes nearby, and what tribes nearby did also affected them, and that conflict over the resources that all tribes needed represented a waste of both energy and resources, and could even risk the destruction of the resources upon which all tribes depended. What sort of resources? Oh, things like the ocean ports, the entire river, the entire lake. The coastline. The farmlands. In other words, the future of human existence and thriving on that part of the continent.

These tribes learned there were actually enough resources for all the tribes nearby, and that tribes joined together over their commonalities of need and proximity could create a human system that generated much more influence and value than single tribes acting apart.

This was an innovation.

Here was the name of this innovation: Nation.

The humans had been tribal. They became *national*.

Nations were natural human systems.

And some tribal humans feared this innovation as a danger that might end tribes, just as familial humans had feared tribes would destroy families, and they were just as wrong. Indeed, this innovation expanded the possibilities of what a tribe could be just as tribes had expanded the possibilities of what families could be. And so nations became the new boundary of the neighborhood, because to make the tribe the outermost boundary of human connection meant living in a dangerous and unsustainable lie that would eventually fall to the greater truth that nations were a more efficient and generative natural human system. There were *more* neighbors, not fewer, and also more opportunity, and more value—and more abuses and harms, too, informed by the same great foundational lie, that some people matter and others do not.

Yet despite these inherited corruptions, the nation was, in many ways, good and useful.

But our story doesn't end there.

What happened next was that some humans within nations began to realize something that had always been true but hadn't yet been realized. They learned that what they did affected the other nations, and what other nations did also affected them, and that conflict over the resources they needed represented a waste of energy and resources, and could even risk the destruction of the resources upon which all nations depend. What sort of resources? Oh, things like viability of the soil and climate and other conditions that produce food. Vegetation. Breathable air. Drinkable water. The global ecosystem. In other words, the future of human existence on the planet. Some people in these nations learned something that had always been true but hadn't yet been known: that there were actually enough resources for all the nations, and that nations joined together over their commonalities of shared human need and a shared human planet could create a human system that generated much *more* influence and value than single nations acting apart.

Here was the name of this new concept: Human.

The humans were nationalist.

They became *humanist.*

But our story doesn't end there.

Humanists began to understand some ancient truths that had been forgotten about connectivity with environments; began to understand that even humans weren't the furthest extent of natural human systems, began to understand that ecosystems are connected to one another just as humans are connected to one another, and that humans themselves are inseparable from their ecosystems. And so humanists began to see interconnectivity existing even on a planetary level.

They became *planetary.*

As a storyteller, I like to look for dramatic settings, so I recommend we set our story about these "humans" right here, in the midst of a great shift from nationalism and humanism into holistic planetary thinking. Let's make this planet the humans live upon spherical—globular. We could call the planet "the globe."

We could call their new innovation into planetary thinking "globalism."

Here's what's going on with our humans in the story as it begins.

Some of the tools of humanism and globalism these humans have developed are empire and commerce and alliance and war and incorporation—which are rough approximations of tools used within families and tribes and nations. Some of these tools are good though imperfect, which means they can be improved, and should be. Some of them are corrupt and harmful, which means they can be abandoned, and should be.

In our story, the human innovation of planetary thinking hasn't entirely taken hold, nor has it put an end to conflict. Our nascent planetary humans are still governed by the bad priorities already present within families and tribes and nations, shaped by bad ideas inherited from families and tribes and nations that have no place within a healthy system, and which have configured their natural human systems into something potentially unsustainable. In truth, the creation of globalism has involved *more* conflict, and *new* abuses, because humanism and globalism are simply more effective natural human systems than nationalism. There are nations that most benefit within the global system of empire and commerce and alliance, and they have used their influence to seize more influence and more benefit, and to use their supremacy on the global stage to exclude many nations from global benefits, or to force these "lesser" nations to accept their terms, and receive global benefits unequally. What sits at the bottom of all these imbalances is an expression of the same great foundational lie: *some nations on our planet matter more than others.*

In our story, this has led to conflict, and many of these conflicts between nations are resolved using the tool that the humans call "war," and it happens a lot. War is a real stinker, as tools go. The humans know this, and yet war has not ceased; unaccountably, perversely, it has increased. However, the humans have begun trying new tools. "Alliance," for example, is a much more effective way of managing conflict than war. "Incorporation" is perhaps the most popular tool, at this particular moment in our story— a thing involving elaborate and effective systems of finance and commerce and jurisprudence, able to deliver astonishing amounts of wealth and benefit to some humans. Unfortunately, while this "incorporation" is startlingly effective at generating and delivering wealth in a targeted way, it remains aligned to the same foundational lies, and is all-too-often configured for abuse, configured to deliver inherited theft and harm to some with the same level of astonishing efficiency it employs to deliver that often-plundered value to others. These humans have incorporated war and theft into their global systems because there are families and tribes and nations infected by the oldest viral human lies, that some people matter more than others; that the people who are *us* matter and the people who are *not us* do not matter at all. And, in our story, these imbalances, applied to a planetary scale, will inevitably have an effect that threatens the future of human life.

It's here the humans in our story find themselves, caught in this centuries-long transition between a *nationalist* realization and a *globalist* one, applying old harms on a global stage, in ways that compromise the entire planet.

So that's our setting.

Here's the conflict of our story, and the stakes: The humans will learn to move into the truth of a connected planet and, having reached the furthest currently imaginable boundary of the neighborhood, begin at last to address the real enemy, which was never any people but rather their oldest foundational lies. Otherwise, they will deny that truth and remain in the lies.

If that happens, our humans will go extinct.

Pretty big stakes!

If we write this story with skill, our readers will hope that the humans do not go extinct. Eventually (and in our story we might introduce at least one crisis that makes this moment more immediate), our humans are going to have to understand that anyone who unnaturally elevates their nation or tribe or family to the detriment, abuse, neglect, and harm of their neighbors on the same planet will be creating a dangerous corruption of everything, including nations, tribes, and families, because, unless these humans make some sort of previously unimaginable interplanetary discovery, *the planet is the natural human system*, because it is where all the humans live.

We should repeat that.

The planet is *the* natural human system, because it is where all the humans live.

The humans in our story won't be able to go back from planetary thinking, because the reality of a global humanity inextricably linked to its planetary systems is, like all innovations, the discovery of something that was always true. Our readers, following the pattern of human innovation and development, will conclude that a peacefully joined, cooperative, noncompeting globe will simply be a more effective natural human system than a globe of competing nations, just as the cooperative nation was a more effective system than competing tribes, and the cooperative tribe more effective than competing families.

This would be a new innovation, and also the oldest one: cooperation.

If the pattern of human history is to be trusted, a unified cooperative globe would create *more* value and potential and opportunity than the nation or the tribe or the family—it would, if our humans let it, create new ties providing the mutual interconnectivity that allows for shared values, which allows for trust, which allows for cohesion, safety, and survival. Our readers might begin to suspect that such an arrangement would, if the humans let it, provide each individual with collective value that is automatic, inextricable, invisible, natural, and inherited, and available only through the innovative creation of a unified non-competing globe—an arrangement within which it would be clearly understood that to harm one was to harm all, in a way that extends to the very boundaries of planetary existence. No common cause with outside planets will yet exist, nor any need for that common cause—not because the humans seek no common cause, but because there remains within human awareness no further common cause to seek. Our humans will have found the outermost boundaries of human interconnectivity.

Let's end our story there for now. And let's create a happy ending for our humans. Let's say the humans lead themselves into the new truth their innovation has uncovered.

But a story can't start with the resolution. We'll need to make this a conflict, to give the story some fizz. Let's start the story at a point where it really looks bad; as if our humans are going to cling to the old unsustainable lies, and choose competition over cooperation, extinction over expansion, life over death.

What would be the scenario that threatens a bad ending? What would that look like?

Well . . . what if we were to find that these humans were still captured by their worst priorities, the ones most aligned with harmful ideas that have no place in a healthy society? If that were the case, they might find themselves encumbered with a leader who always puts himself before anybody else, who always puts his family ahead of any tribe to which he might belong, who always puts the interests of his tribe before that of the nation he leads, and who always puts his nation's domination over the global sustainability of human life. Worse, our humans might have *chosen* that leader, and be seriously considering choosing him again.

Yes. We might start there.

◆ ◆ ◆

It's a sci-fi premise, offered for the same reason as most sci-fi premises. It's not meant as anthropology or history. Understand, I am aware that progressive innovation of natural human systems of family and tribe and nation didn't happen as cleanly or uniformly as presented here—but we know these innovations did occur, because we have these innovations.

It's worth repeating the reason we're contemplating neighbors. We learned a present danger or a present abuse to our neighbor means eventual danger and abuse for us, no matter how much it presently favors us. This suggested that—even if we are only driven by self-interest—we would do well to watch for dangers to and abuses to our neighbors, and then change our human systems to protect them. How far will the change have to reach? To the very boundaries of our neighborhood—our natural human system.

Which demanded the question: *Who is my neighbor?*

And so, after all that, here is my answer:

Who *isn't?*

Suppose we realize that our systems are configured to deliver harm and theft to our neighbors. If we had that realization, we'd have to ask:

Who stole value away from my neighbor's street, and who gave it to my street?

I'll answer these questions with another question, one I've already answered:

Who put my street there?

6. INHERIT

Wait. Me?

Me??

So what, now it's *my* fault? But I didn't *do* anything—how can it be *my* fault? How could *I* have inherited stolen value when

I never set out to do so, when I never took any action to steal? How could *I* have stolen value when there are other houses in my neighborhood that are much *more* valuable than mine, and other neighborhoods in which *all* the houses are much more valuable? How could *I* have inherited stolen value for my house when I personally contribute so much of my time and energy to make sure that *my* house stays nice and retains its value? How could I have stolen if I have been stolen *from*? How can I be a beneficiary of a system of theft if I myself must work and struggle to survive within it? How could I have stolen when I worked for everything I have, when I never asked for anything in my life? How could any of this ever possibly be *my* fault? These are scurrilous accusations I have levied against myself, and I hope you agree. Luckily, I have many defenses from which to choose.

I inherited stolen value? No. I reject the entire concept.

Or . . . .

I inherited stolen value? Yes—from people making their own bad choices, which is why they are where they are, and I am where I am.

Or . . . .

I inherited stolen value? Maybe—but it's polarizing to talk about it. The real problem these days is people who still bring it up.

Or . . . .

I inherited stolen value? Yes—but too long ago to do anything about it.

Or . . . .

I inherited stolen value? Yes—but there's no political support for restitution, and it would be too complex to administer, and it would cost too much time and expense to be practical, and some people might receive benefits they don't deserve in the process, so there exists no perfect way to do it, and that means it's not realistic, and it's very unpopular, so it's better to forget it.

Or, maybe, this . . . .

I inherited stolen value? Maybe. OK. Sure. Yes. Observably so. But one thing has to be recognized, before any other: I didn't intend it, so it has nothing to do with me.

♦ ♦ ♦

I didn't intend it. It has nothing to do with me.
Two sentences, often expressed as one thought.
A neat trick.

♦ ♦ ♦

So, I had no intention to inherit stolen value. And neither did you. And I certainly didn't steal from you, nor you from me; nor did we ever intend to steal from others.
Good job, both of us!
Good job, our intentions!
It's good to not be a thief with intention to steal. To be an intentional thief is a bad thing to be. I'm glad you're not one, and I'm glad I'm not one, either. I just want to get that out there. It is commendable that you and I have not intentionally set out to profit from a corrupt system.
Commendations to both of us!
Commendations all around!
It's not just people in the distant and unreachable past who have suffered theft, of course. We all know that thieves with intention to steal exist. For example, we all know that in the early part of this century extremely wealthy people conspired to steal trillions of dollars from the value of all of our homes, and none of them were prosecuted when the market collapsed as a result, and most of them kept their share of the loot, because taking it would have been theft. For a while we configured our society's laws to make it *somewhat* harder for thieves to abuse the system in that way, but in the interest of stability of the status quo, we let them keep their

jobs and their bonuses and their freedom and their reputations, mostly. They stole value from my house and yours. They got away with it. *The city decided* to let them get away with it.

It stands to reason they'll do it again if they can ... and they can.

The project will involve reconfiguring our natural human system back into the old channels to optimize it even more thoroughly for theft. Once our system is perfectly optimized for theft, the theft will flow in the same way that value does: foundationally, automatically, inextricably. Next time, some small bit of it may come to me, to the extent that opportunity and chance have allowed me to invest in their systems. Some of it might go to you, if you are hypothetically favorably positioned like hypothetical me. If you aren't like hypothetical me, maybe none of it comes to you. Maybe for you, redistribution is only ever a matter of loss, not gain.

Most of it will go to intentional thieves.

They'll get away with it.

The city will decide to let them.

I know this in the same way that I know that every street has a destination, and no street ever reaches its destination accidentally.

And you and I, very fine people of bountiful good intention and ample opportunity but limited curiosity, we'll pocket whatever temporary bonuses come our way as respectable thieves loot the public safe. Thieves of intent will allow some of us to benefit, not out of largesse, but simply as part of the cost of doing business. They intend to get it back from us eventually, anyway. When they decide to take our gains from us, how easy will it be for them to do it? As easy as it was to take from those they robbed before us. Easier, in fact, because now our natural human system—which has a momentum as regards intention—has become even more perfectly optimized for theft, and our incuriosity about the benefit we receive from it will have become so habitual, we'll find it hard to understand how or why we're being devoured. Yes, and when our day comes, the city, built on practiced indifference, will exhibit as practiced an indifference to our fate as we practiced when it was not us but only our neighbors suffering the injustices of an unjust system; and as we fall into poverty, we will be seen as presumed crime and presumed theft, just as our neighbors were, as they fell victim to the theft that left them impoverished.

Do you still think it's got nothing to do with you, just because you don't intend it?

◆ ◆ ◆

Say this: Say I'm driving along and I hit an old lady with my car.

Or say this: Say I discover $12 million deposited into my bank account, and I don't know why.

I didn't intend for these things to happen, yet they did.

So it seems that my intention is not the only controlling factor when it comes to reality.

There's what I *intend*. And then there's what *happens*.

Or: There's what I'd *like* to think is true about me. And then there's what *is* true about me.

People have intentions, it's true, and those intentions matter. From a moral perspective, a practical perspective, a legal perspective, it makes a difference if I ran down the old lady with my car because it malfunctioned, or because I was distracted checking my texts, or because I am the beneficiary of her will and decided it would be better to have her money sooner rather than later, or because I just like the sound my car makes when it hits old ladies. It makes a difference in how the law thinks about me, and it makes a difference in how you think about me, too.

What we intend matters. Hear me: it *matters*.

It's just not *all* that matters.

Whatever I intended, the old lady has been run over, and it was my car that did it, and I was the driver—and I have knowledge of it. Whatever I intended, the money is in my account—

and I have knowledge of it. My intentions matter, yes, but what would we all think of me if I claimed I had nothing to do with getting that money, simply because I didn't intend for it to come to me, and quietly moved it into an offshore account? What would we think of me, if after I accidentally hit the old lady, I drove away as quickly as I could, hoping I hadn't been seen?

Because after all, I hadn't *meant* to run the old lady over. I was just getting groceries.

I hadn't *intended* to take any money that didn't belong to me; it just came to me.

I didn't personally *intend* to cause harm, or to gain wealth.

Therefore, it has nothing to do with me at all.

Right?

Some of you have spotted the error in my metaphor. My examples deal with personal actions, personal decisions, not societal ills that we all inherited from decisions originally made decades and centuries ago—right? It's *me* who did the hit-and-run or who took the money, not some ancestor or even some unrelated party who happened to live in the same place as me in prior centuries. It doesn't mean that a societal ill like (say) systemic racial theft or gender pay disparity or colonial genocide is *my* fault. Somebody else stole that value, not me.

But notice what the personal decision in the metaphor is.

It isn't the accident or the theft, which was in no way tied to my intention, but which nevertheless happened. It's whether, with knowledge of it, I remain in that knowledge or flee from it. It's whether I, in knowledge of my part in the situation, take the responsibility I never sought but which nevertheless came to me.

What if I discover that it was my father facing that choice, taking millions, which I then inherited? Does it still have nothing to do with me? What if even my father was unaware that his wealth was pilfered, and only I have been made aware? Does it still have nothing to do with me? What if it is my child, or my wife, or my friend who hits the lady, and I help cover it up? Does it still have nothing to do with me?

I suspect nobody disputes that my decision to flee the scene of the accident, or keep money that isn't mine, represents a personal decision carrying moral implications. But I hope you also see that my decision to disassociate myself from the situation that exists, using my intent as a rationale, is also a personal decision carrying moral implications, revealing a deeper selfish intention.

In these examples, I have recently acquired knowledge of harm, of loss. The harm and loss are realities. My association with this harm and loss are realities. They aren't made less real simply because my knowledge of the association is new. They aren't made less real if I didn't intend the association, or if I had no control over the association. I *am* associated with this harm, this loss. That association is going to cost me something if I accept it, while if I avoid the association it will provide me an opportunity to keep an unearned reward, or avoid an appropriate consequence. If I were not associated with this harm and loss, I could avoid paying that cost, and I could gain the reward. And so there rises in me a desire, understandable if not particularly honorable, to not be associated with this harm and loss, even though I am.

My personal decision is not whether or not the harm has been done, nor is my personal decision whether or not it has anything to do with me. It did, and it does, and my blameless intentions toward those realities, while they matter on many levels, don't matter a bit to those questions. My personal decision is: first, whether or not to accept the reality of my association with harm and loss; and next, to decide whether I'm going to accept the consequences of that reality, or whether I'm going to insist on focusing exclusively on my blameless intentions.

And that decision reveals my actual deeper intentions.

There might be other people, associated with me, who would benefit from my disassociation from the harm and loss, whose lives might be complicated by my association with a crime, who would not want to see me pay the cost, who might want to see me keep the unearned reward. So perhaps, those who would also benefit might also focus exclusively on my intentions.

And perhaps, if the crime were not personal, but rather societal, you might find an entire society that has decided to focus all moral calculation on a basis of personal intentions to the exclusion of all else, as a way of avoiding any association with knowledge of the reality of their own association with harm and loss. It might be that such a society would heap scorn on even the idea that we share an interconnected life, even though it's clear we do—because to acknowledge we share an interconnected life leads us inexorably back to realities we desperately wish to avoid, because of the costs that are associated with them.

Nor would anyone benefitting from such a society want to notice that the collective decision to disassociate from this reality is itself nothing more than a collection of personal decisions revealing deeper selfish intentions—a spirit of blamelessness, you might say. For such a society, any rationale forgiving the association would be popular and almost reflexively accepted, while any reminder of that association would be seen as offensively polarizing and would be almost reflexively rejected. If we lived in a natural human system founded on harm and loss, we'd inherit a deeply embedded societal expectation to not know or say certain things about harm and loss. And if the knowledge of those things became undeniable, then we would focus only on past manifestations of harm and loss, framed in such a way that suggests they are either already solved or unsolvable. And we'd learn that a good way of accomplishing this is to focus exclusively on what everyone's personal intentions are.

Personal intentions are whatever each person says they are.

They're *personal.*

You can't ever know what they *really* are.

This is very handy, if you don't actually want to know.

If we all focus exclusively on my personal intent, it quickly

becomes impossible for me to ever be (for example) racist, or
sexist, or otherwise captured by bigotry, for the simple fact that
my stated intentions are good. I tell you that I believe racism
is bad, therefore I cannot possibly ever do anything racist, or
benefit in any way from racism—now let's all stop talking about
it. Meanwhile it would be impossible for me to ever discern that
someone else is racist, or sexist, or otherwise captured by a spirit
of bigotry, no matter what they say or do, because it's impossible
to ever truly know their deepest internal intentions, and *they* say
they don't have a bigoted bone in their body, so, since it can't be
addressed, let's not address it—now let's all stop talking about
it. It would be impossible for my family members or friends to
be aligned with systems of injustice, because they are very fine
people: so nice, so good, so generous, and so kind. Their personal intentions are so pure, and yes of course the world has
its injustices, and yes of course those are bad, and yes of course
we should oppose injustice in any cases where somebody is engaged in injustice and openly says "I'm doing this because I love
injustice," but even those cases are individualistic, and the people in my life didn't intend for the harm and loss brought on by that
individual instance of injustice to occur, so what can it have to do
with them? If you think they have intentions other than the ones
they claim to have, it probably means you haven't taken the effort
to get to know them. Now let's stop talking about it.

If we lived in a society founded on harm and loss, we'd learn
that acknowledgement of anyone's association with harm and
loss would be commonly experienced by that person and by the
society around them not as an opportunity for that person to
learn and improve, but as an aggressive condemnation. We'd
encounter a societal expectation that all discussions of harm
and loss be centered around individual exoneration, to achieve
as quickly as possible, and using personal intent as rationale.

How will I ever persuade them if I condemn them?

These aren't irredeemable monsters, you know.

I'd rather appeal to their better angels.

If I were a person of *good intention* in such a society, I might go on giving these defenses, not because I didn't know about my association with harm and loss, but because, deep down, I did know. If I were a person of *good intention* in such a society, I'd decide to not know that I benefit from harm and loss, so as to ensure that my intentions stayed certified as good. Or, if I couldn't make myself believe that, at least I'd make sure it's clear there's nothing I could have done about it; it was all too long ago, and fixing it would be far too impractical politically and economically, and anyway, it's nothing to do with me, or at least it's no more to do with me than with anybody else, so let's just stop talking about it.

And that decision would reveal my actual deeper intentions—the ones that matter.

In such a society, we might find it common for people to suggest that the real racists are the people who always "scream" about racism, that the real sexists are the people who always "scream" about sexism. But imagine a society with enough injustice in it to make people scream. Imagine a people within that society who diagnosed the problem, not as "injustice," but as "screaming." In such a society, if somebody were to blow a whistle on systemic abuse, we might learn that powerful people become extremely interested in the identity of the whistleblower and the particular way the whistle was blown, while demonstrating almost total incuriosity about the identity of the abusers or the particulars of the abuse, and in conducting a meticulous and critical audit of the personal intentions of anyone bringing any complaint of abuse. We might see a systemic reaction against exposure of abuses. We might find that any scant scraps of evidence of bias on the part of the person bringing the complaint are widely published and amplified, and provided as a clear reason to ignore the very real abuses uncovered by the complaint. We might find an inordinate amount of time and energy devoted to the norms broken by the revelation, by the trust lost between the accuser and accused, by the bad precedents set—not by the actual abuse, but by the destabilization and discomfort awareness of abuse has brought. In such a society, intention of the abuser would become not just an important thing, but everything—not because intentions are knowable, but precisely because they are so usefully *unknowable*. We might hear people ask *but where will it all end?*

I've noticed it's a question people ask when they don't want it to end at all.

I didn't mean for that to happen. It has nothing to do with me.

Two separate statements, the first true, the second false, presented as one thought, so that the true statement might lend its truth to the false one.

We can know the truth, if we want to. The value delivered to our streets is intrinsic, and inextricable, and inherited . . . and stolen. This has nothing to do with our intentions. It has nothing to do with whether we were alive when the value was accrued. It doesn't even have to do with whether our direct ancestors were involved. The theft happened, and it has been inherited, because human societies need people, and you and I are people. Our natural human systems needed somebody to inherit its many values, and we became those somebodies. Because the theft came to us through the configurations of our natural human system, we can't separate ourselves from it, any more than we can separate ourselves from the value.

What, then, *can* we do?

To begin with, we can stop saying "that has nothing to do with me."

We can start sincerely asking: "what *does* this have to do with me?"

So let's do that.

7. ALIGN

I feel I should acknowledge a truth about individual choices now, because I think the implications of the previous chapter might have been shocking and offensive to some people, especially to anyone who has believed the dominant cultural lie that the only value that exists is value we ourselves create individually, through our own personal choices and intentions and hard work. So now I'd like to assuage the sensibilities of these rugged individualists.

I'm talking to the individualists now. Huddle in, individualists.

You *do* create value for society through your individual choices. Your decision to be a hard worker, for example, makes society better than if you had decided to be a drunken loafer—provided the work you do assists society rather than corrupting it and draining it for your own benefit, in which case everyone would probably have been better off if you'd become a drunken loafer. Your decision to not personally show overt conscious intentional bigoted hatred to people different from you *does* make the world better than if you had chosen to do so—provided your outward comity doesn't simply provide a normalizing cover that allows you to operationalize secret bigotries and hatreds, in which case everyone would probably be a lot better off if you were less effective at being sly. And, also, to validate you: Yes, we do create value for ourselves through our choices. We do earn things for ourselves through our ingenuity and determination and effort and skill. Our intentions matter. Our choices matter. Our decisions matter. What we personally individually think *matters*. Our achievements and beliefs are real, and they *matter*. By working hard, or by making more wise choices than unwise choices, we frequently *can* create better circumstances for ourselves and others than we otherwise would, specifically because of our individual choices. We should all hope to make good individual choices. We should celebrate such choices.

Rejoice, individualists! Celebrate the individual!

So, when I choose to (for example) maintain and improve my home, I increase its value for myself, and I also help maintain value for the houses around me. That decision matters. But if my positive choices positively affect those around me, then it stands to reason that I'm also receiving the positive effect of the cumulative choices of everyone around me—an invisible, foundational, generative, automatic, inextricable value, the result of an inherited configuration created by the accumulated individual choices of other people who came before. What I'm actually doing through my individual choices is choosing whether or not (and how or how not) to align myself with that inherited configuration.

What I demonstrate when I maintain my house is an alignment with a specific configuration within my natural human system whereby personal wealth is generated through ownership of property. One expectation of this configuration is for the property owner to care for and maintain their property, so that it doesn't fall into disrepair, which would degrade value for themselves and others nearby. This configuration of wealth and ownership of property works out pretty well for a lot of people. It has worked out pretty well for me so far. However, in case you hadn't noticed, it's becoming available to fewer and fewer people, particularly if they are too young to have gotten in when the getting was good—or perhaps it would be more accurate to say, before the getting was made relatively impossible. I didn't get to individually choose to live in a society organized around this configuration whereby personal wealth is generated by property ownership. I only got to individually choose how to align myself with that inherited configuration, and even my ability to choose that alignment is a privilege that simply, observably, as a matter of fact and an item on the news, isn't available to everybody, practically speaking, and the fact that it isn't available to everyone is also a choice...but it isn't an *individual* choice. I have noticed that there are many configurations like this within our natural human system; configurations that are not individual choices.

To give one more example, there is an inherited configuration whereby the ability to live and thrive is a function of one's ability to do valuable work. There's a certain amount of sense to that—something natural, even. For example, if I were sitting in a forest and didn't get to work, nature would make relatively short work of me. So, I work, and I deliver value from my work, and receive value in the form of a paycheck. This configuration of providing the value of work to receive the value of life and thriving works out pretty well for a lot of people. It has worked out pretty well for me so far.

One thing I don't choose when it comes to valuable work is what is meant by *valuable*. Take for example the work of the people who stole all the value from our houses in the early part of this century. That work was—up until that work destroyed almost all the value in the world economy—deemed extremely valuable by the current definitions. That's why the bonuses were so big, and why those who received them were allowed to keep them. On the other hand, the people who do the work that actually keeps a city moving along—road maintenance, say—is considered far less valuable, and serving people food is considered to be almost without value whatsoever. To the extent that I participate in this system of doing valuable work in exchange for life, I align to that configuration, which means I contribute to a spirit supporting and validating the configuration—but again, notice that I don't individually create this or any other social configuration, or individually choose for them to exist. I inherit them, and then I align with them (or not), and then I earn life (or not).

Without the configuration, there wouldn't be anything to align with or against.

You might say the configuration is the controlling factor.

Do you see? By making my individual choice to work hard and maintain my home, I actually demonstrate the existence of an interconnected society, because the configuration of property and homes and work within which I operate is only possible within an interconnected society.

Sorry, individualist. I tried.

Listen—each individual is important. There is enormous value in the power of individual choice. It *matters*. It's just that the effect of individual choice—as much as some individuals might insist otherwise—isn't the only factor contributing to reality, nor is it the most powerful contributor, nor could it be, nor *should* it be—any more than it would be possible or desirable for your personal house to be more valuable than the cumulative value of all other houses in the city.

It's not that our individual choices don't matter.

They simply aren't the outer bounds of human interconnectivity.

Let me ask a question: When did you personally choose your choices?

It's a difficult question, particularly to rugged individualists.

I'll ask some clarifying questions to demonstrate what this question means.

When did you *personally choose* to have a body and a mind that functioned well enough to do the work you do? When did you *personally choose* to be born in a place and within circumstances from which you could develop that body and mind to do what you *personally chose* to do? When did you *personally choose* to not be sick or disabled or infirm? When did you make these individual choices, *all by yourself*? The people who don't have a body or a mind that function as yours, the people who weren't born in a place with the opportunity to develop those gifts, the people who were never offered those choices... when do you suppose they made the *personal individual choice* to be deprived of those choices?

If you can stop providing society with the value of profitability... should you then stop *receiving* the value of our natural human society, which makes living possible? *Can* you stop receiving that value? *Do* you stop providing value to society when you stop providing profit? What should we say about a society that organizes itself to prevent people from receiving life because they're deemed insufficiently profitable? If *choosing* to be profitable is the only way you receive your value . . .what happens if you're no longer able to make the choice? What if you are one of the unfortunate sorts of people who lives inside a human body that will, over time, get old and sick? What if you live in a dynamic world of unpredictable change, in which the reality tomorrow won't be the same as the reality today, and some force might arrive that constrains the available opportunities upon which you have staked your fortune? What if the value you provide is replicated and replaced by human innovation or demolished by natural disaster or human corruption? Should you then be abandoned or destroyed or warehoused away? Should you then suffer and die? Should our society make *sure* you suffer and die? Should our society make sure that your abandonment or death or destruction is made profitable for somebody else? How should we align ourselves relative to a societal configuration that values profit over human life?

Say you *personally chose* to be a hard worker within our existing configuration, and *all by yourself* you manage to become a profitable worker. Congratulations on being industrious! Congratulations for thriving! Industriousness and thriving are good things. But notice: It means that being a hard worker *was an available choice*. It means that profitability was an *available* outcome of that choice. It was an *available* choice because the shared, foundational, generative, invisible, inextricable, configurable, natural human system, which you inherited, within which you operate, from which you partake far more value than you could ever give, provided you with that choice, because you are able-bodied and able-minded enough to pursue the opportunity within a framework of profit and industry, and because the intent of the system within which you exist is that that people should work hard to generate profit.

However, if your society has decided that some people matter and some people don't—that in fact some people have a
supremacy over others—then you might not have choices
available at all, or at least your access to those choices would
have to involve an ongoing persistent effort to overcome society's instinct to view your very existence as deemed unworthiness, and any access to any sort of choice that you were
able to attain while swimming against that societal current
would be instinctively deemed by the dominant supremacist
spirit of that society to be theft. If society had deemed that
punishment was the way to deal with unworthiness, then society might intend that your hard work be compulsory, and
the value received for it be as minimal as possible, and that
the punishment you receive for being unworthy should be as
cruel (and as profitable) as it can be made, and the idea that
you might know a moment's ease would be taken as a sign of
corruption. We would know that this would be society's deeper intention, because it would be what happened. If your body
were to break or degrade in some way, this society's intentions
toward you might instinctively change, because such a society
does not value people who cannot create profit, and you would
quickly find yourself swimming against a similar current. Such
a society would ensure that any healing and care that came to
your unprofitably broken or ailing body be made as profitable
as possible, to the exclusion even of providing the healing and
the care. We would know that this would be society's deeper
intention, because it would be what happened. Even innovation
might curtail choices in such a society, because innovation,
like every other tool, would be instinctively configured to value
profit more than human life.

If you lived in a society in which every person is considered a
part of an interconnected human family, and intrinsically valuable for that fact alone, an innovation that automates your labor
might be an exciting development; an opportunity for you to

pursue new interests, whether or not they were profitable—or, if the work that got replaced were something you'd have done even without getting paid, then maybe you'd go on doing it anyway, providing the unprofitable but creative value generated by work done for its own sake. But if you live in the sort of society I've been describing—where value is measured only by ability to generate profit, guided by the specific dominance of supremacy, energized by the promise of punishment—then the loss of the ability to generate profit, even if brought about by a problem being solved through innovation, could for you become the end of choice, could become death. We would know that this would be society's deeper intention, because it would be what happened. It would be the configuration you would inherit, and your choices would be chosen for you.

So much for individual choice.

◆ ◆ ◆

There's the effect of collective intent—a societal configuration I've called *spirit*.

There's the effect of individual intent—alignment within that configuration.

They both matter. They both matter a lot. The effect of collective intent simply matters *more*, practically speaking, because the collective intent is the empowered intent, and determines the available choices. The value of our individual intent matters more than collective intent in one way: we control it. Therefore, the most important *individual choice* we can make is deciding how to align relative to the configurations of our society and our place within it—which first requires acknowledging many truths that aren't popular in an individualist culture: That you belong to a society; that you exist in the context of that society in ways your intentions will never touch; that you receive more value from that society than you provide; and that you receive choices that other people do not, which provides you the opportunity to receive value others cannot access, with an ease that others cannot access.

I feel like I'm losing the rugged individualists.

Huddle back in, individualists.

I really want you to get this.

Try this: Suppose you belong to a society that has done something good.

For example: Suppose you belong to a society that has organized itself in such a way that when *the city decides*, it represents the voice of all people as equally as possible, rather than giving all power to only one person, like a king or patriarch or warlord, or to a preferred empowered supremacist minority like oh let's say Christians or men or white people, to give some totally random examples. Pretend you belong to a society that has chosen equality and enacted it perfectly, so that everybody has an equal voice in what is meant by *the city decides*. For purposes of scale (given that we are sometimes dealing with hundreds of thousands or even hundreds of millions of people), everybody has a representative who speaks for them in government, but everybody gets to choose the representatives, without restriction. The representatives represent all the people, not just the most wealthy or powerful, and they represent them all equally, and each vote counts the same as everyone else's. In this hypothetical, this means that you have inherited a societal configuration that is dedicated to equality. Equality is the collective intent—and you are a part of it.

And you don't get to choose about that.

The fact that this configuration represents the collective intent does *not* mean every individual agrees with it. In fact, let's pretend it makes millions of people very angry, and they've taught many of their children and grandchildren to be very angry about it, too.

They're aligned against it—but they're still a part of it.

It's so important to realize this. They're aligned against it—but they're still a part of it.

You can choose to not like it, but you're still a part of it.

If you don't take direct action to abet it, you're still a part of it.

If you make yourself completely ignorant about it, you're still a part of it.

Even if you're actively working against it to change it, you're still a part of it—though your individual choice to align against it matters, and may indeed someday help change it. If you belong to an equal society, your choice is not whether or not to be a part of an equal society. Your choice is whether or not to align with it, and, in so doing, with the effort to preserve it or to change it.

We in the United States know about alignment and inherited societal configurations instinctively, even if we are adept at pretending we don't know, whenever it suits us better to not know. We're very proud of having "freed the slaves," for example, and for "saving the world in World War II," and liberating concentration camps, and for founding the world's oldest active democracy, and for the Civil Rights Movement, and for being an economic superpower, and going to the moon, and so on. All those are things *we* did; but we *personally* didn't do these things. People in our country did, years and years ago, often before any of us were born. Yet we seem to understand that we're a part of all these accomplishments and good deeds as inheritors, and we're proud of that inheritance.

What *is* that pride? It's us, pointing toward the good effects of *our* collective intent. It's nothing we did as individuals. It came to us as inheritance: foundationally, generatively, automatically, inextricably.

Here in the United States, many of *us* like to inherit only the good.

This is *our* alignment, and it exists on my street.

OK, rugged individualists. You've stuck with me thus far, and I thank you.

Now I'm going to ask you to really stretch your imaginations:

Suppose you belonged to a society that was *not* perfectly equal, but ran instead on a configuration of specific domination, mediated through supremacist corruption and violence. Imagine you belonged to a society that until fairly recently had not allowed women to vote, to own property, to engage in public life without permission from their husbands, or to make decisions about how their own bodies would be used. Imagine that when *the city decided*, it did not represent the voice of women. Imagine you belonged to a society for which this was also true for people who were not deemed "white." Or who were not property owners, or not Christian.

Imagine now that, even though this society had recently changed, and permitted people outside those original constraints to make their voices heard, it still had preserved many foundational practices that took these inequalities and supremacies as assumed truths, which allowed them to still reverberate throughout the society's narratives of reality and its halls of power. In this hypothetical, if you were a man, if you were deemed "white," if you owned property, if you were a Christian, you'd benefit from all this automatically. In this hypothetical, if you were a woman, or if you weren't deemed "white," or if you didn't own property, or you weren't a Christian, you would suffer just as automatically.

If you were none of these things, you'd suffer the most.

If you were all of these things, you'd benefit the most.

Imagine the full weight of *that* inherited inequality.

In this hypothetical, you would belong to a society dedicated to specific dominance of some, at the expense of others. It would be a society that actually understood the dominated people to be, at a base level, property of the dominating people. If you were somebody recognized by such a society as belonging to one of the dominating categories, you'd have inherited more value—much of it unnaturally diverted, stolen from others to whom it otherwise would have come automatically.

Inequality would be the collective intention, and you would be a part of it.

And you don't get to choose about that.

You can choose to not like it, but you're still a part of it.

Even if you don't take direct action to abet it, you're still a part of it.

Even if you make yourself completely ignorant about it, you're still a part of it.

Even if you're actively working against it to change it, you're still a part of it—though your individual choice to align against it matters, and may indeed someday help change it.

If you belong to an unjust society, your individual choice is not whether to be a part of a just society or an unjust society. Your choice is whether or not to align with or against your unjust society, and in so doing, with the effort to preserve it or to change it.

By the way, the default is "alignment with it." If I make myself ignorant of the collective intent, then I am simply carried along in the current of my natural human system, which will do its work with or without my knowledge or consent or intent, even as I still participate in it.

And until I acknowledge that it exists, I can't align against it.

I have noticed that we in the United States instinctively refuse to know this, particularly those of us who are deemed "white," particularly men, particularly Christians, particularly if we are wealthy. We reject the notion that *we* enslaved the people *we're* so proud of freeing, we reject the idea that *our* heritage doesn't only include a fight that ended chattel slavery in its traditional form, but also a fight to preserve slavery. *We* refuse to admit that *we've* inherited not just the moral authority of the Civil Rights Movement, but also the angry, energized, powerful, violent, and murderous opposition to it. *We* credit ourselves with defeating the Nazis in World War II and helping to liberate their grotesque death camps, but refuse any culpability for having generated the racist practice and supremacist theory that inspired German supremacists to build those camps and fill them.

We Americans—particularly if we are deemed "white"— are very offended at the notion that *we* should not inherit the legacy of all the good *we* have done, but *we* are also very offended at the notion that *we* should inherit any responsibility for harm *we* have done. We're so opposed to the very question "*does* this have anything to do with me?" that it becomes for us a disqualifying question. We give ourselves license to ignore anyone who asks it, for the offense of having asked. And, cocooned in our manufactured unawareness, we are simply carried along in the current of our natural human system, which will do its work with or without our knowledge or consent or intent, even as we still participate in it.

Here in the United States, many of us love to inherit wealth, but refuse to inherit responsibility.

This, too, is our alignment. This, too, exists on my street.

It's important to understand the extent to which collective intent overwhelms personal intent, in order to understand how crucial the matter of alignment is. My alignment with or against the collective intent categorically defines my personal intentions. If I personally choose to align with injustice, that alignment is a fact that overwhelms my stated intentions for doing so. Finding a non-racist reason for joining with a white supremacist political party remains a racist decision. Finding a non-authoritarian rationale for joining with an authoritarian movement remains an authoritarian choice. If I decide to join with a Nazi political party for economic reasons rather than murderously bigoted reasons, I'm still nothing more than a god-damned Nazi. And this, at last, brings us back to Donald Trump and his very fine people—the ones who marched with the Nazis, even though they themselves were not Nazis, as our president would have you understand. He would have us know that a personal choice to make common cause with white supremacists and Nazis should be overlooked, because the people making that choice have discovered some alternate rationale for doing so, which should be taken at face value and treated as entirely exonerative.

But that simply isn't how alignment works.

If I march with the Nazis, bravo to me for not chanting "Jews will not replace us" with my lips, but you can perhaps be forgiven if you notice that I have chosen to chant it with my feet. Bravo to me for all my very fine qualities, but all I have done is lend my goodness to atrocity, and provided atrocity with the shelter and benefit of my fine qualities, which, while still present and real, are now, because of my *individual choice,* tools put into atrocious service, aligned to the purpose of atrocity.

It's not a question of either being a part of the problem or part of the solution. We don't face such easy dichotomies as that. The question before us is *whether or not we can accept the extent to which we are already a part of the problem*—which we are, to the extent that we are beneficiaries of that problem—and align against that, within ourselves first of all.

As a Christian, raised in Christian tradition, I happen to know this is actually a very Christian concept, and I happen to know that it is a very popular notion within conservative Evangelical Christianity in theory, but a *very* unpopular notion within conservative Evangelical Christianity in practice.

I can see why it's unpopular. It's not very easy or comfortable. Accepting we are already a part of the problem means we have to face a second choice, even less comfortable, which is whether or not to do anything about it. How we answer this question determines our alignment.

Rugged individualists, understand this: Our alignment is the most impactful and important personal decision we will ever make. In a very real way, our *individual choice* of alignment with or against our inherited societal configurations *is* our one individual choice.

All our other choices flow from that.

It's not all bad news for individualists, though. Here's some very good news: The power to change configurations rests in the hands of individuals, making choices about their alignment. Just as the power of collective intent matters more, practically speaking, than the power of individual intent, so also individual choice to align with or against that collective intent matters *even more* than the collective intent, and can actually overwhelm collective intent and change it.

When people start to believe new stories aligned against the current way things are, the collective will changes—a change of spirit, creating choices that hadn't been possible before.

Who can change the overwhelming power of collective intent? Who can effect a spiritual change? The same person who put *your* street there. You.

So what kind of world do you want to create?

That is an individual choice we might spend some time contemplating.

Yes, every street has its destination, and no street reaches its destination by accident.

But we shape the streets.

The question of alignment is so vital, because it addresses the question of whether or not we intend for the system itself to change, even if it costs us something—and changing an unjust system always carries a cost, particularly for people who benefit from the injustice. I'd identify the costs broadly as the loss of the unjust value, and the disruption that comes with change.

But the disruption that comes with change isn't optional.

We'll face it either way.

The thing about an unjust system is, it's unsustainable.

And the thing about an unsustainable system is, it doesn't sustain.

You change it or it collapses.

Change will come, either way.

Death is a change, after all.

◆ ◆ ◆

I'd observe that here in my country, which is the United States, *we* do anything *we* can to avoid these choices and these costs and these discomforts and disruptions. *We'd* rather die than face these questions about our foundational spiritual viruses and cancers. Increasingly, more and more of us *are* dying—increasingly of actual cancers and actual viruses, not because these things aren't preventable, but because the virus of supremacy has convinced so many of us to align with a cancerous spirit that insists that we aren't related, that life must be earned through profit, that those who cannot earn have committed an unforgivable sin worthy of death, and that violence redeems that sin.

As the thieves who configured our natural human system toward injustice divert more and more of the shared value of society only to themselves, cutting more and more of it off from more and more of us, those of us who still choose to align ourselves with the thieves rather than engage in radical, active, persistent, determined, informed, and transformative change that is needed to create a sustainable world, choose to align with that inevitable death.

It's an *individual* choice.

Some of us who make that choice call this death "freedom."

Some of us call it "realism."

It's death either way.

Virus and cancer: all either needs to devour a healthy system is for you do nothing—they'll do the rest. Alignment is the choice before us. Perhaps we should think of the compass again. The compass determines the direction. The direction determines the navigation. The navigation determines the course. The course determines the path. The path arrives at the destination. Will we set our compasses to move from unsustainability to sustainability, from injustice to justice, from a spirit of lack to a spirit of abundance, from a broken state to a fixed one? Or will change be forced upon us, as our unsustainable foundational injustices bring us to an inevitable collapse?

So far, too many of us have chosen to set our compasses to staying where we are.

It's an individual choice.

I think that's the answer to the first question: *how did we get here?*

Time to ask the second question.

SPIRIT

REPAIR
(December 2020–October 2021)

1. THE SECOND QUESTION
(December 2020)

He lost—that shit of the world. The pig president. White Evangelical Christianity's bronzed calf. He lost.

That's good.

The person who beat him was a man named Joe.

Joe seems like a nice enough fella, I guess. He's a pretty conservative guy if you go by the way most people in the world track such leanings. I'm not particularly conservative, so this means I disagree with him about most things, but he loves his family—his wife, his kids, even his dogs—or at least he knows how to act like it, and to make displays of empathy, by which I mean he seems to understand that other people exist, and seems to understand why that might matter. He has decades of relevant experience in public service—which includes many horrible errors, but even the errors are at least relevant to the job—and he appears to take the job seriously. He speaks in mostly complete sentences, although he is admittedly not the strongest available candidate in that area, but the things he says mostly align with observable reality, and are mostly centered on matters of consequence rather than the latest demands of his own ego. He probably won't encourage mobs of armed fascists, in or out of uniform, to attack citizens or politicians, for example. These are all novelties these days, when it comes to presidents.

Joe will be a better president than his predecessor, in the same way that a casserole will make a better meal than a festering mountain of turkey shit. The point being: I don't even have to tell you what kind of casserole. However, this is not the same as saying "Joe will be a good president." That matter is still up in the air, and would probably require defining what we mean by *good*.

During his campaign, Joe faced a blistering range of attacks from his opponents, all of which amounted to the sentiment "if this man gets into office, he will enact radical transformative systemic changes to the way things are, all of which are extremely obvious and needed solutions to enormous and present problems that threaten all of our lives." And Joe won by promising repeatedly that he wouldn't do most of those absolutely necessary things, or at least he won *while* promising not to do them. Meanwhile his opponents are still terrified that he will do all these awesome and desperately necessary things he's promised not to do and seems to have no intention of doing. Joe's opponents are convinced without evidence that Joe is controlled by "woke" activists—"woke" meaning people who are aware of the systemic problems we face, and "activists" meaning people who insist that because solutions are desperately needed, we should organize to enact them as soon as possible, with or without the permission of those in power. I'm told this means that "woke activists" are dangerous fanatics and foolish children. I'm told this by "the adults in the room," by which I mean people who know better than the rest of us, and can explain in great detail why improvement and repair and solutions aren't practical or possible or even desirable. The adults in the room live in "the real world," which is the world exactly as it is, to which no changes can be made, and within which nothing can be done about anything, and they know exactly why it's important to never even talk about trying, because if we did talk about trying (they'll explain) then the people who already have spent years calling Joe a socialist might call him a socialist.

A "socialist," by the way, is somebody who thinks that society exists, and that governments should work for the health and thriving of human beings, and that this means that some things that are conducive to the public good are good in and of themselves even if they don't create profit for industry, and therefore many such things—like education, or art, or the judicial process, or medical care, or transportation—should be public goods provided by and for the public, administered by representatives chosen by the public, rather than profit centers run specifically and exclusively to turn a profit. They also believe that profit engines should be regulated, to prevent them from making decisions that would maximize profits but also harm human beings. So that's what a socialist is, and it's one of the most horrible awful things a person can be, and if you don't believe me, just go to the real world and ask one of the adults in the room about it.

Joe was chosen by the adults in the room to lead us specifically because he promised to not be a socialist. As I mentioned, Joe's opponents all already called him a socialist anyway, and they really seem to believe that he is one, but the adults in the room seem to think that it would be even worse if Joe was called a socialist while actually *being* one, because this might lose him the political support of people who have already shown an unshakeable determination to never support him, ever, no matter what. To Joe's credit, he seems to really mean it when he says he isn't a socialist, so I hope all the adults in the room can be reassured for a minute, that Joe will keep seeking the support of people who will never support Joe. The adults in the room could use the chance to relax, I think. I've noticed that they're a rather panicky crowd, endlessly nervous that somebody might actually suggest a transformative and impactful solution to an enormous and pressing problem.

Anyway.

Maybe Joe's opponents are right, and Joe will stop listening to the adults in the room, and start listening to all these so-cialists—these dangerous fanatics and foolish children—and finally do all these desperately needed things that amount to repairing what is broken, and demolishing systems and structures that profit from brokenness.

We can hope.

The adults in the room have many other recommendations. There's a lot of talk now about healing, which seems to be centered on healing the people who aren't wounded—the ones who did the harming, the ones who would like to do a lot more harming, who talk eagerly of their plans to harm. There's a lot of talk now about unifying, without much talk about what we would unify around, or what we would hope to accomplish once unified. There's a lot of talk about compromise, without much discussion about what—or *who*, because it's always who—we would abandon in order to secure this compromise, or what we expect to gain by it, or what Republicans have ever given up in compromise. (That crowd hasn't even conceded the election yet, by the way, and doesn't seem likely to.) There's a lot of talk about how those who want to demolish our democracy and abuse millions of our friends and neighbors aren't our enemy—as if that's something a person gets to choose about people who are actively and enthusiastically attacking them or their loved ones.

And all the people who cheered Trump on, who now refuse to acknowledge that any of the depredations of the past four years ever actually happened, who have already determined not to even recognize Joe's authority, are ready and eager to cheer for the next fascist white supremacist demagogue, or maybe just for the same one again, because a fascist white supremacist demagogue is what they very clearly want. And the adults in the room are already encouraging us to bring these authoritarians back into the very fold the authoritarians are actively trying to destroy—not because the intentions of authoritarians have changed, but because doing so would make things feel normal again, and comfortable, at least for a while. For a lot of people, it truly seems as if all of this has basically just been a parlor game, in which they didn't ever feel the stakes, for which this was mostly about their personal discomfort with the uncomfortable realizations being forced upon them by Trump's grotesquerie. For a lot of people, it seems like the point of the game is to return to a state before our national diagnosis, when some of us could still pretend to not know just how sick we are.

There is, it seems, a desire to not know things already known. I suspect this is because if you know that something needs to be fixed, then you face a choice, which is whether or not to fix it—and if you decide to fix something that needs fixing, then you have to do the work of fixing it, and then you have to pay the price of repair.

There is, it seems, a desire to not do this work or pay this price. This is understandable. Treatment of deadly disease is frightening and disruptive, often radical and targeted in the short term, usually followed by a permanent, holistic, watchful, strategic, systemic restructuring of the way things used to be—to monitor for and prevent recurrence. Radical and transformative treatment is a lot to take on. People tend to not want disruption and discomfort, so comfortable people oppose transformative change. I get it.

However, we all know how sickness works. "Recurrence" is something that happens, for example, if you don't do the work to prevent it.

It's worth wondering: what comes after Joe?

If we don't engage in necessary radical systemic treatment, then I think what comes after Joe is recurrence of the disease, mutation of the virus. So, I think what's needed is radical and transformative change, if we would align ourselves with health. We should actively seek radical remedy and transformational change. We should desire these things as if they were survival itself—which they are. And we're going to have to do it without the support of people who have aligned themselves with our national diseases, which are the status quo, *the way things are.*

We have a lot of work left to do.

It's not clear *we* are willing to do it.

We know things about ourselves that we hate to know, but there's no going back. There are two questions we have to face, now that we have this knowledge. I chose to wait until after the 2020 election to raise the second question, because while the election mattered a great deal, it mostly determined how much damage and harm and pain and theft and murder there was going to be in the near term; but this outcome doesn't mean there won't be any, because the winning coalition seeks to maintain our present system, and these outcomes are what our present system generates. And these questions, which sound simple, but aren't, are the same after the election as they were before, as are the answers.

The first question was about conviction and confession.

It was *how did we get here?*

The second question is about repentance and reparation.

Here's the second question: *What do we do now?*

(October 2021)

Sometimes answers are stubborn.

I've been staring at that question for almost a year now: *What do we do now?*

Joe's answer to that question was simple: We return to business as usual, that's what we do now. Trump was the virus, that's the idea. Defeat the virus, and the system will return to normal, and all Joe's Republican friends will go back to behaving the way they did back in the 1970s and 1980s, back when maleness and whiteness didn't feel so threatened, and open white suprema-cists and progressives all found it much easier to work together to get things done. That was Joe's pitch, and it won him the elec-tion, and he was wrong.

They didn't go back to those earlier comfortable times. Quite the opposite, in fact. The year since the election has proved beyond doubt that the white supremacist christofascist viral mutation of old foundational lies that the Republican Party released into our national bloodstream has no intention of stop-ping just because one major symptom has been displaced as our national leader for the present; it's also proved that our systems, which are optimized to preserve an increasingly untenable sta-tus quo, have no mechanism to address it.

As a result, we are expected to tolerate a growing list of intolerable things.

I've seen hordes of enraged white supremacists invading the Capitol, sent by a sitting president in a nearly successful attempt to overturn an election and murder Congress, abetted materi-ally and legislatively by a Republican Party that has spent all its time since that day working to ensure that the plot remains un-examined and that the next one will be successful and enduring. I've seen Republican governors engaged in a persistent targeted strategy of sabotage against all efforts to contain the Covid pandemic as the death toll mounts and mounts, abetted by a powerful and popular network of propaganda platforms, which day and night issue rhetoric and policy propositions that are increasingly indistinguishable from that of white supremacist and Nazi groups such as the ones who invaded Charlottesville in 2017. I've seen a stolen Supreme Court work diligently with gerrymandered state legislatures to kick over the load-bearing pillars of equality and modern society. I've seen marginalized people targeted for harassment and harm in increasingly open terms, and with increasingly undisguised intention.

There are gun massacres most weeks. Most days, really.

Why? I'm told the answer is complex, and probably so. I've noticed that guns are a common factor to all of them. It seems to me we have so many massacres because people who want to enact gun massacres are very easily able to get massacre weapons—by which I mean guns made for the clear purpose of massacring people. It is very easy to get massacre weapons; certainly, it's far easier for someone to get one than it is to buy or rent a house, or get affordable medical care, or a college education. And it's easy to buy massacre weapons because Republicans refuse to make it difficult to buy massacre weapons, and in fact insist on making it easier and easier, and even brag about doing so, and pose in Christmas cards with their scrubbed pink families all brandishing massacre weapons like some weird pajamas-based cult. They say they do this because they believe that individuals should have the right to use massacre weapons in "self-defense" however they wish to define the term, which really seems inseparable from saying that individuals should have the right to massacre at their discretion—particularly since no matter how many individuals use massacre weapons to murder people, Republicans never stop defending massacre weapons and people's rights to have them without any restriction. And they seem to believe this mostly because they are paid to believe this by a powerful lobby that makes more profit with every massacre, but also because the people they represent believe that they have the right to kill at their own discretion, and greatly resent anyone who questions their judgment and their right to decide who lives and who dies, or to own weapons designed to murder people as quickly as possible, and to own as many of them as they want. They'll tell you that they might need to kill somebody someday, or maybe a bunch of somebodies, and if they aren't able to do that whenever that day comes, they'll tell you, that would be the worst form of tyranny imaginable to them. I'd say we have massacres because we are a society optimized for massacre, and we know we're a society optimized for massacre because disturbed people who want to enact massacres are being accommodated, and the rest of us, who do not want a society optimized for massacre, are not. When *the city decides*, what is meant by *the city* is not most of us, it seems, but only those people who would like to have a world of gun massacres. We have massacres because the people who get to decide such things would rather have a world with massacres than one without. And we know this, because a nation of plentiful gun massacres is what we have.

Also, Democratic leadership appears to have decided that the answer to these massacres, which are not in any way prevented by police in our overpoliced country, is to give the police more money. And they appear to have decided that the solution to systemic police brutality is to give the police more money. I'm just waiting to hear that they've decided that the answer to the baby formula shortage (I forgot to mention: there is a baby formula shortage) is to give the police more money—because if there's one group that needs more funding, oh baby, you'd better believe it is the police, who use civil asset forfeiture to steal more from citizens than any criminal group steals each year, who take so much, and give back so little, and who have convinced themselves they have such a dangerous job they must spend every single moment of it making sure that they are safe even if it means that everyone else is not. They have such an important but dangerous job (unless you look at the actual statistics, in which case you'll see that, no) that they have been assured by our Supreme Court that they cannot face any accountability from anybody for anything they do, provided they establish that they were frightened when they did it, and the legalese for this is "qualified immunity," a term that boils down to, "if a cop wants immunity, they qualify." And the Supreme Court even ruled that if you're a border agent within 100 miles of a border, you're not accountable even to the Constitution for any reason, and you don't even have to say you were scared—you're just an unrestricted enforcer of whatever the fuck you want to say the law is, and if you want to say the law is you, so much the better.

So much for the Constitution.

All these people doing this are allowed to keep doing this. They insist on being treated as if they and their actions are normal, and, as they are treated that way by a cowed opposition and a sleeping media, they have become normal. The people we elected to fix this can't fix it, I'm told. Their hands are tied, I'm told. Apparently stopping the people who are breaking the rules would be against the rules. The people who are allowed to decide about stopping them don't want to stop them, and the people who want to stop them aren't allowed to decide. The Senate Parliamentarian said so. If you don't know who that is, I'll tell you; we learned recently that apparently they are the most powerful person in the world whenever and only whenever everyone whose job it is to do something would rather do nothing and needs somebody to tell them they can't do anything, at which point the parliamentarian shakes their head sadly "no" and everyone else throws up their hands in what they hope is believable frustration.

None of this is popular, yet all of it seems inevitable. Most people want solutions, yet solutions never materialize, even though we quite often know what the solutions are, or at least in what direction they're located. Still, even the hope of solutions seems distant.

The root problem appears to be that we can't get the people who want problems to give us permission to fix the problems, and we can't get the people who claim to want to fix the problems to stop asking those people for permission.

And there are other things, too, but they all seem to boil down to this issue: We can't fix what's broken, because the people who want things broken appear to be in charge of deciding whether or not broken things get fixed.

So, we have our prognosis.

It's not just a virus that we refuse to fight. It's a cancer that we refuse to treat.

So, I've spent a year staring at the question: *What do we do now?*

My answer is: *we realign ourselves to oppose the unjust config-urations of our natural human system* ... and then I delete that phrase, and try again, because at a certain point these things get lost in abstraction.

Change our spirit? Yes.

Change the atmosphere? Yes. Great. Wonderful.

How?

◆ ◆ ◆

My focus is usually on spirit, and rarely on specific action. I think it's more effective to think about what sort of person to be than what sort of thing to do. This frustrates people. *Yes but what actions do you propose? What is your specific plan? What are the five steps to do that?* This frustration is understandable. Actions are something more direct than simply pointing in the direction we ought to go and insisting we can get there. Actions are often measurable. They feel productive. However, I still tend to focus less on specific action and more on spirit.

I have reasons.

Often I simply don't know what to do. I'm still confused and broken. My worldview has been shattered and I'm recon-structing it, so all I'm able to do is share what I've learned, and expound on what I observe. And I'm not particularly knowl-edgeable. When you're a writer who can arrange thoughts in an effective way, there's a great danger that people will start thinking you know something, and then they start looking to you for answers. I'm sympathetic. It's tough to be a disap-pointment, but probably not as tough as being disappointed.

But also, I worry about making global pronouncements about specific actions. Specific actions are *specific,* and thus not all specific actions are appropriate or feasible for all people, while spirit is more generally applicable. You're *you*. You have a specific situation and specific skills and resources and privileges and specific intersections with our unjust and corrupt systems. What you need to do depends on all those things. So what should you do?

Good question: What *should* you do?

Maybe you should run for office, but maybe you know you'd be bad at that.

Maybe you are best at spreading awareness to the confused, or maybe finding the right words isn't your thing.

Maybe you need to call your representatives every day, or maybe you are just trying to keep your head above water and don't have the time for that.

Maybe you need to march. Maybe you need to shout. Maybe you need to make your voice silent so others can be heard. Maybe you need to stay nonviolent. Maybe you need to join a fight. Maybe you have a lot of money and you need to give to bail funds and mutual aid networks and activist organizations. Maybe you have influence and power and prestige, and you need to use them to confront injustice, or maybe you need to give up your outsized influence so others can have a larger share of it. Or maybe you just need to finally give a shit, rather than to decide that the safer thing is to find a reason to be apathetic or cynical—two states which people of bad intent would most prefer for you. Maybe you are in a compromised position under active threat from toxic bullies and you just need to keep yourself safe and alive. Or maybe someday you'll surprise yourself, and discover you need to take extreme unlawful action to keep people under active threat alive. I doubt Miep Gies expected to become a lawbreaker, for example, but when she hid the Frank family, that is what she was. I doubt she imagined she'd build a secret room in her house in defiance of a genocidal police state. I think in an age that was guided by a spirit of murderous order, she was guided by a spirit of truth and hope—truth that every human being carries an intrinsic value more important even than order or law; hope that things can get better. She asked herself "what should I *do?*" and then *did* it, and so did Harriet Tubman, and Martin Luther King, Jr., and many other lawbreakers as well.

What do you need to do? I'd say first realign yourself against what is broken. Become the kind of person that acts in a fierce spirit of love, and then be guided by that spirit. Actions are specific, and can change a situation. They're necessary, but they're situational. Spirit is atmospheric, and can change the world. So, I focus on changing the atmosphere, the spirit.

We must realign. We must change our national spirit.

I type the phrase, then delete it. It's not wrong, but it frustrates me.

Realign. Change our national spirit. Yes. Great. Perfect.

How?

Eventually we do have to get to practicalities. The compass and the navigation aren't of much use without the journey. So, finally, I'm going to propose some actions. To name these actions, I'm borrowing several terms from the tradition I grew up in, which is Christianity—American Evangelical Christianity, to be precise. These actions are focused on the work of alignment, which is a work that each person must perform inwardly on themselves before they can hope to direct it outwardly.

The terms I'm using are: awaken, convict, confess, repent, repair, and redeem.

Here are the actions I propose:

1. Awaken to the truth of systemic corruption and abuse, in all its ugliness.
2. Convict ourselves to the truth that we share responsibility, to transform our minds.
3. Confess our individual and shared involvement, publicly and unequivocally.

4. Repent from that involvement, by agreeing to pay the cost of repair.
5. Repair what is broken, by actually paying that cost and doing the work.
6. Redeem our natural human system, by entering the cycle of the realigning work of repair.

These steps are the work of repair.

They are a process—a progressive and realigning sequence.

They are, incidentally, exactly how we fix . . . streets.

Configuring streets—updating existing ones, building new ones—requires work.

If we wish to maintain our streets, or extend them, or modify them, or build new ones to serve new needs, we would have to . . . do it. Obvious, right?

But some time before we do it, we'll have to realize that there's a need to do it. An *awakening.* And some time after that, but still before we do it, we'll have to accept that doing it is our shared responsibility. A *conviction.* And some time after *that,* but still before we do it, we'll have to determine to actually do it, and make the necessary plans. A *confession.* And some time after *that,* but still before we do it, we'll have to agree to pay what it costs, and modify our priorities toward that end. A *repentance.* And some time after *that,* the work will have to done. And before, during and after *that,* the full cost—in labor, in inconvenience and disruption, in actual money—will actually have to be paid. The *repair.*

This is the work of configuration, of alignment, necessary to any repair or maintenance.

The cost is practical. It's also spiritual.

It's spiritual work. It's also practical work.

It's a process—a generative, sustainable, progressive and realigning sequence.

I think that means it's also redeeming work.

We use these steps to realign our streets. We could use them to realign ourselves—our *individual choice* to realign against our current inherited dominant popular supremacist societal configuration of injustice and abuse.

If enough of us realign ourselves, we'd create a new spirit. Change the atmosphere. Reset the compass. Tell a new story. Whatever metaphor you like.

This would be more than just thinking *I'm against injustice.* It would involve doing the realigning work and paying the disruptive cost. That would be hard—for some of us more than others. But if we did it, the spirit would change.

That's what I think, anyway.

I've been staring at the second question for almost a year now: *What do we do now?*

I think I'm finally ready to answer.

What do we do now?

We fix our fucking streets, that's what we do.

2. BLAMELESS SUPREMACY

Let me tell you a story about Moses.

No, not *that* Moses. Robert Moses.

Wikipedia informs me that Robert Moses was "an American public official who mainly worked in the New York metropolitan area," whose "decisions favoring highways over public transit helped create the modern suburbs of Long Island."

He was never elected, Wikipedia informs me.

An interesting footnote.

Moses built parkways which led, among other places, to Long Island beaches. He set the overpass bridges very low—too low, in fact, to accommodate public transport of the day, which were buses. Buses were the primary option for people in poorer communities wishing to travel to the beach. The poorer communities were largely people deemed "not white," specifically, Black and Puerto Rican populations. The result of Moses' low bridges is that poorer people in the city—who tended to be people of color—did not go to the public beaches, and more affluent people who could afford cars—and who tended to be deemed "white"—did.

This result is not the official reason given for the low bridges, it should be noted. Wikipedia informs me that there are many complexities and rationales that can be offered for the low bridges that are perfectly reasonable and perfectly benign. In fact, if you search Google for "Robert Moses and racism," you may find as a first result a *Washington Post* fact-check that points out, among other proffered exonerations, that the practice of building bridges that wouldn't accommodate buses was widespread nationally, and that Black and Puerto Rican people still don't go to Jones Beach much even though car ownership is more widespread these days. These confessions of widespread practice and persistent ongoing effects strike me as strange proofs to offer that widespread inherited structural racism *isn't* at play, but, in any case, it appears there are those who claim points of view that argue against narratives of Robert Moses's racism and the structural racism of his low bridges. We could go read them, and educate ourselves about them, and maybe we should. Yet it must be said: The result was still the result.

It was a decision that a powerful famously racist man made, with a non-racist rationale offered and accepted by the power structures of his day (and, to some degree, of our day), that happened to have an outcome delivering an adverse effect to people who tended to be disproportionately from racial minority groups—which just so happened to be the groups who mostly white people of the day tended to prefer not to see at what I imagine they mostly thought of as "their" beaches. And so it came to pass that there were not many Black or Puerto Rican people on "their" beaches. They probably didn't think about it, since they didn't have to.

The "not having to think about it" strikes me as the core of supremacy—a system automatically preferring you over others so much you don't even have to know about it when you go the beach.

By the way, I hope you don't think I consider myself a smarty-pants by referencing this story. This is not exactly a scoop I'm bringing you. You may well have heard of Robert Moses and his low bridges long ago, either from *The Power Broker* (Robert Caro's Pulitzer Prize winning history of Moses) or from some other source—particularly if you're the sort of person who is interested in knowing about these sorts of things. You probably have known about it far longer than me, in part because these sorts of things were not featured in my formal or informal education, but also because, I must confess, I was not a very curious person about these sorts of things for many years, even though I would have always told you I was *against* racism. You might say I didn't think about it because I didn't have to. Nevertheless, it's a well-known story, often used to demonstrate the idea of structural racism in civic design, so I'm drawing on its familiarity now.

But I could have used any number of other similar stories.

In state after state, city after city, town after town, other people, who were not Robert Moses, but who held similar positions, made similar decisions: about what sorts of roads to build, and what sorts of neighborhoods to demolish in order to build them, and where to place various parks and libraries and public pools, and what homes to sell in what neighborhoods to what people, and how to value houses when people of a certain color owned them, and thousands and thousands of other choices, and perhaps if we went back and investigated, we'd find that all of those choices were just as blameless as Robert Moses choosing to set his highway bridges low. Perhaps we'd learn that none of these choices were made with racist rationales, but we'd also find that they just so happened to have similar results: the exclusion of some over others, on a basis of race. It might make you wonder, if you were a curious person: How many other stories like this are there? Hundreds, certainly. Thousands, maybe.

Millions? Tens of millions?

Probably so.

There are many tens of millions of people of color in this country, and everyone has a story—don't you have one? And sure, not every story is a part of the historical record, but many stories are, and, though they don't always feature in first-result *Washington Post* fact-checks, we could go read those stories and educate ourselves about them, and maybe we should do that, too.

Interestingly, these decisions about roads don't just cost marginalized people. Eventually Moses' decisions—which were made for whatever reason, but which had the effect of excluding some and benefitting others—cost everybody. Those low bridges are a hazard and a chronic nuisance, causing hundreds of hours of delays and millions of dollars of damage. And, of course, fixing it all would be a massively expensive project, because it would require a great deal of rebuilding— and *who is going to pay for that?* one might ask if one is the sort of person I have been, a blithe and blameless supremacist, in other words: someone who doesn't think about things because they don't have to, who fails to see that everyone is already paying for the current inherited situation, which is already massively expensive, and exclusionary and dangerous to boot. Robert Moses didn't personally make it so that the poorer neighborhoods and communities were disproportionately comprised of marginalized groups, by the way. He just made decisions from the existing reality he inherited, in which impoverished people tended to be disproportionately people not deemed "white." It stands to reason that some other earlier Robert Moses made the decisions that led to that reality, at some earlier point.

Almost all of us are *against* racism now, so one would think fixing the effects of inherited racism would be easy. Ask anybody if they're for or against racism and they'll tell you, they're against. Everyone knows that racism is bad. Even racists know it, which is why they hate being called racist, though they do seem to think that all that racism is or can ever be is direct personal animus, and that all that is needed to be aligned against it is to think "racism is bad." I notice that framing racism that way means one can oppose paying for repairing the effects of inherited structural racism without considering oneself racist, and so those effects— which should be easy to fix, because everyone agrees racism is bad—somehow still never get fixed. It's probably a coincidence, but the effect is still the effect. However, I do wonder: Does the current lowness of the Long Island Parkway overpasses still prevent buses from going to the beach? Are buses still primarily used by people living in poverty, and are people living in poverty still disproportionately people of color?

What have we inherited?

If intention is revealed by what actually happens, and what happened *still happens,* did we not only inherit the effects of racism, but the intent?

I find these are interesting questions to ask.

It seems to me we've inherited a system that has sabotaged itself to maintain the supremacy of its preferred members, by manufacturing designed brokenness, by refusing to pay the lower cost of repair, by manufacturing targeted harm, and by forcing others to pay as much of the higher cost of brokenness as possible, while allowing itself to not know about what it is doing, in order to avoid paying the ultimate cost, which is the blame for doing it—and all of this to maintain a broken belief that societal value is only for those who deserve it. All of this, to avoid the lower cost of inclusion. All of this, to avoid the lower cost of repair. All creating much higher costs as we try to sustain an unsustainable system.

And I think of that as **sabotage.**

As I mentioned, there were a multitude of other Robert Moseses (Mosi?) working at the same time as him, and there were multitudes before him.

And there have been multitudes of Moseses after.

I wonder how many of them were, like Moses, never elected. Lots, probably.

I wonder how many of them *were* elected.

Lots, probably.

◆ ◆ ◆

As I mentioned, we're facing a huge number of serious problems. We have a medical crisis and a housing crisis and an incarceration crisis and a domestic terror crisis and a democracy crisis and many other crises, and looming over them all a climate crisis threatening human existence, which is a pretty big deal if you are a human and existing is one of your interests. We're told that all these problems are extremely complex, which is observably true, but the complexity mostly seems to be mentioned in service of making the case to not seek remedies. We're told that remedies aren't politically feasible, even though they prove hugely popular when polled. We're told remedies aren't possible, even though other countries have successfully enacted them. We're told that remedies can't be afforded, even though the problems are more expensive than the remedy, and we seem to be able to afford the problems, and still have enough money left over to spend the surplus on municipal brute squads and instruments of destruction and punishment, and on lavish giveaways to people who already have more money than they could ever spend—which if one thinks about it for even a moment makes one realize that "we can't afford it" within the context of a huge and wealthy natural human system is an expression of priority, not capability, every single time.

Again, we want to fix serious problems, and yet we don't fix them. In fact, we seem to do anything and everything but fix them, until they start to seem like ways in which society is failing. They almost seem like society is being *made* to fail—which I don't actually think we want. Sure, there are people who want societal collapse but I don't think most do. Some people *claim* to want that, but at the risk of putting words into other people's mouths, I think what a lot of people usually mean is that they want unjust and oppressive systems to fail, so that society can thrive, but our unjust and oppressive systems have become so endemic that they are what we mean when many of us say *society*. And so I can't help but wonder why society should keep failing, when so few of us actually want it to.

If we want to see broken things fixed, why can't we fix what is broken?

And why do so many people insist that things should stay broken?

Here's my diagnosis of what we're up against: an atmospheric, spiritual, institutional opposition to repair, flowing from all our supremacist foundational lies, which has sabotaged the very mechanism of repair itself. There is a process by which things get fixed, and we are witnessing sabotage of that process by people opposed to repair.

We might wonder why people would be opposed to repair.

Before answering, it might be helpful to establish definitions of what I mean by *broken* and *repair* and *supremacy*, in terms as simple and obvious as I can manage.

◆ ◆ ◆

"Repair" presupposes something is broken. How's that for simple and obvious?

Things do break, by the way. Surely, we can agree on that much, even when speaking to people who have chosen to inhabit alternate realities of propaganda and conspiracy.

And generally, the thing to do with broken things is repair them—that or replace them with something better, which is a sort of repair called *improvement*. Things break in different ways, but I'd observe the main categories seem to be natural degradation from wear or time, accidental breakage, and deliberate breakage.

I want to talk about deliberate breakage.

If I break your arm with a shovel, that's deliberate breakage of your arm.

If I lie to you, that's deliberate breakage of our trust.

If I emotionally attack you, that is deliberate breakage of your inner peace.

If I steal your car, that's deliberate breakage of your rightful ownership.

If I pass a law that says you must not be treated as a full citizen, on the rationale that my entrenched bigotry should be recognized and protected as a religious belief, that is deliberate breakage of the shared, foundational, generative value delivered automatically and inextricably by our natural human system. If I overturn a series of laws that safeguard your treatment as a full citizen, I am engaged in a very similar version of this same deliberate breakage.

We might think of deliberate breakage as abuse: theft, harm, violence, lies, cruelty. We might think of abuse that is strategically deployed by someone seeking to achieve some personal benefit as *corruption*. We might think of abuse that is targeted deliberately to cause harm to specific people or groups of people as *hate*. This is abuse, and abuse is what abusive people do. My observation is that abusive people are people who are aligned with deliberate breakage. Or we could express this thought in an inverted way: abusive people are people who are aligned against repair. So, in a society engaged in a struggle against an abusive human spirit, you might find a powerful and energetic opposition to repair. Or, in a society where abuse has become so accommodated that abusers have become comfortable, you might find an all-encompassing and smothering opposition to repair.

The more powerful the abuser, the more their ability to create and enforce a reality where their corruption and hate is defended by general society and by systems of power as normal and respectable, or even kind and generous. In such a reality where abuse has become normal and respectable, eventually even natural and accidental breakages will become deliberate breakage, as those empowered to fix natural and accidental breakages, aligned against repair, deliberately and passively neglect the repair. If you're trying to detect a society that is spiritually and institutionally opposed to repair, you might look, for example, for a society that has enormous institutional problems when it comes to finding the political will and capital to maintain its own roads and bridges.

And (as anyone who has ever observed an abusive person might note) abusers are often powerful, and their abuse is frequently both strategic and targeted—a combination which, when systemized, we might think of as suppression and oppression: *suppression* being strategic and targeted corruption and abuse to prevent theft and corruption and other abuse from being talked about or even known about; *oppression* being strategic and targeted theft and corruption and other abuse, deployed to ensure that theft, corruption and abuse will be permitted or even celebrated, sometimes to such a degree that suppression is no longer needed.

It's all sabotage—a dark mirror of the process of repair.

Sabotage is acquisitive where repair is generative.

It's regressive where repair is progressive.

And unsustainable. It creates brokenness.

It makes collapse inevitable.

Sabotage always costs more than repair, because it takes without fixing, harms without helping, hoards for itself what would otherwise be invested in shared continuance.

Oppressive and suppressive corruption manifests when an abuser—whether person or institution—gains an advantage from something broken, then uses that advantageous position to force somebody else to pay them the much higher cost of not fixing the breakage, rather than paying their own fair share of the much lower cost of repair. Oppressive and suppressive hate usually manifests itself, not through overt statements and actions, but when abusers create supremacist systems to specifically target certain people to shoulder the cost of brokenness, based on their own definitions of which people matter and which don't.

(As an aside, I think this is where we often get corruption and hatred wrong. People will object to the word "hate" in particular, claiming we are taking a reductive view lacking nuance regarding the beliefs or relationships of the individual or institution so charged—but I'd argue this is itself a reductive position that lacks nuance regarding the true nature of oppressive hate. We often think that saying a person or institution is "corrupt" means they are individually unlawful and unrespectable. We often believe that when we say somebody is "hateful" or "part of a hate group" that it means they actively individually have hateful thoughts or take hateful actions. But corruption is often legal and respectable, and hatred is often very polite, even nice, to others and even to its targets. Hatred is often magnanimous, even generous—in specific ways and with specific prerequisites—to compliant individuals within groups targeted for hate. In fact, it's usually only when the supremacist advantage slips that you see the more recognizable, the more overt and direct manifestations, of corruption or hate. If you've ever known an abusive person, maybe you know what I mean.)

So that's what I mean when I say *broken*.

What about repair?

There are a lot of things that aren't repair that are often mistaken for repair.

Repair isn't simply agreeing that something is broken but not moving to fix it.

Many things that might be necessary in the moment to deal with the effects of brokenness aren't repair. For example, being kind to people suffering oppressive systems is good, but it isn't repair, and neither is raising money to help with a specific problem caused by oppression. A workaround isn't repair. A stopgap isn't repair. Somebody managing to survive another year by engaging in constant daily struggle isn't repair. Managing the problem caused by the breakage instead of doing the repair isn't repair—for example, a charity that would evaporate if the underlying problem it manages were to be fixed may be a necessary charity, and the efforts and money expended on its behalf may be admirable, but it isn't repair.

How's this for simple and obvious?

Repair involves actually fixing what is broken and paying the cost for doing so.

Cost. Ah, yes. The primary reason given to not repair things. A real classic.

Repair always involves cost—usually money, but also disruption and inconvenience. (If you've ever experienced road work, or a surgical procedure, you'll know what I mean.) These are natural costs of repair, and the bigger the repair required, the larger the costs.

But also: if the thing that is broken is something that was broken on purpose, then the cost for the person who did the breaking is not just their money and their convenience but also their reputation, because repair always involves public awareness of brokenness and its causes... and if that someone happens to be profiting from the fact that the thing is broken, the cost is not just their money, their convenience and their reputation, but the loss of their advantage, because repair fixes the broken thing from which they profit.

Abusive people and institutions are opposed to repair specifically because they are opposed to paying any of the costs of repair, specifically because the brokenness affords them an advantage—because abusive people and institutions insist on making other people pay all costs of the brokenness they create. And, because they are abusive and strategic, people opposed to repair make their opposition to repair as advantageous to themselves as possible, by making institutional the systemic problems inevitably rising from their individual refusal to repair. And, because they are abusive and hateful, people opposed to repair make sure that the management of those problems is deemed as respectable as possible, and involves punishment of the people already targeted by their abuse.

And that brings me back to supremacy.

◆ ◆ ◆

Let's begin with the couple and their sign.

Maybe you saw them, celebrating the recent murder of bodily autonomy by the U.S. Supreme Court, which this year overturned Roe v. Wade. The sign said WE WILL ADOPT YOUR BABY. The couple are Neydy Casillas and Sebastián Schuff, and they are lawyers who have spent much their time and energy making sure that our laws reflect "Christian values," which is a phrase that usually means things like making sure that people who are gay or trans or otherwise nonconforming to assigned sexual and gender roles are not recognized under the law or protected by it, and that people who don't want to carry babies are forced to do so. It's certainly what it means in this case, because that's the sort of thing Casillas and Schuff have been working on.

Their sign represents a very popular sentiment among religious-minded conservative Christian people. It's a particularly popular sentiment now that the Supreme Court, which has been strategically captured by people like them to represent people like them and only people like them, has struck down a great many fundamental rights and protections, including the right to abortion. The sentiment captured on their sign is: You didn't want a baby, but fear not! Now that you will be forced by law to carry it, we will care for it when it is born.

A lot of people had a lot of reactions to this: a couple performatively giving a self-aggrandizing "solution" to a situation they deliberately worked to create; and meanwhile, hundreds of thousands of children in this country, who Neydy Casillas and Sebastián Schuff did not adopt, live in a foster care system that has been largely defunded down to a shoestring, mainly through the efforts of people like Neydy Casillas and Sebastián Schuff. And of course it wasn't lost on many people that conservative Christians in this country have a history of forcibly raising other people's children as their own, in order to assimilate them away from their parents' values and toward their own. It's a recognized form of genocide, and so for many people the couple's sign carries the credible hint of a historically common genocidal threat that Christianity has, as a matter of historical record, represented.

There are no laws forcing anyone to have an abortion, incidentally, and there never have been. Casillas and Schuff were not being compelled by law to live against their beliefs. That wasn't good enough for Casillas and Schuff, though, or for millions of like-minded people. No, they needed laws forcing other people to follow their beliefs, or to suffer if they refuse.

And they went out and worked hard until they got those laws. And now they insist on being considered good for having done so. And that's supremacy.

◆ ◆ ◆

In this age that refuses to see obvious things and neglects to remember simple things, I keep feeling the urge to repeat simple and obvious things.

If something is broken, it needs repair. If it's something that belongs to me, it is my responsibility to decide whether to fix it, or not. If it's something I broke, it is my responsibility to fix it, too. Repair always carries a cost: money and effort and inconvenience. If I don't want to pay that cost, I might choose not to repair. But if I don't pay the cost, then the broken thing will stay broken.

All of that is simple enough, and innocent enough—though we might all think about the degree to which we find it easier to treat things in our lives as disposable than to repair them. I certainly think about how I behave this way in my life, and the way society is shaped to encourage me toward this behavior.

Let's up the ante.

Let's say I don't make calculations about cost to discern whether or not to fix things. Let's say my main goal is only to avoid paying cost. Let's say I even structure my religion around the idea of an ultimate cost, that others will have to pay, but that I will not. Especially at a societal level, if the broken thing is vital to human thriving, then brokenness carries a higher cost than repair: poverty, ignorance, degradation, sickness, debt, danger. In fact, it often carries a *much* higher cost, one that usually compounds over time as more and more things break and nothing is fixed. If I am somebody whose main goal is to avoid paying any cost, then I am not going to want to pay my share of the cost of any repair, or even the cost, ongoing and lower still, of maintenance—but I definitely won't want to have to pay the higher cost of brokenness. I will have to seize enough power and resources to structure society in such a way that I exclusively own the choice of whether to repair or not, so I can fix only the things that affect me, and so other people can be made to pay all the cost of ongoing brokenness. For example, if I were outraged by laws enforcing school integration, I might methodically spend decades arranging things so that all municipal school funds get siphoned to private school systems I control, under the guise of "parental choice," and then blame the parents of children with no access to those well-funded school systems for the decaying underfunded schools to which they are forced to send their children, and point to the wonderful schools in my own neighborhood as proof that I am a superior parent, and then use my re-established superiority as a parent and a citizen as a pretext to demand more consideration under the law than the parents I have "proved" to be inferior and neglectful. Because I will have arranged matters so that I pay as little of the cost of the brokenness as possible, I will inevitably profit from brokenness—money, yes, but also influence and reputation and a power alignment that gives me preference and position of place, and a supremacy of consideration in any decisions that get made. If I profit from the brokenness, then I will start to see repair itself as a cost. If I profit from brokenness, then breaking things will become an opportunity for more profit. Repair and maintenance will begin to seem like theft to me, particularly if any of the cost of repair falls to me. I will have aligned myself with brokenness: not only refusing to repair, but refusing to allow others to do so, either. Not only refusing to repair, but breaking more things, to further profit from the brokenness.

Let's up the ante.

If I am deliberately breaking things to profit from them, then the responsibility to pay the cost of repair isn't naturally shared. The responsibility is actually now mine alone. If other people notice that the supremacy I claim for myself affords me the power and resources to repair broken things, yet I refuse to do so, they might start to understand me as somebody aligned with brokenness, somebody who bears outsized responsibility for reparation. And if they notice that I helped break it, they might start to blame me for the brokenness. And, if enough people become aware of this truth, they might revoke my supremacy and begin reparation. If they do that, I might have to pay my share of the cost of repair—a cost I have made as high as possible.

And so blame becomes another cost—the highest cost imaginable.

If my main goal is to avoid cost, then, I must become blameless. I will *need* supremacy.

Supremacy is exceptional. It believes in its own exceptionalism. It will always make exceptions for itself.

In a society aligned against paying costs, then, you'll find many people who have decided not to know about their own supremacy, or about brokenness, or their own responsibility for repair. You will find blameless people.

Have you met any?

Let's pretend now, just as a thought experiment, that you and I are among these blameless people, opposed to cost, aligned against repair, comfortable in a supremacy we refuse to acknowledge. We wish to benefit from brokenness while considering ourselves blameless. Some of us will realize exactly what we are doing, and will be working very hard and very deliberately to avoid all costs of repair in order to enrich ourselves and only ourselves, but most of us will have decided to not know; so that while many people who suffer from our ignorance can see we are not blameless, we will sincerely believe we are blameless, and maintain this ignorance simply by learning all the places not to look—a self-aggrandizing logical monkey bars, a worldview that supports only itself and leads back only to itself, but complex enough that we can climb around it with great skill, and convince ourselves that we make sense. Which we do, as long as we ignore anything else that is not the monkey bars.

It will become imperative for us to use our supremacy to create systems that impart to us the benefits of brokenness while hiding the knowledge of brokenness—from others, but from ourselves most of all. We will need to fashion ignorant systems, which will do the abusive work of brokenness without telling of it, even if deep down we know. For us to keep our blamelessness, the system must be held to be perfect. The best ever

created. Exceptional from its inception, from its very foundation. The greatest in history. The envy of all others. The light
of the world. A city on a hill. Perhaps you've heard of such an
exceptional system.

Perhaps you've been told you live in an exceptional nation.

However, an exceptionally perfect system will be, by definition, incapable of improvement. Therefore, any suggested
improvement of the exceptional system must be held to be an
attack on the system. Any actual improvement that gets made
to the system—a law guaranteeing equal treatment under the
law on the basis of race, for example—must be framed as a mistake to be corrected, a betrayal of principal requiring redress,
a loss of greatness to be restored. And so, more and more of
our effort and energy and time and resources will be expended on defending the perfection of our system from the attack
of improvement. And so, the concept of improvement must be
held by us, blameless people all, to be an enemy; every cost of
improvement or even maintenance of the system that does not
benefit us directly must be framed as corruption and theft. And
so, if we blameless people have our way, our perfect system, unimprovable and unmaintainable, will never be improved, and
will never be maintained. Which means that our society will
fall into disrepair, a disrepair made inevitable by our blamelessness—which will leave us facing the impossible problem of the
increasing brokenness our own spiritual alignment against repair has made inevitable. We might be able to hide our accountability for brokenness—from ourselves anyway—but it can't be
denied forever that the brokenness exists. If we hold our broken
system to be blameless of brokenness, we will need somebody
else to pay the cost not only of the brokenness all around us, but
of the blame for it.

If we are blameless, we will need other people to hold that blame.

The problem of brokenness can't be systemic, because our

system is perfect. And we are obviously blameless, so obviously we cannot be at fault.

The cause of brokenness, therefore, must be the people who suffer from brokenness.

The solution, then, isn't to fix our system ourselves, because the system isn't the problem, nor are we. The solution is to fix the other people. And, because we are opposed to repair, we will fix them with the only tool left in our kit, which is punishment. We will need to punish them for causing the brokenness we see—not because we love punishment, but because they have earned punishment. We will punish them, but not to harm them—to redeem them. And then we'll expect to be thanked— because we are blameless, so our control over the lives of others isn't controlling or hateful. No. We are blameless people.

Blameless people cannot be hateful.

We are *loving.*

In this thought experiment, wherein you and I are blameless people, we would use our supremacy to organize our society in such a way that people are forced under threat of suffering to live the way we live, according to the strictures of our consciences (even if we ourselves don't actually live the way we claim). Because we are blameless, we'll claim to do this because we want them to live the best possible way—our way. To prove that our way is the best possible way to live, we'll offer as evidence the fact that we don't seem to suffer any of the costs of the brokenness of the things we refuse to repair. To prove that their way is worse, we'll offer as evidence the fact that they do seem to suffer so much brokenness. And we'll ignore the fact that it is this way because we have made it this way.

We'll claim that we will raise the children we force other people to have, even though everyone can see that we don't want those children, either, even though it's clearly observable that at the moment of birth, they will cease to become useful weapons that we can use against other people and will simply become to us another one of the *other people,* who we insist are to blame for brokenness they are born into and who we demand should shoulder all the blame and cost for it; even though it is clearly observable that we start to blame them for the crime of brokenness the moment they draw their first unprofitable breath.

And if they resist, they will suffer. We'll make sure of the suffering, and use their suffering as proof that they deserve to suffer, and use the fact that they deserve to suffer to justify making them suffer more. And if anyone tries to fix the brokenness that makes them suffer, we'll make sure the attempt fails, and use the attempt as proof that we are being attacked for our way of life, and use the failure as proof that repair will always fail. And I'd call that sabotage, done to avoid the cost of repair, including the cost of blame.

In time, we blameless people will expend all our energy, all our time, all our effort, all our money, fighting to defend our own blamelessness. In time, we'll repudiate even the systems we once claimed to love, as the idea of our perfected blamelessness becomes ever more and more abstracted and recursive. We'll ally with enemies and align ourselves with overthrow of systems we claim to revere. We'll speak in contradiction. We'll harm even ourselves, even (for example) refusing actual vaccines to actual diseases—not because we want diseases but because we have made ourselves instinctively suspicious of improvements. We'll pay any price to avoid paying costs. We'll believe any liar to avoid knowing truths. Our blamelessness will never improve, because improvement admits imperfection, and we insist on being treated as if we are perfect.

Our blameless supremacy will never awake, to know things already known.

Never apologize, which would admit blame.

It will refuse knowledge.

It will hate justice.

It will fall into disrepair.

It's unsustainable.

It will fail.

Systemic failure is the ultimate cost of brokenness—a bill we blameless people will eventually no longer be able to entirely avoid, once the systems we built to consume people have left no one but us to consume. Even if we want to avoid costs, then, we blameless people had better start to learn how we might align with repair.

So, let's think about how.

3. AWAKENING & IGNORANCE

Thank you for engaging in that thought experiment. You are now free to return to being what I'm sure you are, which is a person perfectly comfortable with paying any and all costs of repair, who never refuses blame for any advantage you might receive from systemic brokenness.

I admire you very much for that.

Me, I still struggle with it.

◆ ◆ ◆

We've been talking about a natural, generative, shared, progressive process for repair, and about the idea that each of the steps of this process are being sabotaged by people captured by a dominant popular supremacist human spirit that is opposed to repair, because it wishes to avoid paying any of repair's natural costs—including blame—by making everyone else pay the much higher costs of brokenness. Because they are aligned with supremacy, they are energized by our foundational lies, which insist that some people have earned life and others haven't, that some people matter and others don't, and that violence redeems the offense of failing to earn life. It's worth repeating that the process of repair is *progressive*—by which I mean there is a sequential forward motion to it, with each step leading naturally to the next, and with each step dependent upon the one before it.

Before repair comes repentance—a realignment toward repair.

Before repentance, confession—a proclamation of need.
Before confession, conviction—an expectation of improvement.
Before conviction, awareness—a realization of brokenness.
This is the re-aligning work of repair.
Let's talk about awareness.

◆ ◆ ◆

In 2016, the popular extremist right wing television propagandist Laura Ingraham stood at the podium of the Republican National Convention, electrifying the crowd for approximately 15 minutes. Her speech was about how it was time for people who had already been given disproportionate power to take power back. It was about re-establishing an expectation of respect to be bestowed upon people who had demonstrated very little respect for others. It was a screed against political bias in the media delivered by a major media figure giving a prime-time speech in favor of a political party's candidate. It was about some other things, also, but mostly it was about what speeches at conventions are always about, which is getting people excited about electing the party's candidate as president, and Ingraham, as a major popular figure of her extremist right wing propaganda network, Fox News, was and remains a major figure of power and influence in the extremist right wing political party on whose behalf Fox News very openly operates, namely the Republican Party.

That candidate, in case you'd forgotten, was Donald Trump, who was in the midst of running an openly authoritarian, openly white supremacist campaign—by which I mean that the things he was proposing were authoritarian things, and the ways he was proposing to achieve them were identical to methods recommended by openly white supremacist groups, and he was even using the same words as these groups, the exact same phrases and keywords and memes. This sort of thing proved very popular with the Republican Party's voters, and Donald Trump easily and overwhelmingly received its nomination for president.

Ingraham, who very much wanted this man to be president, finished her speech with the standard signoff of any political figure of modern times, which is "God bless you, and God bless the United States of America." Then she turned to her left, profile to the cameras, and raised her stiffened right arm at the shoulder, teaching us incontrovertibly that the Ingraham Angle is 45°.

It was an unmistakable gesture. It still is. You can go find it online. There's video.

It's certainly possible for somebody waving to a crowd to be caught on camera in a particular instant, the unnatural preservation of the moment creating an illusion of that gesture, but on film, as a gesture—stiff arm from the shoulder palm flat down—it's hard to miss. I guess what I'm saying is, people waving do occasionally achieve that position for a split-second, but they do not make that *gesture*. I don't know if I've ever seen anyone make that gesture by accident.

And, again, it's an *unmistakable* gesture, one we've all seen before, historically most frequently at extremist far-right political conventions in support of supremacist authoritarians.

I'll name the gesture. It was a Sieg Heil. It was a Nazi salute.

We've seen it since then, too. For example, it's the gesture open Nazis made in the days after Donald Trump's election, from the crowd at the Ronald Reagan building in Washington DC, not far from the site of Donald Trump's impending inauguration, where a white supremacist group called the National Policy Institute held their annual convention. Their after-dinner speaker, the white supremacist Richard Spencer, closed with "heil Trump," and though he said it with enough sauce that most media quoted it as "hail Trump," his audience understood him perfectly well, and made the old familiar Ingraham Angle. Like I said, it's an unmistakable gesture—especially hard to mistake in a room full of Nazis. Unless you think they, too, were all waving. Who knows? Maybe they were. It's impossible to really *know* motives.

In the years since, I've frequently mentioned the Ingraham incident, as I think it is emblematic of this moment in time—a gesture somehow simultaneously sly but blatant, which might have been a statement of purpose, or might have been a mean-spirited trolling from a mean-spirited professional troll, or might have been a signal to the open white supremacists (who, as we've well learned, comprise the foundation of the Republican Party's base) that their moment was at hand, or I suppose it might have been a simple mistake, an arm-oopsie—though I have to say that a political convention supporting an authoritarian white supremacist demagogue is a strange place for such a media-savvy and camera-ready person to make such a mistake, and Republicans do seem to keep making "mistakes" in which they seem to be associated with white supremacist leaders and signs and signals and slogans and policies and methods, over and over again. Anyway, the underlying motivation isn't what interests me, and isn't knowable anyway, unless Ingraham ever decides to disclose her motivation, which seems unlikely.

What interests me is the *fact* of the gesture, which exists, and people's response to the gesture, which is to deliberately not know that it exists. A lot of people *really* don't want to know that it was what it was, and is what it is, and they have plenty of help in not knowing it. A day after the incident, an article was written on the website Slate explaining that the gesture Ingraham made *wasn't* the gesture it *was*, because . . . well, because it *can't possibly be*, is what all the reasons offered essentially amount to. You can find the Slate piece without much effort; it's pretty much the only writing from a major media establishment you'll get if you search online for the incident, and if you bring up the incident these days, it's the piece that people who don't want to know about it will cite to you to prove that there is no reason to know about it.

These days, when I bring it up, it's less because I want to raise awareness about Ingraham, who has spent the ensuing years offering far more obvious proofs to her bona fides as an authoritarian supremacist. These days, when I bring it up, it's because I'm fascinated by people who don't want to know things that anyone can know, about a huge number of subjects. The Ingraham incident is so fascinating, because most people don't even want to dispute its meaning. They want to dispute that it even *happened*, even as we can watch it happen. Recently I mentioned it, and somebody told me an amazing thing: they said that they *didn't see any proof* that it was the gesture that it is. And I thought: how odd, to suggest that this observable and unmistakable gesture is something that requires *proof* to exist. How odd, to attempt to establish *oneself* as the person to whom a gesture must be proved, before the rest of us can agree we see it. And what exactly, I wondered, would constitute *proof* that the thing we can all watch on video exists, and was exactly what it very observably is?

To say there is no *proof* that Laura Ingraham made that gesture seems to me identical to saying there is no *proof* that anybody has ever made that gesture.

Proof? Proof... how? Proof of... *what?*

Of an observable thing? It's difficult to miss.

It's also difficult to miss the extreme rise in supremacist hate crimes and hate speech in the ensuing years, directed against all marginalized groups, and in particular the alarming rise among the political right of antisemitism in the United States and in the world. Difficult to miss the Nazis who 5 years ago occupied Charlottesville under the banner of the Confederacy and the name "unite the right," chanting "Jews will not replace us." Difficult to miss the Nazis since. Difficult to miss that some of them were on President Trump's staff, or running for office as Republicans. It's also difficult to miss that Laura Ingraham's propaganda network is, for example, currently, as I write this, engaged in vigorous promulgation of the white supremacist myth known as "white replacement theory," which is the racist myth that animated the Nazis who invaded Charlottesville in 2017, and the ones who invaded Belgium in 1940, the racist myth that home-grown domestic terrorists are using as a rationale for their growing list of massacres. It's difficult to miss that Ingraham's network hasn't stopped doing this even after the "replacement" myth inspired the perpetrator of the recent racist gun massacre in Buffalo. So I guess if people think I'm terribly mistaken about a gesture in 2016 indicating a rise in empowered white supremacist fascism, we could just talk about those sorts of things instead—though I've noticed that the same people who seem to require some sort of ill-defined "proof" of an observable gesture also don't want to talk about these sorts of things either.

It's probably a coincidence. Intentions are *so* unknowable.

A Texas school board just removed all copies of *The Diary of Anne Frank* from their shelves, by the way. Another one in Tennessee just disappeared all their copies of the Pulitzer Prize-winning graphic novel and Holocaust memoir *Maus*. And the problem with these books, and books like them, I'm given to understand, is "wokeness."

Wokeness. A state of being awake.

In original coinage by Black activists for social justice and liberation, "woke," to the best of my understanding, meant a growing awareness of the intrinsic and structural nature of racism. In current coinage, it is used by mostly white mostly conservative people as a slur to mean a great many negative things, but mostly it means "space has been made here for the existence and perspective of people who we think should be attacked and/or ignored."

So the conservative movement in America has met the enemy, and it is awareness.

Simply knowing a thing is broken is the first step of repair.

Anything known was at one point unknown. The step of awareness is a progressive motion, then, from not knowing something to knowing it.

If you were from my Evangelical Christian background, you might think of this step in the work of redemption—that is, repair of our own spirits—as "awakening."

If we claim to know something, it suggests there was a time when we did not know.

We were unaware—asleep to reality, you might say.

Then we became aware. The scales fell from our eyes, so to speak. We woke.

◆ ◆ ◆

Let's see what's up this week in 2022.

Trump transcriptionist Maggie Haberman published an article in *The New York Times* listing reasons that Donald Trump might have stolen nuclear secrets, which is something he did. It doesn't mention the most likely and damning possibility: that he did it to sell them for profit or favors. This is the most likely possibility because profit and favors for himself is the only clear motive Donald Trump has ever had for doing anything. Maybe Haberman forgot to consider the most obvious and damning possibility. Maybe we'll find, even if we discover he did sell them, there will be those who insist we aren't able to "prove" that he sold them, because it will be impossible to discern whether he *knew* he was selling them, or intended to sell them, that maybe he took the secrets and received money for them by accident.

On Tucker Carlson's show, the producers put up a doctored image of Judge Bruce Reinhart, who is facing daily death threats from Trump supporters for granting the FBI warrant that uncovered the theft of those nuclear secrets. The image made it look to any unskeptical eye (and Fox News is nothing if not adept at attracting unskeptical eyes) as if Reinhart was on a private jet with known pedophiliac sex trafficker Ghislaine Maxwell, who is a Trump associate but is not, as far as I can tell, an associate of Judge Reinhart. Later, Brian Kilmeade, who had been the guest host of the episode where the image was displayed, tweeted that *of course* it was a joke—a distinction not made on Carlson's alleged news show. Maybe it was an honest mistake. Intention is *so* unknowable. You could never *prove* that it was intended to target the judge for stochastic terror, if you were the sort of person who had decided such things needed to be proved to you before anyone could observe them.

What else is happening in 2022?

Ah! Republican Senator Chuck Grassley told a crowd that he's for a $35 cap on insulin, which he and nearly every other Republican voted against earlier this month. Maybe he simply forgot he did that. I see no proof he didn't forget that. Can *you* prove he didn't forget?

Republican Senate candidate (and known associate of white supremacists) Blake Masters blasted Democrats for dropping economic relief policies from their bill, which Democrats dropped in part because Masters' party is opposed to them—as is Masters. He actually opposes the thing he's blasting Democrats for not supporting. Maybe he simply forgot he doesn't support economic relief policies. Can you *prove* he didn't forget?

In the House, Rep. Marjorie Taylor Greene is registering her opposition to wind and solar energy, because, as she told her audience, she wants to be able to use power when the sun goes down and the wind is not blowing. This isn't how wind and solar energy works, at all, as we all know, but her crowd does not seem to know this. Greene herself, though not the sharpest crayon in the box, almost certainly knows this too, though I can't *prove* this to whoever it is one needs to prove these matters to, before one can observe that Greene is malicious scum reaping profits by dancing on the Earth's grave before it has even died.

Florida Governor Ron DeSantis, a presidential hopeful who has been pushing fascist anti-democracy and bigoted hatred in his home state to establish his bona fides as a prospective leader of his fascist party, just gave a speech against awakening as a general concept. Here's a bit of it:

> We must fight the woke in our schools. We must fight the woke in our businesses. We must fight the woke in government agencies. We can never, ever surrender to woke ideology. . . . The state of Florida is where woke goes to die.

Imagine opposing, with faux Churchillian cadence, basic awareness as a concept. Imagine hostility to the act of knowing. But we were talking about repair, and sabotage of repair. Let's talk about ignorance.

◆ ◆ ◆

The *opposite* of awakening to awareness is unawareness: remaining in a state of not knowing.

The *opposition* to awakening is **ignorance**: a state of ignoring knowledge.

Ignorance is the most foundational sabotage. Prevent awakening, and the sequence of redemptive work of repair never begins. Here we find truths deliberately ignored, confusion deliberately sown, lies deliberately told.

Lies deliberately told are perhaps easiest to detect; they're so brazen—weaponized ignorances, extreme and obvious propagandas, even bald hate speech; things believed by people who choose to believe obvious lies—because the believer realizes that seeing a person believe an obvious lie is more menacing than seeing a person believing a less obvious one; because the believer realizes that one of the best ways to demonstrate supremacy is to force another person to live according to a lie—and the more ludicrous the lie, the greater the dominance that is demonstrated.

There's also manufactured confusion—the disinformation technique famously described by Trump advisor and far-right propagandist Steve Bannon as "flooding the zone with shit." The more lies there are in circulation, the more people will be confused as to what is true and what is not—especially as the lies become normalized through platforming and repetition—and the more confusion, the more people will start to believe that no knowable truth exists, and that everybody is lying in equal degrees, and to equally malicious ends—a false equivalence which serves sabotage of awareness just as well as belief in lies does.

I think we know about these obvious and blatant ignorances. It strikes me, though, that the hardest ignorances to detect are the truths deliberately ignored—the refusal to observe observable things, in order to frame truth as just another thing that's up for debate, and then to ensure that this debate over truth and falsehood is one that will never resolve, all done while casting oneself as a party interested in truth, because after all, *we're just asking questions here*. It seems to me we're in a culture that is optimized toward this sort of ignorance about awarenesses we'd rather avoid. Ignorance is a sabotage that keeps us comfortable in a supremacy we refuse to acknowledge; keeps us benefitting from brokenness while considering ourselves blameless of the brokenness we cause; makes sure that the cost of repair is made as high as possible, in order to dissuade people away from the natural costs of sustainable repair and to push them toward the much higher costs of unsustainable brokenness.

Here's the awareness I think we're trying to avoid: the knowledge that our core assumptions are lies—foundational lies.

We've believed that we aren't related to one another.

That some people matter and others do not.

That life must be earned by profit or wealth.

That those who don't earn life have earned hard use and punishment and death.

And that violence redeems.

These lies are *foundational lies*, because they go so deep as to be assumed, and once you awaken to them, you see them at work everywhere, not least of all within your own mind.

Your? My. My mind.

I keep discovering I need to awaken, I suspect because repair is not only a process, but a cycle.

I find there are many ways to awaken.

I can tell you how I awaken, when I manage to. I awaken whenever something happens to shock me out of my assumptions, to make me aware of the ways I still align with these foundational lies. I awaken when I stop listening to voices that flatter me or encourage my comfort and complacency, when I instead begin to listen to others who have been aware about these lies and their effects far longer than me, who suffer the effects of them far more directly than me, and can speak with authority of their direct experience of suffering them. I've been awakening more and more often these days, but that also suggests there are many more unawarenesses within me from which to awaken.

But the important thing is to awaken.

As long as we remain unaware of these lies, repair will stay impossible.

As soon as we awakened to them, we've started the process of repair.

If you don't want the natural process of repair to carry forward, you'll need to sabotage that sequence with an oppositional process—an unnatural chain of actions that makes brokenness inevitable. If you want to observe the sabotage of repair, I recommend you look at the ways awareness is attacked, and the places where our foundational lies are accepted uncritically.

And if you are aligned against paying natural costs, the first thing to sabotage is awareness.

You sabotage awareness with ignorance.

◆ ◆ ◆

Above all, a blameless society sabotages awareness in order to claim *knowledge* as the exclusive property of blameless supremacists—a framework whereby a knowable thing cannot be deemed known by anyone unless supremacists first agree to know it; a framework that insists that observable things cannot be observed unless supremacists first agree to observe them; a framework that insists that a lie cannot be deemed a lie unless the liar admits they intended to lie, and that stated rationales for abusive actions must be accepted as valid and true, no matter how long the predictable results of that continued action contradict those stated intentions; a framework that insists that a debate can never end unless a supremacist agrees to end it. It's a framework under which people use the very fact that they refuse to be convinced by truth as proof that the truth isn't convincing, then use the idea that it hasn't been convincing to suggest that it must therefore not be true. It's a framework that empowers fast-talking professional contrarians expert in bad faith discourse, who argue from a position of deliberate ignorance, who demand their opponents engage in the ceaseless futile work of convincing them of truths they've already announced they've decided not to believe.

This is ignorance: the first step in the sabotaging work of blameless supremacy.

It's all done to avoid the natural cost of repair, maintenance and improvement.

And I think that's sabotage.

Why sabotage our awareness? To make ignorance popular, and then to borrow against that popularity to lend ignorance credibility. To make awareness optional, and then make it an *unpopular* option; a difficult burden, one highly undesirable compared to the relative ease of ignorance. To force people to engage in a daily fight to defend their awareness, in order to frame the people engaged in that fight as combative, as a pretext for further suppression of awareness. To unnaturally raise the cost of awareness, and offer ignorance at a discount.

I think it's worth stressing that the way sabotage raises the costs of awareness is *unnatural*. Few people actually *want* to be ignorant, and even fewer actually think of themselves as ignorant. In the same way, most of us want to see problems solved, and most of us want to see what is broken repaired. But the cost of staying aware through a manufactured miasma of daily bullshit drains us, and the imposition of persuading people who have already demonstrated they are unpersuadable daunts us; it's simply easier to not know, to stay quiet, to not take sides, so as to not endlessly reestablish some baseline truth with people who have already decided to occupy an alternate reality, "free thinkers" who have developed memorized catchphrases that they deploy as a ward against any proof of reality you might offer.

Sabotage manufacturers ignorance to make awareness costly, so that people stay away from awareness and resent those who enter into it, until at last they begin to see ignorance as a virtue and a desirable state, and craft byzantine narratives to convince themselves their selected ignorance actually represents a deeper knowledge of sweaty-minded conspiracies to which they have gained the keys. Sabotage of awakening makes ignorance *inevitable*; it's an inevitability that makes the cost of awareness high enough that we will choose ignorance instead. And, when we choose ignorance over awareness, we will continue to live in our foundational lies. But that also means that when we choose to pay the cost of awakening—especially where the cost has been made unnaturally high—we will be aligning ourselves against those lies, and demonstrating our own slow and stammering awakening to others.

And that will reveal our real intentions.

Remember: awakening isn't for people who are awake. It's for those who sleep.

Awakening begins the journey for those who haven't realized a journey is needed.

Here is our work of awakening to awareness: to know the things that are observably true about the unnatural abuses and corruptions within the systems where we exist.

That's it. Know the true things. Especially the uncomfortable ones.

This is my work of awareness. This. You're reading it.

What's your work of awareness? I don't know—you're *you*. You might be far more aware than me, and for you everything I've written (if you're still reading), may strike you as obvious and basic stuff, riddled with inaccuracies, filled with bad framing. Or you might be less aware. Or you might still desire ignorance. Or, based on situational differences between us, it may be all three at once. What I know is that the work of repair starts with awareness, and always carries you further into awareness—a lifetime journey. So let us learn, with a mind open not for things that comfort us, but for things which discomfort us.

Awareness observes.

◆ ◆ ◆

What do we do now? The first thing to do is to awaken to awareness.

Why do we need awakening? The same reason we need to be aware our streets are broken—because repair is a process. Because awakening leads us to discover what is broken, and to a realization: It's up to us to fix it.

We need awakening, because awakening leads to conviction.

4. CONVICTION & COMPLACENCY

Before redemption comes reparation.

Before reparation, repentance.

Before repentance, confession.

Before confession, conviction.

This is the re-aligning work of repair, which might be thought of as the work of redemption.

Let's talk about conviction.

◆ ◆ ◆

A question: Have you ever experienced a sudden and unexpected injury? If not, congratulations on your amazing run of luck... but I presume you have. It's a fairly common human experience. It's part of having a body.

Next question: did you *choose* to make yourself aware of your injury, or did awareness come naturally? Were you given a choice to *not* know you were injured? This may seem like a silly question, in large part because it is a silly question. I know you didn't *choose* to know. Unless you happen to be somebody whose nerves don't work properly, you can't ignore the demand of your body's report. The injury was not an opinion; it was an experience. You had it.

Another question: did other people become aware of the injury? I'd assume so, if the injury was bad enough that you found it worth commenting upon in the moment, or if it were severe enough to incapacitate you in some way, or if you exclaimed in shock, or screamed in pain. I imagine you've at some point had the experience of other people gathered around you, asking questions like this:

Are you OK? How bad is it? What's wrong?

How did it happen? Where does it hurt? How can I help?

These are the questions people generally ask, when somebody is injured. By asking, they gain a deeper and more specific knowledge about your injury, and how best to assist you, and what sorts of things they should do to make you more comfortable, and what sorts of things they should avoid doing so they don't make your injury worse. And, if the injury was bad enough, the assistance might eventually have involved somebody with medical training and medical equipment—an EMT, doctor, nurse, or medic—who asked questions with more clinical wording, but with similar purpose: to gain a deeper and more perfect understanding of your experience of injury. They ask these questions of the injured person, if the injured person is able to answer; they don't ask other people. This is for a very good reason. That reason is this: Nobody understands the experience of the injury like the injured person, because the injured person is the one who is having the experience.

Yet another question: when you were injured, did you complain *politely*? I mean, did you avoid crying or screaming or groaning or expressing emotion or signs of pain? Some people do, I suppose. Maybe you're one of these stoics. I'm not—but we were talking about you. Did you complain *politely*? Were you *civil* in that moment? Did you consider the feelings of the people who *weren't* injured, and how they might feel about the *tone* of your demands?

Maybe this line of questioning doesn't make any sense to you.

It certainly doesn't make sense to me, when I see it happening.

Say you're playing soccer and an opposing player comes out of nowhere and delivers a flying knee to your thigh, landing with the full force of their weight, snapping your femur. Suppose the game doesn't stop. Suppose the people around you don't ask the sorts of questions people usually ask. Suppose when they come running in answer to your cries of pain, instead of asking you questions to better understand your experience and how they might help, they said things like this:

Prove that your leg hurts.

If your leg was really broken, the referee would have stopped the game.

I don't want you to become dependent on stretchers. You don't see us on stretchers, do you?

Why would we penalize the player you claim did this to you? She's having a great game. Why would you threaten her potential? I'm sympathetic to your pain but where does it all end?

We wouldn't want to stop a game everyone's enjoying just because you're struggling.

Your leg isn't my fault. I take care of my own legs. My legs are fine.

It's not my fault. I'm not on the team that did this. I'm on your team.

It's not my fault. I was way over on the other side of the field when it happened.

Why are some people always screaming about legs? I don't even think about legs.

Why did you decide to break your leg?

Or what if they didn't ask questions at all? What if they didn't even come over to see what was wrong? What if they acted as if you weren't even there? What if they made you drag yourself to a phone to call the emergency vehicles? What if the emergency vehicles were staffed by people who wanted to make sure you could pay before helping? What if the vehicles were slow in coming? What if they didn't do as good a job of healing your leg as they're able to? What if their neglect left you with a permanent disability? And what if, after this experience, people said things like this to you:

Nobody's going to ever want to deal with you if you keep bringing up your injury.

I don't think we should go on and on about injuries. All legs should get equal care.

Why are you always limping at me? I wasn't even there that day.

At some point I think you'd come to the conclusion that the people around you didn't actually care about you or your injury.

Perhaps you'd begin to understand the world to be populated by people incurious of injury, hostile to the conviction brought on by that awareness. Perhaps you'd start to learn to simply not trust uninjured people, after experiencing their refusal to care, understanding yourself to live within a culture of neglect.

Now: Imagine if uninjured people started to demand certain assurances from you before they agreed to help you. Say they demanded that you certify them as being blameless of your injury before they'd even consider helping you. Imagine if uninjured people started talking about the impact of your injury entirely in terms of what it cost them to accommodate it—even while using that expense as a justification to refuse to accommodate it. Imagine if you started to understand that your injury, rather than being a reason for you to be accommodated, actually was being presented to you as a reason you needed to accommodate everyone else.

At some point, you'd realize that the culture of neglect you lived in was deliberate and systemic, because it insisted on engaging your injury only on its own terms, and never on yours. You'd understand that the ignorance that fed this neglect was cultivated and defended and maintained. At some point, you'd likely start to mistrust the system, and you'd perhaps start to demand the system be something better than it is. In other words, you'd try to convict a system that refused to be convicted of a responsibility it refused to acknowledge.

Here's my point: It seems to me that when someone is hurt or in trouble, there is a natural human instinct to help. It seems to me that if something is broken, there is a natural human instinct to fix it. If something is wrong, there is a natural human instinct to set it right. People generally tend to give a shit, is my observation. I think of that natural motion—the way awareness of brokenness leads people into a desire to see it fixed—as **conviction**.

What I've been describing here is the disruption of a natural sequence wherein reality of injury leads to awareness of injury leads to conviction to make repairs. An injured person's report of their injury alerts people to it, which convicts them of their natural duty to help, and makes them curious about the person's experience, which hopefully leads to direct assistance. The tone of the injured party in conveying this information really shouldn't be a factor influencing this sense of conviction, beyond perhaps providing uninjured people with some clues as to the extremity of the injury.

Injury is a reality; an experience, not a choice. There is awareness of the injury, and there is the experience of injury. Two different things. If you are interested in healing, you have to listen to an injured person, and accept their narrative as authoritative to the experience of injury, which they have had and you have not. And if you don't want to listen, and you'd rather trust the authority of your own uninjured belief about the nature of injury, then it has to be assumed that you have some intention other than healing.

I ask myself: Who am I listening to about injury? And how am I listening to them? Who am I *not* listening to? And what reasons am I giving myself to not listen?

I ask, because I find it vitally important, if I want to align myself with repair, to hold to the conviction to repair, because holding to conviction continues the progressive work of reparation. Indeed, I keep discovering I need to re-enter conviction, because in a society of systemic injury, repair is not only a process but a cycle, and so I keep awakening to new awareness, leading to new conviction.

Conviction isn't for the person who already has entered conviction; it doesn't exist for their awareness. A person who has entered conviction already knows the truth, that repair is a process that requires much more than simply wanting things to change.

Conviction is for those who observe it in others.

Conviction pulls people along who are a step behind.
Conviction brings awareness to those who are still unaware.

◆ ◆ ◆

It's 2022 now as I write this. Let's see what's happening in 2022.

In recent days, fascist Republican state governors Ron DeSantis and Greg Abbott have been engaged in a bit of light human trafficking, for funsies. It's like this: Some of the most vulnerable people in our country are asylum seekers and immigrants fleeing political and economic upheavals, many of which *we*—by which I mean our nation and our economic and political structures—helped cause. Our country's policies toward these people once they arrive here are broken and cruel and unjust, leaning deeply into our blameless society's supremacist foundational lies, which insist such people simply do not matter. DeSantis and Abbott have a big problem with these cruel and broken policies—to wit: they aren't nearly cruel or broken *enough*—and they have seen disturbing signs that these policies might get marginally less cruel and broken and unjust, so they've used their power to make sure that in their states, our country's responses to these vulnerable people are made as harsh and unjust and broken as possible.

As it happens, there are people here in this country who actually believe our policies should be more open, welcoming, and accommodating; who even believe we share some collective responsibility for living in a country whose policies have created instability and collapse elsewhere; who want to make our existing policies less harsh, more just, less broken; and who are, as a result, utterly opposed to the direction taken by people like Ron DeSantis and Greg Abbott, and say so, and some even do something about it. These governors/fascists are *enraged* about the existence of people opposing them; enraged about this persistent belief in, and expectation for, repair of what is broken;

and so they have decided to demonstrate their rage by busing and flying refugees to various places where their opponents' political parties are in power, in what they clearly frame as a punitive act against those places—a stunt that not only potentially breaks human trafficking laws, and aligns these governors with similar tactics of supremacist Jim Crow officials from our nation's recent past, but reveals their assumption that they do not see refugees as people, but as punishment. Moreover, they're doing so in a maximally cruel way: deliberately offering these immigrants lies and misinformation, deliberately offering no advance notice of what they intend to the authorities and organizations at the chosen destinations, deliberately transporting human beings under false pretenses to unknown locations— in the most recent example, to Martha's Vineyard, which is a known bastion of the sort of wealthy liberals that fascists like Ron DeSantis insist are the traitorous socialist globalists who cause immigrants to come to America in order to destroy America, a nation largely populated by immigrants. And this belief of DeSantis' is a vile lie sometimes referred to as the "replacement theory," and it is a belief shared by Nazis, like the Nazis who invaded and captured Charlottesville in August 2017 under the banner "unite the right."

The governors' idea appears to have been to create as much chaos as possible, in order to use the chaos they created to demonstrate that refugees and immigrants cause chaos. The idea appears to have been to make the situation as disruptive and costly and systemically unworkable as possible, in order to demonstrate that migrants are not people but rather a disruption and a cost, and that systems built to support and aid them are always costly failures. The idea appears to have been to manufacture a problem, and then to take their opponents' reaction to the problem they themselves manufactured as evidence that everybody *actually* agrees with their grotesque and inhumane belief that immigrants are not people, but problems. And they are supported by a consent-manufacturing media apparatus that will report on the matter and deliver their desired framing, even if the people of Martha's Vineyard actually mostly responded to the unexpected influx of immigrants with kindness and charity.

DeSantis and Abbott are doing all this to demonstrate that people who despise immigrants and other kinds of refugees should be allowed to go on not caring about their fellow human beings without the consequence of being understood to be inhumane—not because it is good to be indifferent to human suffering, but because they have furnished themselves with adequate proof that people who claim to care are just pretending, that all other people are secretly just as indifferent about human suffering as they are. DeSantis and Abbott and their supporters don't want to be good. They just want to reassure themselves that everyone else is similarly bad. And they rejoice at any slight hint that this might be true, even if those hints come from scenarios of their own making.

And, as mentioned, these actions may well qualify as human trafficking, which is a crime against humanity. And in DeSantis' case, it was almost certainly a crime of misappropriation, since the migrants he flew over weren't even from his own state. And probably it was criminal obstruction of the government as well. So, once again, we have multiple open crimes committed by powerful sitting Republican office holders, for the sake of bigotry and cruelty and greed and political gain.

I am told there's an Attorney General in Washington DC for just these sorts of things.

Oh well, I guess.

What else is happening in 2022?

Oh! Joe Biden recently moved to forgive college debt, and conservative America lost its mind, insisting that this would crash the economy or make people stop working or explode every bald eagle in Wyoming and immolate every flag in Montana or I don't know what all else, but it certainly caused conservative America a lot more heartburn than trillions given to already-wealthy billionaires so they might piss it away on luxury items like apocalypse survival bunkers or yachts or space travel or judges or Senators. Anyway, one rationale that conservative America settled upon for their opposition to this massive relief from decades of predatory debt was that it wasn't fair to people who had already suffered from predatory debt over the decades—which, as many people have pointed out, is simply a sociopathic and selfish rationale against improvement as a general concept, as if curing cancer would be unfair to those who had already died of cancer. Do their objections mean they want to expand the relief to also include the people they claim to be concerned about—that is, to offer restitution to people who already paid their college debt?

Hey hahaha let's change the subject!

Let's see what else is happening in 2022.

This summer, during testimony before the Joint Legislative Budget Committee, Arizona Department of Corrections Director David Shinn said Arizona communities would "collapse" without cheap prison labor. So I guess our mass incarceration problem isn't a problem after all. I guess the economy depends on it. Being a felon is practically patriotic.

And hundreds of people will die today in this country from Covid, which is over. Yesterday it was over, and hundreds died from it. Tomorrow hundreds will die from it, and it will still be over. Millions suffer the effects of long Covid, which is also over, and our workforce is facing shortages across a wide range of essential industries and service sectors—a situation that is totally unrelated to millions of deaths and millions of disabilities, because, again, Covid is over. We're done with it. It is *over*. If it kills or disables you, it's important to remember that ignoring your death or disability is also an important part of it being over.

I could go on. I could go on maybe forever.

But we were talking about repair, and sabotage of repair.

♦ ♦ ♦

The *opposite* of conviction is uncertainty—an inability to decide on a proper course—and saboteurs of repair will foster uncertainty by sabotaging our awareness with ignorance.

The *opposition* to conviction is **complacency**—an active unwillingness to take a known course.

We've been talking about repair as a progressive process with sequential steps, which ends with doing the actual work of repair and paying its costs, but begins with awareness ("the thing is broken") and proceeds to conviction ("the broken thing should be fixed, and we share responsibility for fixing it"). And we've been talking about a blameless society, opposed to all natural costs of repair, including the cost of blame—that is, the cost of being exposed as people aligned toward maintaining brokenness, and making others pay the much higher costs.

If you are aligned against paying natural costs, the first thing to sabotage is awakening to awareness of what is broken, and the next thing to sabotage is the conviction that what is broken should be repaired, and that we all share a responsibility for making it so. If you don't want to see the natural process of repair begin, you'll need to sabotage the natural sequence of repair with an oppositional process—an unnatural chain of actions that makes brokenness inevitable.

You sabotage conviction with complacency.

Here's a thing I do sometimes. See if this sounds familiar. Sometimes, when I see something that isn't as it should be, I talk about how it *should* be different than the way it is. Sometimes, when I see somebody being treated by society as if they don't matter, I talk about how they *shouldn't* be treated that way. Sometimes, when I see somebody announcing their intention to do something harmful and cruel, I talk about how we *ought* not to permit that.

Should. Shouldn't. Ought.

Maybe you're like this, too. I doubt I'm unique.

There seems to be an expectation hard-wired into us—that old natural human instinct—that it would be better if broken things were fixed, if hard things were made better, if cruel things were made kinder. So we talk about what *should* be, imagining a better state of reality, with some expectation that together we might create that better state of being—in fact, it's a belief that changing it is a shared responsibility, and is, in many ways, the reason for society to exist: to make the work and pain and striving and harm and struggle and sickness and cruelty of the natural world less, not more.

After awakening to something broken or wrong, it's natural to move toward imagining something different and better, and then, having imagined something better than what is, to expect that improvement to happen. In fact, it seems to me that nothing ever changed without conviction that *the way it is* should change. So that's what I try to do, and probably so do you. And, because I try to start with the premise that the world is the neighborhood, and that everybody matters as much as I do, I enter into a conviction that things should improve, not just for myself, but for everybody, and that if anybody is treated in an unjust or abusive way, it's something that *ought* to be changed.

You probably try to do this, too.

What's truly interesting is the response I see, when conviction of any kind is sent out into the world. I don't know if you've noticed it, but I bet you have: Whenever conviction enters the world, there rises up an opposition that immediately moves to eliminate it, negate it, neutralize it, and destroy it. What rises is a different human urge, which appears just as instinctive as conviction: the urge to *not* give a shit. And I'd call that urge complacency.

If you're like me, you'll have noticed that complacency takes many forms.

When something cruel or atrocious is proposed, and I say

that shouldn't be, I find I'm quickly assured that the people who say they intend to enact cruelty or defend brokenness don't *really* intend to do the cruel broken things they are clearly trying to do, or that the atrocious things that have been proposed can't ever possibly *really* happen. Or else I'm told that other atrocious things, which are already happening to others, will work themselves out somehow, and anyway they will certainly never happen to *us.* I'm told this by people who share my awareness that things are broken and cruel and hard, but they're *optimistic* that everything will work out, without anyone having to do any work.

These are people who say "I don't think that will ever happen" about things that are already happening to other people—because when they say "that won't happen," what they clearly mean is, "I don't think that will ever happen to *me.*" Optimism, I've found, is a popular way to not give a shit, by deciding that our broken human systems are self-repairing, self-healing, and self-correcting. It's a way to deal with awareness without entering conviction.

I've been optimistic before. Maybe you have, too.

Sometimes, when I look at something that has been broken, and talk about how things *should* be, I'm asked what my plan is, in such a way that it's clear the interlocutor doesn't think *any* plan will work; or I'm told that my aspiration is very cute, but it will never happen because the system is impossibly broken and can never be fixed no matter what happens; or I'm told that it doesn't matter because nothing matters and everything has gone far too far, and we're doomed. These are people aware that things are broken and cruel and hard, but they're *cynical* about solutions; they've constructed their identity around not being able to be hurt by atrocity, by ensuring they'll never be surprised by it. Cynicism is another way of not giving a shit, by deciding that our human systems are so broken that they can't possibly ever be fixed, to such an extent that even the desire for repair is naïve and foolish.

And I've also been cynical before. Maybe you have, too.

Sometimes when I talk about what *should* and *shouldn't* be,

I'm given reasons why the cruel thing that's happening isn't really happening, or why the cruel thing that's happening isn't actually cruel, or why the cruelty is necessary to achieve or preserve some other good thing. Sometimes I'm told that, while brokenness is regrettable, it's inevitable, that fixing the broken thing would be impractical, even unwise; might devastate some sector of the economy, or make us all less safe or free, or compromise us in some way that might be uncomfortable or inconvenient or unpopular. Or I'm told we just don't have the votes, so even suggesting the measure is foolish and impractical. These people are aware that things are broken and atrocious and cruel, but their commitment to *institutionalism* convinces them that the institution is the primary thing to defend, rather than the principles the institutions purport to uphold. They perceive the ways brokenness itself has been incorporated into the system, and decide that the brokenness not only *is* the system but *ought to be*; that the natural disruptions and costs that would attend repairing our institutions are far more threatening to those institutions than the slow inevitable collapse of refusing to repair them. And institutionalism is another way of not giving a shit, by seeing brokenness as so fundamental to society that repair itself is perceived as impractical, unwise, frightful, and ruinous.

Have I ever been an institutionalist? Yes, I'm afraid I have.

Sometimes when I talk about what *ought* to be fixed, I'm even told that people suffering cruelty and brokenness *deserve* cruelty and brokenness. I'm told why they don't matter, and why their suffering isn't tragic—and more than that, why their suffering is righteous and good and necessary, even desirable, in order to better shape their behavior. Or I'm told that because *these* people have already suffered from the cruelty, it's not fair that *others* should now be spared. Or some person will explain they are indifferent to suffering and brokenness and injustice because they believe that people who claim to care about such things are only pretending—as if their perception of others' indifference licenses their own. It's an almost incalculable *indifference* toward injustice and suffering, but it, too, is a reason to not give a shit.

Have you ever been indifferent? I hope I haven't.

I fear the truth of the matter isn't very flattering.

Sometimes when I say *should* and *shouldn't* and *ought*, I'm offered pure misdirection: some decoy or another, some deflection or false dichotomy. Have you ever heard this one? When the topic is providing for some basic human need, I'm often told that *if you give a man a fish, he'll eat for a day, but if you teach him how to fish, he'll eat forever.*

It's a metaphor. The idea is that it's more effective in the long run to provide a person with the sustainable means of production than it is to simply gift them the temporary output of production to meet an immediate need.

Which is true.

I can't help but notice, though, how often it is that the person who deploys this aphorism doesn't *actually* support providing people with sustainable means of production, and doesn't even seem aware that's what they're suggesting. They don't want to break up the commercial monopolies overfishing the waters, or subsidize easily affordable fishing schools, or offer no-interest loans on boats, gear, and tackle backed with government collateral. They just mean they don't want feed the hungry guy. The *actual* reason for deploying the aphorism seems to be to neutralize our conviction to feed hungry people. In fact, if faced with a conviction that we ought to create more sustainable economic models—to teach a man to fish, in other words—many of us would just as willingly point to immediate material needs as a reason not to do so. This, not because we wish to see immediate material needs fulfilled, but merely because, as sabotage-minded people, we don't want to see *any* cost that we might have to pay. So people will argue against universal medical care because they claim spending on universal care for everyone while veterans still go without care would be horribly disrespectful to the sacrifice of our brave fighting men and women, and then those same people will vote against increasing medical care for veterans because there isn't enough money.

The underlying philosophy doesn't seem to be "give a man a fish" *or* "teach a man to fish."

The underlying philosophy appears to be "these are *my* fish."

Sometimes when I look at brokenness and say "that should be fixed" I notice people using the very fact that the brokenness is structural and systemic as the reason not to fix it, a sort of manufactured *helplessness*. The idea is to take the problem and cast it as endemic—simply an inevitable part of the way things are. When a problem can't be solved, after all, you don't have to solve it—which means you don't have to pay any costs of repair—so "endemic" is exactly the way that blameless supremacy wants to frame every problem.

I could use gun massacres as an example. In fact, I think I will.

Notice that Republicans don't *just* enact policies to make gun massacres inevitable—crucially, they start with the premise that gun massacres *are* inevitable, and build their policy out from there, and then when gun massacres occur, the only thing to do is to mourn, and anyone pointing to guns as the clear and obvious cause must be cast as an unseemly monster making political hay out of tragedy, by demanding solutions that would make such tragedies less likely. And notice: Massacres themselves, which reinforce the exact notion of a dangerous and scary world that we know makes people want to purchase massacre weapons, are absolutely crucial to establishing and maintaining the illusion of this worldview, and so massacres must exist—even though we know they can be prevented, even though we have ample proof of this, even though other people in other countries don't live this way.

A massacre *has* to be an unsolvable problem, precisely because it is solvable. The act of even suggesting a solution *must* be cast as unseemly, precisely because solutions already exist, because conviction—the notion that solutions are possible and we share a responsibility to seek them out—is a part of the process of repair, and repair leads to natural cost, and a blameless society is opposed to any cost it might have to pay.

So we need more guns, which did not stop anything, to stop bad people with guns, who nobody can stop, except for good armed men, who did not stop them. We have guns, and we always shoot people who need shooting, unlike bad people, who shoot the wrong people, and we know they were the wrong people to shoot, because they were not shot by us. The guns are needed to enact good violence, and bad violence reinforces that need—and the worse the bad violence, the more it reinforces the need, the more "unsolvable" the problem becomes, and thus the more blameless those who refuse to seek solutions become, and the more unseemly those who try to seek solutions are made to seem.

We're talking about guns and massacres.

We could be talking about anything, really—anything at all.

If I am somebody who doesn't want to enter conviction, I'm going to need to overcome the natural instinct to give a shit, by finding a reason to not give a shit, and, because not giving a shit about others can cause reputational damage, by then providing to others my reasons for not giving a shit, and, because the sight of other people giving a shit will expose the ways I have decided not to give a shit, by also coming up with reasons to believe that those who still act as if they do give a shit don't actually give a shit either. What I've noticed about people who don't want to give a shit is that they don't put much priority on whether the reason they give makes sense, or is logically consistent with any previous reasons they've provided, or whether their reason demonstrates any sort of basic human empathy, or any moral or ethical or even basic understanding of the problem.

The main priority appears to be not giving a shit.

Any reason will do.

I think the reason there are so many different types of complacency—indifference, institutionalism, cynicism, optimism, false dichotomy, deflection, disassociation, learned and manufactured helplessness—is because complacency, by definition and as an aspirational goal, doesn't give a shit. Any path will do for complacency, as long as it arrives at not giving a shit, and once it doesn't give a shit, it doesn't give a shit why it doesn't give a shit, and if it needs to change the reason it doesn't give a shit from one reason to a completely oppositional and contradictory reason, it'll do so without hesitating, because when it comes to reasons to not give a shit, complacency doesn't give a shit which reason it uses.

It's all in service of a worldview that tries to extract the maximum value from our natural human system without paying anything back; that treats the problems this corruption causes as inevitable, unsolvable, and requiring violent punishment to manage. And it's all to avoid paying the cost of solutions. If you want to observe the sabotage of repair, I recommend you look at the ways conviction is attacked, the places where we are encouraged into the great apathies of optimism and cynicism and institutionalism and indifference, and in the ways we're offered false dichotomies—these logistical games of three-card monte, where unless we look closely at the ever-moving hands, we never notice that the lie is the notion that we have to choose, never notice that it is entirely possible to both teach a man to fish *and* give a man a fish, so we never do anything—which was always the point of the game.

◆ ◆ ◆

Above all, blameless supremacy sabotages conviction in order to claim the right to define **problems** and **solutions** as its exclusive property; the license to treat as invalid any attempts to address problems if supremacists have not agreed that the problem is a problem; the license to treat any attempt to actually solve the problem as a threat against the established order; the license to establish and defend a framework that systematically forces people other than themselves to pay the abusive costs of brokenness, then to use the fact that they themselves have unjustly avoided the cost as proof that the cost is avoidable, then to use the fact they have avoided the costs of brokenness to blame anyone who hasn't avoided those costs for the crime of failing to do so, then use that crime as a rationale to further punish those who have most suffered the effects of injustice, then use the expense of the punishment as a rationale that the punishment should be made profitable. Supremacy puts people into impoverished and unstable conditions that ensure the rise of social and economic turmoil, then casts those who suffer that turmoil as the reason for the turmoil, in order to cast them as undeserving of relief or justice. And then supremacy pours money into charities that are organized to carefully flatter supremacy's own sense of blamelessness, and into institutions designed to punish human problems at a profitable markup rather than sustainably solving the problems at a lower cost.

Blameless supremacy demands a cruel management of the problems it causes, and it is willing to pay extravagantly for the cruelty, as long as it doesn't have to pay the natural cost of blame.

And it's all to avoid the cost of repair, maintenance, and improvement.

And I think that's sabotage.

Why sabotage our conviction? To make complacency popular, and then to borrow against that popularity to lend complacency credibility. To use that credibility to further increase complacency's popularity. To force people to engage in a daily fight to defend their conviction that better things are possible and what is broken needs repair—in order to frame the people who engage in that fight as combative and unrealistic, as a pretext for further suppression of conviction. To make conviction an unfavorable position to hold, a difficult burden to maintain, and highly undesirable compared to the ease of indifference. To establish repair as morally unsupportable, a waste of resources bestowed to undeserving people who have not avoided brokenness. To make conviction hard, and painful, and draining, so that people stay away from conviction, and resent those who enter into it. To unnaturally raise the cost of conviction, and offer complacency at a discount. It all amounts to sabotage: a learned and categorical opposition to solutions.

Sabotage of conviction makes complacency *inevitable*; it's an inevitability that makes the cost of conviction high—high enough that people will choose complacency instead. And, when we choose complacency over conviction, we will continue to live in our foundational lies. But that also means that when we choose to pay the cost of conviction—especially where the cost has been made unnaturally high—we will be aligning ourselves against those lies, and demonstrating our conviction to others—because conviction builds resolve for the journey in the hearts of those who hadn't believed a journey was possible.

Here is our work of conviction: To understand that an awareness of injury is not the same as the experience of injury. To cultivate the voices of the injured, and hear them. To read their words. To learn from their stories. To step out of the way when they ask. To step in the way when they ask. To hear the ways we are hurting them, and believe their report, and change. To learn to recognize the seduction of ideas that flatter our complacency, and reject those ideas. To learn to recognize the discomfort of conviction as the discomfort that comes with good work.

This will lead to further awareness, which will lead to further conviction—of course it will, because this work is not just a progression, but a cycle.

So let's reject empty optimism and cynicism and institutionalism and learned helplessness and manufactured indifference. Let's expect things to get better. Let's demand that they do. But most of all, let's hear from those who are injured—particularly when their report of injury leads us out of comfort and toward paying some cost.

Conviction listens.

◆ ◆ ◆

What do we do now? The second thing to do is to enter conviction.

Why do we need conviction? The same reason we need to know the streets are broken and understand how to fix them—because conviction leads to understanding our responsibility for the work, and to proclaiming that responsibility as a new idea in the world.

We need conviction because conviction leads to confession.

5. CONFESSION & DENIAL
Before redemption comes reparation.

Before reparation, repentance.

Before repentance, confession.

This is the re-aligning work of repair, which might be thought of as the work of redemption.

Let's talk about confession.

◆ ◆ ◆

Back in the early 90s, many of us would laugh at a skit on Saturday Night Live called "It's Pat." In the skit, there was a person whose gender presentation was so ambiguous as to be impenetrable to the people with whom this person came into contact. The person's name was Pat, which is not a gendered name, and this left the people who were discomfited about Pat's ambiguous gender presentation no closer to a comfortable resolution than they had been before. The people around Pat would ask leading questions designed to deduce Pat's gender, and Pat would give answers that were ambiguous, further frustrating expectations. Pat's depiction was comically grotesque in the manner of many SNL characters, such as Goat Boy, and skits featuring Pat were often preceded by a theme song, in the manner of many 90s SNL skits, such as Massive Head Wound Harry. Pat's theme song started out with the line "What's that? It's Pat!" The joke about Pat was that Pat's existence was socially uncomfortable to the others around them. The point of view character of the skit was not Pat. The point of view belonged to those made uncomfortable by Pat's presence.

There was even an "It's Pat" movie, but I haven't seen the movie. Perhaps the movie told different jokes with different premises. It sort of would have to, to stretch out to movie length.

There are people who say of entertainments like "It's Pat" things like this: *you could never make that sort of thing today.* Something I've noticed about this is that very seldom does somebody who says *you could never make that sort of thing today* ever say why we would *want* to make that sort of thing today. I've also noticed this: nobody who says such a thing seems to notice all the ways we still absolutely *do* make that sort of thing today.

Which is interesting.

But we were talking about confession.

◆ ◆ ◆

Here's a brief and limited history of my experience with confession.

A few years ago, Twitter made it possible to quote-tweet people by pushing a button, and people across this land have rejoiced ever since. The GIF reactions alone—such joy! We Twitter users have really gone to town when it comes to quote-tweeting. I sure have.

There came a day when somebody pointed out that by quote-tweeting toxic people and their toxic statements, you're actually teaching the Twitter algorithm to boost their toxic platform and message, even if your intention is to criticize or mock them and their message, and so, all things being equal, it would probably be better to not quote-tweet toxic people. I remember being annoyed by this suggested imposition on my behavior. After all, clicking the button is easy, and I like easy things. But I started doing what a lot of other people did around that time, which was to take screenshots and comment on those instead. It took a few more steps, but it did rob the toxic account of juice from the algorithm. Take that, toxic accounts! Take that, algorithm!

After a while, I noticed an account that would comment on every tweet of mine containing a screenshot, to the following effect:

> *Please make your content available to blind and low vision people, who do use social media, by adding alt-text when tweeting images, especially when they're the point of the tweet. OCR isn't equitable, nor always accessible.*

They were polite. They were also persistent and repetitive. And I remember being annoyed by this suggested imposition on my behavior. *God*, I thought. *Where does it end?* Or words to that effect. But in time I started to put the alt-text into my images. It's a few extra steps. Sometimes I still forget. Sometimes, honestly, I decide not to, because I'm rushed or maybe I just don't feel like it. And I suppose when I do that, people with impaired vision correctly assume that in the moment I make that choice, I value my time more than I value accommodating their presence.

I can tell them my reasons.

But I can't say I don't know.

Also, around this same time, there came people who pointed out that even screenshots of toxic accounts and people still promoted those people and their accounts, and put their views in the feeds of people who were being directly targeted for harm and abuse by those comments, and so maybe it would be better just to comment on their message without spreading it directly. And I remember being annoyed by this suggested imposition on my behavior.

God, I thought. *Where does it end?* Or words to that effect.

But also, slowly, I began to put toxic stupid people into other people's feeds less than I once did. Not never, it should be noted. But less.

And I can't say I don't know.

Even later on, I remember reading a series of messages from various people—polite but firm—that suggested that words like *stupid* (a word you may or may not have noticed I just used) or *idiot* or *moron* actually turned learning and developmental disabilities into invective that equated the people who struggle with those things with bad behavior or even evil intent, and were therefore probably best not used at all.

And I remember being annoyed by this suggested imposition on my behavior.

Really? You can't even say "stupid?" But what if something is stupid?

Where does it end?

But somewhere along the line, I've noticed that I don't really use those words very much anymore. I've found more precise ones. When someone is being ignorant or foolish or toxic, I tend to call them an ignorant toxic fool, which is what they're being, rather than equating their deliberately harmful behavior to people who have learning disabilities. I guess, because I was listening, I stopped asking myself "why *can't* I say 'stupid?'" and started asking myself "why do I *want* to?" Sometimes I still say "stupid," because I think "damn, that's pretty stupid," and I want to say "stupid" and I don't want to think about all that. You'll never guess what: it turns out I still absolutely *can*. Nothing is preventing me.

And, when I make that choice, I have my justifications, and some of them might even be good. Or maybe I'm in a context where nobody who would be harmed by my using that word could possibly hear me use it. So that's great, I haven't hurt anybody, maybe, as long as the assumptions I've made about the people in my surroundings are correct. Hooray for me! But ... I'm still aware of those meanings and those effects, and I'm still passing on their use as normal. And what I've discovered is, knowing that makes me *want* to do it less and less, even though I still *can*.

I may have my reasons, and I can give them.

But I can't say I don't know.

Somewhere earlier than any of this, I put my pronouns in my Twitter bio.

This, I'm told by people who consider themselves free thinkers, is a reason to automatically reject anything I might say.

And sure, they can reject what I say.

But they can't say they don't know.

Somewhere earlier than *that*, my wife and I decided to put one of those signs in our yard, which proclaim the sorts of things about basic decency and shared reality that people like me used to believe could go unsaid, before so many people in our lives proved they can't go unsaid at all. The sign is sort of embarrassing in its earnestness, I must say, but it says what my family and I want it to say, so it stays. And then somewhere in there, we hung a pride flag from our front porch. And there came a day when we were told by a real estate agent that a deciding factor in the sale she had just made of the house across the street was that rainbow flag. It seems that flag said something to the new owners about openness and welcomeness and freedom and liberty and equality for all that the stars and stripes no longer do, if indeed they ever did.

And the people who live around us can't say they don't know, and neither can I.

I'm not trying to pat myself on the back, here. In fact, I'd like to draw our focus more on what I got *wrong* than the fact that I'm getting it a *little* more right now: the times I *don't* use alt-text, the times I *do* feed the algorithm beast, the times I *still* say "stupid" when "ignorant" is more precise, the times I still do use words I'm beginning to suspect aren't really appropriate, but I use them anyway, because I've decided to prioritize my own ease.

And I'd like us to focus on the progression.

This started with awareness, and then led to conviction, and then finally led to me actually changing what I communicate through my behavior and language. And I'm inconsistent, and sometimes I'm clumsy, and I'm sure sometimes it's what the goddamn kids today call *cringe*, which means that I am not at all cool for doing it, and also that many times my actual actions show that this presentation is performative rather than substantive. But first there came awareness, and then conviction, and then an actual change in the things I said and how I said them, along with as close as I could manage to a clear-eyed look at what it means for me to have participated in a blameless supremacist society and how I still participate even after I have started to change. And that led to making my language more inclusive, so that when I spoke, I wasn't leaving somebody out of my assumptions about what was meant when I said *we*.

Which I think is a **confession** of what is broken and what needs to be repaired.

People opposed to repair really, really, really hate inclusive language.

It's interesting to think about why.

I think this is because they sense innately that inclusive language inevitably will lead to people thinking about marginalized people where previously they had just been able to ignore them, and that awareness will lead to more inclusion, and that inclusion will create a more inclusive society, and a more inclusive society will inevitably lead to repair, and to repair's natural costs. I think it's because acknowledging brokenness exposes the brokenness of those who refuse all blame. So when they oppose inclusion, they're confessing, too— confessing an opposition to inclusion.

And that brings me back to "It's Pat."

The reason I brought up "It's Pat" isn't that the skit was promoting a lie—not exactly.

The reason I brought up "It's Pat" is because the skit was actually trafficking in a *true* observation, which is that for some people, gender can be complicated, or ambiguous, or not made immediately obvious to observers by its presentation, and this can make other people uncomfortable. The skit took this fact and turned Pat into an object of fun, by framing Pat's existence as obviously grotesque and off-putting, and by taking as its point of view the people made uncomfortable by the presence of Pat. It confessed the discomfort, and then normalized it. It framed the people who were *already* deemed "normal" as even *more* normal by the very fact of their discomfort, and people like Pat even *less* normal, by dint of having produced that discomfort.

It presented Pat as a problem to be solved.

Unspoken in this but unavoidably present lurked the idea that there are people who matter, and there are people who don't. A skit from Pat's point of view could be made, and it could be funny, but it would be a very different skit. For all I know that's what the movie was.

Perhaps you think I'm making a bit much of a 30-year-old comedy skit.

Probably so.

Perhaps you think that by critiquing it, I'm *attacking* the makers of "It's Pat."

That's an interesting interpretation. What's interesting about it is the perspective it's choosing.

Why do we seem so optimized to see this critique as an attack on cis people who made a skit about a nonbinary person instead of a defense of the nonbinary people they were making the skit about? I'd argue it's because we don't even think about whose perspectives we automatically prioritize.

"It's Pat" was not alone in its cultural space, and it wasn't the most toxic example of transphobia, and transphobic material isn't the only thing we can find lurking in the video archives of the early 1990s, which I believe was the dawn of television. The characters made uncomfortable by Pat in "It's Pat" weren't always badly intentioned people, and I suspect the people bringing Pat to the screen were not badly intentioned people, either, nor was I a badly intentioned person when I watched "It's Pat," and when, like much of America, I laughed and laughed and laughed, and then did a bad "It's Pat" impression the next day at school along with my passable impression of Wayne Campbell and my pretty decent impression of Hans and Franz. Did I do my impression within sight of a person who looked at Pat and saw themselves as the object of my fun? I don't know, for a very specific reason: I didn't care enough to think about it. But it was a pretty crowded cafeteria.

Am I *attacking* the people who made and broadcast "It's Pat?" If so, I'm attacking myself, too. I was a part of "It's Pat." It was what it was. I was who I was. I find it to be an apt example.

This is why I decided to put pronouns in my social media bio, even though I am assigned male at birth and masculine-presenting, and to my knowledge have never caused anybody any confusion on that point. It's a simple thing that acknowledges a similar observation as the one "It's Pat" was making—which is *people exist whose gender presentation is ambiguous*—but makes it in such a way as to put people with ambiguous gender presentation—and other people who are otherwise nonconforming to cultural standards around gender—at the center and (hopefully) accommodates them, rather than centering people like me whose gender presentation conforms to the dominant societal expectations.

Trans and nonbinary and other gender nonconforming people

exist, and their lives *matter*, in the same way my life does—which isn't an obvious thing to say in this society. The world is full of people who want to make their discomfort with the existence of such people into the problem to be solved, and demand that power solve that problem for them by making such people not be visible parts of the world, and, if power is wielded by blameless supremacy (as it often is), then power will choose to accommodate the uncomfortable people in this demand. This makes the world a much more dangerous place for nonbinary and otherwise nonconforming people than it is for me. If they are the only people putting their pronouns in their bio, then it's just another way that they are making themselves visible in a world where that isn't safe to do.

However.

If people like *me* do it, then a person who conforms to what blameless supremacy deems "normal" will be framing *them* as normal, despite their lack of conformity, and will be framing people's discomfort with the existence of others as the problem to be solved, and those made uncomfortable by the existence of others as the ones with the responsibility to solve it. It's a confession that gender nonconforming people exist, and matter. And thus, in a tiny, microscopic way, it brings such people into the sphere of *normal* by spending the tiniest bit of the automatic privilege that puts me in that sphere and keeps me there. It's a simple confession about my conviction of the way things aren't, and the way they should be.

It's quite literally the least I can do, if I actually care.

When we confess the existence and importance of nonbinary people, we create a word in which people might still decide to cast nonbinary people as grotesque objects of fun, victims of an undesirable and hilarious predicament, a problem for the rest of us *normal* people to solve on behalf of ourselves. We *can* still do that. But now people might ask: why do you *want* to?

And they can't say they don't know.

It's worth noting that nobody cisgendered should really care about whether I or anybody else has pronouns in their bio or anywhere else. It *shouldn't* matter to them, particularly since they seem so obsessed with the notion that anyone should be *allowed* to say anything, so my decision to declare pronouns should be something that is zero problemo for them.

But—and you will certainly know this if you've ever done it—it is not zero problemo.

It is a *big* problemo.

Blameless supremacists do care, and so they reveal that they actually don't believe that other people should be allowed to say what they want. The pronouns in my bio bothers them—a *lot*.

What bothers them, I think, is that it is confession, because confession doesn't just affect me, or marginalized people.

My confession affects *them*, and they *know* it.

A world in which *everyone* announces their pronouns becomes a world with an expectation that they should announce their pronouns, too. A world in which *everyone* confesses that gender is not a simple binary, and that people who don't align with simple binaries exist and matter, is a world where they will be expected to behave as if such people's lives matter, too. It's a world where they'll be expected to change, or else face a social or professional consequence.

And they *know* it.

It's happened before, creating a more open and just world, a world within which they feel compelled to say *you just can't say what you think anymore.*

Which is why confession is part of the realigning work of repair.

We're talking about pronouns. We could be talking about many things, where some people have experienced systemic abuse or theft or injury and others haven't. We could be talking about racist microaggressions or even systemic macroaggressions within our economic and judicial systems. We could be talking about sexual harassment or gender pay inequality. We could be talking about how our society generally, or our health care industry specifically, sees people who are overweight. We could be talking about many things.

A blameless system insists *we are beyond reproach.*

But confession... confession says *we have been wrong.*

Confession accepts blame, and then changes.

A blameless system, then, will abhor confession.

A system based on abuse will resent confession and attack it.

If someone refuses to pay costs, they're going to need to sabotage confession.

They're going to need a way to say "I don't know" about things they know, a way that allows them to not even know they've decided not to know.

Confession isn't for the person making the confession; it exists neither for their awareness or their conviction. The person making the confession already knows the truth, and already expects it to get better. Confession is for those who hear it. Confession pulls people along who are a step behind. Confession brings conviction to those who still live in the lie.

◆ ◆ ◆

It's 2022 now as I write this. Let's see what's happening in 2022.

On the supremacist conservative propaganda outlet Fox News, host Jesse Watters called homeless people "an invasive species." If you're the sort of person who gets alarmed, that might strike you as alarming talk. It seems to me to be a public confession of how conservative supremacists see unhoused people—not as neighbors in desperate need, demonstrating a great brokenness in our society requiring repair, but as the problem itself, a danger and an expense, a separate species requiring a more final solution that is *almost* stated, but not quite, not yet.

It makes me think of the leaning benches.

See, the thing is, many subways in Brooklyn (and elsewhere perhaps, but the story I saw was about the benches in Brooklyn) no longer have benches, they have these wood leaners affixed to the walls, canted at a steep angle, which are pretty much useless for any tired commuters to rest on. However, they are *also* useless for any unhoused person to sleep on—which is why they exist.

So: our economy is leaving more and more people without shelter—a basic need—and our government seems aligned with those who share the prevailing belief that any relief sent the way of unhoused people is a moral hazard and a theft. The civic solution has become to make our cities inhospitable and violent to people who are unhoused, in order to drive them out. However, if a city is successful at that, then unhoused people will not stop existing; they'll merely go to other cities, which—because those cities also share the prevailing belief—choose to also make themselves inhospitable and violent for unhoused people. If a city doesn't make itself inhospitable, it risks being excoriated as a place run by dangerous fools, with its glut of unhoused persons in their public spaces made to represent not that city's alignment with basic human hospitality, but its incomprehensible accommodation of a swarm of dangerous pests.

The ultimate result of all this is that our cities appear to have entered an inhospitality arms race, with each state and city scrambling to be the most inhospitable to unhoused people, even as our dedication to inhospitality configures our society in ways that make a growing population of unhoused people not only likely but inevitable, and which almost always costs more in dollars and cents than simply providing housing to people without housing. Nor are dollars and cents the only cost— because now we all have to live in cities that are making themselves deliberately unhospitable and violent to human beings, which can be a problem, if we also happen to be human beings.

Anyway, that's why tired people in Brooklyn can't sit down while waiting for the train.

We don't always say it out loud, but look to the benches and you'll see us confess who we are. The leaners are a gesture toward function, without providing the actual function. Unhoused people are a confession that we have decided to make growth of capital and the interests of property far higher priorities than caring for the basic needs of people. Our leaning benches are a confession that we have decided to do without a functional city in order to be cruel instead of kind to the people we've failed. They are a confession that we believe there are some people who matter and others who don't.

The benches are confessing our alignment toward creating a world of unhoused people, the same way that policing and prosectuion and incarceration statistics confess our alignment toward criminalizing Black people. And yet, somehow, we never get around to knowing what we're confessing, because all these confessions seem to be shrouded in a deep institutional denial that has created and enforced in our minds a reasonable doubt that we might not be doing what we can all see we are definitely doing.

And I think that's sabotage.

◆ ◆ ◆

The *opposite* of confession is silence—a refusal to speak a demonstrable truth—and saboteurs of repair will foster silence by sabotaging our conviction with complacency.

The *opposition* to conviction is **denial**—a deliberate and outward repudiation of the truth, and a physical demonstration of the lie, that reinforces both the lie and the license to abuse others that the lie bestows.

Denial might be best thought of as a confession of something untrue, to force confession of truth out of the public sphere. It's a leaning bench of discourse, a gesture toward truth with nowhere for truth to actually rest. Denial can be propaganda, or a book promoting a lie, or a literal demonstration—like very fine people marching in solidarity with actual Nazis in defense of monuments erected to honor traitors who fought a murderous war to maintain and expand the institution of human slavery, while claiming that their rationale to do so has nothing to do with bigotry. Or it can simply be defending the people who elected to march in common cause with Nazis as very fine people. It could be insisting that the cause of the war to expand and preserve slavery, and those who fought for that cause, are a blameless part of one's heritage. It could be insisting that everyone else accept your definitions of your heritage, and your exclusive license to define it.

Yet denial, like any lie, has its limits.

However we chose to deny our intentions, the results of our actions confess to the truth.

We've been talking about repair as a progressive process with sequential steps, moving from awakening to conviction, and ending with doing the actual work and paying the costs of repair. And we've been talking about a blameless society, opposed to all natural costs of repair, including the cost of blame—that is, the cost of being exposed as people aligned toward maintaining brokenness, and making others pay its much higher costs. If you are aligned against paying natural costs, the first things to sabotage are awakening and conviction. But if awakening and conviction begin to creep into the public sphere, it will become imperative to sabotage confession with denial.

Under denial, blameless supremacy insists that already known things be treated as unknowable, and that indestructible skepticism be applied to solutions for solvable problems that it has already decided cannot be solved. Denial uses this position of unassailable ignorance and impermeable complacency to ensure that supremacy is allowed to keep itself blameless for any neglect.

Notice how blameless supremacy will frame any confession of brokenness exclusively in terms of individual guilt, and individual accusation, rather than systemic guilt and systemic culpability. *Guilt*, because guilt must be proved, which means it can also be disproved. *Accusation*, because a false accusation is a crime wherein the victim becomes the accused, and the criminal becomes the accuser. And always, always, always *individual*—because someone making a confession of systemic brokenness is making a systemic confession—and while a blameless society will of course defend their blameless system, they'd much rather defend the reasonable doubts surrounding their own unknowable and unprovable individual motivations, which allows them to never even touch the systemic brokenness that was the subject of the confession.

Confession of brokenness identifies abuse and its victims, and carries an expectation of repair. Denial converts confession into an accusation, which changes not only the forum—from something that has been *observed* to something that must be *proved*—but even redefines the victim and the crime.

The crime is no longer the abuse—now the crime is the accusation of abuse.

The victim is no longer the person harmed by the abuse—now the victim is the abuser.

Because the abuser has been self-established as the victim of accusation, the abuser can now counter-accuse. The abuser's accusation is against the act of confession itself. Soon we're not even arguing the subject of the confession—which was some exposure of systemic abuse. Now we're arguing whether or not the abuser has been psychologically or reputationally harmed by the exposure, and we're trying to fix not the brokenness of our system, but the reputation of the person who was profiting from the damage. It's all designed to keep us talking about guilt and blame, rather than what we were talking about—which is turning ourselves into people who are aligned with repair instead of brokenness.

Remember that thought I told you I had, again and again?

Where does it all end? is what I asked myself.

Denial keeps us locked there, inside *where does it all end?* so that we'll never realize that the topic should be repair and improvement rather than making a critic shut up, and we never ask the most important question we can ask about the process of repair and improvement, which is this: Why would we *want* it to end?

It is improvement. *It* is progress.

If action leads to results, and results confess to the truth, then by improving we'll always be confessing to the need for the next improvement; by repairing we'll always be confessing to the need of the next repair.

Which is actually good news, if we're doing the work of repair.

If we're engaged in the work of improvement, *why do you want it to end?*

The real answer is: *it never ends.*

Think of it. We might *never* stop improving.

We might *never* stop hearing new voices.

We might *never* stop learning, and growing and changing.

We might not want to, once we started. I think that's good, actually.

I'd suggest only somebody who thinks they're blameless already would fear such a prospect, or frame the call to improvement along lines of accusation and guilt.

Denial keeps us frozen in a fear of *being* wrong, rather than moving us into a desire to avoid *staying* wrong.

◆ ◆ ◆

Above all, blameless supremacy sabotages confession in order to claim the right to define **fault** and **blame** as its exclusive property. It insists on drawing the fault lines in ways that create doubt as to what it is doing, and then insists that we certify the doubt it has manufactured as reasonable.

It all amounts to sabotage: a refusal to accept any true confession; a demand to receive reconciliation while having done nothing to reconcile, a demand to be given redemption without reparation.

Why sabotage? To make denial of truth popular. To borrow against that popularity in order to lend credibility to denial and make the observable results of actual actions disputable. To force people to engage in a daily fight to confess the truth about what is broken—in order to cast people who engage in that fight as annoying guilt-tripping scolds, as a pretext for further suppression of truth. To make confession of truth hard, and painful, and draining, so that people stay away from truth, and resent those who enter into it. This is a sabotage that makes denial of truth inevitable, and an inevitability that makes the cost of truth high—high enough that people will choose lies instead.

And remember, it's all to avoid the threat of improvement; all to avoid the costs of repair; all to preserve the profits gained from forcing others to pay the higher costs of brokenness.

This is denial of truth: the third step in the sabotaging work of blameless supremacy.

And this is my work of confession.

This, literally. This book. It's my work of confession.

It's about all the things I failed to see. It's about me confessing new truths to myself that have been entirely obvious to injured people I failed to hear. And, because I'm not blameless, I'm still improving. And because I'm still improving, I'm almost certainly expressing these ideas in ways that reveal still-existing ignorance. This makes it a little scary to write; not because I might be criticized for it, but because some of the criticism, when it comes, is likely to be *accurate*—at least the criticism that comes from those whose voices I am trying to hear. There's a temptation to not write it, certainly a temptation to not publish—and this temptation exposes to me the ways I'm still aligned with my own blamelessness. The idea that I'd rather not even speak than face accurate criticism... what is that? That's alignment with blameless supremacy.

And what if I *do* face accurate criticism for exposing my ignorance? Will I receive social or professional consequence?

Maybe I will—though I've noticed that these consequences usually attend *inaccurate* criticism for having confessed something true—the standard fate of the whistleblower—because a blameless system usually moves to protect those who face accurate criticism and to prosecute those who bring it. I think a far more likely result of *accurate* criticism is this: I'll lose more of my blamelessness. I'll have to accept that I have been wrong. I'll be offered a chance to learn how to grow and improve, if I'm willing to listen.

My compass will become more accurate. And I think that's a good thing, actually.

What is your work of confession? It depends on who you are and what social license has been bestowed to you. Here are some suggestions: Discover the things you didn't know, and then call attention to them. Use your own previous ignorance as your authority to speak about ignorance. Learn where our foundational lies bestow you with an unfair measure of attention and power, and use it to confess the lie, which will help dismantle it. Stop using the fear of having your remaining ignorance exposed as a rationale to avoid speaking the truth you've learned. Don't enter into confession with your motivations rooted in blamelessness, as a duty you hope to perform once, discharge quickly, with a final resolution as your target—instead, enter into it as an opportunity to engage in an endless progression of improvement, a cycle of awareness and conviction and confession that makes you better and better without ever believing that you have become perfect. Most of all, speak bravely, speak unpopular truths, and speak to be heard.

Confession proclaims.

◆ ◆ ◆

What do we do now? The third thing is to confess.

Why do we need confession? The same reason we need to agree it is our responsibility to fix our broken streets—because confession builds a general awareness of brokenness, and a general conviction that we ought to repair. We confess, because it tells a new story, it introduces a new idea, and that changes the spirit within our natural human systems, which changes what is possible. We confess, because when we confess, it helps other people change for the better, and realign toward repair.

We confess, because confession leads to repentance.

6. REPENTANCE & OPPRESSION

Before redemption comes reparation.

Before reparation, repentance.

This is the re-aligning work of repair, which might be thought of as the work of redemption.

Let's talk about repentance.

◆ ◆ ◆

What is repentance?

Jewish traditions talk about repentance as a return. The word in Hebrew is tshuva.

This is what I think about when I think about repentance.

I want to be clear and I want to be careful here. I was not raised in any Jewish tradition, nor do I claim any authoritative knowledge in those traditions. My understanding of tshuva was first gained in non-Jewish Christian spaces, though I have since begun supplementing that understanding with Jewish voices who can speak to it with greater authority. All this to say, I reference the concept and practice of tshuva with respectful intent, and in genuine hope that I honor it. However, even given the admitted limits of my understanding, I do find it useful to consider repentance along the lines of a return.

With a return, you go somewhere. Then comes awareness that you're in the wrong place. *Oh shit, I'm in the wrong place.* Then comes a confession that you're in the wrong place. *Hey, I think*

I took a wrong turn. Then comes a turn, back toward the right place. Then you actually do the work to go back—the return. And it's a journey.

That's repentance.

These elements are all very important, I think, as is the sequential order. I also note that this is how repair of streets work—both the travel upon them and the fixing and maintenance of them. It's how the repair of *anything* works. If you don't turn, you won't get back, even if you keep walking. If you just turn, but don't walk, you won't return even if you're facing the right way.

Why would one return?

There are many reasons, but let me suggest that all of them boil down to "you want to get back to the place you were before you went wrong." In the case of both travel and repentance, it's generally understood that being in the wrong place is the result of going in an incorrect direction. You're in the wrong place, and you should return to the right one.

But what if the place we came from *also* isn't the right place?

What if the place we want to go is a return to an ideal, a place we've never been?

To what, then, should we want to return?

I'd suggest we return to being works of art carrying unsurpassable worth—a state we can only truly inhabit if we recognize it in all others, and a state we can only truly inhabit if we're first completely honest about where we are and the direction in which we've been heading. We need to return to our natural human system, which provides a value that is shared, invisible, foundational, generative, automatic, inextricable, configurable, and inherited, delivered to us not because of anything we did; but because there was a need for a *you* and a *me*.

Perhaps you see why I find it useful to begin with art.

Perhaps you see why I find the idea of a compass so foundational.

Recalibrating our compass back to our best ideals and taking a journey based on that recalibrated direction is good work— repairing work, even. In fact, repentance strikes me as the process of repair applied to spirit.

But now what?

What if we want to do the realigning work of repair? If what we want to fix is a system based on unsustainable foundational lies, we're going to have to align ourselves against that system, even as we are a part of it—to stop accommodating the spirit that animates those lies, especially in the places where those lies accommodate us.

We might need to do more than fix our roads, if our roads are killing our neighbors. We might need to replace them with something new. And this will be inconvenient, especially if we are the people for whose convenience the roads were first built.

It may be uncomfortable. Journeys often are.

People who want to avoid the discomfort of a journey will do everything they can to make any journey as uncomfortable as possible, to discourage movement.

I think that's sabotage.

Let me tell you a story.

◆ ◆ ◆

Say your name is Joe but I insist your name is Jean.

Let's say you believe your name is Joe because that's your name.

Let's say I insist your name is Jean because I believe I have the right to name you as a function of who I understand myself to be, and I believe you do not have the right to name yourself as a function of who I understand you to be.

Let's say this plays out in a number of other beliefs I have about your identity, and the way you choose to live. Again and again, you establish yourself on your own terms, and again and again I refuse your *self*, in a way that makes it clear that my right to accept or refuse you is a core part of how I see myself.

Perhaps you've seen this scenario play out in thousands of different ways, and wondered: What *is* that?

I'll tell you what it is.

It's supremacy.

It's a belief that I am supreme. Supreme over you, to be precise.

I am demonstrating the dominant core belief in our society—the foundational lie—that there are people who matter, and I am one of those, and there are people who do not matter, and that you are one of those. I am attempting to impose a reality founded on that belief, under which I am the one who gets to define you, and your right to exist is not a foregone conclusion but something that will be established and mediated by what I and other people who matter are comfortable allowing. I'm establishing that *my* understanding of who you are is more important than *your* understanding of who you are.

I'm establishing my license to permit you to exist.

It so happens I am wrong, by the way. I actually believe a bunch of unsustainable lies about you and me and how society is supposed to work. *Unsustainable* because a society that believes some people do not matter inevitably becomes a society optimized to destroy people, and a society optimized to destroy people will do that as long as there are people, and society is made up of people—so if you're a person, you might want to oppose me and my supremacy. I'm wrong, and not only wrong, but wrong in ways that endanger everyone, including myself.

You have beliefs of your own in this scenario.

You believe I am a supremacist asshole. *Supremacist* because I believe I have supremacy over you, and *asshole* because that is an asshole thing to believe.

It so happens you are correct about me.

Now, let's say I have power behind my supremacist beliefs. Let's say our natural human system has been unnaturally configured in ways that force you to live in my lie instead of your truth, and the legal and political apparatuses of our society also impose a reality under which I am the one who gets to decides the limits of your ability and your right to *be*.

Now I am not just a supremacist, but an *oppressor*.

I am an oppressor, because power agrees with me that I am supreme. My view is accommodated over yours, even though my view is a lie, even though the accommodation hurts you and dismisses you and your identity. I am an oppressor, because my supremacy rules the day.

But what I believe is still a lie. And I am still a supremacist asshole.

I oppose you, but it is not my opposition to you that makes me oppressive, it is my empowered and accommodated supremacy. If power agreed with you about me being a supremacist asshole, for example, you would not be an oppressor, even though you oppose me. You would not be an oppressor, because your view is not a lie, and power accommodating your view would not hurt the person you oppose—me, in this example—or dismiss me or my identity; it would merely prevent me from doing that to you.

This may all seem obvious and repetitive, but in an age of empowered liars, I've found it can be instructive, even powerful, to repeat true things.

Thanks for your patience.

Now that this is out of the way, there is a massive problem in my country that I'd like to bring to your attention, because I've been given to understand by the adults in the room that this problem must be solved before any other problem can be solved or even considered.

This makes it *the supreme problem* we face today.

A pretty big problem!

Here is the supreme problem: conservatives have not been made perfectly comfortable yet, and that is something they find extremely oppressive. So it's a problem of oppression. They're being oppressed. Listen to them; they'll tell you. They won't *stop* telling you. Let me lay it out for you. We could use conservative evangelical Christians as an example; since I'm an evangelical Christian of sorts, I'm pretty close to this one, and I can really get into the weeds.

We evangelical Christians believe our way of living is the best way to live.

Ask us. We'll *tell* you.

Fair enough, right? Most people try to live in the way they think is best, is my observation. But we *really* believe our way is best. We believe this because as we understand it, our way of living is the way God instructs people to live (you might say it is just *our* interpretation of *our* understanding of God's instruction, and that there exist rich Christian traditions that do not line up with these interpretations of evangelicals in the United States, and that there are even other religions besides Christianity that have their own ways of looking at these questions, but that's very oppressive of you to say).

Anyway, these are religious beliefs, and we have freedom of religion in this country, so evangelical Christians are free to hold them. So far, so good, I guess.

Here's where the supreme problem comes in for us conservative Christians: there are people who *don't* live our way, and yet they seem, if left to their own devices, to *also* live meaningful lives of satisfaction and joy. They *exist*, these other people. They don't seem to need the conservative Christian way of living to find satisfaction or meaning or morality or joy.

To conservative Christians, this is an aggressive act against conservative Christians—an *oppressive* act. Let me give some examples of what I mean, so you can understand the terrible plight of a conservative Christian in the United States today.

Gay and trans people exist, for starters, as do other people who do not conform to the gender norms that conservatives consider standard. This is a pretty big problem for us evangelical Christians, especially if we're conservative. It's not because we *hate* queer people, and I have been told it's very important you understand that. It's because we are deeply convicted that being queer is a wrong way to live, and not only will result in suffering, but *ought* to result in suffering, and if the suffering isn't forthcoming then we will naturally find it necessary to demand laws that will make the suffering happen. Furthermore, we evangelical Christians don't feel we should have to show any sort of tacit approval of gay people by being forced to interact with them in any way that might be construed as approval or tolerance of behavior we personally disagree with, because if we did that, it might give gay people the idea that they *don't* deserve to be punished forever and ever in ceaseless torment, and that wouldn't be a very loving message for us as Christians to deliver.

These beliefs find many forms of expression.

For example, many conservative Christians believe we Christians should be able to own and operate businesses without having to serve gay people in any way that might be seen as approving of or even tolerating the existence of gay people's gayness, and we believe we should be able to enter any public space we want without ever having to see or hear any positive or even neutral acknowledgement that gay people exist, which we find oppressive to our way of living. Most of all, we believe that our children should not have to encounter queerness at all, and certainly not in any sort of positive or even neutral or tolerant way, which might indoctrinate them into dangerous modes of tolerance and empathy for people who are going to suffer the eternal torment that everyone deserves and everyone is going to get except us. Again: We conservative Christians don't *hate* queer people. It is *so* important that you understand that. We just don't *agree* with queer people—with their existence, I mean. A queer person exists, and a conservative Christian disagrees (often very respectfully and politely) with that existence as a matter of deep personal conviction. So we think that the question of queer people's existence should be mediated by the question of whether or not we conservative Christians personally agree with it, and the degree to which we are comfortable with it, and that queer people should be permitted to exist in the world only to the degree that conservative Christians agree they may exist, or else conservative Christians get very uncomfortable, and what so many non-Christians forget these days is that Christian comfort is much more important than anyone else's, and failing to realize that is oppressing Christians on religious grounds. The right to be queer ends where a conservative Christian's line of sight begins, you might say. It's a religious belief, remember—a loving one. And we do believe in religious freedom. And who would set themselves in opposition to love?

And that makes evangelical Christian discomfort part of our supreme problem.

Hopefully by now you can see why *existing* is a very aggressive and discomforting thing for queer people to do to conservative Christians, and such an oppressive problem to be solved. But in case not, let me break it down in a bit more detail for you.

Right now these conservative Christian beliefs aren't being respected—not perfectly, anyway, not yet. Right now, society and law to a certain degree expect that gay people will be treated equally under the law, as if they were human beings, the same as anyone else. This means that we Christians are forced to do terrible, difficult, awful things, things like explaining the existence of queerness to our children, and that's very hard to do without making it sound as if we bear personal animosity toward queer people (which let's be sure to remember we do *not*), all while still ensuring our children are very clear and sharp on our deep conviction that being a queer person is an absolutely unacceptable thing to be, so much so that should any child of *ours* make that choice, that child should expect to be shunned and have core aspects of their life and identity rejected, because any loving

Christian is so sure that being queer *will* cause suffering and ostracization and harm, that we will lovingly make sure that it *does*.

Making this clear to our children gets much much *much* harder when gay people are allowed by society and by law to exist
in public spaces in the same way as anybody else, because what
happens *then* is that our children can clearly observe that queer
people actually are not being rejected by anybody but bigots,
and that there are ways of living other than the strictures of
conservative Christianity that can lead to meaningful and moral
lives of satisfaction and joy, and *that* could mean that instead
of being the loving grateful people they claim to be, their parents—*us*—might actually be bigots, and our way of living might
not be best after all. And that might lead them to wonder if conservative Christians *actually* live lives that are more moral and
more full of satisfaction and joy than all others, or to wonder if
even conservative Christians themselves actually live the way
they claim to live, or just use their moral posturing as a pretext
to virtue signal while pushing their own comfort and their own
supremacy. All of this equal treatment under the law and by
society is especially dangerous to us Christians because some
conservative Christian children are themselves actually gay.
And that, my friends, means that there is a very real danger that
conservative Christian parents won't have the option of shunning
their gay children to punish them for being gay, or shaming them
into pretending they're not gay, because their gay children would
instead have the option of shunning *them* and moving on with
their lives in a society that accepts them as they are.

But don't worry! Conservatives spent the last four decades
capturing the courts using shocking and scandalous abuses of
power and massive bribes. So now they are solving the queer
question, and many other questions as well. There are laws
coming and laws already here designed to walk back all that
oppressive societal and legal acceptance of other people; laws
that make it illegal to talk about being queer, and illegal to get

married to your chosen partner if you're queer, or to have and raise children if you're queer, or to exist around children or patients if you're queer, or to enjoy equal protection under the law for employment if you're queer; laws that make it perfectly OK to not provide medical care or prescription medication or even delicious cakes to queer people if you have convinced yourself Jesus wouldn't want you to. And there are laws coming and some already here that prevent recommended and often life-saving medical treatment to trans children.

So rejoice! A lot of people who deserve to suffer are going to be made to suffer! Very lovingly! Our supreme problem is being solved at last!

But sometimes uncomfortable conservatives are so uncomfortable with the existence of other kinds of people, they can't even wait for laws. Librarians are being hounded out of their libraries for shelving material that treats queerness as normal, and treating queer people like the equal human beings that they are. And conservatives are even shutting down libraries in their own towns, because they'd rather have no library at all than have a library that makes them feel uncomfortable. And the Texas Department of Family and Protective Services is struggling to function, because nearly 2,300 employees have quit, following Governor Greg Abbott's prosecutorial policy of targeted investigations of parents of trans children. And an Oklahoma English teacher was just fired, for providing students with a QR code link to the Brooklyn Library—a link providing electronic copies of books banned by conservative school boards for the crime of promoting awareness. And a Nebraska school board just closed a school newspaper after the student journalists ran a Pride Month issue. And in many place children are going to start having their genitals inspected before they can participate in sports, and are increasingly being bullied and harassed for not conforming to gender norms, and a lot of people are going to suffer torment and die, and so on, which (let's remember) is exactly what conservative Christians believe all people deserve, so I imagine we Christians will become a bit more comfortable with things than we were before.

There aren't any laws forcing conservatives to live a "queer lifestyle" that I'm aware of, by the way. I'm not even sure what the "queer lifestyle" might be, other than simply living your life as a queer person, and there certainly aren't any laws forcing Christians to be queer, other than the law of nature, which observably results in some Christians being queer. I don't believe there has ever been a law that's even been suggested that would force conservative Christians to get abortions, or to restrict an adult from being around children because the adult was Christian, or to dissolve Christian marriages, and so forth, nor will such things occur if conservative Christians lose their battle with those opposing them.

But queer people do seem to be advocating that this not be done to them, and far too many people seem to be agreeing with queer people, and very divisively refusing to listen to conservative Christian reasons for making sure queer people suffer, so we have a lot of work to do to solve our supreme problem. Because all of this acceptance and tolerance and inclusion is very very very uncomfortable for Christians, especially conservative Christians, especially male Christians, especially white male Christians—dangerously uncomfortable. I say *dangerously* because if a certain type of conservative white male Christian is allowed to stay uncomfortable too long, they might lose their patience that these people will *eventually* suffer and be forced to hurt somebody themselves. Ask them. They'll tell you. You probably won't even have to ask.

But people in the queer community aren't the only ones causing our supreme problem, I fear. We have the oppressive problem of women, for example, who have bodies and even sometimes have ideas about what should be done with those bodies and who should get to make decisions about those bodies, and some of those things even include life-affirming and often life-preserving medical treatments, such as abortions. And this simply isn't acceptable to conservatives, who haven't agreed to allow women to exist in that way. So we're going to have a lot of laws about abortion, too, and as a result we know that a lot of pregnant people are going to suffer and die, and a lot already have suffered and died, and conservative Christians know this perfectly well, but at least they will be spared the uncomfortable sight of women and queer people and others living meaningful and moral lives of satisfaction and joy without first securing conservative Christian permission to do so.

And so on.

And it's not just the conservative Christian supremacists! There are conservative white supremacists, for whom the existence of Black people who can vote is very oppressive, even though Black people are not trying to keep white people from voting. And there are conservative wealth supremacists, who believe that people with money deserve to live and people who don't have money don't deserve to live unless they can be made profitable, and so find the sight of any expenditure that exists simply for the public good without thought to profit to be very oppressive, even though they would remain hugely wealthy even if they were taxed in a way commensurate to the value they had received from society.

And there are many other types of supremacists as well, all experiencing another facet of our supreme problem. I could have written just as long an essay explaining each one of them, and they would all follow pretty much the exact same pattern and logic, and reach the same conclusions. There's a lot of overlap between types of supremacy, but certainly wealth supremacists might not be white supremacists, and white supremacists might not be Christian supremacists, and male supremacists might not be any of the other three, and so forth—yet they all believe one core thing, which is that some people matter, and other people do not, and that being asked to acknowledge the right of other people to exist in the same way as them (or even to be forced to confront the sight of people living differently than them) is deeply oppressive.

Honestly, there's a *lot* of overlap between supremacies—more overlap than points of difference. Supremacists seem to have unified around their belief in supremacy, to the point where the particulars of supremacy don't seem to matter much to them, and they mush into each other, until a conservative Christian might identify their wealth supremacy and their male supremacy and even sometimes their white supremacy as core components of their Christian supremacy, far more than (for example) any of the diametrically opposing things that Christ actually taught. And a conservative Christian supremacist might learn that some politician they support actually doesn't live in *their* way of living at all, and actually might have even (for example) paid at least one girlfriend to have at least one abortion, and threatened to murder his wife and children on multiple occasions, and so forth, and yet that conservative Christian doesn't hesitate for even a moment in their support for that politician, because even though the politician has made a mockery of their stated religious beliefs about abortion and family, he did win the Heisman trophy, and he still intends to help conservative Christians establish their domination over the bodies of women, and that was really the point all along.

This intersection of competing supremacies, by the way, is how it can be that conservative Christians feel oppressed by the sight of women exercising control over their own bodies, even though many conservative Christians *are* women. And you might resolve many other seeming contradictions within conservative ideology as well, simply by observing that for a supremacist, the particular flavor of their supremacy might matter, but ultimately it is the general idea of their supremacy that is supreme. It's almost as if what matters most to a supremacist isn't the stated principles or strictures of their stated ideologies, but simply their ability to establish and enforce their dominance over others.

But we were talking about repair.

First you awaken to awareness of brokenness and connectivity. *This is broken, and it is something shared between all of us.* Then you move to conviction, based on that awareness. *It should be fixed, and it can be, and I bear some responsibility for fixing it.* Then you move to confession, a public airing of this awareness and conviction, to change the atmosphere of what is considered good and what is considered possible.

But before we can repair, we have to actually realign our beliefs and intentions and resources: away from an alignment with a spirit that profits from brokenness by making other people pay the higher costs; toward an alignment with a spirit of repair and a willingness to pay our share of the lower costs of repair.

And I think of this realigning as **repentance**.

If we want to fix a supremacist system, we're going to have to engage in oppositional repentance—a return to our natural human system that stands in direct confrontation to blameless supremacy. Which will be inconvenient and uncomfortable, especially if we are the people for whose convenience blameless supremacy was established.

This means that, if we're going to enter repentance, we're going to have to make other people's survival more important than our comfort or our convenience.

We need to seek repair, and when the question comes *yes but who's going to pay for that?* we have to be willing to put up our hands.

If we want repair, we're going to have to pay the bill.

◆ ◆ ◆

The *opposite* of repentance is resentment—entitled sullen anger at the sight of people moving the world toward repair—and saboteurs of repair will foster resentment by sabotaging our confession with denial.

The *opposition* to repentance is the fourth sabotage: **oppression**.

The first three sabotages comprise suppression. Ignorance suppresses awareness; complacency suppresses conviction; denial suppresses confession. Suppression means you stop repair before you even have to fight it, by convincing people to not fight. But blameless supremacists are certainly willing to fight if they have to.

Oppression is a show of strength, meant to cover its great weakness—because oppression is what happens when blameless supremacy gets desperate. Oppression means suppression has failed, and now people are actually moving to align themselves with repair, which means that repair is about to happen, and that will mean paying the costs, including the cost of blame.

Blameless supremacists will do anything to prevent that from happening—*anything*. They'll raise the stakes as high as they must to preserve their supremacy. They'll harm whoever they can, as much as they can. Blameless supremacists will destroy society itself before they pay for their share of it.

As, I'd argue, we can very easily observe these days.

Above all, blameless supremacy sabotages oppositional repentance in order to claim as its exclusive property the right to define, and to **define people** most of all. It insists on imposing a reality founded on that right, under which it gets to define what human experience is permitted to be, under which a person's right to exist is not a foregone conclusion, but something that will be established and mediated by what supremacy is comfortable allowing.

Blameless supremacy claims an exclusive right to define oppression as the discomfort a supremacist is made to feel, by the existence of undeserving people who do not matter, living outside the boundaries of supremacist permission. Blameless supremacy claims an exclusive right to hurt you, and then define whether or not you were hurt, and whether or not the definition of *you* it forces you to live should bother you, and whether or not the attempt to control and define your existence should be allowed to be seen as the hate it is, or whether it must be praised as love.

And I think that's sabotage.

Why sabotage? To make realignment toward repair difficult and unpopular, by leaving all control and leverage and priority of place in the hands of those opposed to repair. To make all the steps of sabotage easier and more popular than the steps of repair. To borrow against that popularity to lend credibility to oppression, and to make the perspective of oppressive supremacists the dominant one, to the point that opposing oppression is itself framed as an oppressive act. To establish every flavor of supremacy as the preferred natural order, and any existence of human beings outside of those bounds as oppressive aggression to be punished. To force people to engage in a daily fight to exist as themselves—in order to frame the people who engage in that fight as aggressors to the preferred natural order, and then to use that framing as a pretext for further oppression.

Oppression exists to make oppositional repentance hard, and painful, and draining, so that people stay away from repentance, and resent those who oppose oppression. It all amounts to sabotage: a refusal to align toward repair, in favor of an alignment toward brokenness.

This is a sabotage that makes oppression inevitable, and an inevitability that makes the cost of repentance high—high enough that people will choose blameless supremacy instead.

And remember, it's all to avoid the threat of improvement; all to avoid the costs of repair; all to preserve the profits from the higher costs of brokenness.

This is oppression: the fourth step in the sabotaging work of blameless supremacy.

What is our work of repentance?

Here's my suggestion: find your comfort, and investigate it.

I want to be clear and I want to be careful here.

I'm not asking you to *seek* discomfort.

Comfort isn't bad in itself. Comfort is a necessary aspect of being human, and we all could use a bit more comfort these days. Just find your comfort, and investigate.

And maybe ask: where does my comfort depend on the discomfort of others?

A blameless society expects its members to participate in a shared blamelessness—in the reflexive act of giving first priority to the accommodation of the desires and preferences of its members, no matter how harmful or morally indefensible their actions and beliefs, because doing so preserves our own comfort, too. I think the answer to this problem is, we have to stop accommodating supremacy's ignorances and complacencies and denials, even though accommodation is more comfortable for us than opposition. And too often, we choose the mutual comfort of giving that accommodation.

So let's repent of all that.

This may be uncomfortable work, and it may bear a heavy cost. But it's worthy work, and a sustainable and just world is a reward worth the price.

Let's do that work. Let us refashion our priorities and our society until *justice* becomes the way of ease, until it is enacting injustice that carries the heaviest burdens and costs. May we never abandon our friends and neighbors and parents and siblings for the sake of comfort, or to avoid the cost of repair. May we always increase the awareness of injustice, and thus the discomfort of conviction, and thus the visibility of confession, and thus the inevitable growth of the momentum toward a new human spirit with a new intention.

Most of all, let us repent with our whole being, and let us change.

Repentance transforms.

◆ ◆ ◆

What do we do next? After repentance, the next thing to do is to repair. You might say *reparation*.

Why do we need repentance? Because if you realize you're going the wrong way, and stop, and determine to go back, then you have to turn yourself back in the right direction before you start walking again.

We need repentance because until we repent, we'll never set our compasses for a return. We need repentance, because it points us back home—a home many of us have dreamed of but never seen. We need repentance, because until we have repented, we haven't agreed to pay the cost of repair, which means we'll never pay, which means the work won't ever happen.

We need repentance, because it leads to reparation.

7. REPARATION & WAR
We're almost there.

Awakening brings us to conviction, brings us to confession, brings us to repentance, brings us at last to reparation, where the work gets done, where the cost gets paid. When reparation repairs not just our nation's streets but our national spirit, repair might also be thought of as the work of redemption.

Let's talk about reparation.

◆ ◆ ◆

A compass will only take you so far.

The compass is not the journey. Even the navigation is not the journey. Moreover, the compass and the navigation are useless without the journey, which is not meant to disparage the compass. The compass is vital. It's the first thing. It *has* to be the first thing. Without the compass, we don't know we need to move, or where we're going, and we can't make adjustments on the way. Without a direction and a destination, we'll never imagine a new and better location to which to move. Nor is this meant to disparage the navigation. The navigation is vital. Without a plan on how to get to where we want to go, and tools to measure and track our way, we'll never know how to arrive at our destination, or whether we're nearer or farther from it, or even whether or not we've arrived.

The compass and the navigation are the *first* things.

But . . . the compass and the navigation are *only* the first things.

Without the journey, there is no movement: no departure, no progress, no arrival.

Without repair, nothing gets fixed. Right?

Awakening doesn't result in repair, if awakening doesn't convict you. Knowing the streets are broken doesn't fix the streets if you don't care that they are broken. Your conviction doesn't fix the streets, unless you confess it. If you care whether or not the streets are fixed but keep it to yourself, the streets will remain broken. Your confession doesn't fix the streets without repentance. Saying that the streets need to be fixed but not re-aligning toward fixing them leaves them broken. And repentance doesn't fix the streets if, once realigned toward reparation, you never actually enact the repair. It doesn't matter if you agree to fix the streets, if you don't actually fix them.

Awareness, conviction, confession, repentance . . . these will set your compass, but eventually you have to get moving. So why, after doing all of the rest of the work of repair, would we fail to get moving? I'd suggest it's because there's real risk to moving. While the compass and the navigation represent the idealized forms of our intentions, the journey has no such advantage. The journey's advantage is also its disadvantage: the journey will be real. The journey is guaranteed to involve adventure and failure and setbacks and unfortunate happenstance and unexpected obstacles and challenges and complexities, and unforeseen successes and benefits and gain.

The journey can be expensive.

The journey can be dangerous.

The journey is *hard*.

The journey might not succeed.

If the journey is long enough, not everyone will see the end of it.

Because of this, we can expect to find many people who *agree* with the compass—the direction in which to travel—and also *agree* with the navigation—the plan for how to get there—but who, when it comes time for the journey, decide they'd rather not go.

And for those people, blameless supremacy is there, ready to provide reasons to not go.

We should be clear about what reparation is. It's literally repair. It's fixing what is broken—*whatever* is broken. Restoration of material loss, to be sure, but also dismantling lies and replacing them with truth, rejecting false understanding and replacing it with better understanding, replacing complacency with the natural human instinct to give a shit, replacing false denials with true confession, turning from a path oriented toward our foundational lies and onto a path oriented toward a belief in a shared natural human system; deconstructing supremacist structures and replacing them with structures that accommodate all.

When people hear "reparation" they tend to think "money." And sure enough, reparation can involve money—and probably should, as long as money is still how value is most easily distributed in our natural human system. But money is only the simplest way reparation is paid.

Remember, a system based on corruption and abuse—which is theft and harm—generates blamelessness precisely because blamelessness holds itself to be perfect, and as perfection cannot be improved, so blamelessness acts as a bulwark against the cost of paying for improvements. A system based on abuse wants by its very nature to avoid paying any cost. As such, a blameless system will treat the idea of reparation as dangerous foolishness and an existential threat. It will go to any lengths to prevent a world in which reparation is even a possibility. But the *reason* a blameless system attacks every other step in the realigning work of repair is because a blameless system knows that those steps inevitably lead to this moment of payment, and it knows full well—on the deepest levels of intention—that reparation will cost them more than money. They know it will cost them something even more valuable, available even to supremacy's most impoverished adherent, which is the bedrock of supremacist power: the inheritance of unimprovable unfixable exceptional blamelessness.

Reparation, as you're probably well aware, is not a popular word these days. To me, this is as good a way as any of detecting just how aligned we are as a society with brokenness. If I am opposed to paying any costs, then I am also opposed to every one of the steps in repair's process. And, as blame for brokenness is a cost of repair, if I am opposed to paying costs, then I must create a narrative of my own blamelessness. And, as remaining in brokenness carries a much higher cost than repair, I must find other people to pay those higher costs—which means creating a narrative that some people matter less than me, and in fact are the cause of the brokenness, and therefore deserve all cost and all blame of brokenness. And it is this last thing—this belief that I matter more than others, or that I matter while others do not—that makes me a supremacist. So, to be a person opposed to the costs of repair—that is, opposed to reparations—inevitably means joining with blameless supremacy—becoming a blameless supremacist. And, if a society is one where most people say they want to see broken things fixed, yet repair never comes because they oppose reparations, one could conclude that such a society is, at its core, a blameless supremacist society—a society that sabotages the process of reparation and never lets itself know about it, to avoid paying any cost.

There are so many reasons to not pay the cost of reparation, aren't there?

Here are just a few:

It's unrealistic, it's impractical, it's too complex, it would be too expensive, the abuses happened too long ago, the abuses can't even be proved, it's hateful, it's divisive, it's disruptive, it's un-helpful, we aren't ready as a culture, other people would never go along with it, it wasn't my direct ancestor doing the stealing, it wasn't your direct ancestors stolen from, it wasn't actually that bad anyway, the beneficiaries will become lazy and depen-dent, some of the people who would benefit are very wealthy already, the beneficiaries don't deserve it, I'm not convinced it's a good idea, I don't see proof it's necessary.

There are so many reasons to not pay.

There's always a reason to not take the journey toward repa-ration and justice.

Those who oppose repair will make sure of it.

I think that's sabotage—deliberate sabotage of the natural, progressive, redemptive, realigning process of repair.

I'd like to name this sabotage now.

But first, I think it would be good to review, one last time, how repair gets sabotaged by blameless supremacy. Just as the process of repair is a progressive and restorative sequence, so sabotage is a series of regressive and violent steps.

Any awakening to awareness is sabotaged by deliberate man-ufactured *ignorance.*

And, if ignorance fails, blameless supremacy attacks any conviction that arises from awareness with a *complacency* that uses any excuse it can find.

And, if complacency fails, blameless supremacy attacks any confession of awareness or conviction with a *denial* that casts oppressors as perpetual victims, and casts victims as aggressive oppressors.

And, if denial fails, and people actually begin to align their beliefs and resources and intentions toward repair, then blame-less supremacy abandons the suppressive tactics of ignorance and complacency and denial, and attacks repentance through an active *oppression*, which makes awareness and confession of truth, and conviction and intention to repair, and the very existence of people who supremacy deems do not matter, into crimes.

And if oppression fails? If people actually start to repair what is broken, and maintain what has been abandoned, and improve what has stagnated, what then? What does blameless supremacy do when supremacy itself starts to fail?

Blameless supremacy will always fight every step of the process leading to reparation.

But—it will go to war to prevent reparation itself.

Will? Has.

Does.

The final sabotage is **war**.

Literally, war.

◆ ◆ ◆

War arises from supremacy's point of greatest weakness, so supremacy only wages war once all its other sabotages have begun to fail, once repair has been made so inevitable by redemptive movement that reparation actually starts to happen. If all previous sabotage fails, and the actual repair begins, blameless supremacy will start to actively destroy our natural human system.

My country is the United States. Let's talk about my country's Civil War.

My country's Civil War was a war fought to preserve and expand human slavery, and it failed. And I find it usefully accurate to call it not The Civil War, but The Failed War to Preserve and Expand Slavery. It strikes me that the most common mistake we make about The Failed War to Preserve and Expand Slavery is to think of it as something that *happened*, instead of something that *happens*—a murderous urge, opposed to natural costs, present in the very founding of our nation, continued as a tradition and a heritage ever since. Supremacists have been fighting this war against other people throughout the history of this nation. It seems to me that it's been a war waged without cease.

And yes, there was a time in my country's history, from 1860 to 1864, that this war flared into battles between armies of U.S. citizens opposing one another on battlefields. That war, again, was waged to safeguard and expand the right to own other human beings, with the justification that those other human beings were Black, and whiteness was self-evidently supreme. So the war was waged over the right to protect and expand the white supremacy that undergirded the slavery that allowed whiteness to profit from brokenness, and this was a brokenness it caused by making other people—those they enslaved, but also anybody else who had to compete against an economy founded in free labor—pay the much higher costs of brokenness. The supremacists who fought for this sad and destructive and unsustainable cause saw this cause as their heritage. You'll never guess: they claimed to be blameless. They said it was everyone else's fault. These wagers of war said *they* were the victims of aggression. Their descendants—some of them moral descendants, some of them literal descendants, still say so.

Go ask them if you doubt me. Don't expect polite answers.

So that was an easily recognizable war. But the war didn't really end at Appomattox any more than it began at Fort Sumter. The war still happens every day.

Question: What do I mean by *war?*

It's hard to know where to start.

I could start almost anywhere.

Life expectancy for Black people is only 71.8 years compared to 77.6 years for people deemed "white," according to the Kaiser Family Foundation.

Let's start there.

That's a difference of 5.8 years, according to the math I just did in my head. According to the last U.S. census, there are 41.1 million Black people in the United States. In the next 75 years or so *something* is going to steal 238.38 million years of Black people's lives. That's 3.07 million full lives over the next 75 years, if life expectancy is 77.6 years. That's almost 41,000 people a year, every year.

I had to use a calculator for all that.

In the United States, *something* is stealing life—a *lot* of life—from Black people. It's killing the equivalent of 41,000 full lives a year, or about a tenth of the full loss of life the United States endured in World War II, every year. If that *something* is intentional, I think we should think of it as war—a genocidal war, no less.

Let me put my cards on the table and flip them over: I think that *something* is supremacy, and I think supremacy is intentional, so I think that *something* is war.

Literally, war.

I know that this way of framing the matter can result in a lot of argument and dissent, and if these words are ever widely shared, I daresay they will have that result. And I think it will be very interesting to see how many of the arguments against this framing will utilize blameless supremacy's sabotages. It will be interesting to see, for example, how many arguments are formulated and offered in an ignorant spirit that is incurious about the problem, demanding to establish as a first priority the idea that this discrepancy is *not* intentional, and is in fact caused by any number of factors that are unknowable and unsolvable, to such a degree that any attempt to know these factors or address them or solve them is dangerous foolishness, and that any facts presented in an attempt to know or to solve these factors should be preemptively considered inadmissible and unacceptable.

I think it will be interesting to see how many of those arguments are formulated and offered in a complacent spirit that makes it clear that the argument is being presented in order to find reasons *not* to solve the problem of racially based lifespan discrepancies in the United States, or to find reasons to not even see it as a problem, or to suggest that the problem cannot be solved, or should not be solved, or must be solved exclusively by Black people who are having millions of years stolen away from them, because—since it is Black people who suffer from it—it is a *Black problem.*

I think it will be interesting to see how many of these arguments are formulated and offered in an oppressive spirit, that makes the case that the thing stealing millions of years from Black people is Black people themselves; that they are somehow naturally and unavoidably to blame, or in some way intrinsically physically or spiritually defective, fated to—or even deserving of—the loss of these millions of years.

I think it will be interesting to see how many of these arguments are formulated and offered in a spirit designed to sabotage our awakening to awareness of the problem, and our conviction that it is a problem, and any public confession of the problem, and any alignment toward repair of the problem, and most especially any actual repair and any cost of repair of the problem.

How many of the arguments will be formulated and offered in such a spirit? A lot, if my previous encounters with such arguments serve as any indication. Almost all of them, actually.

And what I think is most revealing is the hostility that inevitably attends these arguments, whenever there is any attempt to know or broadcast this fact about racially based life expectancy; the anger that arises whenever there is an attempt to locate the causes; the atavistic, almost instinctive rage that erupts whenever it seems that our systems might actually be aligning to try to address those causes; the way that any actual attempts to do so are spoken of almost exclusively in terms of cost, the way that cost is spoken of almost exclusively as theft, the way accusations of theft are used as a rationale to promote and excuse further violence and marginalization and harm, and to ensure that any efforts to address the problem are made to fail, and the way the manufactured failure is used as proof that any attempts to repair are fated to fail.

And I think these reactions to solving real problems actually reveal the deeper intention, the true intention—an intent to not repair our most foundational brokenness, which is supremacy itself. Which demonstrates to me that it was intentional all along.

And I think that's war—a civil war that never stopped, that has been there since our very founding, the war of blameless supremacy against the process of repair, waged against the bodies and lives of people it demands must pay the high costs of a brokenness it refuses to fix, so it can avoid paying even the costs of its own blame for having done so. It's a determination to overthrow the government if the government ever even hints that it might stop being oppressive to people who supremacy believes have not earned life and have therefore earned oppression.

It's a determination to destroy everything, to unnaturally force everyone to pay the ultimate cost rather than personally suffer paying any natural cost.

It's a war our Founding Fathers started when they ratified accommodations to supremacy into our Constitution (right next to the soaring words about universal human freedom and equality that we might someday hope, finally and at last, and for the first time, to live up to). This is why armed supremacists captured the Michigan State Capitol in 2020, when it became clear that the government expected them to participate in efforts to contain a deadly virus, to do the tiniest things in order to help protect the lives of their fellow citizens, including those citizens who they in their supremacy deemed unworthy. This is why murderous insurrectionists attempted to overthrow the government and overturn democracy in 2021, when it became clear that our democracy—despite bestowing upon supremacists massive structural and institutional advantages of over-representation—was no longer as effective a tool for enshrining their supremacy as it once had been.

It's our Foundational War.

We're still fighting it.

We inherited it.

◆ ◆ ◆

Here's the thing: I started with life expectancy among the demographic of Black U.S. citizens. I could have started in a lot of other places.

That was the hard part of even starting.

I could start almost anywhere, really, because when you have a supremacist society, supremacy appears everywhere. I could have started with any of the other statistics in the medical arena that help explain the racial discrepancy in life expectancy by diagnosing the telltale symptoms of white supremacy: the way that Covid harms Black communities disproportionately; the way that medical care facilities and doctors treat Black patients differently than white patients; the ways that lack of access to abortion disproportionately harms Black people; the ways almost any breakdown of our heath and public apparatus disproportionately affects Black people; the ways it literally steals life from Black people.

Or I could start by talking about the effects of wealth supremacy or property supremacy, and how they ensure that people without property and wealth are thought of as lesser, and how those without property and wealth are made to struggle to survive as a result, and how all of this robs people without property and wealth of opportunity for property and wealth, steals their time and energy and resources until it becomes almost impossible for them to generate enough profit to be permitted to exist for a while longer; how it makes people without property or wealth disproportionately more likely to experience insecurity and deprivation of food and water and shelter, and more susceptible to poor health and illness and disease and pain and assault and brutalization and early death. The way these supremacies steal the lives of impoverished people—literal years of their lives, in ways that are statistically measurable, because they are the people forced to pay the higher costs of brokenness by blameless suprem- acists who refuse to shoulder their own share of the lower costs of repair, in order to go on profiting from an unnatural system designed to consume human beings.

Or I could start by talking about the effects of all these supremacies within our apparatuses of lawmaking and legal enforcement and prosecution and punishment, and the way all punishment is disproportionately levied against people without wealth or property, and the ways it resists enforcement of any real consequence against those with wealth and property, until as a practical matter "crime" actually must be understood not as in- fractions against the law's letter, but rather the act of existing as a person whose life has been determined to not matter. I could talk about all the statistically measurable ways this enforcement system exists to protect property and wealth rather than people, and the violence that causes, and the ways these systems prof- it by imprisoning human beings in greater numbers than any other nation in the world, and the conditions of hidden legal slavery this manufactures. I could talk about the lives it steals— literal years of human lives, and the profits this generates for already wealthy people.

Or I could start with all the ways that this application and operation of the supremacist apparatus of law encourages blameless supremacists to see society as exclusively theirs, and to resent any incursion into society by anyone who is not them; or how our lawmakers ensure that supremacists, puffed up with entitlement and resentment, never lack for targets or massacre weapons that make violence and massacre and terror and in-surrection not only a likely response to any attempt to repair all this inequality and supremacy, but an inevitable one. I could talk about the inevitable conclusions that must eventually be reached: that the reason we have a political apparatus that op-poses any attempt to curtail massacres is because that political apparatus desires massacres as a matter of policy and strategy; that massacres should be seen not as isolated events, but as a shadow war, fought by terrorists in uniform and by civilian terror cells, radicalized and armed by a far-right supremacist political apparatus that protects supremacist terrorism, allows it to par-ticipate at scale in our law enforcement and military, and insists on bestowing to supremacists the ability to kill those it believes need to die, and to call its murders "self-defense," as a founda-tional component of what it calls "freedom."

Or I could circle all the way back around to talk about the ways white supremacy guarantees that all the adverse effects of the application, operationalization, and enforcement of wealth supremacy and property supremacy just so happen to ensure—as a matter of historical record and a matter of current public policy—that wealth and property are disproportionately more difficult for Black people to acquire and hold, and that the pun-ishments for failing to acquire them fall disproportionately upon Black people, stealing from them hundreds of billions of dollars. I could talk about how this theft of wealth and property inevitably steals life—literal years of literal lives, in ways that are statistically measurable.

Or I could talk about how male supremacy ensures that it all falls more heavily on women.

Or I could talk about how able-bodied supremacy ensures that it all falls more heavily on people who are sick and disabled.

Or I could talk about how Christian supremacy ensures that it all falls more heavily on people who do not adhere to suprem-acist interpretations of Christian dogmas.

Or I could talk about how gender supremacy ensures that it all falls more heavily on people who are gay and trans and intersex and nonbinary.

And the more I did this, trying and failing to start, the more we might begin to think that the whole thing is a connected web of overlapping and interlocking supremacies, of wealth supremacy and male supremacy and white supremacy and Christian supremacy that in actuality is all one supremacy; a supremacy that different people decide to participate in from different levels of privilege seeking different advantages, but which all amounts to a picture of murder and suicide: of a man with an empty gas can and two torches standing atop the prow of a lone sinking boat aflame in the middle of an icy ocean, laughing at the horrified faces of everyone else as the deck tilts toward the sky, and screaming: "Enjoy swimming, you fuckers! This boat is MINE!"

That's the final joke, you know; the punchline: everyone dies. Supremacy is designed to eat people, and so, if you are a person, it will eventually eat you.

Everyone's life expectancy is sinking.

Blameless supremacy enacts its war against repair, for brokenness; against sustainability, for unsustainability, against an attainable generative society, for an impossible individuality; against life, for death. It's a war being waged by supremacist saboteurs fighting for the right to be allowed to sink our shared boat, just for the privilege of being last to drown. This is our Foundational War, which we have inherited, in which we don't get to not participate; we just get to decide how we want to fight, and how we want to align ourselves.

It's a war being fought over whether or not humanity intends to consume itself.

Supremacists are fighting to make sure that humanity does consume itself, and many of them think that after it does, they'll all go to a gated community that they call "heaven."

I dare to hope you have aligned yourself in opposition to that. I think we had better win.

◆ ◆ ◆

The *opposite* of reparation is brokenness—disrepair, degradation, injustice, theft, corruption—and saboteurs of repair will foster brokenness by sabotaging our repentance with oppression.

The *opposition* to reparation is the final and greatest sabotage: war. Literally, war, that old desire of our foundational lies. Literally genocide and slavery.

Let's talk about something basic. Let's talk about water.

Let's talk about the town of Flint, MI, a town of 95,000, where people went years without drinkable water, and some still don't have it, nearly a decade later. You can learn that Nestlé (whose former chairman and CEO, Peter Brabeck-Letmathe, believes that water should be sold as a commodity rather than protected as a human right) donated 1.6 million bottles of water in relief to Flint, and you can also learn that Governor Rick Snyder, who presided over the strangulation of Flint, sold Michigan aquafers to Nestlé for $200 a year, but you won't usually discover both things in the same place, with lines clearly drawn between these two very proximal points.

Yes, and also Louisiana Attorney General Jeff Landry is delaying funds needed to operationalize the Sewage & Water Board of New Orleans, funds that this city of 400,000 needs for flood response—in retribution for that city not complying with Louisiana's harmful and predatory abortion bans.

Yes, and now, in the year 2022, Jackson, Mississippi, a town of 163,000, has had no water for months, after decades of neglect of its infrastructure.

And Puerto Rico, a U.S. territory of over 3 million people, suffered a power outage for weeks this year due to a hurricane, on the 5-year anniversary of the hurricane where it was left without power for nearly a year by politicians who refused to recognize that *they* were *us*.

The people of Puerto Rico happen to be mostly brown people, it just so happens. The people affected by the neglected water emergencies in New Orleans and Jackson and Flint are predominately Black people, it just so happens.

Nothing racial, I'm often told. It just happens that way. Noticing race in these situations is the real racism, I'm often told.

The American system, which is an exceptional system, is blameless.

We could expand this globally, to look at how we are dealing with climate catastrophe generally, and the disasters that are coming and the ones that have already come, and the populations that we are making pay for our neglectful convenience in so many ways, including lack of access to potable water. We could talk about the ways supremacy plays into climate injustice, to ensure that the burden for climate catastrophe will fall first and hardest on those who had least to do with the causes. We could talk about how those people are most often people of color, people in poverty, people considered by supremacy to not matter.

We could talk about so many things.

We could talk about almost *anything*.

If you confront a blameless supremacist about this, you'll learn that there are a host of reasons why this doesn't have anything to do with them, why those who suffer are to blame for their suffering, why they themselves feel no responsibility for it and resent the suggestion they should, and use their resentment as an excuse to pursue accelerated retributive harm—all rationales designed to negotiate away a simple fact about water, which is that human beings need drinkable water to live, and without it they die, so if you prevent people from having access to drinkable water, you're killing them, and if you decide to enter into a human spirit that makes access to drinkable water a matter of deserving it, you're aligning with a spirit that will eventually make genocide and war not only likely but inevitable, to such a degree that it has to be considered intentional. Supremacy is the willing and unnatural reconfiguration of our natural human society—which provides its shared, foundational, generative inheritance of benefits automatically and inextricably—so that it instead delivers inherited harm and inherited theft, while passing on the cost of responsibility to the victims, so that it consumes more and more people to the benefit of fewer and fewer.

It's war.

◆ ◆ ◆

Above all, blameless supremacy sabotages reparation in order to claim **society itself,** and all the value it naturally delivers, as the exclusive property of blameless supremacists, in order to establish a framework whereby any systemic or individual violence committed to keep society as its exclusive property is automatically seen as justified self-defense, and any claim of ownership of society from anyone else is seen as an aggressive act of theft, justifying whatever retributive and punitive aggression that comes in response.

And I think that's sabotage.

Why sabotage?

To make supremacy popular, and then to borrow against that popularity to lend it credibility, and then use that credibility to further increase supremacy's popularity. To force people to engage in a daily fight to defend a just claim for reparation, in order to frame the people who engage in that fight as the aggressors, as a pretext for waging further war against them. To make repair an unfavorable option, a difficult burden, and highly undesirable compared to the relative ease of capitulation to supremacy. To make repair hard, and painful, and draining, so that people learn to instinctively avoid repair, and resent those who enter into the progressive redemptive work of reparation. To recontextualize the natural act of repairing what is broken into an unacceptably aggressive act of war. It all amounts to sabotage: a refusal to fix broken things, to avoid paying any of a society's natural costs, while reaping all of a society's benefits.

It's the promise that before you can repair things that are broken, you will have to fight people who would rather die than see broken things fixed. And people quite naturally don't want to fight. So, at every stage of the process of repair, blameless supremacy threatens escalation and offers de-escalation; a higher and escalating cost for refusing to accommodate supremacy, and a significant discount for accommodating it.

The offer is this: uncomplicated relationships and comfortable rewards for those who show neutrality to ignorance, who provide compromise to complacency, who offer exonerations to those who deny any responsibility for brokenness, who appease brokenness by agreeing to stay in our broken frame. And the threat is this: discomfort, vilification, and attacks against those who are biased enough against supremacy to insist on witnessing to the reality of brokenness; attacks against those who are hopeful enough to believe that repair is possible and to demand it; attacks against those who possess the moral clarity to know who is benefitting from the higher cost of brokenness and who is being forced to pay; and attacks against those who enter into an unshakable solidarity with people who suffer from our broken culture of blameless supremacy. The purpose of the offer and of the threat is this: to make sure the cost of repair is always made unnaturally higher than the cost of brokenness, for a long enough time, so that people learn to desire brokenness and fear repair.

War is the final threat, the final escalation. War is blameless supremacy's response to repair; it's the determination to destroy and kill rather than suffer unacceptable natural costs of repair and maintenance and improvement. Again, this is literally war—

something which steals people's lives in ways that we can detect and observe. Supremacy is a sabotage that makes war and genocide and slavery inevitable, to such a degree that supremacy and war and genocide and slavery should be considered commingled.

And remember, it's all to avoid the threat of improvement; all to avoid the costs of repair; all to preserve the profits from the higher costs of brokenness.

This is war: the final step in the sabotaging work of blameless supremacy.

You can always tell when sabotage has taken hold; it's when you see people who claim they want solutions accommodating the people opposed to solutions by accepting their framing, and using it as a reason to not take the journey their compasses have set.

If you accept their frame, you'll always be inside their picture.

It strikes me that we've all been living inside a frame built by saboteurs for a very long time. It strikes me that almost all of us are, to some degree or another, very fine people. This strikes me as the ultimate mirror that won't let us see ourselves; the ultimate bubble.

Let's pop it.

◆ ◆ ◆

Time to tell a different story.

Time to talk about a different frame.

Repair reframes.

Repair pays.

Repair redeems.

A question: *what does it redeem?*

REDEMPTION
(October 2021–April 2023)

1. THE BIG QUESTION
What do we do now?

We fix our streets.

How do we fix our streets?

We change our compass—our national spirit, our global atmosphere.

We change our spirit by moving the frame.

We move the frame by telling a new story.

Let me tell you a story.

◆ ◆ ◆

When my kids were little, we lived by a park, which is still there even though we don't live by it anymore. The park has a small and little-cared-for playground, a couple basketball courts, some picnic tables—the usual park stuff. Also, it has a large cement floor next to a little house.

The floor is in the shape of a swimming pool. The house is a pool house.

Was a pool house.

The cement floor is a cement plug, filling what had been a public swimming pool in a public park. What happened to the pool? I don't know the particulars of this particular pool, but we know what happened to many public pools. We sabotaged them.

We.

In the 1950s and '60s in the U.S., municipalities started to integrate their public swimming pools, in part due to legal mandates, in part perhaps because of the fact that segregation is cruel and unjust, and people have always known that, no matter what people say now about "a different time." So, municipalities—whether voluntarily or not—made public spaces available to everybody. A simple thing. A good thing. The right thing.

What happened next was this: White people violently rioted. In *The Sum of Us: What Racism Costs Everyone and How We Can Prosper Together,* Heather McGhee writes of one example of this fun revival of an old white-supremacist tradition:

[T]wo hundred white residents surrounded the pool with "bats, clubs, bricks and knives" to menace the first thirty or so Black swimmers. Over the course of the day, a white mob that grew to five thousand attacked every Black person in sight around the Fairground Park.

What happened after *that* was this: Municipalities closed the swimming pools.

It was a choice.

The city decided.

Cities could have left the pools open, and used law enforcement to put down the violent rioting of white people willing to fight for injustice. Cities were certainly every bit as comfortable using law enforcement to put down crowds of protesting people back then as they are now. But they didn't, because the cities were oriented to accommodate the psychological and physical comfort of the people it deemed "white," even if what the white people wanted was morally indefensible, obviously illegal, and clearly made things worse. It might be useful to coin a word to describe this strange phenomenon, whereby cities accommodate one group over another, even if the preferred group's preference is to harm the public good.

How about this word: supremacy.

I want you to pay attention to an important distinction now, as it's one that's usually missed—I'm tempted to say *purposefully* missed, but intentions are always so unknowable.

Here is the distinction: The violent white people were supremacists, but the violence of the white people wasn't the supremacy. The decision of people with the power to accommodate them anyway—*that* was the supremacy.

The accommodation is the supremacy.

The accommodation *is* the supremacy.

So, because of the supremacy of people deemed "white"—because of *white* supremacy—perfectly good public swimming pools closed. It was a withering of the commons—and it was not exclusive to pools. We could be talking about schools. We could be talking about housing. We could be talking about many things. Because of the supremacy, the public sphere, which existed for public use and public benefit, withered and died. In fact, the courts decided that if white supremacist people wanted to use the channels of our natural human system to deliver harm to the community to which they belonged, then the systems that existed to accommodate them should be allowed to deliver harm.

Again, Heather McGhee:

Draining public swimming pools to avoid integration received the official blessing of the U.S. Supreme Court in 1971. The city council in Jackson, Mississippi, had responded to desegregation demands by closing four public pools and leasing the fifth to the YMCA, which operated it for whites only. Black citizens sued, but the Supreme Court, in *Palmer v. Thompson,* held that a city could choose not to provide a public facility rather than maintain an integrated one, because by robbing the entire public, the white leaders were spreading equal harm.

Now, it wasn't true that the harm *was* being spread equally, but it was the position of white supremacists that the harm was being spread equally, and our systems were oriented to accommodate the abstracted stated intentions of white people as accurate, even if that position, when put into practice, was observably false. And so, because of the supremacy of white people, the courts agreed with their little white lie, which was that white leaders were spreading harm equally. And we could be talking about crumbling streets. We could be talking about access to the vote. We could be talking about access to health care. We could be talking about many things. The courts agreed to accommodate the desires of supremacists, and to find their nonsense rationales credible, and so delivered a supremacist verdict, by which I mean it was a verdict aligned with blameless supremacy. I'd argue this means it was a verdict aligned with sabotage of the process of repair.

And so, these days, most cities don't have very many public swimming pools. Instead, they have cement floors in the middle of public parks abandoned by white people who wanted a less-functional society and a less-valuable public commons, and moreover were willing to pay for it; who wanted inequality and injustice, and moreover were willing to fight for it; who were supported by a city oriented to accommodate their desires over the clear mandate to maintain a functional city. There was no legal remedy to counter this. It's not illegal to close public swimming pools, after all. And it's not illegal to pay for a private club, even if the cost of that club acts as a barrier along lines of affordability to something that had once been a public good, and even if "affordability" just so happened to affect racial minorities more than those who deemed themselves "white."

Over the next decade, millions of Americans who once swam in public for free began to pay to swim rather than swim for free with Black people, as desegregation in the mid-fifties coincided with a surge in backyard pools and members-only swim clubs.

Let's make it three for McGhee:

In Washington, D.C., for example, 125 new private swim clubs were opened in less than a decade following pool desegregation in 1953. The classless utopia faded, replaced by clubs with two-hundred-dollar membership fees and annual dues. A once-public resource became a luxury amenity, and entire communities lost out on the benefits of public life and civic engagement once understood to be the key to making American democracy real.

I guess the reason I'm thinking about the swimming pools today is because, as you may have noticed, there's a pandemic on, and elected officials are killing thousands and thousands of their own constituents, and moreover doing so seems to be a prerequisite for these officials, if they want to retain the loyalty of the people they're killing, and a lot of us are curious why.

It's understandable to be curious. It's a curious thing.

Just to state the facts: we're entering year three of a global pandemic. Before it began, the White Christian president disbanded our pandemic task force, to save money. In year one, he told everyone the pandemic was a hoax. He downplayed the coming severity even though he had been told better by people more knowledgeable than he. He suppressed the report of the numbers of infections. He decried the use of masks. He fought with governors who tried to take the recommended precautionary steps. He withheld needed supplies from those governors. He suggested junk remedies. He caught the virus himself and made no attempt to not spread it. He promoted news services that spread outright misinformation designed to increase the spread.

Hundreds of thousands of people died. And a large and vocal minority, tens of millions of mostly white people, didn't support him despite it, but *because* of it.

They loved him for spreading the virus, and still do.

These days there are, thankfully, vaccines, which prevent transmission in many cases and death in almost all cases—at least until a variant pops up that can circumvent the vaccines. And, of course, if we continue to accommodate the preferences of people who would rather not get the vaccine, then eventually we will see the emergence of such a variant, and back to square one we'll go. And that's exactly what supremacists all seem to want.

Republican elected officials are doing everything they can to prevent the vaccine's adoption, and doing everything they can to sabotage our new president's frequently bad strategies, in favor of even worse strategies, or preferably no strategies, and the new president often seems willing to accommodate them. They cast endless dispersion and doubt on the vaccine. They oppose all mandates and regulation related to public health recommendations. They promote junk remedies and sources of disinformation. They even fine and penalize businesses that require vaccines for entry. And, increasingly, it is their constituents who cause our schools to close, who choke our hospitals past the breaking point, who die on social media broadcasting their swan songs of regret, and yet they don't stop, because the large and vocal minority of mostly white people who vote for them don't support them despite it, but *because* of it. They *expect* it. They *demand* it. They seem to want the societal collapse that a pandemic brings, and they are willing to pay an increasingly steep price for it, and—in order to justify this preference—are willing to abandon our shared reality to such an extent that it has become almost impossible to interact with them.

There was an extraordinary recent parade of Covid deaths that occurred within the lower echelons of the conservative anti-reality propaganda ecosystem (a network of podcasts and radio shows and blogs and vlogs and who knows what else, all dedicated to buttressing the alternate reality that supremacists demand be created for them to accommodate their false beliefs). These were not the national figures—massively famous and popular individuals on mainstream platforms who broadcast the most popular and insidious lies—no. The national figures *knew* they were spreading lies. *They'd* gotten the vaccine, and then hidden the fact from their audiences by treating any question of their vaccination status as the most personal possible thing you could ask, as if they had been asked their favorite sexual position. No, these were the tiers below, the ones who spread the lies they receive from the upper echelons—the ones who actually believe the lies, and actually didn't get the vaccine, and then got Covid, and then died, having done their part to ensure the deaths of hundreds or thousands or hundreds of thousands, and I suppose their families mourned them, but many of the rest of us are going to save our first tears for all their victims. Some of them even expressed regret for their choices in their final days, as they learned that you can get millions of people to believe lies about a global pandemic, but you can't get the virus to believe it. Some expressed regret, yes. Most held their positions right to the end, convinced that the thing that was happening could not possibly happen, because "the libs" had said it would happen.

And the question you might be asking is: *why?*

Why does this large and mostly white conservative minority want to spread a deadly virus? Why are they willing to sacrifice knowable reality and even their own lives and the lives of their loved ones in order to accomplish this?

My guess is, it's the swimming pool.

◆ ◆ ◆

I'm a middle-aged white guy, very privileged, so I'd say I first became aware of the fact that white conservatives not only were opposed to an equal society, but would literally rather see society collapse than see an equal society come about, around the time we elected a Black man as president. I realize this reality must have been detectable long before, but I do think that when Barack Obama was elected, something significant shattered in the conservative psyche. To my perspective, it feels like we elected a Black man as president—a pretty conservative (by any reasonable and traditional definition of "conservative," anyway), very status quo, very steady-as-we-go Black man, but a Black man nonetheless—and white conservative America perceived that the exclusive swimming clubs of power and influence they had created as a fortification against the rising tide of equality had been irreparably breached; decided it was time to take the swimming pool of American civic life and cement the whole thing over.

Again, I'm a middle-aged white guy with a lot of privilege, so forgive me a moment of almost impossibly naïve reverie here, but . . . there was a point not so long ago when we really did seem on the verge of potentially trying something new—a system built on real equality and justice, where accommodation would be made for all. I mean, I knew we weren't there yet and never had been, and had never even really been close—I'm naïve, but I'm not so naïve as to suggest otherwise—but it did *seem* like we might be making a try at it. We had for decades a functional Civil Rights Act, a Voting Rights Act, abortion rights. Gay people could get married. We all agreed that Nazis were bad, and that the problem to be solved when it comes to Nazis involves figuring out how best to keep them marginalized, not figuring out how to have perpetual open public dialogue with them to better understand their grievances, and anyone who suggested that white nationalists and white supremacists and Nazis would make good presidential advisors were considered suspect. There was that, at least.

It was a fool's hope, perhaps, but there did seem to be a hope, a belief that there might be a possibility that we'd actually create a pluralistic society where the response to people who were different from you could never be "make them not exist," or "make them have to be somewhere other than where I am;" a society where people who wanted to see harmful and morally indefensible things done to other people wouldn't be given preferential accommodation, simply because they had been baptized in the supremacy of their self-declared whiteness or their maleness or their Christianity.

But...even if it didn't seem likely we'd ever fully achieve this possibility, we knew there existed a large, vocal, mostly white conservative minority, who believed the possibility of an equal society was very real, who saw the coming possibility that society might no longer be arranged to give maximum accommodation to them and their desire to comfortably oppress others, and experienced that possibility as not only fearfully oppressive, but an existential threat to their fortunes and identities—to their supremacy.

And now we all *also* know—if we're still willing to observe reality—that this large and vocal minority is willing to do literally anything, no matter how destructive to public well-being and even to themselves, to prevent any part of that possibility from coming to pass.

They're ready to cement the totality of human society over.

They're willing to fight for their supremacy, and they're willing to pay.

How much are they willing to pay?

Anything, it turns out.

Even their own lives.

A question: *Do* you want an equal society of reparation, where broken things are fixed?

Another question: What are you willing to pay for it?

Why do conservatives want to spread Covid even though it collapses our shared society? is the wrong question, I think. To my mind, the right question is this: Why do conservatives want to bring about the collapse of our shared society?

I think the answer is the *shared* part.

It's the same reason that conservatives mostly no longer participate in our shared reality.

Reality isn't attractive to them, if everyone else is there, too. They don't want to share.

On some level, they seem to *want* the system to collapse specifically because the system now seems to be oriented in such a way that it will make them share. Hospitals, schools, roads, bridges, infrastructure, government, democracy—the whole "American experiment," whatever the hell that means, all needs to come crashing down. It seems to be their intention. Anyway, whatever their intention, it's certainly what they're doing.

I presume many white conservatives actually think they'll survive the coming hoped-for systemic collapse. I expect white conservatives are so used to having their physical and psychological comfort accommodated above any demands of justice or peace or stability that they on some level truly believe that, even after society crumbles, reality itself will bend to serve their needs. I presume they believe there will exist some private swimming club for reality itself, to which they, rugged individualists all, can buy membership, where the unjust and harmful society they insist upon will have not collapsed, but will go on serving them and only them.

And maybe so.

It's admittedly true that our supremacy-oriented society is likely to give them a preferred shot at survival during any systemic collapse they might help bring about. The wealthier these white conservatives are, the better the chance that they will be able to find some island upon which to perch after the flood takes it all away. But in my opinion, they'd collapse society anyway, even if they knew they wouldn't survive, for the sake of their supremacy. Their demand is a society that caters only to them, and they'd rather see it all fall than lose that privilege, and they're willing to pay for it. They're willing to kill for it and die for it. They expect their leaders to enact an increasingly self-destructive supremacy, as a prerequisite for their ongoing loyalty.

So that's what their leaders are doing, on their behalf.

Again, according to our law, there exists no legal remedy for an elected official who decides to deliver harm and death and destruction—other than removing them in elections, that is. But perhaps you've noticed that the large and vocal mostly white conservative minority is also hard at work destroying the apparatus of elections, and, again, there exists no remedy for an elected official who decides to deliver destruction, even destruction of elections. We can't stop supremacists from breaking the rules, because the rules, which are supremacist, won't allow it—which is how we can tell they are *supremacist*. And, to one extent or another, many—*most*—of us also accommodate supremacy, we people of awareness and conviction, people who confess that we see brokenness and want to see it fixed.

Why would people of awareness and conviction and confession accommodate a supremacy that makes sabotage inevitable? I fear the answer isn't so comfortable. Those of us who accommodate blameless supremacy do so because we operate within blameless supremacy, too.

Blameless supremacy offers us luxuries.

Refusing to accommodate supremacists will mean giving up those luxuries.

And we like luxuries.

So the remedy to all this is uncomfortable, by which I mean that for many of us it will involve moving from comfort to discomfort. At long last, to the extent that we do, we all have to stop participating in blameless supremacy. At all. Anywhere. By any means. If we can fix the broken supremacist urge within ourselves, we will join with a changing spirit, a realignment of the national compass.

We'll change the atmosphere that we all breathe.

We'll change the scope of what is possible.

This leads me to another question. It's the big question.

Here's the big question: *How?*

◆ ◆ ◆

How? How do we overcome the many sabotages of blameless supremacy?

I've been staring at the big question for years.

I think the answer is, we become people who reject our blamelessness and accept the reality of our inheritance. We become people who pay costs of repair rather than costs of brokenness, even if the cost of repair might be momentarily higher. A large and vocal mostly white minority of supremacists are willing to fight for their supremacy, and they'll pay for it with their lives if they must. It's why they get their way. They'll cement over our shared society, if we let them—and we're letting them. We're *accommodating* them.

I'd say it's time for us to take their supremacy and cement that over, instead.

You want a shared society of equality and repair and maintenance? Good. Me too.

We need to be willing to fight for it—and to pay the cost of the fight.

Or else we'll pay the steeper cost of accommodation.

This means we'll have to become people who can detect supremacy, and who refuse to accommodate it, and are willing to accept the discomfort that comes with that.

It means we give up our own blamelessness, and become people of repair.

Good. But again: *How?*

Well . . . how do we accommodate supremacy?

◆ ◆ ◆

I find it useful to understand sabotage of reparation as a process, with its own regressive steps; each with its own luxurious accommodation.

There is sabotage of our awareness with ignorance, accommodated by **neutrality.**

There is sabotage of our conviction with complacency, accommodated by **compromise.**

There is sabotage of our confession with denial, accommodated by **exoneration.**

There is sabotage of our repentance with suppression, accommodated by **reconciliation.**

There is sabotage of reparation itself with war, accommodated by **surrender.**

Here's an observation: repair of streets involves tools.

It stands to reason that repair of our spirit, our compass, our atmosphere also involves tools. Some tools—wealth, certain skills, certain aptitudes—are specific, and only available to some. But I think some tools are available to us all, so I'd like to focus on those. What I hope to do now is expand on each enablement—each accommodation of each blameless supremacist step of sabotage—and try to name and describe five universal tools that we all can access, that will help us become people of awareness, convicted of our responsibilities and aligned with repair, rather than blameless people aligned with avoiding cost. Is it the *complete* answer? Certainly not. But maybe it can be the beginning of *an* answer. When I look out in the direction my compass points, it's the furthest landmark I can see.

Here we go.

2. NEUTRALITY & WITNESS
The first accommodation of blameless supremacy is an accommodation of the first sabotage—that is, accommodation of

ignorance, which sabotages awareness, which sabotages the redeeming work of repair.

Let's call this accommodation **neutrality**.

Neutrality is so pervasive, it's hard to know how to start.

How about I start with a beer commercial?

◆ ◆ ◆

"Beer commercial" is a little reductive, I confess. It was a commercial for the National Service in the UK, sponsored by a beer company. But "beer commercial" just has a little more fizz to it than "commercial featuring a mass-produced lager promoting a National Service program," so let me call it a beer commercial. The beer commercial came out several years ago; if you're curious about watching it, Google is your friend (and I might recommend "Heineken worlds apart" as your search term). It was approvingly shared recently by people I consider intelligent and well-meaning, by people who are doing good work to make the world better. It's also a great example of accommodation of ignorance. Here's how it goes: first, we hear voices of people we're about to meet, over title cards, which read:

TWO STRANGERS DIVIDED BY THEIR BELIEFS MEET FOR THE FIRST TIME

. . . and we see a large warehouse and three pairs of two strangers entering . . .

NEITHER KNOWS ANYTHING ABOUT THE OTHER OR WHAT THE EXPERIMENT IS ABOUT

. . . and we see them wordlessly walk over to some instructions and begin to read . . .

IS THERE MORE THAT UNITES THAN DIVIDES US?

. . . and then we watch the experiment unfold. The experiment involves the three pairs (there are three iterations of this experiment cut together in montage, so in each case it's just the pair alone, not the three pairs together) taking pieces scattered around the warehouse and assembling them. The pairs, naturally united into an easygoing camaraderie by the shared experience of a modestly challenging task, eventually realize they've assembled a bar. The bar is stocked with Heinekens. The pair is instructed to open two bottles, then watch a video, which shows interviews with themselves conducted at an earlier point. The pair watches the video and learns that their fellow worker is somebody who disagrees with them fundamentally on a matter of importance to them. Then, having already been confronted by the essential humanity of their ideological "other," they both have to decide what to do with this new knowledge. This is the experiment.

Will they have a beer and a chat with their new workmate?

Or will they withdraw from a new friend, over a disagreement?

Each pair decides to sit down and have a conversation with their new friend over a beer.

The idea is: Hey, if we get to know each other over shared work, we'll learn we aren't that different. Shared work brings people together. Join the National Service.

And I thought: how awful, how grotesque.

To make human beings drink Heineken.

◆ ◆ ◆

It's 2022 now, as I write this.

Let's see what's up this week in 2022.

Joe Biden gave a speech warning about the dire threat to democracy posed by the group he dubbed "MAGA Republicans," whom he correctly identified as fascists. Most people of even basic awareness would simply refer to this group as "Republicans," but the president made a point of drawing a deliberate and sharp line between Trump insurrectionists and regular Republicans. He needn't have bothered; Republicans as a whole responded by angrily identifying with MAGA Republicans, and decrying a president who would give a speech so corrosive to unity. "Unity" is suddenly apparently a very important matter to a political movement that just overturned Roe v. Wade and is passing anti-gay and anti-trans legislation, and which has spent my entire adult life pursuing a strategy of disenfranchising Black people, and which defends as justified every extrajudicial murder of every racial minority by police (or just people who like to pretend to be police), and I could go on, but honestly either you observe things that are obvious, or you don't, so, here's a period to end this sentence.

And sure enough, our consent-manufacturing apparatus heaved into gear, worrying that the president's factual words might be corrosive to "unity," without much thought given to what we are meant to unify around in order to unify with Republicans, or who we'd have to abandon in order to achieve that unity.

Joe Biden has spent his entire presidency trying to rehabilitate the image of Republicans, by the way: preaching a vision of a unity in which Republicans have steadfastly shown no interest. He even campaigned on it. He told us that once Trump was gone, we'd see a real difference in his friends across the aisle. He said we'd be really surprised.

His friends have responded by calling him a commie extremist and a sundowning puppet and a thief of the election he decisively won, and they've threatened political violence should any appropriate legal consequence befall their rabbit-eyed foundation-shellacked god prince, the White Christian president, Donald Trump.

And the White Christian president held a rally in Pennsylvania last night. At the rally, the former president bashed trans women and told his cheering throngs that Democrats are against God, among many other things. There is little reason to expect a show of concern about politicians saying things corrosive to unity similar to what we've enjoyed in response to Biden's much more measured and deliberate words.

I have not been surprised by this, I must say.

I wonder if Biden is surprised.

The current president—a man who has sometimes bent over backward to speak flattering lies about blameless supremacists—at last spoke a simple truth that is clearly observable, which is that the Republican Party is a fascist movement (he said "semi-fascist," but we take our crumbs of truth where we can). In response, a lot of people took time out of their busy schedules to make sure they expressed outrage at these "unprecedented" infractions against comity and unity and other virtues—virtues they spend the rest of their time demonstrating their clear contempt for. Meanwhile, the TV news networks, who breathlessly covered every fart of the Trump presidency, decided not to air Biden's speech—which, let's all remind ourselves, involved a sitting president speaking of a clear and present and easily observable threat to our democracy, and naming the threat, and asking for unity against it.

They aired re-runs instead.

They decided the speech was political.

Apparently they don't like it when politicians are political.

Apparently they think unifying to defend democracy is a controversial subject.

They like to stay *neutral*.

◆ ◆ ◆

Awareness is what I think is being sabotaged. Did I mention that? I think I mentioned that. And awareness is a part of a process of repair, a process we might call *reparation,* a process we might think of as a spiritual alignment toward being a people who repair and maintain rather than neglect and destroy. And sabotage is a process, too, a regressive mirror of the progressive process of repair—ignorance for our awareness, in order to defend supremacist blamelessness from the threat of improvement.

I want to repeat these points about *process*, because I think it's important to understand that these steps are work, with a predictable outcome, and it's also important to understand how all of these steps tie into one another and bleed into one another. I also want to think about process, because every time somebody gives witness to the injustices in our society—remembering the way that injustices are foundational within our history, discussing how injustice threads throughout our national story like a dominant theme in a symphony, naming the ways we hide our brokenness from ourselves, naming the people who have suffered the higher costs of brokenness, naming the people who profit from those higher costs—we suddenly hear blameless people fretting about *divisiveness*; people who have, strangely enough, rarely worried about divisiveness before.

They say things like *how can you simply condemn half the country because of different beliefs?* They say things like *that sort of polarizing rhetoric leaves no room for nuance or for people to change.* They say things like *you're treating these people as if they're irredeemably bad, and you'd feel differently if you got to know them.*

Notice the way these statements smoothly slide away from making any value judgements or clear observations. Notice how they position the problem to solve as being different *beliefs* without naming those beliefs or measuring the effects of those beliefs upon others. Notice how these statements insist on crediting people whose beliefs target others for harm with some deeper nuance beneath their intent—and notice how the people who are targeted for that harm are allowed scant room for nuance themselves. Notice the demand that we all create narratives of redemption on behalf of people who are violently opposed to any sort of redeeming work.

I think it's interesting, the assumption that witnessing to injustice would be understood as a de facto condemnation, rather than a challenge to improve. I think it's interesting, the assumption that a person who has already done the work of observing things through a new lens has neglected nuance, when doing so requires greater nuance than simply using the old lens. I think it's interesting, the assumption that a person witnessing to injustice would be assumed to simply *not know* the people enacting that injustice, since there is a massive mainstream far-right political movement in this country, and we all know people involved in it or aligned with it—friends and neighbors and colleagues—and we know that some of them are indeed very fine people.

All of these interesting assumptions rely on establishing and maintaining neutrality. Neutrality is a rhetorical tool that in a healthy context can be a very good thing—can in fact be an outcome of health and general good will that people of good will should desire in the same way that they desire any healthy contexts. But in unhealthy contexts, neutrality merely participates in abuse by never acknowledging abuse, and by believing abuse's rationales and excuses without ever marking what abuse actually does.

This neutrality is a *luxurious* neutrality, because it costs the person employing it nothing, and makes somebody else pay its often-exorbitant fees.

Let's go back to the beer commercial.

◆ ◆ ◆

A lot of people found the beer commercial inspiring, and though I didn't find it inspiring, I can see why that would be. Human connectivity is naturally inspiring. It would seem churlish to oppose it. When two people encounter each other, they are forced to observe something undeniable and powerful, which is the essence of one another's humanity. This creates connection, and connection makes othering and hatred more difficult to achieve—and that *is* good. We *should* seek such connection. I truly believe that. I'd even drink a Heineken to achieve it, if that's what was required of me. But let's return to the title card:

TWO PEOPLE DIVIDED BY THEIR BELIEFS

Three sets of two people, in fact, running three different iterations of the experiment. The commercial shows us these divisive beliefs, right at the beginning: clips from the video the two will later be asked to watch, after completing their task. There's a feminist who believes that women should be treated as equal human beings, and a man who believes that feminism is man-hating twaddle. There's an entrenched climate denier, and a man deeply concerned about climate catastrophe—that which is coming and that which is already here; those who will suffer and perish, and those who already have. And there's a trans woman who believes she is a person who deserves to exist, and an anti-trans bigot who believes that trans women don't exist.

And I have to ask myself: Are *all* these beliefs divisive?

Do *both* people within these pairings have beliefs that need changing?

Are they divided by . . . *beliefs?*

Is *that* the problem we're trying to solve?

I can't help but notice that the commercial elides the truth, which is that the trans woman has not failed to understand the bigot's essential humanity, but the bigot has rejected hers. The feminist has not failed to understand the essential humanity of men, but the anti-feminist is staunchly opposed to her humanity and believes that it threatens his, even as he threatens hers. The climate activist is not misaligned with a basic important component of modern reality, but the climate denier is. The climate activist doesn't actually have to learn anything about climate denial, and he doesn't have to convince the denier in order to believe the truth, or for that truth to be true—nor, I have to say, does there seem to be any evident interest on the denier's part to learn; he only desires that his nonsense be listened to, and greatly appreciates the climate activist's apparent willingness to spend his time doing so. Maybe after the commercial shoot was finished, the climate denier listened, and learned—but maybe not. The commercial is incurious about that matter, choosing instead to focus on whether or not these two *get along.* And I have to ask myself why attempting to change a mind that has already made itself reality-resistant is a good use of a climate activist's time, when it's far more likely that the denier's takeaway will be a reinforcement of his already-existing belief that people ought to listen to his counterfactual bullshit, and that it's good and healthy when that happens.

Neither does the feminist actually have to learn that men are people, because she already knows that, and while the conversation she is asked to have might convince the anti-feminist that women *are* equal people, it might just as easily reinforce his clear belief that his anti-female positions should in no way preclude women from treating him as if he's an awfully good bloke—after all, *she* got to know him!—when in fact she would be absolutely correct to understand him to be the threat he actually is to her well-being, absolutely correct to perceive the ways that he, despite his current situational approval of her specifically, has made himself generally comfortable with denying her essential humanity.

And then, there's this:

When an anti-trans bigot is suddenly confronted with the fact that they have been working alongside a trans woman, and are confronted with the fact that they have *already* accepted the trans woman's essential humanity, they must now decide whether or not to remain in their new awareness, or reject it and retreat to their previous ignorance, and this is a *hugely* dangerous place for any trans person to find themselves, which anybody who has spent any time listening to trans people can tell you. As the beer commercial depicts it, the bigot—after making a "joke" of stalking off and rejecting her—chooses to accept her humanity. But he might just as easily not have—and rejection was the least of the dangers present in that moment. A trans woman in that position doesn't have to make the same calculation as the bigot, because she never denied the bigot's essential humanity. She merely has correctly insisted that she be allowed to exist in society on the same level as cis men.

A trans woman in that position has a very different calculation to make.

She must decide whether or not she is about be assaulted or killed.

Yes—even in a controlled setting like a beer commercial.

Do you think that's dramatic? I would bear witness to the simple fact that it's the reality. I could provide statistics on hate crimes and murders of trans women, but honestly if you're curious you can find them, and if you have to be convinced in the year 2022 then I have to suspect you've decided not to know. And then our commercial—and all of us, too, if we find the commercial inspiring—expect this woman to have a beer with a person she rightfully ought to understand as a credible threat to her health and well-being and even her life, because of choices he has made about what to believe about people like her. We ask her—no, we *expect* her— to treat this man who is a threat to her physical well-being as if he has already proved himself to be as harmless a person as he expects everyone to understand him to be, even though he has firmly established he is not. We ask her to share a beer with that credible threat. And if she does, then he will receive the message that he's just as good as her.

And it's all performed for his personal benefit and growth. It's not for hers.

And he will be treated as if the personal growth has happened, even if it hasn't.

And she's doing it—she's being *compelled* to do it—for her safety.

And if she refused to do it, then she would be the one who failed the experiment, not him.

She would have rejected *unity.*

She would be *divisive.*

The beer commercial highlights the fact that each participant sees the other as a threat on some level, whether emotional or intellectual or physical, but ignores the fact that in each pair there is one person who is entirely wrong about their assessment, and another who is *entirely correct.*

And that's neutrality, in the context of accommodating supremacy.

It lays the burden of changing the minds of bigots and fools upon the very people who are endangered and drained by them, without even acknowledging it is doing so. It takes bigoted beliefs and puts them on the same level—that is, as a divisive problem—as the simple existence of people who make bigots uncomfortable. It neutrally equalizes two very different demands: the demand to be thought of as a human while actually being a human, and the demand to be thought of as good and safe while holding beliefs that are harmful and dangerous. It reassures people who have chosen bigotry (and other deliberate and harmful ignorance) that the problem isn't their personal ignorance in which they have specifically chosen to participate, but a general divisiveness; that the problem of divisiveness isn't that their ignorance makes other people pay a high cost for simply living, but that they, the ignorant party, haven't been *seen* properly, *listened* to enough, or *respected* sufficiently—even though they themselves have refused to see or listen or respect.

The commercial stays neutral about matters that aren't neutral. It's designed to make comfortable people feel inspired, which I know, because that's what it did. I probably watched it years ago. I might have been inspired by it then. Earlier in my journey of awakening and awareness, I certainly have watched videos like this, and have been inspired by them from a place of comfort. My awareness was sabotaged, and I enabled the sabotage by entering into a luxurious and vapid neutrality. I'm sure I still do so in many ways I don't even realize.

We've been talking about a beer commercial, but we could be talking about thousands of other messages that come to us every day. The sabotage of our awareness is something in the national spirit. Between the malicious mainstream of conservativism and the rest of us can be found a thin but permeable rind of respectable individuals committed to the proposition that there exist two and only two sides, and that both sides are equally good and equally bad, equally right and equally wrong, equally respectable. It's an active ignore-ance, ostensibly performed in the name of depolarization and comity, but actually designed to maintain a comfortable relationship with blameless supremacy—which we know, because a comfortable relationship with blameless supremacy is what it actually achieves.

◆ ◆ ◆

Neutrality is what happens when the process of repair stagnates at awareness. We see brokenness but we don't want to know what is broken, or why, or by whom, or who is harmed. We'd rather that those who suffer the brokenness do the necessary work to survive in a broken world that harms them, and we celebrate them when they agree to do that work, and we scold them if they won't.

Neutrality offers persistent and ongoing credulity in response to deliberately ignorant and debunked positions, and bestows upon credible and proven perspectives a persistent and indestructible skepticism.

Neutrality entertains public conversations about the right of different people to exist, without including the people affected by the conversation into the conversation.

Neutrality is "just asking questions."

Neutrality is "only saying what lots of people are saying."

Neutrality is "genuinely curious."

Neutrality "plays devil's advocate."

Neutrality ignores power and aggression in matters where power imbalances and abusive aggression are the primary factors; it ignores readily available solutions to problems to focus exclusively upon obstacles to those solutions; it ignores the adverse effects of abuse upon the abused to draw focus onto the adverse effects upon abusers that attends any exposure of their abusive behavior; it refuses to draw distinctions between truth and untruth, between what *is* and what is *claimed*. It isn't interested in exposing a lie as a lie, it's only interested in presenting the lie next to the truth, usually between advertisements, and then speculating like day traders over which one the public will decide to believe. Neutrality absolves itself of any accountability for delivering objective truth, takes no sides between harmful and helpful, conspiracy theory and actual threat.

Neutrality will tell you: it only reports. *You* decide.

Reality is optional, if you are one who is offered the luxury of neutrality.

Most of all, neutrality *always* takes the perspective of blameless supremacy as the given presumed default, reinforcing ignorance's claim upon reality by positioning reality as something ignorant people get to decide whether to be *persuaded* by or not. Neutrality always takes ignorance's refusal to be persuaded by the truth as evidence that the truth is not persuasive. Neutrality remains indifferent to awareness because awareness carries a cost. Neutrality doesn't take sides, to avoid the cost of being thought of as divisive. Neutrality keeps silent in the face of lies, to avoid the cost of being thought of as argumentative. Neutrality accepts the framing of ignorance and never interrogates it, but only makes sure that it is seen as understandable, which it accomplishes by understanding it without criticizing it.

Neutrality isn't neutral.

Supremacists sabotage awareness with ignorance. But the accommodation is the supremacy, and neutrality makes ignorance successful. You'll know our awareness has been sabotaged, because you'll find that even very fine people who seem to agree with progressive motion toward repair begin to accept blameless supremacy's framing: that knowable things are unknowable, that both sides are equally bad, that the most ignorant side must be persuaded of truth in order for the rest of us to accept truth and act on it, that awareness is a burden, and that those who pursue awareness are tiresome. Once we've agreed to occupy the frame of the blameless society, we remain inside their picture. We never take the journey our moral compasses have set, because we have decided to not even know that movement is needed.

It's important to note, all of this is done in service of avoiding repair; all done in service of a worldview that decides every day to live in an alternate reality, untethered to knowable and observable fact, all to avoid paying the cost of awareness.

It's sabotage, and accommodation of sabotage.

So now I want to answer the big question, which is *how do we fix it?*

I want to talk about **witness**.

◆ ◆ ◆

Let me give you some examples of witness before defining it. Let's name the abuse. Let's name the virus that keeps mutating in our natural human system. Let's name the cancer that eats systems that would otherwise be healthy.

Let's call the virus supremacy.

White supremacy, male supremacy, Christian supremacy,

able-bodied supremacy, wealth supremacy, cis-hetero supremacy; all of it a toxic desire to make certain people the preferred
and default predetermined elect who must be accommodated,
and others the abandoned and invisible cast-offs who must always do the accommodating—guilty for their own suffering,
and therefore responsible for forgiving those who oppress them
to maintain the blamelessness of their oppressions, worthy of
any further suffering they might experience and deserving of
any bad use to which they might be put.

Supremacy. A thing that has no place in any healthy system.
A spirit that must be eradicated completely and then guarded
against to prevent further mutations and variants.

Let's name the virus. Let's call it supremacy.

And let's call the cancer capitalism.

I can already feel sphincters tightening.

Let's put it this way instead: Our country has cancer of the
capital.

Am I saying business or entrepreneurship or enterprise or
markets are *bad?* I am not. Remember, a cancer is different from
a virus, because a cancer grows out of a healthy structure until the purpose of the structure is not the health of the body,
but of growth of that structure. I'm talking about a spiritual
configuration that makes growth of capital the *primary purpose*
of society. I'm talking about something that would otherwise
be healthy and natural, even vital—in this case, commerce—
metastasized into growth not of commerce but of capital, improperly prioritized within a natural human system, until it
promotes only itself rather than the system, until it threatens
the entire system with collapse.

Capital is not a philosophy, or at least it shouldn't be. Capital
is, I suspect, a tool that enables finance and entrepreneurship
and enterprise when put to its proper use. If heavily regulated
within a healthy system I suspect it could potentially prove apt
at growing wealth for a great number of people, and I say that

because that's often what it does even in our present unhealthy system. I say "I suspect" because it's hard to know what it would do within a healthy system, given the degree to which its improper elevation contributes to our current system's unhealth.

A picture might help: Think of a furnace. A furnace's function is to produce heat, which is vitally useful whenever you need heat. It will still produce heat, even if you fed it living human bodies. But to say that you should not fuel a furnace with living bodies is not the same as to say you are against furnaces or heat. So with capital. It's a tool. It shouldn't ever be an overriding philosophy. It shouldn't shape every aspect of society around growth of itself. It shouldn't be allowed to calculate the worth of human beings by their ability to generate profit for itself. Capital understands profit, not life and liberty and human art, and to use it to mediate and govern constructs intended for human thriving (systems of justice, or health, or education, to give just three obvious examples) will inevitably turn humans into products for capital to consume.

Capital, like any tool, has no desire for human beings one way or another, and so like any tool, it matters very much whose hand wields it and to what purpose. A chainsaw has no care for whether it cuts through wood or flesh; it cares only for the cutting. Capital, therefore, would in a healthy society be permitted to exist only to the extent to which it accomplishes the larger goal of human thriving, and human harm should be the limit beyond which capital is never permitted to grow. Or let me put it another way: if somebody has lung cancer, you try to eradicate the cancer, not the lungs—and not to destroy the lungs, but to save them. Nobody who is fighting lung cancer is seen as being anti-lungs, but as somebody who is trying to preserve lungs for their proper use. And, while many do oppose capitalism in order to end capital's use as a tool entirely, even if you are somebody who would like to preserve capital's use, it might be wise to align with the fight—because until we make human thriving our primary goal, we'll never be able to discover what that proper use might even be. In fact, anyone who wants to preserve capitalism should seek heavy regulation and radical transformation of what capitalism is now into something that is sustainable and healthy, because cancer never wins—when the body dies, so does it.

For this reason, I would encourage any staunch capitalist not to think of social systems (or "socialist" systems) as oppositional to systems of capital, any more than you would see your house's ductwork as oppositional to your chainsaw. Socialism is another tool—a less dangerous one than capitalism, to my mind, but one which also shouldn't be the *purpose* of society. So maybe someday we should be on the lookout for cancer of socialist systems . . . but we don't have cancer of the social systems, no matter what the dominant narratives insist. Everywhere we look, our social systems have atrophied and nearly died in favor of privatization, not because doing so returns better results for human beings, but because cancer grows wherever it can, and in this country we have cancer of the capital.

So let's name our cancer. Let's call it malignant Stage 4 capitalanoma.

And let's name the organizations around which our virus and our cancer congregate. Let's say it so it's said: The Republican Party is an organization energetically dedicated to the demolition of any hope we have for an open and free world of global pluralism and equality and democracy. It is currently led by Donald Trump, a wanton criminal and a proponent of white supremacist ideas, white supremacist policies, and white supremacists, and there is within the party a long queue of wanton criminals and white supremacists lining up to inherit his mantle. The party seeks to effect an endless free fall into retrograde supremacist fascism that engages every possible bigotry to pursue its goals of maximalist corruption and abuse. It is actively working to demolish democracy and centuries of social progress. It has set its sights on every one of our finest aspirations about ourselves as a nation, and intends to steer us back into all of our most shameful traditions and habits—in the name of its own self-righteousness, to the satisfaction of its own ego and greed.

No, wait. This is getting too wordy.

Let's name it in as simple a way as I can manage.

The Republican Party is a supremacist hate group.

It's many other things as well, but just to boil it all the way down, that's what it manifestly is: a supremacist hate group. It's not pretty, and it's not comforting, and it's not nice, but it's true.

This means that anybody who belongs to the Republican Party belongs to a hate group. And anybody who votes for Republicans provides direct political support to a hate group. And anyone who works with the Republican Party is working with a hate group. And anyone who gives a platform to a member of the Republican Party is platforming a member of a hate group. And anyone who belongs to a religious movement, the majority of whose members provide the enthusiastic, activated, sustaining spirit energizing the Republican Party, is part of a religious movement that energizes a hate group.

Again: not pretty, not comforting, not nice. Just true.

It's one of the great problems of our fraught current moment.

Some will point out that calling the Republican Party a hate group is very divisive and biased, to which I can only note that belonging to a hate group is also very divisive and biased, whether or not anybody points it out—and being biased against (and divisive toward) hate groups is actually a very good and necessary thing. It's really a question of what you choose to be biased against, and what you intend to divide yourself from. If you refuse to divide yourself from a hate group, you will by definition be dividing yourself from the people the hate group hates.

Some will point out that by calling the Republican Party a hate group, I'm talking about millions and millions of people, as if hate groups cannot possibly gain the allegiance of vast numbers. But popularity doesn't make a hate group any less a hate group—it simply makes the hate group popular and empowered . . . and there have been popular empowered hate groups before now.

Some will suggest that I should get to know some of these people who are Republicans, and I'll find that they're very nice actually; as if it is possible to live in most places in this country without knowing a great many Republicans, many of whom are nasty and many of whom are indeed very nice, in roughly the same ratios as any other group of people; as if history doesn't teach us that every popular hate group ever formed wasn't full of nice and respectable people. The respectability and niceness of a hate group's members doesn't make it any less a hate group— it simply makes the hate group insidiously respectable . . . and there have been popular, empowered, insidiously respectable hate groups before now.

Some will respond to this by telling me that I'm talking in part about people that they love very much, as if I'm not also talking about people that I love very much, as if there has ever been a popular hate group that didn't result in painful inter-personal conflicts between people on either side of the divides that those hate groups deliberately create. The fact that a popular hate group's members are known and beloved to us doesn't make it stop being a hate group—it simply means that the hate group has become entangled into all of our lives, which makes the fact of its existence more painful and complicated for those of us who feel compelled to fight it—and which in no way distinguishes it from any other popular, empowered, and insidiously respectable hate group that has ever formed.

Some will respond to this by pointing out that many people who support the Republican Party don't do so out of hatred, but from some other motivation, or because they have been confused by misinformation and propaganda; as if this distinguishes adherents of the Republican Party in any way whatsoever from other popular, empowered, respectable hate groups throughout history—all of which swelled their ranks with people motivated by something other than hate: enticed by reward, cowed by fear of reprisal, cocooned in ignorance, confused by propaganda.

Some will point out that the Democratic Party is very bad also, and note all their many failings, as if the failings of some second group to adequately defend the dignity of human art, or to oppose a hate group when empowered to do so, in any way justifies belonging to that hate group. (Though incidentally, while we're here, we should witness to the fact that the Democratic Party, while not a hate group, and while in many important ways aligned against the overt hatred of supremacy, is, particularly at the levels of senior leadership, committed to neutrality in the face of witness—to not knowing things already known; to accommodation of those captured by the spiritual virus of supremacy with practiced neutrality on matters that should not be neutral; to a desire to return to a "normal" that consumes human beings, provided that the normalcy creates comfort for the already comfortable—and fundamentally opposed to the systemic, watchful, radical remedies that extreme illness requires. And we should probably witness that the reason they are that way is because they generally see capitalism as a philosophy rather than a tool, and at least one reason for *that* appears to be that they have noticed that doing so gets a high-enough measure of support from enough of us to guide their reasoning—which suggests that we might do well to tell them that we no longer support such things, and would prefer representatives who don't support such things, either.)

Some people will argue that the Republican Party is not a hate group, to which I can only respond that all these statements are based on decades of observing what the Republican Party has done, validated by its trajectory of ever-accelerating aggression and intolerance and violence toward marginalized people.

Some will point out that Republicans say many of the same things about those who oppose them, as if we don't know that an abuser's first defense is accusing others of their own exact infractions, to sow confusion and doubt; as if it's not possible to simply witness the ways in which observable reality doesn't match their claims at all; as if the natural response to somebody who has abandoned reality isn't to stop taking their claims at face value.

The reason we can say that the Republican Party is a supremacist hate group is that we've seen politically empowered and popular supremacist hate groups before, and they acted like the Republican Party acts now. The Republican Party is a hate group, not because of what it says it intends, but because of what it is actually doing. What it is doing is waging war, for all intents and purposes—war against those it would abuse and harm and exclude, to secure the territory of its own cultural, political, and societal dominance and impunity; a war it claims to be enacting as victims of aggression, even as it pursues shocking aggression against its targets—which is what a hate group does.

These are very confrontational and charged things to say.

Why should we say such things?

I'll tell you why I say them.

I say such things, because the way you change the atmosphere is by replacing current ideas with new ones. I say such things, because all of the objections I addressed above demonstrate the current dominant thinking, and all the observable truths that those objections exist to counter represent radical ideas outside the mainstream. I say such things, because the current idea is that the Republican Party is a legitimate and respectable participant in our political process and civic lives, one of two sides in our government, a partner with whom we must work to solve problems—and I believe we need to witness to the truth, which is that it is a hate group, a supremacist confederate party, and, like all hate groups, it is a corrupt and authoritarian saboteur of healthy natural human systems, who through its own actions has delegitimized its claim to power, with whom we can never work to solve problems, because it wants to entrench those problems, and sees the solutions as existential dangers.

I say such things, because I know them to be true.

I say them, because in an age optimized for lies, speaking truths is a new idea.

I say them, because speaking new truths is the start of changing the atmosphere for the better.

And I think that's witness.

◆ ◆ ◆

Here's what I mean by **witness**: the simple act of observing what is happening, and speaking to it with the authority of that observation, without the need to appeal to further authority. In short: You have the authority of your own experience; to observe what you have observed, and to say that you have oberserved it, and to know that you know it. Witness is simple. It's not an argument. It's not a rationale. It's not a justification. It's an observation. It speaks the truth without asking permission, and it rests on your ability to simply perceive what is perceptible to you, from the unique perspective you find yourself in.

For example, to say "I am grieving your involvement with the Republican Party, because I can see very clearly that it is a supremacist hate group that is dismantling democracy and deliberately abusing people for its own benefit, and I can clearly see that your support of it degrades your essential humanity and your many fine qualities," is witness.

Notice the value of aligning your witness to a core principle grounded in universal justice: it doesn't have condemnation built into it, but rather a recognition of essential humanity and a clear path back to it, for anyone who would care about your opinion enough to seek that path. Notice how it doesn't shift a person's responsibility to change their harmful beliefs away from themselves and onto anybody else. Notice how it names the thing without negating the essential humanity of the person who has believed an inhumane lie, but also without negating the essential harm of the lie the person has believed. Notice how it allows you to see a person's goodness and niceness and other fine qualities clearly, without forgetting that these very fine qualities are what people lend the movements they join; that it is the fine qualities of its members that fascist movements find so valuable to use, because they provide atrocities with the trappings of goodness. Notice how this leaves the door open to further conversation with people who have genuine curiosity to converse— without obligating a threatened person to engage with someone they ought to understand as a threat, without obligating a person who has awakened to awareness to engage in endless bad-faith argument with somebody who has refused awareness. Notice how, while a person hearing your witness may wish to debate against it, witness isn't an invitation to debate, nor do you have to engage in one or win one for the act of your witness to remain exactly as it is. Notice that witness can be heard and seen by others, who might be encouraged or moved by it, and who might start witnessing themselves—which I would say counts as persuasion much more than permission-seeking debate with unpersuadable people. Witness names what is wrong. It gives language to the challenge. It labels the map for those who want to take the journey. Witness is, in unacceptable times, a statement of observation about something that you find unacceptable.

And another thing—maybe the most important one: **Witness repairs awareness.** Witness breaks a morally vacant neutrality, by making self-evident things evident once more to people who had hoped to avoid knowing them. **Witness increases the cost of ignorance**. It increases the cost of sabotage and blamelessness, which might bring people to your side who would have entered awareness if the cost had not been made so high, and which raises the ideological overhead for blameless people whose main goal is avoiding the lower cost of repair so they can profit from the higher costs of brokenness. Even to simply say "The Republican Party is a supremacist hate group," or to begin to talk about all the unacceptable things it does, and why you find those things unacceptable, begins to bring these truths into common currency. If it happens enough, then these truths will become the common understanding about the Republican Party, and what membership in it means, and that will be preferable, because it will be an understanding of truth rather than a retreat into a comfortable and luxurious falsehood.

This has been the fate of hate groups in the past, by the way, when the atmosphere changed, and suddenly belonging to one or supporting it or believing in its tenets was simply no longer possible without receiving a social consequence that had never been a worry before. Membership in the KKK used to be a common and respectable thing, for example. It isn't anymore—or at least for many long years it was possible to believe it wasn't. The KKK were the heroes of one of cinema's earliest blockbusters, *The Birth of a Nation*. That would be unthinkable today. Being a member of the KKK has long been considered totally unacceptable.

So it can be with today's hate groups.

To be a witness to simple truths is to fight blameless supremacy's sabotage of awareness. You'll know this, because if you start to witness, those convicted by it will begin to attack your authority to bear witness, by making sure the price is as high as they can make it—recriminations, arguments, mockery, ostracization. So you'll know you've begun to witness, when you start to pay.

I think witness is a powerful tool in our fight against supremacy, available to everyone.

It expands the frame. It moves the spirit. It changes the atmosphere. It tells a new story.

It raises the cost of blameless supremacy and its many sabotages.

Witness takes us out of ignorance, and increases awareness, which makes conviction inevitable.

And that's what I think repair looks like.

3. COMPROMISE & HOPE

The second accommodation of blameless supremacy is an accommodation of the second sabotage—that is, accommodation of complacency, which sabotages conviction, which sabotages the redeeming work of repair.

Let's call this accommodation **compromise**.

To understand compromise better, I'd like to dig back into complacency.

◆ ◆ ◆

Sabotaging our conviction involves making people believe that better things are impractical, impossible, or even undesirable; it establishes a complacency that goes so deep into shared cultural assumption it becomes invisible as blamelessness itself, until complacency—optimism, cynicism, institutionalism, indifference, learned helplessness—becomes the preferred setting.

Why are so many of us so afraid of solutions—so afraid even to seek solutions?

Many of us are, you know. Have you noticed?

Maybe an example would help. Let's talk about a big problem. Let's talk about poverty, and then two of its symptoms that are reaching a crisis point: houselessness and student debt.

We know what poverty is. It's the condition whereby people chronically do not have enough basic resources to thrive, or even live. And we know the cause. The cause of poverty isn't that resources don't exist, but that our natural human systems, which deliver value to all humans, have been unnaturally configured to prevent basic resources from coming to every human. And so I think we also know the solution, which is to reconfigure those systems into more natural channels, to provide basic resources to people who don't have them, and keep doing it until the state of poverty ceases to exist.

We also know what causes people to be unhoused, which is (to state the bloody obvious) the fact that many people cannot afford shelter. That this is the cause of houselessness suggests that one root component of the problem is the fact that we have made acquiring shelter a matter of being able to afford it in the first place. This suggests a solution, which is to provide shelter to those who don't have it, regardless of their ability to pay. We have the resources to do so, and in fact we know it would cost less in dollars and cents to do so than the cost of managing millions of unhoused people—to say nothing of the deeper costs of living in a society that cruelly abandons people to harm and death for the crime of not being able to afford shelter.

And we know what causes student debt, which is (to state the bloody obvious) people not having enough money to pay for college, in a world where trying to survive without a college degree is very difficult. That this is the cause of student debt suggests that one root component of the problem is the fact that we make people pay for their education in a system that values profit more than education. This suggests a solution, which is to make education free, or at least to greatly subsidize its costs; to reconfigure our spirit so we treat education as an investment rather than a profit center—to treat our children as if they are our future rather than a product, which would generate for us far more value than the profits their tuition brings. And by the way, we know this, not just because it's sort of obvious, but because we've done it before, in the postwar period, for people deemed "white." And it created massive wealth—for people deemed "white." I could continue this act of witness about poverty, but I'll just stop there.

I think there are a few ways you could receive this witness. Perhaps you're aligned with it, and eager to create a world where we'd begin these repairs. I'd say that represents your conviction. Or maybe you're bothered by what I've presented. Maybe you think these solutions are simplistic, or impractically costly, or even dangerously impossible.

OK. Let's talk about that.

Perhaps these simple truths concern you with their simplicity. Perhaps you'd like to tell me that the problem is actually far more complex—and I agree, to an extent. The summaries I presented are generalized. The problems *are* more complex than that, but those complexities only matter if we agree that the problem *is* a problem, and actually start the repair. At the bottom of it, our compass can always point us to these basic truths, which are general: what the problem is, what the cause is, and what the solutions are—which are almost always matters of determination to overcome the complexities, not ability to do so.

Or perhaps these simple truths concern you with their cost. Perhaps you'd like to tell me that the expense would be massive—and I agree, to an extent. Repairing poverty, homelessness, and college debt *would* be massively expensive—but those massive costs would only emerge if we actually engaged in the repair. Meanwhile, we spend *even more* to manage the problem, and those higher unnatural costs are ongoing, because they begin with the premise that the problem should be ongoing; and worse, they don't provide benefit of repair—they don't *fix* anything. Moreover, those unnatural costs go far deeper than money, because brokenness is a cost that levies a high interest upon the human spirit, and drains not only our bank accounts, but our joy, our energy, our will, our potential, and our time. Acknowledging that repair is expensive is a necessary and important part of planning the journey toward repair, but a refusal to acknowledge that brokenness cost *more* than repair is a load-bearing pillar of all our most expensive lies, which are designed to avoid paying the cost of repair.

Or perhaps you feel there is a moral hazard to these simple

truths. Perhaps you feel that if we just *give* people housing and education, then they will become dependent—and I agree, to an extent. However, I want you to notice the degree to which this belief uses a lens of separation; the degree to which this view depends on the foundational lie that we aren't related to one another; the degree to which it completely abrogates the truth, which is that we are part of a shared society. It's not so much that those who would receive the value of housing and education from our natural human system would become dependent, so much as the act of delivering those values would align us with the deep truth that they have *always been dependent* on our shared society, and so have every one of us, and moreover (and most crucially), *we are dependent on them*. We need people to be educated, if we want to live in a world of educated people. We need people to have shelter, if we want to live in a world that is not grotesquely cruel. If people are abandoned by us to live lives without shelter and education, then we live in a human system that has been unnaturally configured to abandon people. If you think seeing people dependent upon our natural human system for shelter represents a moral hazard, I'm not going to debate you, other than to observe that it is a far greater moral hazard to allow people to freeze to death on the street because our natural human system has decided it can't afford them.

So yes, our problems are complex, and solutions will be expensive, and there will be hazards. But leaving broken things broken creates greater complexities which we would avoid if we actually performed the repairs, and focusing questions of cost only on money is itself a massive oversimplification, which ignores the great massive ongoing costs of brokenness. And the hazards of a journey toward sustainable and generative repair are far less than the hazards of remaining in unsustainable and cruel brokenness.

But brokenness is what you can expect to see in a country that has decided we are not related to each other, and that life must be earned, and profit is how you earn it, and that violence redeems. Blameless supremacy, captured by complacency, holds that brokenness is best ignored, but when the cost of disrepair grows unignorable, then it insists that the problem is unsolvable, so that it will not have to explain why it refuses to solve it. And then—since our blameless society is already oriented toward violence and the idea that life must be earned—it will always conclude that the unsolvable problem is best managed through the already established tools of punishment and profit, with all assistance mediated exclusively not through questions of what people need, but of what people *deserve*.

Either you *deserve* basic human needs, or you *deserve* punishment. This is the outlook of supremacy. Once you're in supremacy's frame, you will believe that solving a problem for somebody who doesn't *deserve* it would no longer merely be impractical or unrealistic, but morally wrong, and dangerously disruptive to society. Once a management system based on who is *deserving* has been established, then those who suffer because of the problem can be converted from the victims of the problem to the causes of it, and solutions themselves can be converted into problems best avoided.

In such a society, you might find a great fear of spending a single dollar, if that dollar has the slightest danger of being delivered to hands deemed undeserving. You might find people are willing to spend five dollars to prevent that one misappropriated dollar. You might find poverty and homelessness and college debt increasing in such a society, even if it has resources to give poor people money, and unhoused people shelter, and students education. You might find for-profit prisons in such a society. You might find that such a society imprisons more people than any other in the world, and spends more of its money on weapons and the military than any other, and arms its police until they take on the appearance and bearing of an occupying military, and refers to all this expenditure as "defense" no matter how aggressive it becomes, and "safety," no matter how many find themselves endangered by it.

You might find such a society facing an epidemic of gun violence in schools, and responding by investing not in vigorous sweeping national gun control, but in bulletproof bookcases and backpacks for schools, in more police, in more guards, in more guns, in services that teach our children that school is a place where you need to be ready not only to learn but to be shot. You might find that those who suffer most from a problem receive the most suspicion that they might be profiting from it and the most blame for causing it. You might find many problems approached not with the intention of solving them for good, but managing them forever. Yes, you might find exactly that, in a society that has believed old foundational lies rooted in blameless supremacy and exceptionalism.

But the conversation only rarely gets even this far.

Usually, the sabotage of conviction happens much earlier in the process.

Why are so many of us afraid to seek solutions?

I fear the answer isn't so comfortable. I fear it's because we are in the blameless society, too. We want to enter conviction, but the cost has been made too high, and we're incentivized against paying our share of the lower cost of repair, if somebody else remains to pay the full higher cost of brokenness— and blameless supremacist society will always make sure that the cost of conviction is high, and that there is somebody else to pay the cost of our complacency. So, we will always find very fine people who have decided to accommodate our blameless society's complacency by agreeing to abandon their conviction for a more comfortable and convenient (some might even say *luxurious*) **compromise**—an ongoing orientation toward capitulation, ostensibly performed in the name of strategy and mature realism, but actually designed to maintain a more comfortable relationship with supremacy. Which we know, because a more comfortable relationship with supremacy is what it actually achieves.

Wait. Pause.

Compromise is a bad thing?

Compromise is *bad?* Isn't compromise *necessary?*

Isn't it the realistic thing? The mature thing?

Isn't it what the adults in the room do while all the ideological children whine about their utopian pie-in-the-sky fantasies?

I hear you.

Let me tell you a story.

◆ ◆ ◆

In 2018, the U.S. president whose name escapes me at the moment disbanded the U.S. pandemic response team, which had been established by his predecessor. Old What's-His-Name was shutting down a lot of things set up by his predecessor around that time. This might have seemed petty and political and biased to a news media that typically hates bias and petty politics, but this move was about reducing costs, and we don't like paying costs, and anyway we weren't in a pandemic at that moment, and as a society we have a habit of mocking expenditures on prevention of bad things that haven't happened recently.

In 2019, a virus showed up called Covid, and Old What's-His-Name did nothing about it, which is a polite way to say that he actively and categorically opposed doing anything about it, even going so far as to lie about what he already knew the effects were going to be, and to oppose the testing that any epidemiological response would include, and he pushed quack remedies, and...look, it feels like a fever dream, but...I'm *pretty* sure he suggested we apply sunlight to the lungs and inject disinfectant. This would have been very funny, if it hadn't been such serious business—which it was, because this virus is virulent and airborne and deadly and disabling, all qualities that land solidly in my top 10 least-favorite attributes for viruses.

Anyway, our public health apparatus moved to do the sorts of things that are necessary in times of an airborne virulent deadly disabling virus, and most of us—because we did not want to become dead or disabled, or cause others to be dead or disabled—moved to comply. This included directives to wear masks in public, and to shelter in place, and to close down all non-crucial businesses, and to pay people relief money while they were sheltering in place, and so forth. And the bodies piled up and our infrastructure (which, to avoid costs of maintenance, had not been maintained to prepare for a pandemic) creaked dangerously, and our health care workers quickly were strained to the breaking point, and while all this was going on, Old What's-His-Name did everything he could to oppose and undermine efforts to contain the virus: he refused to wear a mask, or to shelter in place, and continually insisted that we all return to normal, which to him mostly meant that we stop acting as if we were in the global pandemic we were in. Old What's-His-Name, who was not all that big into subtext, was quite shockingly clear that he opposed fighting the virus specifically because to fight the virus meant acknowledging the virus, and acknowledging the virus carried a responsibility to do something about it, and doing something about it would get us into money. Even worse, that money would have to be paid by people who had almost all the money in order to pay people who didn't have much of it, and, given our dominant cultural belief that people who have money deserve life and people who don't have money don't deserve it, paying people to live who weren't doing the work necessary to earn life began seeming extremely morally hazardous, especially to people who were wealthy—people like (perhaps coincidentally) Old What's-His-Name himself.

And all the people who looked to Old What's-His-Name

for identity and meaning and purpose took on his viewpoint—
which was that the attempt to keep people alive wasn't worth
the cost, and that in fact the cost of keeping people alive was
theft, and was in fact the worst possible form of tyranny. And
then there was a general politicized opposition to masking, on
ostensibly moral but observably selfish grounds—and in my state
some of these heavily armed emotional and moral toddlers came
and took over our state capitol and tried to kidnap and murder
our governor, a woman who Old What's-His-Name was vilifying
on a daily basis while refusing to send my state much-needed ven-
tilators, for the crime of having elected such a woman.

The upshot was, we got people back to work as quickly as
possible, and shut down the relief money as quickly as possible,
and we created a relief loan system that made a top priority of
ensuring that nobody undeserving got any money, which meant
that it was administratively difficult to get the money, which
meant that it was far easier for people who had money to get the
relief money than it was for people without money to get it, which
turned it into a boondoggle that benefitted for example wealthy
ex-NFL player Brett Favre but not maybe as many people who
for example actually needed it, and we had a massive tax give-
away to the wealthy, and some massive corporate bailouts, and
then we saw the greatest increase in wealth disparity of all time.
And I suppose that, for those who happen to share the dominant cultural view that people with money deserve money
and people without money don't deserve money, this was all
very comforting. During this time, we crossed the threshold of
100,000 people dead, which was pretty easy for us to do, given
that people were dying by the thousands every day. The New York
Times called it "an incalculable loss," which it was, for many reasons, not least because we refused to calculate it.

And then another million people died, and so forth.

And we've seen a near-daily barrage of opinion pieces insisting that the pandemic is over, from the day it began until now,

most of which make the point that people who insist on acting as if we are in the global pandemic we are in are very distracting and annoying to everyone else.

And last week, the New York City Transit Authority put out some new posters promoting a "you do you" masking policy, which frames mask wearing as an entirely personal choice—the exact framing that the followers of Old What's-His-Name demanded two years ago. One gets the sense (if one is me) that the purpose of this campaign is to curtail harassment not of people who *don't* wear masks, but of those who *do*—of those who still choose to commit the offense of reminding people that the virus still exists, which reminds non-mask wearers of the ever-present conviction to do something about it.

I'm not sure if we ever got around to learning how much money we saved by shutting down the pandemic response team in 2018, by the way.

It must have been an incalculable amount.

◆ ◆ ◆

It's 2022 now.

Let's see what's up in 2022.

Well, we've replaced Old What's-His-Name with Old What's-His-Face, for starters. That's promising. What's-His-Face (as previously mentioned) is a guy named Joe, and Joe promised to be better about the pandemic. But Joe just took an interview where he said the pandemic was over, even though a hundred people died today, and a hundred died yesterday, and a hundred more will die tomorrow, even though the stories about long Covid are many and devastating. And earlier, Joe's administration announced that Covid was a "pandemic of the unvaccinated," by way of encouraging people to get vaccines, to be sure, but also by way of supporting the by-now quite popular belief that those who don't get the vaccine *deserve* what they get, because of the choices they've made. And, sure enough, there are people who have chosen deliberate ignorance, and decided they'd rather die than get a vaccine, and Covid has sure enough taken many of them up on that proposition; but there are millions of immunocompromised people who cannot get the vaccine for health reasons, and we all know it. They are the ones who are now paying almost all the costs of our ongoing brokenness. They are having the pandemic so that we don't have to have it anymore, and more and more of us are pretty comfortable with that.

And we aren't subsidizing home tests anymore, at least not as of this writing; Republicans are still as opposed to the tyranny of tests as they are opposed to the tyranny of vaccines, and there are enough Democrats that agree to accommodate them that I guess there won't be any more funds for it, and I guess there's nothing to be done about that. And nobody wears masks pretty much anywhere, but we're asked to respect the choices either way. It's a *personal* decision now, whether or not to spread a deadly and debilitating virus. If you look around, you'll see it: We have won the victory over ourselves, successfully overcoming the natural human instinct to give a shit.

Two years ago, most people were of the view that we ought to do whatever it took to contain and oppose a global pandemic, a view reflecting the great truths that we all are related in ways we can't extricate ourselves from, and it is the responsibility of the healthy to see to the well-being of the sick. But a loud minority insisted that the only thing that mattered was acting as if there was no pandemic, and that the only viewpoint that mattered was theirs, and the only risk they were taking in flouting health guidelines was to themselves, and that any deaths that came were inevitable, and therefore to mourn the deaths that came was an unseemly display of politicization, and to expect anyone to participate in caring for the sick was not only unrealistic but immoral theft and authoritarian tyranny, deserving whatever violence those who suffered it decided to enact in retaliation.

And eventually, most of us who held the former view have come around mostly to the latter point of view, or at least we decided it was easier to accommodate it.

They got everything, and they gave up nothing.

I'm given to understand this was a *compromise.*

Where was I?

Ah yes. As I said, somewhere in there we crossed a million deaths. If you are savvy about how chronological time functions, you'll have already realized this happened sometime after the 100,000 deaths, which is the number *The New York Times* told us was an incalculable loss. The million deaths passed with relatively little fanfare, as *The New York Times* had joined most other publications and broadcasts and opinion pieces and other pillars of our consent-manufacturing apparatus in telling us that the million deaths were not so much incalculable but inevitable, because all viruses are endemic, so we didn't have any significant period of mourning to mark the occasion of 10 times an incalculable amount.

I guess we got better at calculating loss.

Republicans are running for office this year, by the way, as they tend to do. It looks like they might just win. Having shut down the pandemic response task force, they promise to shut down most other government functions as well, for the unspeakable crime of taking tax money from citizens and using it to take care of citizens.

Think how much money we'll save!

But we were talking about compromise.

◆ ◆ ◆

I think it's important to reiterate that every accommodation of supremacy involves invocation of something that is positive in times of health—the fruits of a healthy society. Neutrality, for example, even though it enables sabotage of our awareness when applied to a deliberate ignorance, isn't inherently bad. Neutrality, when applied in healthy times, allows many valuable things: open-mindedness, exchange of ideas, unbiased journalism on competing proposals for solving the same problem. It's only destructive when it's improperly applied to deliberate ignorance, specifically because it sabotages our awareness.

So too with compromise.

When you have multiple parties that all agree that there is a problem to solve, but don't agree on the methodology to solve it, compromise is an excellent tool for negotiating those differences—and even when two parties don't agree that there is a problem to solve, it can certainly be the responsible and realistic choice to give up some of your preferences on pursuing a solution in order to achieve most of your main goals and establish a better position from which to achieve the rest. If those making the compromise understand how the compromise is getting us all closer to an end goal of repair, and understand the strategic worth of what they are gaining, and what their opponent is giving up in exchange, and how they intend to use their better position to achieve further goals along the same path, then yes, compromise can be appropriate and necessary. All too frequently, though, we see a compromise that exists only for the sake of itself, a compromise that chooses to give up everything while getting nothing, all for the sake of compromising rather than repairing, not because the compromise brings us closer to repair, but because compromising is what responsible people do, in healthy times—and we want to live in healthy times, so we agree to be seen compromising.

Supremacy *knows* this. It knows that even in unhealthy times, there's an instinct to pursue the trappings of health, and supremacy capitalizes on this instinct to achieve its ends. We won't be offered actual health, because health requires repair, so instead we'll be offered a luxurious compromise, which will cost us nothing for now, and will force others to pay unnaturally exorbitant rates—and many of us will take that offer, giving up our conviction without thought to an endpoint, never noticing that supremacy is giving up nothing and never will, without remembering that supremacy has reneged on every promise it's made in the past.

Compromise is an excellent tool in certain situations. It's always a terrible final goal. If we set our compasses toward compromise as our final destination, we'll never go anywhere.

And blameless supremacy knows that, too.

There's a thing I wrote on Twitter years ago that still gets passed around. It goes like this:

> *Meet me in the middle, says the unjust man.*
> *You take a step toward him.*
> *He takes a step back.*
> *Meet me in the middle, says the unjust man.*

I think this little scrap of free verse gets passed around because it describes something we have all seen: a sabotaged conviction accommodated. What supremacy asks us to do is more than compromising on our *method* for achieving a solution, or to horse-trade one goal for another. The demand is that we compromise on our conviction *to seek any solutions at all.*

And again, I ask:

Why are we afraid to seek solutions?

Somewhere along the line we agreed that true solutions ought not be pursued, because they are doomed to failure, or are impractical or unnecessary, or are impossible, or even dangerous. Somewhere along the line we agreed to not try for good and necessary things, not because we don't want them, but because we imagine somebody else doesn't want them, and, fearing this imagined opposition will defeat our attempts to enact improvements, we concede without trying. Somewhere along the line we agreed to replace healing with symptom management, and to allow that management to be mediated by questions of who *deserves*.

Those who wanted repair agreed to stop trying to repair what's broken.

Those who want things broken agreed to keep things broken.

It was a compromise.

Compromise is what happens when the process of repair stagnates at conviction. We're aware of brokenness, but we refuse to agree that brokenness needs fixing. Supremacists sabotage conviction with complacency. But the accommodation is the supremacy, and compromise makes the complacency successful. You'll know our conviction has been sabotaged, because you'll find that even very fine people, who seem to agree that progressive motion toward repair is needed, begin to accept blameless supremacy's framing, and talk about the natural final destinations of justice as something intrinsically impossible or even undesirable.

People who want immigration reform will start by assuring everybody that "nobody wants open borders," even though open borders should always be our desired goal, because a country with open borders has achieved such a state of peace between neighboring countries, such a mutual fulfillment of basic human need, such a reduction of strife, that controlled borders between them have become unnecessary.

People who want to reduce police brutality or mass incarceration say things like "nobody wants to abolish the police" or "nobody wants to abolish prisons," even though a land without police and prison should always be our desired goal, because a land without these institutions is one where peace has taken such natural sway, one whose laws are so just and whose institutions so well-attuned to their spirit, that enforcement no longer requires a violent apparatus.

People who want economic justice say things like "nobody wants education to be *totally* free" or "nobody is saying we

should just *give* people houses," even though it is far less expensive—from not only a moral standpoint but a practical economic
one—to care for everyone rather than to pay the cost of not doing so; even though the only reason not to do so is because we
have believed expensive lies that life must be earned.

In a compromised society, you'll hear outright proclamations
of despair, instinctive reactions against any hopeful statement
or aspirational strategy. You'll hear "good luck doing that in *this*
political atmosphere," as if atmospheres can't be changed, as if
the sight of somebody trying a difficult necessary thing can't inspire others to believe in new possibilities. You'll hear "but what
is your *plan* for doing that?" asked in such a way that it conveys
the clear meaning "I don't want to plan on doing that."

Or—how about this one?

You'll hear people denigrate something as "utopian." Have
you ever noticed that one? Scoffing at the notion of utopia as
self-evidently wrong-minded? Imagine it: people so opposed to
utopia that they don't just work to prevent it; they fear it, and
convince everyone else to fear it, too.

It's a compromise.

You'll hear many things like this, in a compromised society—
self-inflicted sabotages of end goals we should all seek, even if
a perfected state is unlikely. It's a subtle despair, a belief among
people who consider themselves well-meaning that not only is a
perfected human system unattainable, but so unattainable as to
make even the desire for it a dangerous and fearful thing.

Once we've agreed to occupy the frame of blameless supremacy, we remain inside its picture. We never take the journey our
compasses have set, because we have agreed that not moving is a
preferable option, even if we know not moving is unsustainable
and ensures disaster. We've agreed in thousands of tiny conscious and subconscious ways with the saboteur's framework:
that the uncertainty of the journey guarantees certain failure,
that our present unsustainable status quo is safest because it is

most familiar, that change is impossible and therefore undesirable, and that we can never take any journey without first securing the permission of those who refuse to go. And all of it rests upon a sabotage of our conviction: a refusal to believe better things are possible, or that we can bring them about.

It's important to remember that all of this is done in service of a worldview that tries to extract the maximum value from our natural human system without paying back, then treats the problems that this corruption causes as inevitable, unsolvable, and needing violent punishment to manage. And it's all done to avoid paying costs.

It's sabotage, and accommodation of sabotage.

So now I want to answer the big question, which is *how do we fix it?*

I want to talk about **hope**.

◆ ◆ ◆

Hope is often seen as a mushy and naïve thing—and it can be, of course. There's a form of hope that is just another form of indifference, a hope that looks at what's coming and simply hopes that it won't come, or insists "that won't happen," not because it won't happen, but because acknowledging that it already is happening would draw us toward the inconvenient conviction that we might have to do something about it.

I'm talking about something different.

I'm not talking about a hope that crosses its fingers and closes its eyes and wishes for the best, or a hope that just keeps its eyes on the ground and refuses to look at a problem that it insists will solve itself. That's optimism, hope's counterfeit, which is just the friendliest flavor of complacency. I'm talking about a hope full of rugged resolve; an uncompromising hope that looks clearly at a dire situation and refuses to look away. I'm talking about a hope that allows you to look at unlikely but necessary change, in full awareness of how unlikely that change is, and to try for it anyway—not because the change is likely but because it is necessary; because somebody has to try, and you are somebody. This is the sort of hope that makes you fight even when victory is far from assured. This is the sort of hope that refuses to hand its opponent easy wins simply because support seems scant and a loss seems likely. This is the sort of hope that rallies in the final minutes and brings the crowd to its feet. It's the sort of hope that is willing to pay a high cost for victory when defeat isn't an option. It's a hope that is willing to be beaten and then try again. It's the sort of hope that changes what can be done.

It's a hope that makes unlikely change possible, then likely, then inevitable.

I hope you'll agree, we need a lot of unlikely change.

If you agree, I have good news: Unlikely change happens all the time. In fact, most major changes throughout our history—emancipation, women's suffrage, the New Deal, the labor movement, the Civil Rights Movement, gay marriage, the 40-hour work week, the weekend, democracy—were *extremely unlikely* at some point beforehand; before, that is, they all actually happened. They failed and failed and failed and failed and failed... until they succeeded.

You know what this means? It means that uncompromising hope is the tool *realistic responsible adults* use to solve problems in the real world, while optimistic and cynical and complacent children compromise over the management of fixable problems they have already agreed to not fix, with people who have already declared their inflexible opposition to all solutions.

So how does hope work?

The same way it always did, I'd guess.

First, expect change. If you don't expect it, start expecting it. Really expect it. Expect the people who you voted into power to use that power to bring it about; or, if they can't bring it about, to advocate for it ceaselessly in the faces of those who are standing as obstacles to it, and to always maneuver to make it more likely, not less, and to at the very least stop making the persistent case for why it can't happen. And think big—think huge. Make your demands for change the perfected endpoint of the change, because it's only by doing this that you will secure any sort of compromise that actually moves you toward your goal. Don't start with the compromise position. Point toward the destination. Make your opponents compromise with *you*.

Express your expectation by demanding it. Demand it constantly and consistently. Tell people who find your goal to be "unrealistic" the truth, which is that every improvement we've ever had started out as unrealistic and impossible, and that the human spirit is, if it is anything, an agent for changing possibility itself. Refocus naysayers from the challenges of the journey, back to the absolute necessity of the destination. Counter those who complain of cost with the reality that remaining in brokenness is always the more expensive option, carrying unending costs that bring no benefit.

Give your demands weight by issuing consequences for those demands. If the people you empowered to bring about necessary change refuse to use that power to bring it about, use the same levers you used to empower them to disempower them. This could mean supporting somebody else in a primary or even general election, if a suitable optional candidate presents themselves, or working to identify and promote suitable optional candidates, or even *being* that candidate. It could mean joining protests against a person you voted for. It could mean calling their offices and agitating for them to do better. It could mean a great many things, but it will always mean delivering the understanding that your support for our leaders is contingent on their seeking real repair. The flip side of this is celebrating and encouraging those people when they do the right thing, and positively reinforcing their actions to bring about necessary change. Not all consequences are negative consequences, and we'd do well to remember that—but align your consequences with action toward necessary change.

Realize permission isn't required. Realize that you can work within power and institution if it aligns toward unlikely change—but if those institutions capitulate to complacency and enter into a spirit of learned helplessness, realize that you don't have to make their failings your own. Demonstrate your own power by working toward change independent of that power and those institutions. Find people already aligned toward necessary change, and adept at organization and agitation, and lend them what you have to give, whether it is skill or labor or money or simply the moral weight of your support and your presence.

Finally, repeat. The hope I'm talking about is a cyclical hope that never stops looking for improvement and repair. It's a hope whose journey isn't derailed by the knowledge that the journey is hard, because it has a clear vision of the terrain and knows the difficulty full well. It's a hope that understands that the world is changeable, and we can change it.

It's a hope that knows that few victories arrive without defeat as a preamble.

It's a hope that never accepts incremental losses and calls them gains.

It's a hope that works for what it expects and demands what is needed.

It's a hope that refuses a purposeless compromise.

It's a hope that rejects cynicism's predetermined defeat, even while it clearly perceives the depth and scope of the problem.

It's a hope that knows that there are people of bad intention, who hope for a less equal, more authoritarian, corrupt, bigoted country, who hope to restore authoritarian supremacy and fascist hatred to full strength, and, because they hope for it, they have been achieving it.

It's a hope that knows we can make a better, kinder world, where even people of bad intention will be cared for. It's a hope

that knows we should make a sustainable world that supremacists will hate and fear, even as it sustains us all—even them.

To resolutely hope for unlikely change is to fight a blameless society's sabotage of your conviction. You'll know this,
because as you move into hope, those convicted by the sight
of people acting in uncompromising hope will begin to attack
that hope as unrealistic and foolish and divisive and dangerous
and wrong. They will make sure the price for your hope is as
high as they can make it—so you'll know you're there, once you
start to pay.

Compromise makes complacency cheap, and maintains
comfortable relationships with profitable abuse. But **hope
repairs conviction**. Hope dissolves the urge for a directionless
compromise that has no goal other than itself, by demanding
necessary repairs, and by refusing to accept managed brokenness.
Hope increases the cost of complacency—and may move to
your cause many complacent people whose only goal is to avoid
cost. The hope I'm talking about is a generative hope, which
realizes that the sight of people enacting hope might inspire
other people to hope as well, and knows that as the ranks of
those who expect and demand change swell, the more that unlikely but necessary changes will become possible, and then
likely, and then inevitable.

I think hope is a powerful tool in our fight against supremacy,
available to everyone.

It expands the frame. It moves the spirit. It changes the atmosphere. It tells a new story.

It raises the cost of blameless supremacy and its many sabotages.

Hope takes us out of complacency, and increases conviction,
which makes confession inevitable.

And that's what I think repair looks like.

4. EXONERATION & CLARITY

The third accommodation of blameless supremacy is an accommodation of the third sabotage—that is, the accommodation of denial, which sabotages confession, which sabotages the redeeming work of repair.

Let's call this accommodation **exoneration**.

Notice, I say *exoneration*, not redemption—because as any good conservative Republican Christian can tell you, redemption involves somebody paying some cost. . . and blameless supremacy opposes paying any cost.

Sabotage of confession involves a certain level of desperation on the part of blameless supremacy, because confession can only occur once awareness and conviction have broken through the protective wall of blamelessness, and *that* means that society is getting dangerously close to repairing broken things, which will create natural shared costs. It's worth thinking about how exoneration works in a blameless society dedicated to its own exceptional supremacy.

◆ ◆ ◆

It's 2022 now. The attorney general of Arkansas recently had an interview with Jon Stewart that went badly—for her, anyway.

Here's what happened.

Arkansas Republicans recently passed a law that makes it illegal for parents of trans children to seek recommended and often life-saving medical care. This was done for a very simple reason: if you are sabotaging our natural human system, you are harming people, and if you would like to remain blameless for doing that, you're going to need somebody else to blame.

Government is, at the root, the way we organize and administer our shared society, and the Republican Party, which controls large parts of the government, is organized around the foundational lie that we are not related to each other, and that therefore there is no shared society. For this reason, it's dedicated to making government fail, so it governs while insisting that government always fails, and then to prove it, it makes sure government fails, and as government fails people, that failure harms those people, and that harm makes people angry— including Republican voters, who are disproportionately harmed from a national perspective by all this because they are disproportionately represented by the kinds of people who they choose to vote for—people who deliberately cause failure and harm. And all the people in the state of Arkansas who are not Republican voters are harmed as well, and mostly are disproportionately harmed from a statewide perspective—harmed *more* than the significant harm that comes to Republican voters from Republican governance—and that increased harm appears to be all Republican voters really want from governance, so they go on voting for failure that harms them, which encourages Republican politicians to keep on delivering failure and harm. The danger for Republican politicians would be that those harmed people might someday start to blame that harm on them, the people who caused it. So, to avoid that blame, Republican politicians find it useful and necessary to identify some group (usually a group with the least power and representation) to blame and punish for all the failure and harm that Republican politicians cause. And there's always somebody to blame and punish.

Trans people are currently the group that Republicans are most directly targeting for the sort of abusive harm and injustice and cruelty that their supremacist voters want to see enacted, and so they are using their power to persecute and terrorize and harm and kill already-marginalized children and their parents, in order to consolidate their power with a group of mostly Christian fascists who would like their own ideas about morality to be given supremacist consideration above all others, above even the consensus of medical professionals—a consideration that involves making sure that anyone who doesn't conform to their way of living suffers, as proof to others that suffering awaits anyone as a natural consequence of failing to conform to their way of living, and as satisfaction to themselves that their way of living is the best way of living, specifically because it does not result in similar suffering, and as justification to them that any punishment and suffering they deliver to people for not conforming to their way of living is not the product of their hate but a proof of their deep, guiding, paternalistic love.

It sounds bad, because it is bad.

It sounds cruel, because it is cruel.

It sounds bigoted, because it is bigoted.

Many Republicans know how this all looks to people outside of their voting base. So they go out and tell their own story about their intentions—a story of denial. They claim that what they *really* want to do is allow more choice, even though what they are actually doing is constraining choice. They claim they want to protect kids, even though they are targeting kids. They claim to be interested in fostering health, even though they're preventing health.

So anyway: the attorney general of Arkansas.

She went on Stewart's show, in order to put this narrative of denial out there.

Now, Stewart is known as a liberal guy, and the Attorney General of Arkansas certainly knew this, so I think she expected Stewart to oppose the anti-trans bill, and debate her on it. I don't think she was expecting what happened, though.

In the interview, Stewart didn't *debate* her, as such. He simply, calmly, repeatedly refused to accept her lies, and called them out as such. He told her that what she was saying wasn't true, and that he knew she knew it, and then he told her why he knew she knew it, by continually returning the conversation to the facts of what was actually happening: that there is a medical consensus that Republicans are not only ignoring but criminalizing; that the data they offer in support of their position is cherry-picked and manufactured, the stories they offer as rationale are specious outliers, and their claims about their true intentions are, quite literally, unbelievable. He used examples that laid bare the fact that she, the attorney general of Arkansas, would never permit herself to be treated the way she was treating so many others. He didn't make much attempt to disguise his contempt, which I think is appropriate when encountering a deliberately cruel person engaged in deliberate acts of cruelty. He ended by expressing his hope that she, the attorney general of Arkansas, never had to deal with the sort of terrible cruelty being caused by her, the attorney general of Arkansas. And then he expressed his sincere hope that the vile Republican bill she was supporting would get struck down. These are the sincere hopes of any decent person in this country today, and in my opinion can serve as a litmus test as to whether a person is decent in the first place.

Now, all of this was very cathartic for anyone who knows the truth about what Republicans are—which is a supremacist hate group energized by every kind of bigotry. It surely didn't convince many people who refuse to acknowledge that basic truth, and no doubt it would be good for us to understand that the hypocrisy that Stewart exposed will do no damage to supremacy among supremacists, because for supremacy, hypocrisy is a virtue designed to establish and demonstrate supremacist dominance. And certainly there are conversations to be had here regarding Stewart's privilege—his ability to be heard where trans people are ignored—and other conversations to be had about the utility of platforming hate in any way, even for the sake of exposing its hypocrisy, given that for supremacists the sight of supremacist hypocrisy in action appears to serve not as a shameful deterrent, but rather as an energizing encouragement.

But for now, I want to focus on the attorney general's reaction to Stewart's approach.

She was caught totally flat-footed by the sort of basic opposition to counterfactual nonsense and malicious self-exonerating

lies that ought to be a baseline standard of any journalistic encounter. She was visibly flustered to encounter this sort of opposition, clearly unprepared to talk about basic details in support
of her position, and even said at one point that she—her state's
top lawyer—hadn't prepared to have some sort of *legal* discussion about this *law.*

It's almost as if she had prepared for a different experience.

It's almost as if she were expecting her goals to be opposed
in the abstract—*what would you say to those who claim that
what you are doing is . . .?*— and expected that her claims about
her intentions would be accepted at face value, and passed into
common currency by a politely oppositional but mostly neutrally curious interlocutor. It's almost as if she was expecting
to be allowed to have the truth of what she and her party were
actually doing to be smoothly ignored, in favor of a framing
that treated her vile abusive bigotry as the sort of normal and
reasonable position a decent person might hold, about which
decent people could calmly and pleasantly disagree.

Maybe she should have seen it coming. Maybe she should have
remembered another time Stewart famously refused to play ball,
back in 2004, when he went on Tucker Carlson's show *Crossfire* and
told so much truth about the nature of toxic shows like *Crossfire* that it may have resulted in the cancellation of *Crossfire.*

But maybe she had seen Stewart's jokes from *The Daily
Show* in decades past, the ones in which he casually employed
anti-trans slurs. Or maybe she'd seen his recent defense of
his friend Dave Chappelle's repeated almost-pathological
trans-targeting material, whereby Stewart defended Chappelle
as a person he, Jon Stewart, was sure had different intentions
than the ones Chappelle had already proved himself to have.
Or maybe she saw one of many *Daily Show* interviews Stewart
conducted during which he was chummy with Republicans
about the atrocities they were committing back then, or some of
his MAGA-exonerating sound bites following Trump's election,

about how Trump voters aren't all hateful people, a truth that elided the deeper truth that millions of nice people had voted for overt hate. Or his speech at his "March to Restore Sanity" event, where he said that what needed to happen was for "both sides" to come together.

But it seems that Stewart's perspective may have changed in recent months and years.

Certainly his approach changed in his interview with the attorney general of Arkansas.

It might have been a warning sign to her, when he started his program by calling himself out for some of his own previous ignorance. It might have seemed a clumsy attempt to some, and it might have been "too little too late" for others, but it also might have served as a flashing red light to the attorney general of Arkansas, that this was somebody who had achieved enough basic awareness and conviction about what was broken in our society to begin his program by picking apart his own unearned blamelessness, and confessing it as part of a larger confession of the truth he had received.

But we were talking about exoneration.

◆ ◆ ◆

Exoneration is what happens when the process of repair stagnates at confession. We are aware of the brokenness in our society; aware of injustice and abuse. We agree that what is broken should be repaired, and that we share in a collective responsibility to join in the repair. But we don't progress from there. We don't realign ourselves away from our own blamelessness, and as a result we make our first priority our own comfortable relationships with people aligned against repair. We engage in a *luxurious* **exoneration**, which costs us nothing, while making other people pay its unnaturally exorbitant rates.

We extend forgiveness to people enacting abuse, and we extend it from unabused safety, as self-appointed proxies for the people they actually abuse. We ignore the abuse that is *actually happening* to focus on self-aggrandizing stories of personal intent from people doing the abuse. We take the complexity of their rationales as evidence that the issue is complex. We agree to allow supremacists to claim their place as the central protagonists of society. We agree that their abuse is up for debate, by debating them about it. We demonstrate that we agree that ending abuse is a matter they get to decide, by making our attempts to persuade them our only strategy for stopping them. We turn our first attentions to establishing a redemptive path for the abuser, before thinking of establishing a safe path for their victims, before even acknowledging the fact of the abuse, before noticing that the abuse is ongoing. We immediately jump to redemption before doing the work of repair, and never think to establish whether or not the abuser has the slightest interest in any sort of redemptive work.

We say things like "we don't want to make forgiveness impossible" and fail to notice if forgiveness has even been asked.

We treat a true accusation of abuse not as a revelation of brokenness needing repair, but as if it were an attack on the future potential of the abuser.

We find a person from a marginalized group who has a perspective that flatters our own comfort, and we use their perspective as a pretext to ignore all other voices from that group.

We hear women tell of the harm male supremacy does to them in the world and we say "not *all* men." We hear Black people tell of the harm white supremacy does to them in the world, and we say "not *all* white people." We hear what Christian supremacy is doing in the world, and we say "but those aren't *real* Christians."

We use a framing of ignorance to challenge awareness.

We use a framing of complacency to challenge conviction.

We might do well to wonder: *Why* do we do this?

I think we do this because even though we see the brokenness and want to see it fixed, we don't want to pay the cost of our own supremacy and blamelessness, wherever we intersect with supremacist identity. This is where the urge to say "not *all*" comes from: We agree to align with repair, but only if our own reputation is certified as blameless first. Our alignment with justice carries a prerequisite that we be seen first and foremost as blameless for injustice, which makes establishing our own personal goodness a higher priority than actually doing the systemic repair. And so, instead of entering into confession of what is broken, we enter into a more comfortable agreement with blameless supremacy, agreeing to focus only on whatever fine qualities we share, and then using those qualities to exonerate ourselves for the ways we still profit from brokenness. We live in denial, believing that we can align our intentions with justice without doing the work and paying the costs—which ensures that repair never happens.

Exoneration forgives abusers on behalf of the abused.

But more than anything, exoneration exonerates itself.

Blameless supremacists know this, by the way.

Supremacists sabotage confession with denial. But the accommodation is the supremacy, and exoneration makes denial successful. You'll know that confession has been sabotaged, because you'll find that even very fine people who seem to agree with progressive motion toward repair begin to accept supremacy's stories of its own good intentions, and ignore what it is actually doing to actual people. Once we've agreed to occupy supremacy's frame, we remain inside its picture. We never take the journey our compasses have set, because we have agreed that supremacy is a reasonable position to hold, as long as the people holding those positions insist that their intentions are good.

So now I want to answer the big question, which is *how do we fix it?*

I want to talk about **moral clarity**.

Let me tell you a story.

◆ ◆ ◆

The novelist and Bokononist spiritual teacher Kurt Vonnegut once wrote a story called "All the King's Horses," about a man, captured in war, forced by a dictator to play chess for his freedom. The dictator had in his possession a giant board, and huge pieces the size of real people to fill that board, which could be moved by servants. The large board made it a novelty, but the size of the board didn't change the game. It was still just a game—a *respectable* game.

However, in the story, the dictator added a wrinkle: the pieces would be replaced by real soldiers who had been under the command of our hero. If a "piece" was taken, that soldier would be immediately executed. Then the dictator added an even more shocking wrinkle: three of the most strategically vulnerable pieces would be embodied not by soldiers, but by the man's own wife and children. Suddenly it wasn't a game of chess or a classic battle anymore. It was something else. It carried a different moral weight, one you would absolutely call unacceptable—not a respectable game, on any level. Anyone playing such a game would only do so because they had been compelled by those with the power to force them to do so.

Speaking of moral weight, there was a multi-layered moral in the story about the futility inherent in the very nature of war— the sort of thing at which Vonnegut was particularly adept. Read the story. It is in my opinion good, and you'll also catch any of the details my shoddy memory missed or got wrong. What I'd like to point out about the story is this: It demonstrates that the stakes change the game, even if the board and rules remain the same.

Got it?

Not the rules.

Not the board.

It's the stakes that define the game.

Now I'm going to make a confession to you, because you are my friends, and that fact makes me feel safe unburdening myself.

Here it is: I like being thought of as a reasonable and respectable person.

Being thought of as reasonable and respectable is pleasant. It's nice. It comes with a lot of tiny microscopic benefits that assist me in my daily life, some of them practical, others social. If I'm thought unreasonable and unrespectable, it creates a lot of tiny microscopic difficulties in my life, some of them practical, and some of them social. I'd rather avoid this. If you are somebody like me, who likes being thought of as reasonable and respectable, and likes keeping things cool between yourself and others, you do what I do, and play a game—a *respectable* game.

The respectable game involves me doing and saying things that I think people will find reasonable and respectable, and which affirm their own respectability and reasonableness. I do things like trying to understand what the other person is saying, and making them feel as if their thoughts and feelings are reasonable, too. And usually, if somebody I'm dealing with has a preference on a matter, and I don't feel too strongly myself, I just let them have their way, because I don't really care. And if I do have a preference, I perform a calculation as to whether my preference is strong enough to advocate for it, or if I'd rather just make the social interaction expedient and let the other person's preference win out. And if I do advocate for my own position, I try to do so in a reasonable and respectable manner, so as to indicate to everyone involved and anyone observing that both of us are, despite our difference of opinion, reasonable and respectable people. Even if we can't agree, I'll frequently seek a compromise. And even if, at the end, we still disagree about the matter, and one of us is entirely disappointed, we both usually will make overtures to one another, to make sure it's understood that, while we disagree, our positions are both understandable and reasonable, and affirm that we are both respectable and reasonable people even in the midst of the present disagreement, and while we might be disappointed if things don't go our way, we'll still be friends, and we'll accept the outcome.

Even though we disagree, we are still aligned. And that's how sometimes I wind up eating at a restaurant that's not my very favorite.

Playing the respectable game doesn't distinguish me very much from other people, by the way. Most people play the respectable game, if they want to be thought of as reasonable by others. This is how people have learned to operate in the world, and it's a good thing, too. It is a respectable game, and it has reasonable rules, and I've notice that playing it makes daily interactions a lot more pleasant and easy to navigate.

The game allows for disagreement, but not strife, so when you want to have disagreement without strife, which is hopefully most of the time, the respectable game is a very useful and necessary tool, because disagreeing while remaining fundamentally aligned is what the respectable game does.

Notice that the primary goal of the respectable game is not actually to win an argument. The primary goal of the respectable game is *to be thought of as respectable while playing it.*

The respectable game is an exonerative game. It says: Our difference of opinion doesn't mean either of us is morally or factually or intellectually bad. It says: Even though we disagree about this matter, I still find your position acceptable, and I still find you respectable.

Something else I've noticed: When people play the respectable game, the atmosphere doesn't change. So if you're wondering how to make necessary changes to spirit or atmosphere, I would observe that the respectable game doesn't accomplish that. In fact, the respectable game *reaffirms* the existing atmosphere, when both people are playing it—even if it involves disagreement. I presume you've all played this game, and seen it played. I presume you've noticed how disruptive it is when somebody refuses to play, and doesn't allow that the other person is respectable, and refuses to compromise—and the *atmospheric* change that occurs.

This is why most people play the respectable game over things like pizza toppings, but people generally do *not* play the respectable game over things like "why are you passing laws that target me for harassment and menace and harm?" or "why are you inspecting my child's genitals before they can play sports, and harassing them about their gender presentation, and staking out public bathrooms to scream at them about 'grooming'?" You refuse to play the respectable game when you really care about what you want, and you find the alternative unacceptable.

Refusing the respectable game says: I do not exonerate what I see here.

It speaks of opposition and a willingness to engage in strife.

It changes the game.

Refusing the respectable game tells people: I find your position unacceptable, and therefore we are no longer aligned. It says: This position changes my opinion of you. It says: This position of yours will involve a cost to you—the loss of my regard, and perhaps a cost to your reputation and respectability in larger society, as well.

Some people *never* play the respectable game. Have you ever known a person like that? A person who habitually breaks the rules of the respectable game carries atmospheric change with them. But, if that person refuses to play the respectable game over even minor things like where we should all eat lunch, that person starts to be thought of as a very unreasonable person, which can create its own costs. So most people are hesitant about refusing to play the respectable game. I sure am. And I suspect most people are like me. Most people like to be thought of as a reasonable and respectable person. And most people don't like paying costs.

But that means there is an advantage to be gained, by refusing to play the respectable game. If only one person is playing the respectable game, then the respectable game moves the atmosphere in the direction of the player who is playing a confrontational game—even if that person is still strategically *pretending* to play the respectable game. The unreasonable person usually gets the restaurant they want, in other words, unless somebody else gets sick of their bullying shit, and also stops playing the respectable game with them.

If neither person plays the respectable game, that's when we have conflict—a fight.

Sometimes a fight is inappropriate.

Sometimes *not* fighting is what's inappropriate.

The difference is distinguishing between *acceptable* and *unacceptable*.

The difference is understanding that it's the stakes that define the game.

What's needed here is moral clarity.

Fighting carries its risks. Some of them involve getting physically or reputationally hurt, or misunderstood, or attacked, or threatened. Some of them can involve becoming a target yourself when you might have stayed safe otherwise.

But there's this: *Not* fighting carries its own risks.

What's needed here is moral clarity.

In Vonnegut's story, the math was simple. The man who played chess was forced to play, not only on his own behalf, but on behalf of his "chess pieces." The stakes were his own life and those of everyone else under his care. If he refused to play, then both his life and those of his soldiers and family would be forfeit. So, he played—not because he wanted to play, but because humoring the dictator's cruelty was the only way to defer tragedy. I don't fault his math, and I daresay neither do you. In the story, as soon as rescue arrived (spoilers), the man no longer wanted to play. If he had wanted to continue the game, I would fault his math, and I bet you would, too.

So I'd say it's important to understand who is forcing others to play a cruel game, and who is being forced to play. Wouldn't you?

Allow me to make some adjustments to Vonnegut's premise. Let's say I'm the man in the story. Let's also say I'm not a commander of soldiers; I'm merely somebody who dedicated my life to mastering the respectable game of chess, and thus I know the game and revere it, and my reputation has grown with my skill, and so when a cruel dictator decides he would like to amuse himself, and draws his political prisoners and random citizens for a deadly game, he invites me to be his opponent.

Let's say I do the math and tell myself that even though in my secret heart I deplore this practice, I should play the game. After all, I tell myself, I am a very skillful player. I will know best how to play games that minimize casualties. So let's say I agree to play the game. Maybe my arithmetic is correct; maybe I save a few lives for a few days. And, through my play, I gain the respect and admiration of the dictator, who gives me many benefits—some practical, others social.

Let's say I never ask the "pieces" what they would like me to do.

Let's say that I never even contemplate attacking the dictator to end this horror—not because I agree with the dictator, but because to physically fight one's opponent violates the rules of chess, and I cannot imagine anything more dangerous or destabilizing—not even daily murders—than abandoning the rules of my beloved respectable game.

I expect the day would come when nobody could tell the difference between my intentions and purposes and those of the dictator, even though—on the field of the game—I have opposed him every time. I expect the day would come when people correctly realized that the question of whether I sincerely oppose the dictator's practice in my secret heart is immaterial to what I am actually doing. I expect the day would come when I discovered my skills had taught the dictator how best to extract the maximum carnage from a skillful player trying to minimize carnage. Were my story being essayed by a writer with a flair for dramatic irony, I might have this realization as I finally recognized my own family among the pieces on *both sides*.

It would be a terrible lesson.

It's a lesson coming, I fear, for many of us.

In a game of chess, the purpose for both people is to play chess, and to win. Both people are engaged in the same game. They are aligned with playing that game. It's respectable and mutually beneficial. In Vonnegut's game of chess, one person is engaged in a struggle for his own life and the lives of those in his care, and the other person is engaged in a cruel and murderous amusement. The two players aren't playing the same game, and there is a recognition of that fact. The opposing player is positioning himself between his opponent and his opponent's target—which is the correct place to position yourself, if you are forced by circumstance to play in a cruel game. In my modification of Vonnegut's story, both people are once again playing the same game, perfectly aligned with cruel intent. In that story, I did not place myself between the dictator and his targets, and I maintained an illusion of respectability for our cruel and murderous game.

Again: the stakes define the game. Not the board. Not the rules.

And some stakes make a respectable game very wrong to play.

What I've noticed these days is, no matter how obvious the cruelty, no matter how murderous the amusement, there are a lot of people who still insist on playing the respectable game, who insist on having it credited back to them as virtue, who insist that it's only by engaging with those with whom they say they disagree that they can persuade them over to the right way of looking at things.

But you know what? I don't see many practitioners of the respectable game actually trying to persuade supremacists that they're wrong. I see them seeking out and finding the bigots willing to play the respectable game with them, not to identify

points of disagreement, but to identify their points of agreement, and stack as many of them as they can on top of the growing pile of corpses they've both agreed to ignore. And really,
why *would* masters of the reasonable game try to persuade supremacists away from their supremacy? They only oppose each
other on the board of personal belief, but both are clearly aligned
as a first priority with playing the same supremacist game of
luxurious mutual exoneration, no matter how dire the stakes
become. No, respectable game practitioners aren't trying to persuade *supremacists*. They tend to save their powers of persuasion
for *unrespectable* people who are refusing to play the respectable
game. They don't want to persuade homophobes to stop being
homophobic; they want to convince gay rights activists to play
the respectable game by exonerating homophobes—because
the point of the respectable game is not what you are trying to
accomplish, but how you are perceived. Somebody whose first
priority is to play the respectable game tends to platform the
bigots they claim to disagree with; but they don't tend to platform the activists with whom they claim to agree. Have you
ever noticed that? Do you see?

It's *breaking* the rules of the respectable game that changes
atmosphere.

Moral clarity breaks those rules.

◆ ◆ ◆

Moral clarity occurs when you see things as they are, and refuse to see things as they are not, even when seeing things the
way they are impeaches yourself, even when it would be more
comfortable for you to see things as they are not.

With moral clarity, you first look within. You begin to see the
unacceptable ways that you yourself benefit from supremacy. You
start to understand your own complicity, and your own imper-
fections. You begin to push against your own moral simplicities,

against your belief in your own moral purity, your own impunity, your own unassailability, your own terror of ever being thought wrong. In other words, you find your own sense of supremacy within yourself and begin to demolish it—which teaches you how to recognize and demolish supremacy outside yourself.

I tie moral clarity to confession because moral clarity is, like confession, an outward expression of an inner journey. When you confess to the truth, it's the opposite of demanding blame-lessness. It's entering blame and finding yourself there, too— not to live in the guilt, but to see things as they are with enough clarity to leave blame behind, through actions that will confess your true intentions, which are the ones that actually matter, because they govern what actually happens.

Which is why it's not accusation, but a confession.

It's an observation of an observable thing.

And it starts within.

It no longer says *that has nothing to do with me.*

It asks, at long last: *what* does *that have to do with me?*

And then it finds out. And then it knows.

And then it tells.

Moral clarity is what happens when you combine witness with hope. It allows you to act as a witness, implicating not only yourself but your blameless system, pointing to a brokenness that anyone can perceive, but which everyone—everyone respect-able, anyway—has agreed not to perceive. You're delivering an awakened belief that things are not as they should be, and an uncompromisingly hopeful declaration that better things are actually possible, despite the costs and difficulties, if we all work toward them.

Moral clarity frees you to speak with authority from exactly the place where you have been wrong, from exactly the place where other people like you are still wrong, in ways that those people cannot deny. Moral clarity is like a vaccine to the great virus of supremacy, delivering awareness and conviction of

brokenness throughout the system, allowing the system to recognize supremacist blamelessness wherever it appears, and to
demolish supremacy by repairing what supremacy has broken.
Instead of exonerating abusers on behalf of the abused from a
position of luxurious safety, moral clarity confesses abuse *from
the position of an abuser,* not out of some self-serving guilt, but
out of a deep awareness and conviction. It's a confession about
abusive society that abusive society finds far more challenging
to deny, because it comes from within itself.

Again: Moral clarity isn't about guilt. It's about healing. It's
about fixing broken things.

A blameless society, founded in supremacy, hates this, because
moral clarity inevitably makes supremacy pay a higher cost—and
supremacy is, above everything, opposed to paying costs.

Exoneration makes denial cheap, and maintains comfortable
relationships with profitable abuse. But **moral clarity repairs
our confession**. It demolishes exonerative games that comfortable people play over unacceptable stakes. **Moral clarity
increases the cost of denial**—and might move to your cause
self-exonerating people, living in denial, whose only goal is to
avoid cost. To speak with moral clarity about yourself and your
place in the world is to fight blameless supremacy's sabotage of
confession. You'll know this, because as you use moral clarity to
confess your awareness of truth and your conviction to repair,
blameless people will begin to attack that clarity as divisive and
polarizing and dangerous and wrong. They will make sure the
price for speaking with clarity is as high as they can make it—so
you'll know you're there, once you start to pay.

I think moral clarity is a powerful tool in our fight against
supremacy, available to everyone.

It expands the frame. It moves the spirit. It changes the
atmosphere. It tells a new story.

It raises the cost of blameless supremacy and its many sabotages.

Moral clarity silences denial, and sharpens confession, which makes repentance inevitable.

And that's what I think repair looks like.

5. RECONCILIATION & SOLIDARITY

The fourth accommodation of blameless supremacy is an accommodation of the fourth sabotage—that is, accommodation of oppression, which sabotages repentance, which sabotages the redeeming work of repair.

At repentance, blameless supremacy becomes desperate. Whenever a lot of people not only signal their awareness and desire for repair, but actually start to talk about doing the actual repair, it creates a natural human spirit of repair, and a spirit of repair will inevitably start fixing things and paying the costs for doing so—which is completely unacceptable to someone opposed to paying costs. Finding something unacceptable carries a conviction to fight it, which is why it's at this moment, as supremacy starts to lose its blamelessness, that we'll find a blameless supremacist society highly motivated to fight repair with an active and persistent oppression. Oppression is a showy demonstration of strength, but one that reveals a great weakness—a fear that it might be losing.

We've come a long way.

Our awakening to awareness is sabotaged by deliberate ignorance. Our conviction that what is broken ought to be fixed is sabotaged by ignorant complacency. Confession of our new awareness and of our growing conviction is sabotaged by ignorant and complacent denial.

And, as I perceive it, each sabotage is accommodated by its own enablement.

Ignorance, accommodated by incurious neutrality.

Conviction, accommodated by vacuous compromise.

Denial, accommodated by self-serving exoneration.

The enablement of the fourth sabotage—the sabotage of our repentance with oppression—is something I name **reconciliation**.

Reconciliation is very popular in our society, I've noticed—provided it costs the person offering it nothing. If it carries a cost, I've noticed, reconciliation is treated as if it were punishment. We can see cheap reconciliation everywhere, if we look around.

Let's look around.

◆ ◆ ◆

It's 2022 now. Last week, Paul Pelosi—whose wife, Nancy Pelosi, is the speaker of the House of Representatives—was attacked in his own home by a hammer-wielding maniac. It was an assassination attempt, inspired by the narratives and propaganda now offered daily and nationwide by mainstream Republicans.

Let's start there.

Paul Pelosi's attacker was chanting "where's Nancy," which is what the January 6 mob was chanting as they invaded the U.S. Capitol. In case you forgot, January 6, 2021, was the previous time the Republican Party tried to assassinate the sitting speaker of the House (as well as the sitting vice president, and many others). I say "the Republican Party tried" because the mob was sent by the leader of that party, Donald Trump, who was at that time president; and the Republican Party has worked tirelessly and shamelessly ever since in defense of that mob, and the leader who incited them, and the members of Congress who provided them material and strategic aid; and also the Republican Party has worked tirelessly in pursuit of that mob's cause—which is the abolition of our democracy, the installation of a supremacist authoritarian theocracy, as well as the implicit threat of the prosecution or murder of the Democratic leadership, which is the sort of thing they love to chant about in their rallies.

Anyway, the guy with the hammer thankfully didn't kill Paul

Pelosi or Nancy Pelosi—but it was an assassination attempt by the Republican Party all the same. We've learned from the record he left behind—15 years of blogging—that the assassin's mind had been packed with standard murderous components of modern conservative belief: Holocaust denial, climate change denial, transphobia, racism, voter fraud theories, screeds against "pedos," and other things, none of which distinguish him in any way from mainstream Republican candidates and office holders, or from messages now emanating from the Republican propaganda arm of far-right media figures spread across many and various platforms and channels. And what happened is what happens as a matter of standard practice in times like these, when the obviousness of what the Republican Party is becomes inescapable. What happened was: The Republican Party and its propaganda wing did everything they could to establish that the culprit sprang from some other ideology separate from theirs, and made it clear that this attack had nothing at all to do with them, and that the culprit acted completely on his own, and what they expect is for the Democratic Party to build bridges to them, members of the Republican Party, who are the very people who have made this political violence not only likely, but inevitable.

It's a demand.

It's a demand that we not know all the things they've done to deliberately foster an atmosphere of rage and political violence that has created a growing population of potential free-range political assassins, and a demand that we not know the ways they have supplied their potential assassins with a list of political targets for that rage. It's a demand that we not understand the clear intent that is communicated by all these things they've done, or the way they align with each act of violence made inevitable by that intent. It's a demand that we fail to observe the clearly observable fact that the brokenness enabling each instance of political violence exists specifically because the

Republican Party opposes any cost of any repair or improvement. It's a demand from people disinterested in making friends with us that we make friends with them. It's a demand from those who divide us to come together. It's a demand to unify with people who scorn unity. It's a demand to establish peace with those who intend to continue to wage war.

It is a demand for **reconciliation without reparation**—a reconciliation that will not only be cheap for the reconciled abusers, but free, whose cost will be ongoing harm, borne by those the reconciled abusers intend to go on harming.

It remains to be seen to what degree the rest of our media will pick up and promote that demand in response to this latest infraction, or the extent to which public sentiment will accept it, but if the January 6 insurrection and hundreds of other infractions are any indication, the answer will be "to a great degree" and "to an overwhelming extent." I don't see Republicans framed very often as what they have clearly revealed themselves to be—which is an insurrectionist party and a supremacist hate group, seeking to overthrow democracy in order to install a corrupt autocratic theocracy on behalf of supremacists. To do so would break journalistic neutrality, which has clearly become a more important principle than the journalistic commitment to expressing the clear truth. And I still meet people everywhere who consider Republicans a reasonable option that reasonable people might choose and still be thought of as reasonable, instead of what they are, which is a national suicide pill, unhinged from reality, and eager to make even worse atrocities even more inevitable. And sure enough, there seems a very good chance that they will be empowered to do that, by an activated supremacist minority and a complacent middle, using voter suppression and outright intimidation and malfeasance and structural imbalances they've leveraged even further to their benefit.

If that happens, I expect to see what happens every time supremacists come to power.

I expect to see voices elevated that instruct us to, first, ignore everything about what supremacy intends to do and is already doing, and, next, to focus on acknowledging the supremacist perspective to be a reasonable one, and on easing supremacist discomfort—which happens to be a discomfort with the simple existence of people supremacists hate, whose perspectives we will not be encouraged to understand and whose own discomfort we will not be expected to ease. I expect to hear that the supremacist victory should serve as a rebuke to those seeking equality, and a proof that the demands for equality went "too far."

And if they lose these elections they are predicted to win? I expect to see the exact same thing: narratives centering supremacists and their distress and alienation, warning us against going "too far" in our opposition to those who have already gone too far, warning us against leaving behind those who are determined to stay behind even as the rest of us go ahead; warning us against painting them with a broad brush even as their positions are painted in the best possible light; warning us against condemning them and writing them off even as they are being exonerated; warning us against leaving them with no path back to reconciliation even as reconciliation is once again offered to them for free. I expect to see what we always see: a frame that casts the discomfort of supremacists as the central problem to solve, and the comfort of supremacists as the chief priority to pursue, and validates as reasonable and justified their threat of violent retaliation if we set any priority other than these.

After all, I expect to be told, *what are we to do?*

If we oppose them, won't it just cause *more* violence?

And anyway, am I saying they're all *evil* and should just be *abandoned?*

There are tens of millions of them!

Where is the room for *redemption?*

Shouldn't we be open to *reconciliation?*
Hold that thought.

◆ ◆ ◆

I'd like to return to an central point about these enablements;
neutrality and compromise and exoneration and reconciliation
aren't *inherently* bad things. They are tools, which all have appropriate and necessary uses, and in fact are important parts
of any healthy progression toward repair. People of bad intent,
because they are aligned with a human spirit that is inherently
abusive, are skilled at abusing these potentially good things, using them as justifications for their bad intentions and abusive
actions. They do this by fouling the progressive order of repair;
by demanding each tool be deployed *before* it would be appropriate, by demanding the fruits of repair while refusing to plant
repair's seeds.

Neutrality, for example, is an important quality for any
mind to possess if it would make itself open to new ideas and
experiences, which can lead to cycles of deeper growth and
awareness and improvement and discovery. It's only when it is
removed from the process of repair that neutrality becomes an
enablement. It's only when neutrality is used out of order that it
becomes toxic. To establish your neutrality before first becoming aware of systemic abuse and brokenness, or bearing witness
to what is actually happening, or deciding that broken things
must be fixed, is a neutrality designed to stagnate the process
of repair, because it refuses to distinguish between what is and
what is not, or to contemplate what should be. Neutrality must
come *after* awareness and conviction, not before. Once you
know this, you can easily detect people who are aligned with
blameless supremacy, because they will demand neutrality only
if it comes *before* awareness and conviction, only if it is sure to

sabotage repair, allowing them to avoid paying the natural costs that attend awareness and conviction.

Compromise, too, can be an important component of an open mind negotiating between various perspectives that are all aligned toward an attempt to repair the same complex problem—which allows us to use our diversity of perspective to find the very best solution. It's only when it is removed from the process of repair that compromise becomes enablement; only when it's used out of order that it becomes toxic. Any compromise made before establishing a public understanding—that a broken thing is in fact broken and that the only valid options for discussion must involve repair—is a compromise designed to stagnate repair, because it refuses to consider the end toward which compromise is being deployed. Compromise must come *after* confession, not before. Once you know this, you can easily detect people who are aligned with blameless supremacy, because they will demand compromise only if it comes before a mutual understanding of what the problem is and a mutual determination to solve it; only if it is sure to sabotage repair, allowing them to avoid paying the natural costs that attend confession.

And even the urge to exonerate can be an important process of repair; useful for recognizing and celebrating growth and positive movement, for perceiving when somebody who had been aligned with brokenness begins to enter awareness, begins to be convicted, begins to actually change their intent—things that are perceptible in what they say and do. Exoneration is necessary, if we are to recognize the ways that somebody has changed for the better, if we are to celebrate positive movement and encourage further positive movement. The exonerative urge can be very important for repair. It's only when it is removed from the process of repair that it becomes enablement; only when it's used out of order that it becomes toxic. Any exoneration offered before its beneficiary actually repents—meaning they agree to pay the natural costs of repair, and start to pay them—is an exoneration designed to stagnate repair, because it only confesses a desire to repair, but remains aligned with brokenness. Exoneration must come *after* repentance, not before. Once you know this, you can easily detect people who are aligned with blameless supremacy, because they will demand exoneration for having participated in the problem while still participating in the problem and opposing any solution, allowing them to avoid paying the natural costs that come with repentance.

So it is, too, with reconciliation without reparation.

Let's examine what reconciliation looks like when it is put in its right place, as a part of a system aligned to repair.

◆ ◆ ◆

If somebody abuses somebody else, and a third somebody enables that abuse, then the relationship—between the abused party on one hand and the abusers and enablers on the other—has been broken by the abuse and the enablement, and the abused party has experienced the harmful effects of abuse. But the abused party is not the only person harmed by abuse. The abuser is also broken by their own abuse, and the enabler is broken by their enablement of it. They are broken inside themselves, by aligning themselves inherently with supremacy, by choosing unsustainable lies instead of natural, generative, sustaining truths.

But even though they are broken, they are responsible for the brokenness.

And the responsibility they carry is the responsibility to enter into a spirit of repair.

They? We.

We? I.

Me.

Because I'm the one who put my street there.

When I harm someone, the responsibility I carry is not to first establish repair of the relationship I have broken. The responsibility I carry is to repair the brokenness within *myself*, which includes accepting that the damage caused by my abuse means I may not achieve reconciliation with those I have harmed, and reconciliation is not a matter I will get to decide, and that the realigning work of repair is worth it *for its own sake*. If I have made myself supreme over others, and harmed others, I must ask: How does a supremacist repair the brokenness within themselves?

I think the answer is, the same way anything else is repaired. The process of repair seems to be the same for broken roads or broken systems as it is for the human spirit or anything else: awakening, then conviction, then confession, then repentance, and then finally repair, which always includes paying the costs.

If the abused party doesn't desire reconciliation, and the abuser refuses to accept that decision, but instead uses this rejection as a reason to return to abuse, and uses their abuse to force the abused party to make a show of reconciliation with them anyway, and demands their enabler exonerate them on the basis of that show—and if the enabler extends that reconciliation to them, forgiving them on behalf of the abused party—then there has been no repair, because the abuser and the enabler never truly abandoned their supremacy, or repaired the brokenness inside themselves.

The abuser doesn't get to dictate the repair of the relationship they have broken, and the enabler doesn't get to decide that the reconciliation should happen or has already happened. Abusers and enablers only get to align themselves with repair of their own brokenness, which means rejecting a supremacy that would demand they receive those things from victims without doing any reconciling work.

But if an abuser acknowledges their abuse, and the enabler acknowledges their enablement, and both realize they are to blame, and then speak that knowledge and realization, and then change their behavior so that they no longer engage in abuse and enablement, then the brokenness within them is at least at the beginning of repair, because they are no longer aligned with their blameless supremacy over those they have harmed. Then and only then, the relationship with those they have abused might be repaired, and then only if the harmed party desires it. And if the harmed party does desire it, and engages that repair by joining with the abuser and the enabler in a new relationship free of brokenness, that is reconciliation within a healthy framework of repair.

We don't see much of that these days, though.

What we see instead is reconciliation *without* reparation. It's an appeasing reconciliation that insists that the brokenness caused by abuse is the responsibility of the abused, not the abuser, to repair, by forgiving the abuser before the abuser is even sorry.

It's a demand—a demand for appeasing reconciliation.

Appeasing reconciliation is what happens when the process of repair stagnates at repentance. We are aware of the brokenness in our society, aware of injustice and abuse caused by a belief in supremacy. We agree that what is broken should be repaired, and we share in a collective sense of responsibility to join in the repair. We even proclaim the need for repair publicly. But we don't progress from there. We don't align ourselves away from our own blamelessness, but choose to realign ourselves with it, and as a result we make our first priority our own comfortable relationships with people aligned against repair. We engage in a luxurious reconciliation, which costs us nothing, while making other people pay its unnaturally exorbitant rates.

Appeasing reconciliation holds that some submissive posture exists, which marginalized people can (and should!) take toward the blameless supremacists who harass and demonize and menace and harm them, a submissive posture that would be deferential enough to preclude or at least blunt supremacy's promised oppression, and that it is marginalized people's responsibility to seek that submissive posture, find it, and hold it indefinitely, in order to secure the psychological comfort of those who abuse them—and that by doing this, the marginalized people will *earn* the right to live, a right that can only be given to them by supremacist abusers, as a gift. It's a position that almost always involves abandoning some group that is the subject of particularly energized oppression, almost always framed as a way to protect different marginalized groups that might otherwise be subject to that aggression as well, almost always offered by a person who is not a member of any of the targeted groups, and almost always framed as a strategy.

What does appeasing reconciliation demand we give up?

It's never a *what*, actually. It's always a *who*.

The *who* is usually whoever is being targeted for particularly energized oppression at the moment.

In response to oppression, appeasing reconciliation offers up a nesting doll of ostensibly strategic capitulations, an endless series of retreats allegedly in search of an opportunity to advance which never arrives, because appeasement always prioritizes the convenience of those who oppose progress over the existence or survival of those who require progress to survive.

Appeasing reconciliation will offer up trans people in order to get the votes of people who "will never accept" trans people, so that we can protect, oh, let's say, gay marriage. But appeasement will just as easily offer up gay marriage rights in order to get the votes of people who "will never accept" gay marriage, so we can, oh, let's say, safeguard the vote. But appeasement will just as readily offer up voting rights in order to get the votes of people who "have legitimate concerns about voting security" in order to, oh, let's say, protect a woman's right to abortion. But appeasement's practitioners will just as readily make alliances with forced-birth anti-choicers, in order to, oh, let's say, protect trans people from oppressive anti-trans laws.

And round and round we go.

Appeasing reconciliation seems to never notice that people whose favor they intend to curry are always on the verge of providing support that they never quite provide, because there is always some issue that makes them too uncomfortable, and so their support for justice will always stay contingent on safeguarding some other injustice.

Appeasing reconciliation claims to be aligned in favor of repair, but never actually aligns with it; always speaks in favor of justice, yet always seeks the support and permission of people who are made uncomfortable with some facet of justice; always speaks in defense of those who most suffer injustice's effects, yet always scolds those same people for making the demand for justice too troublesome to ensure the perfect comfort of those made uncomfortable by justice's demands.

Appeasing reconciliation teaches oppressors that people will abandon the effort for justice if it turns into a fight, which incentivizes oppressors to turn any attempt for justice into a fight.

Appeasing reconciliation teaches bullies who want to avoid the cost of a fight that there exists no appetite to fight them.

Appeasing reconciliation teaches oppressors that the violence they enact to defend their own blameless supremacy will always be treated as valid and reasonable—and teaches those oppressed by that violence that their allies in the fight against blameless supremacy will always abandon them, and so encourages them to give up on their conviction that change is possible.

Appeasing reconciliation of abuse encourages abuse. No, it's even worse than that—appeasement of abuse *incentivizes* abuse. It makes the cost of abuse low. It accepts the offer of surrender on behalf of other people who have not agreed to surrender and who will never be offered peaceful terms. The appeasement offered by reconciliation without reparation makes the spiritual realignment of repentance expensive, and difficult, and unpopular.

So now I want to answer the big question, which is *how do we fix it?*

I want to talk about **solidarity**.

Let me tell you a story.

◆ ◆ ◆

When I was a child, they let us out of the classroom twice a day as I recall. You can only hold 25-40 children inside a room the size of an average gas station for so long before the molecule turns unstable and I assume the teacher needs a few stiff drinks, and you can't really have children in the room for that, so we'd go outdoors to scream and pound on each other for a while and hurl ourselves into the air or into walls like sentient superballs, and that was recess as I recall. Again, it was a long time ago. It was the olden days: the eighties—the *nineteen* eighties.

I do remember one recess game that was popular. It was called "smear the queer." This was basically tag with a ball added. Whoever held the ball was "the queer." Everybody else chased "the queer." You could hit "the queer" as hard as you wanted is my recollection. The thing to do was to get "the queer" on the ground and then everyone would dogpile on, maybe with an elbow or a knee thrown in. Then when that was over, you'd throw the ball in the air and whoever the ball landed closest to would have to be "the queer," and usually a guy wouldn't want to take the ball and would be forced to take it, if he wasn't tough enough to force somebody else to take it. It was a rough game, with pretty much all the boys playing it, taking turns being "the queer" and then taking turns in joining the mob brutalizing "the queer." And some of the tougher guys could choose kids they wanted to brutalize by making them play.

If you refused to play, that automatically made you "the queer."
We all played.

Nobody in this game ever fought on behalf of "the queer."
Nobody even considered it. I certainly did not consider it. Anyone doing so would have broken the game so fundamentally that
it would have stopped making any sort of sense. I do know this:
being "the queer" was not fun. You didn't particularly want to
be "the queer." You'd do what it took to avoid it. It wasn't a thing
questioned, this playground game. Fighting was not allowed,
but unless serious injury occurred there was no problem that
I recall with all the boys taking turns getting beaten for being
"the queer." I don't know how we knew about this game. I guess
the way we knew all the other games; somebody told somebody
who told somebody who told everybody else. An older brother to
a younger brother, maybe, just a sort of inheritance of tradition
and knowledge.

It was just a game. A playground game.

This was pretty much my only exposure to the concept of
"queer" back in the olden days. Sure, I heard rumors—of men
who wanted to marry men, is how I recall being told about it—
but it was in the same category as hearing about werewolves,
or Freddy Krueger. There weren't *really* gay people, at least not
if they knew what was good for them. We had words for these
sorts of mythological people besides "the queer," which we deployed freely at one another, usually as a casual insult. I won't
print those words here, because we "can't" say those words anymore—which means we *can*, but not without receiving awareness that by using those words we've done actual harm to actual
people, and I'm told that the delivery of this awareness means
that these are far more polarized and divisive times today than
they were back in the olden days, when video games cost a quar-
ter a play, and schoolchildren played "smear the queer," and calling each other slurs meaning "homosexual" didn't mean you
thought the person was something as terrible and mythological

as *gay*, it simply meant you thought the person was worthy of contempt, or bad, or socially maladroit, or dumb, or you just didn't like them, or (in a certain tone) it meant you were getting ready to beat up the person you said it to, or sometimes it meant nothing at all.

Speaking of *dumb*, there was a kid in our grade who didn't learn in class as easily as the rest. We had a word for him and people like him, too, which again we deployed liberally about him, but also among each other as an insult. We had words for all *sorts* of people. They all meant basically the same thing, or at least they all felt like they meant the same thing when you were called them, which is that you were the guy who'd been chosen to hold the ball. I won't print them here, because, again, these are much more polarized times, when nobody agrees about what is funny and you *can't say anything anymore*, because *everyone* is offended so easily and *nobody* just relaxes, and that makes things harder for *everybody*, is what I am told.

For people who believe that everyone is too easily offended these days and should just relax, I expect the olden eighties were indeed a fine time, because everybody who saw us play smear the queer was pretty relaxed about it, and none of them were offended, as far as I could tell. It was a much more relaxed time for *everybody*, I'm sure, and *we* were far less polarized. The unpolarized eighties were a halcyon time; there were all kinds of words you could say without anybody ever delivering any awareness to you about it at all. Nevertheless, even in the eighties, there were words we generally knew you *couldn't* say. These were words that people could use with impunity when our parents and grandparents were children, in an even *less* polarized time, when racial slurs came easily, with no social consequences whatsoever. I had a vague understanding that back in the sixties there had been some *very* polarized times, and now, following those times, everyone agreed those words that had been OK prior to the sixties were mostly no longer OK, so we were no longer polarized. (I still heard those words all the time, by the way. I just noticed people took care of their company before using them.)

And twice a day we went out for recess, and played our games—which were just games.

Somewhere around that time, Ronald Reagan's press secretary told a lot of jokes on the record about AIDS—the disease that was killing thousands and thousands of gay men, the disease that the Reagan administration was ignoring to fatal effect, and everybody in the room on *both sides* laughed and laughed and laughed. The punchline was that thousands of gay men were dying. I don't know how *both sides* knew this was funny. I guess the way they knew all the other jokes were funny, or the way we learned our playground games; just a sort of inheritance of shared knowledge about what was funny. They, like schoolchildren, seemed to think that gay people were no more real than werewolves. There was no real controversy at the time about this incident, no significant outcry, or at least nobody that *mattered* complained. It was the olden times: the nineteen eighties, a far less polarized time, when the world's most powerful government leaving people to die by the thousands from a virus was funny, and everybody agreed with that, or at least kept quiet about it if they didn't. These days, when the government lets thousands of people die from a virus, there's lots of yelling and fighting about the damage to human dignity and the loss of human life, and the ways we treat disabled and immunocompromised and other marginalized people as disposable. People were yelling and fighting about human dignity and the loss of human life back in the nineteen eighties, too, by the way. It's just that back then *we* found it much easier to ignore.

And I'm informed this means *we're* far more polarized now.

I think a lot about this: how polarized *we* all know *we* are right now, and what a problem *we* all know it is. It's a real problem, I'm told. *We've* never been more polarized within *our* lifetimes, at least that's the word.

We and *us* and *our* are such interesting words. They leave a trail. You can usually follow them back to the lair of their underlying assumptions. "*We* have never been more polarized as a country," for example, says something very clear about who is considered a part of this country, and who is not. If one becomes adept at following the trail of pronouns, one might almost start to observe that the idea of "polarized" is very much a question of whose perspective you've decided to take up, and where you set your poles. One might almost start to realize that even neutrality is a way of taking a side. One might even start to understand the deeper meanings of a blameless society's strange hostility toward precision, when it comes to pronouns.

But I get it; I really do. I see what is meant by "polarized." Family relationships have grown cold. Friendships fray. There's invective on the airwaves on *both sides*. Rhetoric is superheated on *both sides*. There's a lot of anger on *both sides*. And, if you're a marginalized person of middle age or younger, this is perhaps a particularly terrifying time, because the worst intentions of those who wish to harm you have rarely in living memory been so near to political actualization, and those who will normalize literally anything in order to maintain a comfortable order have never worked so hard to make the worst intentions of the worst actors seem as if they're perfectly normal.

But *both sides* are fighting.

There's a lot of *strife*.

And I've been talking about gay people, but we could be talking about many things.

To give just one example of very many, we could talk about democracy.

On one hand, there are people who want everybody to have equal access to the ballot, and on the other, there are people who would like to further entrench and expand our country's history of disenfranchisement of racial minorities, and to see election results they dislike overturned completely—and they're doing it. But, while many of the people who claim to want everyone to have equal access to the ballot seem quite willing to compromise with the people who want to dismantle democracy (almost as if accommodating those people was their automatic reflex), a lot of other people seem to really mean what they say about defending democracy, and have become uncompromisingly angry and hostile toward the people who want to dismantle democracy, and people who want to disenfranchise minorities are certainly willing to fight about it. People who want to disenfranchise minorities are showing they're willing to threaten and harass and even *kill* for it, if they decide the police aren't doing so efficiently enough on their behalf.

So, there's a fight. And that's distressing.

The resulting strife of this fight is very damaging to the national fabric, I'm told. Probably so! But I'm not convinced it's more damaging to the national fabric than the dismantling of our democracy, which is the project of the disenfranchisers, and always was. Disenfranchisement isn't new, and the fight against it isn't new, either; it's just awareness of the fight that's new for a lot of otherwise unthreatened people. And, perhaps, from the perspective of disenfranchised people, those times when few others fought beside them (or even acknowledged that there was a fight) felt *more* polarizing than now, when more people are fighting and refusing to stop fighting for the sake of comfortable politeness—even if that means that there is more fighting now, even if that means there is more *strife,* more discomfort, for people who are used to feeling comfortable and going unopposed.

We're talking about democracy now, but we could be talking about climate injustice. We could be talking about wealth disparity. We could be talking about access to public spaces. We could be talking about insulin prices. We could be talking about anti-trans bathroom bills, or anti-awareness education laws.

We could be talking about many things.

Maybe for people who suffer systemic disenfranchisement,

the fact of the fight isn't newly polarizing, because the fact of the fight has been a reality every day of their lives. Maybe it's not the fight itself that's distressing so much as the fact that there are people willing to fight to enforce and expand systemic disenfranchisement, supported by people willing to ignore it. Maybe the increase in strife actually feels like the first fluttering sign of *solidarity*—one they've seen go dormant far too many times to place much hope in, perhaps, but nevertheless certainly not polarization. Because when people fight beside you as you struggle for dignity and life, then you are *less* polarized from them, not more. This seems obvious to say, but it's apparently not—because, remember, it's become received knowledge that at this time of strife *we* have never been more polarized on *both sides*.

We? *We* who?

Both sides? What does *both* mean?

◆ ◆ ◆

Think of this respectable modern idea of fighting against polarization on *both sides*.

You know, that great narrative formulation of our modern age: *Both* sides.

The two sides. The only two sides you have to consider.

Please, name the two sides.

We might use the standard way of looking at "both sides," which is to frame it around whether or not somebody agrees or disagrees with a proposition. Take gay marriage. You *agree* with gay marriage. I *disagree* with it. We are *both sides*, though neither of us is gay. We might point out that this framing allows two people who are unaffected by a topic to discuss the topic in a way that erases the person directly affected by the harmful proposition—actually takes them completely outside of it, by postulating two sides, and not including the person affected as either of those two sides. We might point out how this advantages a person who wants to keep the harmful proposition in circulation forever. We might therefore postulate that a better way of framing "both sides" would be to view the two sides along lines of "those who are affected" and "those who aren't affected."

You *agree* with gay marriage, I *disagree*, but neither of us have our humanity up for debate. We are one side. And then there are gay people, for whom marriage is a case of being a part of society or being shunned from it. The other side.

I think that's a better framing, for sure. We should use that framing, if only to understand the ways our thinking has been warped by modern "both sides" narratives, and stop treating real toxic ideas that really harm real people as if they are bloodless abstractions that merit debate.

But I suspect it's still the wrong framing.

I think the problem is the word *both*.

What if humanity is a gem instead of a playing card? What if there aren't *two* sides? What if there are *many?*—almost infinite in number, and not oppositional, but cooperative? What if we saw the sides as different kinds of lived experience? What if a lot of us changed our framing in *that* way? What if, as a result of this reframing, we weren't just suddenly more sensitive as a society, but much more aware? What if there are hundreds of millions of us, billions maybe, all acting in a spirit of growth and improvement, acting on a shared understanding that all human beings are intrinsically valuable in and of themselves, acting with a shared commitment to hearing and accommodating a truly extraordinary array of lived experiences, acting from an increasing awareness of the ways our current societal structures and assumptions have failed to honor the humanity of human beings, and united in a determination to fix those failings? What if there is, as a result, a momentous shift transpiring, right now, a massive explosion of voices heard, as people take back their own rightful license to exist as themselves, as others try to listen and learn and change and improve?

Think of all the different things we're learning about how to live together, about how best to honor the essential humanity of one another. Think of all the different perspectives available. If you are a fan of nuance and avoiding simplistic arguments, think of the *complexity* to be found here. Think of how much work there is to do in order to be a society that arranges itself, not around enforcing a single default way of being human, but around embracing the full spectrum of what being human can be. Think of the challenge of it. Think of how much more we'll have to listen, to live peacefully in a society where so many different types of people exist. Think even of the inconvenience, the accommodation we'll all make, as we make room in areas where we've been given a surplus of space, for those who have been given none. Because just as the accommodation of supremacy is what empowers the supremacy, so the accommodation of equality and diversity is what empowers equality and diversity.

Now think of the people who don't want to participate in that—and more, who don't want anybody else to participate, either, and are willing to harm people to prevent it from happening. Think of all the people who would rather just *not* listen, and *not* learn about things we might do that would make it easier for other people to live, all in defense of their own perceived right to do as they please, without ever being "oppressed" by receiving knowledge of their harmful impact on others. Think of all the people trapped in their own unimprovable blamelessness, who treat even the suggestion that they might have harmed somebody—or spoken out of ignorance, or benefitted from an unjust configuration of society—as an unforgivable assault on their freedom, one that demands immediate retribution. Think of the people who consider even the mention of the existence of other types of people to be disruptive and disturbing, and think of the violence they are willing to see enacted in order to smooth over that disturbance in their lives. Think of the people whose perspective is that they are the only side that matters, and that all other people, by insisting on taking an equal place in our society, by insisting that their perspective also be heard, by insisting *we deserve to live, and you are making that difficult*, represent an existential threat.

Now realize that this supremacist side, which refuses to participate in humanity—*they* are habitually framed as one of the two and only two sides that is meant when we say *both sides*.

Really? The people who don't want to participate in our shared humanity represent *half* of the entire ideological equation here? If they get their way, and pass all their laws designed to preserve their own blameless supremacy, and pave over the global swimming pool, is it really only *one* side that loses?

Think how much more stagnant "both sides" framing makes us. It takes the gorgeous multifaceted gem of society and smashes it flat. Think of how much we'll miss. Think of what we'll fail to learn. Think of how simplistic supremacist arguments are, no matter how complex they make the rationale. Think of the improvement that won't happen. Think how far behind we'll fall.

Think of the voices we'll never hear, the accomplishments we'll never see.

Think who will be harmed. Think who will be killed.

Think who *already* has been harmed and killed.

Our mission is honoring everyone's basic humanity in a spirit of solidarity, and it's a challenging mission with many problems to solve and many bumps along the way. When people enter into a spirit of blamelessness and domination, they have a completely different mission—an unacceptable one, a spirit that isn't a side in that project, but an obstacle to it.

The problem with even talking about "both sides" is, it promotes people acting with abusive intent and a politics of domination to the level of one of two equal "sides," with literally every other way of being human lumped together as the other "side." That elevation is the core of the supremacist belief system, and we're accommodating it.

The problem with even talking about "both sides" is, it validates the worldview of people with abusive intention, by considering their politics of domination an acceptable outcome, and so they win before we even start, simply by having us accept their premise of only two sides, their premise that obstacles to the existence of all other sides represent fully half of the human equation. When you accept the "both sides" framing, the conversation immediately stops being about figuring out how best to honor the essential humanity and basic needs of everyone, and becomes about which people to exclude.

This idea there are only two sides, and supremacists are one of them?

That's *their* framing. It's a lie.

People who want to end polarization by listening to *both sides* say they are doing so because they recognize the debate is a complex one, but listening to only two sides is kids' stuff. It's a product of shallow understanding and an immature spirit. Truly open-minded people don't have time for that. Open-minded people are listening to too many other sides, and aren't interested in leaving any of those sides out. Open-minded people understand that learning to accommodate all the sides isn't weak, but strong; not closed, but open. Which is why—if you want unity—you mustn't treat everyone working together toward the goal of a just and equitable world as an equal "side" to the people who are being active intentional obstacles to that goal. This is what makes people who accept "both sides" framing in the name of "unity" so toxic. If you engage "both sides" in this way, you are actually aligned with a politics of domination and abuse, even if you are arguing against the politics of domination and abuse.

I'll repeat that: even if you are arguing against.

That's where we are right now. That's how our culture sees *both sides*.

That's our spirit. That's the atmosphere.

So let's change the atmosphere.

We change the atmosphere with new ideas.

Here's a new idea: There are not two sides, but many.

Here's a new idea: We don't need to listen to *both sides*, be-cause *we are the sides*, multitudinous in number, and we are listening to each other *already*.

Here's a new idea: The people who refuse to repent of their blamelessness don't get to be one whole side in a binary. They aren't allowed to force us all into one side, and then wait for us to beg them for our permission to exist.

Both sides?

We *are* the sides.

We are the sides.

We are the sides.

◆ ◆ ◆

There were real people indicated by the slurs and words we used to use on the playgrounds in the eighties, which *we* "can't" say anymore. Perhaps those real people experienced those golden olden times—when those words were given free license and *nobody* got offended and *everyone* was much more relaxed—as a *more* polarizing time than right now, when using those words will at least create some controversy, even if that means there is more visible anger and argument at the dinner tables and on the airwaves now than there was before.

I have to say, if I were a gay teacher at my elementary school in the eighties, I might have experienced that time as extremely polarizing. There were things that *couldn't* be said back then, too. It's just they were different things than slurs. In those days you *couldn't* say things like "actually, *I'm* gay'" or else you'd be carrying the ball. You'd become "the queer," and if you wanted to know what that meant for you, you only had to watch the boys playing at recess, or listen to *both sides* laughing at the press secretary of the president of the United States about tens of thousands of dead gay men. Criticism would be the least of it. Criticism still *is* the least of it, even in these times that have more protections for and awareness about gay people ... protections and awareness that are what make *us* more polarized, as many very fine people will remind us. Perhaps this hypothetical gay teacher at my elementary school back in the eighties, who today sees families and churches breaking up because a critical mass of their members are no longer willing to go along with the anti-gay bigotry of the rest, does not experience this as an increase in *polarization*, but of *solidarity*, even though they recognize an increase in overall strife.

Yes, and what do *we* mean when *we* say "*we've* rarely been so polarized," anyway?

What if instead we introduced new ideas?

What if instead we said "It's been a long time since awareness of the reality of injustice has been made so unavoidably present to otherwise comfortable people?"

What if instead we said "It's been a long time since so many people have become so violently resentful of the moral demands of justice?"

Let me suggest something that might seem counterintuitive to many of us, who are used to comfort: **At this time of increased strife, we have rarely been less polarized as a country.** Am I saying we're not polarized? Far from it.

I'm saying we're misunderstanding what polarization even is.

When people say "this polarization is tearing *us* apart," by *us* they don't ever seem to mean "the people our society ignores and harms, either for identity or fortune; the people we ignore for our own lazy comfort." That is a polarization they insist on entrenching; that is the cause they fight for. When people say "this polarization is tearing *us* apart," by *us* they seem to mean "the critical mass of people who before now were willing to license our own injustice." And yes, many people, who resent the inconvenience of that fight, or who have no stomach for it, experience this strife as polarization. They experience it as being treated as a *them* for the first time. Even though nobody is trying to disenfranchise them or take away their bodily autonomy or risk their health and welfare, increasingly people are simply no longer willing to date them or debate them or prioritize their comfort above the survival of others. Again, for many, I suspect the increase in this kind of strife isn't experienced as polarization at all, but solidarity.

So, where do you set your poles?

Are you opposed only to fights? Or are you actually interested in what people are fighting for? Do you see each fight as an *increase* in polarization? If so, be honest with yourself about the assumptions you're aligning with, about who in your worldview is allowed to be *we* and *us* and *ourselves,* and who isn't.

Consider the idea that treating certain people as if they don't matter enough to care about or fight for their dignity and their lives—and doing this so thoroughly and effectively that society treats them as if they are nonexistent and disposable—creates a much deeper polarization than any fight over the holiday dinner table or on the airwaves over whether or not it's good to do so.

And: the more peaceful that subjugation, the greater the domination of those who would dominate, and thus the greater the true polarization. Consider a corollary, that as people stop going along with this unnatural injustice, it will decrease the peace of that subjugation; will increase resentment and strife, for as long as there are people still willing to fight to subjugate others. But the strife isn't polarization. It's distressing, but it's not polarization. The strife is the first early sign that we might be willing to *stop* being polarized by bigotry and injustice.

We are still very likely to treat gay or bi or trans or nonbinary, Black or brown, Muslim or Jewish or Sikh or Hindu, or undocumented, or disabled, ill, neuroatypical, impoverished, or unhoused people, and many others, too, as if *their* lives and dignity don't exist, or at least don't matter enough to fight about.

But more and more of *us* are unwilling to do that to *them*.

We are insisting that *they* are actually our friends and neighbors and parents and siblings—everyone is, because the planet is the neighborhood, and always has been—and that *their* lives have the same value as *ours*, and *they* deserve protection from those of *us* who would mistreat *them* as if *they* were not *us*, too.

Some of *us* insist on behaving as if all of *them* are actually *us*, because they *are*.

Which means *we* are increasingly unwilling to keep comfortable and normalized relationships with those of *us* who insist on treating our friends and neighbors and parents and siblings in this global neighborhood as if *their* lives don't matter. And yes, *we're* willing to fight about that with some others among *us*—not because *we* see ourselves as separate from *them*, but because *we* know that even though we're fighting *them*, *we* realize that *they* are actually *us*, too . . . and *we* demand better from *ourselves*.

It's not a separation, but a new unity. It's not the beginning of "us versus them." It's the end of it. Or, I hope, at least the beginning of the end of it.

It has to be said, even if we're less polarized than ever, we're still a very polarized country, and always have been. There exist many willing to fight for the subjugation of other human beings, and they are supported by a critical mass of comfortable and indifferent people, because supporting injustice remains the path of ease. There are still people who want to smear "the queer," and they'll always find somebody they can force to pick up the ball and run, as long as everybody continues to treat it like a game, or at least not care enough to notice. And some people *are* those humans, who have had no choice but to hide or fight their whole lives. And for those same people, the sight of ostensible allies willing to reconcile in order to reduce visible strife and maintain their own comfortable relationships would represent not a diminishment of polarization, but rather a demoralizing and entirely expected reversion to our polarized norm.

What is the strife about, after all? It's a fight. Not a new one, even if awareness of it is new for some of us. It's a fight over whether all humans matter enough for us to care about their dignity and their lives. This seems like a worthy fight, and worth the strife. We should hope that those among us who have picked up this old fight for the first time continue it, not abandon it—if we are interested in *decreasing* our national polarization, that is. Anyone fighting on behalf of "the queer" will start breaking the game of oppression so fundamentally that it will stop making any sort of sense . . . as a game.

So let's do that.

Let's break the game.

If we do, maybe we'll become even *less* polarized than we are now, even as strife increases.

And I think that's solidarity.

◆ ◆ ◆

Supremacists sabotage our repentance by trying to smother it with suppression—ignorance, complacency, and denial—and if they cannot suppress it, then they try to strangle it with oppression—to make the very act of aligning toward repair a punishable one. But the accommodation is the supremacy, and our reconciliation with oppressors is the accommodation that makes oppression successful. You'll know our repentance has been sabotaged, because you'll find that even very fine people who seem to agree with progressive motion toward repair begin to accept blameless supremacy's framing: that the way to achieve justice is to run from it, apologize for it, ask for change around the margins of the picture without ever changing the picture itself, without ever thinking to move the frame to allow the entire painting to be viewed.

Once we've agreed to occupy the frame of blameless supremacy, we remain inside its picture. We never take the journey our compasses have set, because we have opted not to oppose things that must be opposed; decided to not even know that opposition is needed.

It's important to note, all of this is done in service of avoiding repair; all done in service of a worldview that decides every day to enforce a system in which people do not matter if they don't make profit for others, in which others will never matter simply because of who they are; a world in which repair is seen as theft, in which those who are deemed unworthy are punished for the crime of not mattering, in which those who are punished are blamed for their punishment, and made to pay as much of the higher burden of brokenness as possible, so that a constantly shrinking elect can enjoy the profits. Part of our work of reparation, then, needs to be the repair of repentance. The way you repair repentance is through an uncompromising and persistent solidarity.

Solidarity is what happens when you bring witness and hope and moral clarity to bear, all together. It's what happens when we become aware of societal brokenness, and begin to carry a rugged expectation that it should be fixed, while clearly and publicly noting the difference between what is being broken and who is being harmed and who is doing the breaking and the harm, and then at last we refuse to align with the breaking and the harm, not because we see ourselves as separate from the harm or the blame for it, but because in our shared humanity we recognize a greater unity. Solidarity opposes supremacy, not because it wants us divided, but because it recognizes the deeper truth, that we are all already unified, in ways from which we cannot extricate ourselves. Solidarity understands that there is no "us" and "them," but only a great "us," and refuses unity with any foundational lie or human spirit that would create a "them" to destroy.

Solidarity is tolerant of supremacists without being tolerant of supremacy—because supremacists are human art, and because tolerance is the very lowest bar of justice's ladder. We will oppose supremacists, of course, and we will fight their abuses, and in that opposition we will have to fight them in whatever venue they force the fight, but in fighting them we will be creating a world supremacists will hate and fear—that is, a world of equality and repair that cares for everybody, even them—and we will tolerate supremacists in ways that they refuse to tolerate others. If we enter solidarity, we will not disinherit supremacists of their universal birthright—which is a claim to justice—simply because we know the human spirit they follow to be evil and their beliefs to be malignant and twisted. If a supremacist gets cancer, we will see they are treated without having to worry about cost, just like anyone else. If a supremacist struggles to make ends meet, we will see them with a roof over their heads, enough food in their belly, clean water to drink, and health care that is free at point of delivery. In solidarity we will see that a supremacist's labor will not be exploited, and ensure that even a supremacist should be able to determine what happens to their bodies, and should not have to worry about how they will live once their bodies become too old to earn money through work. If a supremacist's evil beliefs lead them to harm others, we in solidarity will see that their physical safety is a chief priority in their apprehension, that their trial is fair, and that their sentence is carried out without violence or retribution or cruelty or exploitation. We think that the children of supremacists should be well-educated and, if they come to school hungry, should be given food to eat, without having to earn it, or prove that they deserve it for any reason other than the simple fact of their hunger. In solidarity we will, even as we despise a supremacist's bigotry and the vile lies around which they have organized their lives, not withhold from them the shared, invisible, foundational, generative, automatic, inextricable value that our human system naturally provides them, because we recognize that they are humans, and we recognize that they are art, even if they fail to recognize it themselves. If we enter solidarity, we will recognize the deeper

unity of our shared humanity, will recognize that even supremacists are *us* too, in ways that supremacists, acting from what they
call love, cannot ever bring themselves to recognize in others.

Solidarity is less interested in decreasing polarization, and
more interested in where it sets its poles. Solidarity is only interested in a unity that unifies against supremacy and oppression,
not one that seeks to unify with it. Solidarity demonstrates
to blameless supremacy that its oppression with be met not
with appeasement, but with determined opposition. Solidarity
teaches those harmed by blameless supremacy that their allies
will not abandon them when the cost grows high, which allows
them to hopefully trust them as allies rather than rightfully
suspect them as enablers. Entering solidarity is where the rub-
ber meets the road, because it specifically means paying costs
that you could easily avoid through appeasement.

Solidarity repairs our repentance. It refuses to offer a facile
and cheap reconciliation to those who refuse to pay any cost of
repair. **Solidarity increases the cost of oppression** for those who
pursue it, and, since those who pursue oppression are people who
are opposed to every cost, solidarity makes blameless supremacy
desperate and dangerous, because it exposes supremacy for
what it is, and makes the cost of blame inevitable.

You'll know you've entered the discomfort of solidarity,
because those exposed by your solidarity will oppress you, to
punish you for rejecting their comfortable offer; will try to strip
you of the determination to oppose, by making the price of
solidarity as high as they can make it—so you'll know you've
entered into a spirit of solidarity, when you start to pay.

I think solidarity is a powerful tool in our fight against supremacist sabotage, available to all.

It expands the frame. It moves the spirit. It changes the
atmosphere. It tells a new story.

It raises the cost of blameless supremacy and its many sabotages.

Solidarity refuses an appeasing reconciliation and strengthens collective repentance.

And that's what I think repair looks like.

6. SURRENDER & DEFIANCE

The final accommodation accommodates the final sabotage.

The final sabotage is war.

Literally, war.

The final accommodation, then, is **surrender**.

Let's talk about it.

◆ ◆ ◆

It's 2022 now. *Late* 2022.

A couple weeks ago, we here in the United States had an election. Maybe you heard about it. In case you didn't, let me give you the results. The Republican Party, which represents the interests of supremacists (wealth supremacists, Christian supremacists, white supremacists, male supremacists, and so forth) failed to win back the Senate and may have even lost a seat there by the time all the dust settles. But they did win the House by a razor-edge margin and a bunch of state governments and governorships, too. And their most prominent and popular new fascist won his governor's race down in Florida handily, and he's banning books in classrooms, and doing a lot of other things as well, and a lot of people are very excited about his chances to bring open fascism back to the White House in 2024. However, it must be said: The supremacist party known as Republican didn't have as good a time of it in the elections as our media predicted they would, and in fact had a far worse time of it than history would suggest a party in their particular position should have had.

And that is some cause for hope.

There is very good reason to think that this disappointment for supremacist people everywhere came about because voters were concerned about what Republican supremacists said they intended to do once in power. For example, there is evidence voters were concerned about the literal end of democracy. Democracy, for those who haven't heard of it, is a newfangled power-organizing mechanism whereby representation in government ultimately lies in the hands of the people through the act of voting for representatives and proposals. It's a way of putting the matter of "the city decides" into all hands, to the degree that is practicable, in a way that honors and reflects the great truth that the value of society comes from the people who make up that society, and that therefore power should exist for the benefit of all people, and that therefore the most foundational levers of power should be in the hands of the people as much as possible, and the structures of incentives should be set in such a way as to encourage power to act primarily for the benefit of people, rather than some other priority, such as (oh let's say) property, or profit. And democracy is the best way we've found yet to operationalize this great truth, so democracy is generally seen as a positive arrangement by those who believe in fundamentally true things about the worth of humans.

Democracy is generally seen as a very bad thing, though, by people who believe the great lie that all a society's value comes only from and should go only to certain people who matter, that any value that goes to people who do not matter represents unacceptable theft, and that thieves deserve any punishment that comes to them no matter how violent that punishment is; who therefore believe that government should exist only to safeguard the privilege of people who matter and to ensure the punishment of those who do not. This is the supremacist position, and you can hear that position presented uncritically any time you switch on the news.

Where was I?

Oh yes!—democracy.

Voters were concerned about the end of it, it turns out.

And voters were also concerned about bodily autonomy—mostly the bodily autonomy of people who can get pregnant, but also of anybody who might want access to instruments and tools of reproductive health, and maybe of 12-year-old girls who don't want to do things that conservative Christians and other supremacists are forcing them to do, such as submit to a genital examination in order to play middle-school volleyball, or be forced carry their rapist's baby. There is and was a very good reason that voters should have been concerned about what handing power to Republicans would mean for bodily autonomy, because Republicans have spent decades talking about their supremacist intention to establish theocratic control over everyone's bodily autonomy, and 2022 was the year when, after decades of scraping away at legal protections, they finally got their fingers all the way under the linoleum and started to rip up the flooring. The 50-year-old national right to abortion is now completely gone, thanks to a captured and corrupt partisan supremacist majority on the Supreme Court, and Republicans immediately pivoted from this victory to begin talking with real energy about restricting and banning things like contraception and IVF, and so on. And there is very good reason to believe that voters should have been concerned about what handing power to Republicans would mean for democracy, too. For example, a whole lot of Republicans ran very directly on effectively dismantling democracy—first, by achieving positions of power that would allow them to control elections, and then by using those positions to create as many unfair advantages as possible for their side, and then by ignoring and overturning any results that didn't favor them. And those Republicans who weren't running on specifically anti-democratic propositions did not in any way withdraw their support from those who were. They were clearly on board, either with their direct support or their undergirding silence. Any of the very few not on board with full supremacy have by now been bounced from the party by supremacist Republican voters, who have been taught that they can have openly supremacist candidates if they demand them, and so they now expect and demand nothing else.

So, yes: There was plenty of reason for voters to believe that Republican supremacists all meant exactly what they said, and there was very little reason (none?) to believe they didn't.

Voters also had history to consider, if they were astute.

The 2022 midterms didn't represent the first assault on bodily autonomy or democracy by supremacy. Supremacists have been waging a war against the ideals of democracy and bodily autonomy—and also equality for all, liberty for all, the pursuit of happiness for all, freedom for all, and many other things—from the very foundation of our nation.

And I think that's war.

Again, I mean *war* literally.

◆ ◆ ◆

Time for a brief and very incomplete reverse chronology of American supremacist war:

On January 6, 2021, a large group of partisans, incited by then-president Donald Trump, swarmed the Capitol with the intention of overthrowing our democracy and killing as many members of Congress that opposed them as they could, and they almost did it, and they enjoyed the political and sometimes even tactical support of practically every single Republican office holder, both before and after the event. They did it because they believed the election had been stolen, and by their actions it's clear that by "stolen" they meant "Black people voting." I say this because in the months after the election supremacists all around the country (mostly white Christian supremacists but there were all types) were up in sometimes-literal arms at polling places, demanding literally opposite things, depending on whether or not the votes in those places were predominately white ("count every vote") or Black ("stop the count").

And "stop the count" eventually became "stop the steal," which eventually became an attempt to overthrow the U.S. government and install a theocratic fascist dictator who would accommodate their supremacy.

It was an act of war.

And some months before January 6, 2021, in Michigan, a large group of armed supremacists captured the State Capitol, protesting mask mandates, demonstrating their exclusive ownership of the people's government, and demonstrating their right to carry massacre weapons unharassed by police as clear evidence of that exclusive ownership. They were protesting against mandates designed to curb the spread of a virus that was disproportionately killing and harming people from various groups and segments that supremacists have deemed unworthy of life, and they were livid over the idea that they should be asked to act as if those people mattered. So they captured the state house. Later some of them plotted to kidnap the governor.

It was an act of war.

And a few years before that, Nazis marched with other very fine people who were apparently not Nazis, to defend statues honoring the murderous traitors who waged war to protect and expand the institution of human slavery. They marched and chanted Nazi slogans, and I suppose the very fine people with them who were not Nazis just marched but did not chant, or just chanted but didn't mean it, or they meant it but they didn't, you know *mean it* mean it. And one of them ran over a protester named Heather Heyer with a car and killed her. It's a murderous act, running over protesters with your car; and not incidentally, it's an act that Republican lawmakers have been trying to legalize before and after Heyer's murder, with proposed laws that would make it legal to run over protesters with motor vehicles.

It was an act of war.

And for decades before that, and on into this present day, Republicans (you might be thinking "not just Republicans," and good for you if so; we'll get there) have made sure that anybody who wants to enact a massacre is given easy and unrestricted access to tools that will allow them to kill as many people as possible as quickly as possible, and then used the massacres they've made ubiquitous as a pretext for making massacre weapons even more ubiquitous, and they've held themselves blameless when people inspired by their propaganda use those massacre weapons to massacre the targets of that propaganda. And they've made sure that police can operate in as brutal a manner as they desire in the neighborhoods they occupy, neighborhoods which some of us have noticed happen to be predominately Black in their demographic makeup. Incidentally, some of us have also noticed that this dynamic has led to police forces recruiting the exact types of people who seem to very much enjoy being brutal to Black people. And whenever the people protest this brutality, the police have rioted, making sure that the protest was maximally violent, then using the violence they created to frame the protest as violent. And whenever police riot, armed supremacist militia groups use the violence the police have created to swarm to the area, ostensibly to provide support to the rioting police— and in one recent police riot, one baby-faced militia member from Illinois killed a couple people in Wisconsin and got off the hook for it in court and is now a celebrity in supremacist circles, and a prominent speaker at supremacist conferences like CPAC and Turning Point USA and maybe the Republican National Convention in a couple years. And supremacists have enacted many other policies as well, all designed to make sure that people who they believe don't matter are treated as if they do not matter.

These are all acts of war. Supremacists even call these things "war." Wars on crime, on drugs, on poverty, all of which have harmed those who suffer most from crime and addiction and poverty, all of which have disproportionately lowered their life expectancy and quality of life, all of which have stolen actual years of freedom and life from actual human beings.

And for decades before that, laws known colloquially as "Jim Crow" were permitted to proliferate in states that refused to function as democracies. These laws delivered to Black people not only disenfranchisement but open terror and violence, with the full support of the moral ancestors of today's supremacist party, who were at that time (as a matter of historical record) mostly Democrats, so I think we've learned that supremacy doesn't mind changing its name and its symbols as long as the supremacist intents and the supremacist outcomes remain. The promulgators of Jim Crow marched with sheets instead of red hats, for example, and they put a D next to their name back then at least as often as they put an R, but they carried signs emblazoned with many of the exact same slogans that seem so familiar today, about communist infiltration and Jewish infiltration and their perceived Christian values of segregation and white supremacy. Jim Crow grew out of a series of compromises and surrenders with supremacists who were enraged by the sight of people they thought of as lesser participating in democracy and society, and these supremacists expected to have their outrage accommodated, as it had been since the Civil War, and, as it had been since the Civil War, it was accommodated.

And the Civil War—the traitorous mass-murder event enacted by mostly Southern promulgators and defenders of the institution of human chattel slavery—was itself the inevitable endpoint of a long accommodation with that unsustainable institution, the endpoint of accommodations with supremacy which made a lie of all the very fine principles our founding documents enshrine, from the moment those documents were drafted until today. Until the Civil War, the entire American South was, in effect, a genocidal concentration camp, a centuries-long house of nightmares, and wealthy people from North and South profited from it. We could talk about liberty and equality and freedom, but any casual observer could see what we as a country were truly about.

And some observers weren't so casual.

As a matter of historical record, American chattel slavery and Jim Crow apartheid inspired German Nazis, who formulated their own brand of supremacy on the foundation we set. And yes, there was a war, then, too—in Europe and the Pacific and Africa. The whole world, really. It was a World War, to use a term I may have just coined, and if so then I expect royalties for its use. We don't "both sides" that war much, I've noticed—depending on who I mean by *we*. We certainly "both sides" the Civil War, and all the other supremacist acts of active and passive war that came trailing after it like sharks trailing a slave ship. We certainly "both sides" the war that is happening in Europe right now, which is the belligerent attack of Ukraine by Russia and its supremacist leader, Vladamir Putin, a despotic man whose despotism is greatly admired by supremacists in America.

Our supremacists seem eager to take the supremacist side of Putin's war.

They campaigned on doing that, too.

And we certainly make sure to fulfill the supremacist expectation that the rage and violence of modern supremacists—their acts of war—will be accommodated. Depending, again, on who is meant by *we*, because some people don't get offered the opportunity to accommodate supremacists. They only get the opportunity to submit to oppression and suffer from that oppression, or else defy oppression and suffer even more from the retaliatory war that is waged against them.

And I haven't yet even mentioned our centuries of supremacist war against the many Nations of people native to this continent, which continues to this very day. Failing to mention them doesn't distinguish me much from many others in this country, who don't want to deal with the thorny matter of living on stolen land right next to the people from whom it was stolen. Our endless, inherited, foundational war is a war we don't acknowledge, I've noticed.

I think that's sabotage.

As I perceive it, each sabotage is a regressive process, the dark mirror of the process of repair. And, as I perceive it, each sabotage is accommodated by its own enablement; a tacit agreement with supremacy by people who claim to not ascribe to supremacy's goals. Why would people of awareness and conviction, engaged in confession and repentance, accommodate a supremacy that makes sabotage inevitable? The answer isn't so comfortable. Those of us who accept it do so because we are in the blameless society, too. We want repair, but the cost has been made too high, and we're instinctively optimized against paying our share of the lower cost of brokenness, if somebody else remains to pay the full higher cost—and blameless supremacy will always make sure that the cost of repair is high, and that there is somebody else to pay the cost of our foundational wars.

The accommodation of the final sabotage is something I'd name **surrender**—specifically, a pre-defeated agreement with supremacy to not oppose any supremacist aggression. I'd call it an accommodating surrender: a surrender offered, not because the resources and ability to oppose supremacy's intentions have been exhausted, but simply to avoid the cost of opposition entirely, and receive the benefits from having done so.

We can see accommodating surrender everywhere, if we look for it.

Let's look.

◆ ◆ ◆

Surrender is the final accommodation of supremacist sabotage, and, just as the act of reparation depends upon all the previous steps in repair's progressive process, just as the act of war depends on all previous steps in sabotage's regressive process, so the final accommodation of surrender depends upon and uses all other accommodations.

Surrender involves a deliberate neutrality about matters that demand perception, an apathetic compromise on matters that need principles, an exoneration of abusers for their abuse that launders their unbelievable denials into common currency, and an appeasing reconciliation with a supremacist oppression so encompassing and instinctive that it becomes almost invisible. All of this is ostensibly performed in the name of peace and comity and depolarization, but is actually designed to maintain a comfortable relationship with supremacy—which we know, because a comfortable relationship with supremacy is what it actually achieves.

Maybe you know what I'm talking about.

Maybe you see the ways that people in high positions who claim to know better often don't do better and sometimes don't even try, even when they could.

Surrender is what happens when the process of repair stagnates before payment. We are aware of the brokenness in our society; aware of injustice and abuse. We agree that what is broken should be repaired, and we share in a collective sense of responsibility to join in the repair. We even proclaim the need for repair aloud, and align our thoughts and behaviors away from brokenness and toward repair. But we don't progress from there. We don't make repair a higher priority than avoiding cost, and in so doing, we remain fundamentally aligned with the foundational priority of blameless supremacy, which is to avoid paying costs by making other people pay them.

Surrender avoids the violence of opposing supremacist aggression, and in so doing makes the greater violence of supremist domination inevitable.

Surrender happens when we agree that repair should only be attempted if it generates a profit rather than a cost—which incentivizes supremacists to make sure that any attempt at repair is as costly as possible, and that all brokenness becomes as profitable as possible.

Surrender is what happens when we agree that only those

who work full-time jobs and meet certain qualifying metrics deserve support and care and aid—acquiescing to the supremacist notion that for most people the right to live is connected inexorably to the act of earning it. And so our support for relief is contingent on every recipient being seen as deserving—which incentivizes those who oppose relief to create classes of the undeserving, and to target and highlight those undeserving people, and to make the process of means testing as complex and difficult and costly as possible.

Surrender only supports the demand for justice if it remains perfectly free of strife—which incentivizes supremacists to make every demonstration for justice as violent as possible. Surrender looks at an oppressive police force larded with white supremacists acting as a brutal and oppressive occupying force, and gives it increasingly more money and resources, trusts it to improve itself, and calls that safety. Surrender looks at the highest incarceration rates on the planet and worries not about incarceration but crime; looks at our profitable gulags of enslavement and torture and seeks to gain even more profit from human bondage, seeks to increase the number of crimes that might be prosecuted, increase the numbers of those imprisoned, and increase the excesses of prosecution; looks at our alignment with structural punishment for its own sake and calls that justice. Surrender looks at the largest army in history, which has been badly used by people of ill intent for wars of convenience, and increases its budget every year for less and less security and less and less return, and calls that defense. Surrender looks at a supremacist political party that has spent decades actively dismantling democracy, justice, and every protection of every marginalized class, and tells us that this party is not the enemy of democracy and justice, but a necessary opposition, filled with good friends of good will, whose ongoing strength and vitality we must ensure.

Surrender looks at bigotry next to it on the pew and demands nothing of it, while expecting the target of that bigotry to bestow upon the bigot gifts of performative forgiveness and exoneration, without receiving any confession of wrong or expression of regret; expects the person suffering brokenness to extend to their abusers reconciliation without reparation. Surrender does all this, and calls that unity, without thinking of the disunity that attends every surrender to the supremacist urge to abuse.

Surrender looks at people marching in common cause with Nazis and gives them credit for not being Nazis, by extending an indestructible credulity to the excuses the marchers have made for themselves for having made such common cause.

Surrender teaches oppressors that their threat of war will always be treated as valid and reasonable, and that their acts of war will always go unopposed. Surrender teaches those who suffer supremacist acts of war that their fight against blameless supremacy will be a fight they must engage in without allies, and encourages them to surrender, too.

It teaches people struggling under oppression that they will be abandoned, and so encourages them to give up on their convictions and surrender to the endless violence of domination.

It teaches bullies who want to avoid the cost of a fight that there exists no appetite to fight them, which incentivizes further bullying.

Surrender claims to seek justice, then sets itself against the demand for justice, and against every tool used to fight for it. It frames witness as bias, hope as naïveté, moral clarity as sanctimony, and solidarity as divisiveness.

Surrender values not peace for all but comfort for itself.

Surrender doesn't distinguish between aggression and opposition.

Surrender wants not justice but respectability.

Surrender always negotiates against itself.

Surrender agrees with supremacy that the worst thing possible is cost.

Surrender agrees with supremacy that only some people matter.
Surrender refuses to fight sabotage, so that it can join it.

Surrender encourages war. No—it's even worse than that.
Surrender *incentivizes* war. It makes the cost of waging war low.
It accepts the offer of surrender on behalf of other people, who
have not agreed to surrender, and who will never be given any
offer for anything like peace.

This is a luxurious surrender; it is a state of *being surrendered*.

Supremacists sabotage our attempts to repair with suppression and oppression, and if that doesn't work, then they wage
war on people who suffer most from brokenness—war on disabled and sick people, on racial and religious minorities, on
women, on queer people, on impoverished people, and so on
and so on, a machine designed to eat people that will never run
out of people to eat. But the accommodation is the supremacy,
and our surrender to aggression is the accommodation that
makes war successful. Once we've agreed to occupy the frame
of blameless supremacy, we remain inside their picture. We
never take the journey our compasses have set, because we have
seen that repair needs a fight, and we have decided not to fight.

So now I want to answer the big question, which is: *how do
we fix it?*

I want to talk about a tool available to everyone. I want to
talk about **defiance**.

What do I mean by defiance?

Glad you asked.

◆ ◆ ◆

The regressive sabotaging process leading to war is, at its core, a
sabotage of repair itself. I think a reminder is appropriate: this
is about reparation—about becoming people who, in a society
optimized to create unsustainable brokenness, engage in the act
of repair. It's about being people who are committed as a first

priority to repair no matter the cost, because we are people of repair, not people of cost-avoidance. And for this reason, I think defiance must, at its core, involve paying the cost of repair. As long as there are people willing to make that cost a fight, then defiance will mean a fight.

There's a type of person who when I say "a fight" immediately thinks I'm calling for violent and armed battle.

Well? Am I?

No. I don't call for it. I would hope to avoid it.

But I do recognize that fights sometimes get there.

Accommodation of supremacy is how fights get there, in case you're wondering.

Can defiance of supremacy involve the sorts of thing we typically associate with violence and war? Armies in fields and pitched battles and guerrilla actions and destruction of property and riot and all that? It can get there, if supremacy is accommodated to such a degree that it is empowered to wage literal war against the rest of us. And I think we all know it sometimes does get there, and that those who fight in defense are different than those who fight in aggression. We stand with Ukraine and against Putin, I hope, because we can recognize the difference between aggressor and opposer, between abuser and abused. We stand with Black Lives Matter against the violence of American policing for similar reasons, I hope, and would have stood with the Civil Rights Movement against the violence of Jim Crow, I would hope. And I hope we are glad the Confederacy didn't win its vile war to expand and defend human slavery, and that the Union, despite often self-interested motivations, was successful at putting it down. And I dare hope we're glad the Axis powers were opposed and defeated. So yes, it can get there—but we should also hope not to accommodate supremacist sabotage so far that such grave actions become inevitable. It would be better by far to choose a progressive series of earlier non-violent defiances, which prevent supremacy from gaining access to the mechanisms of war.

What else could defiance be? Can it be breaking unjust laws to protect human beings? It can get there. I hope we all agree that the people who operated the Underground Railroad acted justly. I hope we feel the same way about those who hid Jewish people and gay people and others from Nazis. I hope we feel the same about doctors today, working in authoritarian states like Ohio and Arkansas and Florida, who must now either surrender to our foundational war or risk their careers and their freedom to provide pregnant people safe abortions and trans children with life-saving medical care. Yes, it can get there—but we should also hope to not accommodate supremacist sabotage so far that such desperate acts become necessary. It would be better by far to choose a progressive series of earlier defiances, which never permit supremacy to seize the reins of power and law.

Can defiance involve ostracizing and shaming? Can it involve separation, and the end of relationships with friends and family members? I think it can get there, depending on the dynamics, depending on who needs to be protected, and from whom. But we might hope to choose earlier acts of defiance, which might prevent it from getting to that point.

So yes, defiance can involve a physical fight for those able to engage in it, and it might involve supporting the struggle even if it gets physical for others, but certainly let's not start there. Let's hope to avoid that cost, not by pre-surrendering, but by choosing earlier battles that might rob supremacy of the power to pursue war unopposed. And we must remember that avoiding or engaging in conflict is not the point of what we are trying to do when we engage in the work of repair. The point is repair, if we intend to be people of repair. Therefore, our fight is not primarily against broken people but against brokenness itself. And in a society optimized for brokenness, any act of repair and any payment of any cost is a defiant act.

I'll say that again: in a supremacist society, any act of repair is a defiant act.

And so is any payment of any natural cost of repair.

What do we do about this supremacist society?

Well, there's a lot that needs fixing. There are many costs.

What can you fix? What can you pay?

Contemplating these costs and the enormity of the struggle to repair all that is broken can feel frightening and overwhelming. I know—because that's how I feel, too. It can feel like shouldering the weight of the world. What can one person do against . . . *everything*? How can one person change the world? How can I fight what I hate without becoming what I hate? It's a lot. It might make you want to give up. It might almost feel like it's *designed* to make you want to give up.

Let's start here: Can you choose awareness instead of ignorance? Can you know about brokenness and reject incurious neutrality? Can you listen and learn about abuse and aggression from those who suffer its effects, and can you do it without insisting on reestablishing your own ignorance? Can you be aware of something that is uncomfortable to know about your country or your society or your place in it? Can you accept that there are ways that your experience is incomplete, and that there are other people who have a deeper and more complete understanding of the corruption and abuse and brokenness of our broken society, specifically because it is they who have been made to suffer the costs? Can you listen to those voices without feeling the need to impose your voice? Can you bear witness to these hard truths, even though knowing it is harder than not knowing? Can you reject the supremacist advantages ignorance gives you? Can you pay the cost of your own blamelessness?

If you can do that, do you know what that is?

It's repair. It's defiance.

Can you be convicted by that new knowledge? Can you choose conviction instead of complacency? Can you believe that repair is both necessary and possible? Can you expect it enough to demand it, even if it seems unlikely? Can you reject valueless complacency, refusing to accept all the various reasons you're given to not care, choosing instead to engage in an uncompromising hope for better things, even though most people believe better things are impossible or undesirable, even though caring is harder than not caring? Can you pay the cost of your own comfort?

If you can do that, do you know what that is?

It's repair. It's defiance.

Can you proclaim your awareness and conviction of brokenness, simply and clearly, with moral clarity that sees your own place within the brokenness and then refuses to deny it, speaking of the ways you benefit from it honestly enough that it exposes that brokenness, even for those who benefit from it but deny they do, even if it makes for uncomfortable conversations and strained relationships? Can you hear truths about the ways supremacy benefits you without making your first priority celebrating your good intentions, or having your goodness validated? Can you accept some of the blame for supremacy even though supremacy offers you blameless reconciliation without reparation? Can you pay the cost of your own automatically presumed goodness?

If you can do that, do you know what that is?

It's repair. It's defiance.

Can you change your priorities and your determination, away from comfort and ease and toward the costs of repair? Can you convert your conviction into action? Can you commit to unwavering solidarity with people who are threatened by oppression, and take on some of the threat even though you don't have to, and risk losing some of your reputation with those who would reward you for staying out of the fight? Can you enter places where space to lead and speak and be heard and believed and to receive opportunity and advancement is automatically bestowed to you, and then, rather than claim those gifts, step out of that space, so it can be taken by others whose voices are seen as disruptions, whose presence is seen as intrusion, whose advancement is seen as a threat? Can the struggle to repair become one in which you aren't the primary protagonist? Can you pay the cost of your own supremacy?

If you can do that, do you know what that is?

It's repair. It's defiance.

Can you refuse to surrender your commitment to repair, even if those who are opposed to repair make sure the price for doing so is high—even personally high to you? Can you fight in whatever little way it is given to you to fight, in order to insist on repair? If you find yourself asked to take a bit of the higher costs of brokenness, which usually are given entirely to more marginalized people, can you take that cost on? Can you support a movement toward sustainable justice even if it costs you money and property and safety? Can you become more aware, more convicted, more aligned with repair today than you were yesterday? Can you pay the cost of whatever profit you receive from unsustainable brokenness?

If you can do that, do you know what that is?

It's repair. It's defiance. Defiance, defiance, defiance.

A willingness to pay the natural costs of repair, and a determination to take on the higher unnatural costs of sabotage whenever necessary.

Defiance.

So: Who will pay the cost of your decisions? Yourself, or somebody else?

Who will pay the costs of sabotage? The blameless saboteurs, who insist on avoiding every cost? Or those they would harm with every cost imaginable?

Surrender makes war cheap, and maintains comfortable relationships with aggressors.

But **defiance repairs the very process of repair itself.** It demolishes pre-defeated surrender, and **increases the cost of waging our supremacist foundational war**—and might move to your cause many already-surrendered people whose only goal is to avoid cost.

How can we fix our broken society?

We can make the cost of sabotage high, that's what we can do—using the individual tools of skill or wealth or resource we've been given, yes, but also using the tools available to us all: simple witness, uncompromised hope, moral clarity, unshakeable solidarity, and committed defiance—all of which make the cost of supremacy, and of accommodating supremacy, high.

Witness makes the cost of ignorance high. It exposes ignorance by speaking to what *is,* without trying enter ignorance's obfuscating smokescreens to argue over varying degrees of what is *not.* It exposes the efforts to hold on to ignorance in the face of truth as deliberate acts intended to strangle repair in the cradle of intention. It exposes those holding a valueless neutrality between truth and lies, revealing their methods as the enabling self-interested cowardice it is. In so doing, every act of witness lowers the cost of awakening for everybody.

Hope makes the cost of complacency high. It exposes complacency, by believing that better things are not only possible but necessary. It exposes the efforts to maintain complacency in the face of brokenness as the morally lazy selfishness it is, rather than the pragmatic realism it claims to be. It exposes compromise as a negotiated collusion, designed not to establish a better foothold toward repair, but rather to establish a more comfortable position from which to stop caring about what is broken. In so doing, every act of hope lowers the cost of conviction for everybody.

Moral clarity makes the cost of denial high. It exposes denial as self-interested fraud by always drawing focus to actual results and actual outcomes. It exposes denial's attempts to cast itself as both wrongly-accused victim and sympathetic jury by refusing to participate in enabling exoneration, especially self-exoneration. It exposes the instinct of non-threatened parties to offer exoneration to abusers on behalf of the abused as the self-interested conspiracy of supremacy that it is, rather than the fair-minded tolerance it claims to be. In so doing, every act of moral clarity lowers the cost of confession for everybody.

Solidarity makes the cost of oppression high. By refusing to abandon those who suffer oppression's effects, it exposes oppression as a cruel attempt to maintain and expand supremacy. By refusing to accept oppression's abuses, solidarity exposes oppression as the absolutely unacceptable abuse that it is, rather than the self-defense it claims to be. In so doing, solidarity lowers the cost of repentance—that is, spiritual realignment—for everybody.

And all of this, taken together, is defiance—a willingness to fix brokenness and fight sabotaging supremacy, wherever it is found. A blameless society, founded in supremacy, hates defiance, because it inevitably makes supremacy pay a higher cost for waging war—and supremacy is, above everything, opposed to paying costs. Or you might say, a bully hates a fight. Even a bully willing to fight hates a fight, because what a bully most loves is cost-free cruelty, and achieving cruelty without having to pay the cost of a fight is what the bullying is for.

For this reason, I think you'll know that you've entered into a spirit of reparation, when you start to repair what's broken and notice that the cost of doing so is much higher than it ought to be, and then, crucially, if you pay the higher cost anyway.

Defiance repairs, and in its defiance refuses to accept anything other than repair.

One other point about war: Supremacy only progresses to war when all its other less costly sabotages—ignorance, complacency, denial, oppression—have started to fail to such a degree that repair has actually begun and the abuser is forced to fight a defiant opponent to preserve their unjust advantage. You see? War for an aggressor is not a position of strength. It's a position of weakness.

It's the last gasp of a failed spiritual movement based on a vile lie. It's an indication that reparation is near. All the more reason to not abandon the fight. All the more reason to not surrender. All the more reason to choose defiant repair instead.

I think defiance is a powerful tool in our fight against sabotage, available to everyone.

It expands the frame. It moves the spirit. It changes the atmosphere. It tells a new story.

It raises the cost of blameless supremacy and all its many sabotages.

Defiance refuses accommodating surrender and pays to fix what is broken.

And that's what I think repair looks like.

◆ ◆ ◆

What do we do now?

We keep going, of course. Reparation is a cyclical process—it's *the* process. Awareness to conviction to confession to repentance to reparation leads into more awareness, all of which requires some cost but all of which pays us back with reparation—a more sustainable way of being, one that is more open, more aware, more free, more peaceful, and less costly.

Why do we need reparation?

On the surface, this may seem like a silly question. We need to repair what's broken, because if we don't, we'll continue to live in an unsustainably broken world—one that will inevitably break us. We need reparation, because reparation *repairs*.

But just as supremacy and repair are movements governed by our collective human spirits, I think there exists a spiritual aspect to repair. We need reparation, because it leads to the thing that blameless supremacist abusers want to be given without paying, which supremacist enablers want to give them for free on behalf of those they abuse.

Repair reframes, and repair pays.

But also, repair redeems.

A question: *what does it redeem?*

7. THE VINEYARD & THE MOUNTAIN

If you're still reading, I think I can consider you a friend.

I say this in hopes that you might forgive me for bringing you all this way and not getting around to this question until now.

What does repair redeem?

Really: What are we redeeming, exactly?

We should probably know, if we're doing the work of redemption.

◆ ◆ ◆

It's 2022. Let's see what's happening in 2022.

The leader of the Republican Party, its presumptive 2024 presidential front-runner, is Donald Trump, believe it or not. This week he met with Nick Fuentes for a strategy session. Nick Fuentes is, it just so happens, a Nazi, by which I mean an open admirer of Adolf Hitler, who ascribes to Hitler's worldview and advocates for his policies, and calls for a "holy war" against Jewish people. The leader of the Republican Party met with him, for a strategy session. It was an accident, we're told. Trump didn't know who Fuentes was, which is odd since ex-presidents don't tend to just have random breakfasts with people they don't know anything about, and also because Fuentes was one of the Nazis who marched in the murderous "Unite the Right" Charlottesville demonstration five years ago. These were the Nazis who, if you recall, Trump later defended as very fine people—though, if you recall, there are many who insist that Trump wasn't defending the Nazis, but rather the non-Nazis who marched with the Nazis for apparently non-Nazi reasons. Anyway, Republicans insist it was an accident, this meeting with their leader and an open proud Nazi. Republicans have had many of these accidents in recent years; so many, in fact, that an attempt to catalogue them all would probably double the length of what is already a pretty long book.

So many accidental confluences with Nazis.

Man. Boy oh boy. Republicans are *so* accident prone.

In a completely unrelated story, last week a man already known by local authorities to be a danger to others entered a Colorado Springs LGBTQ club and shot and shot and shot until the patrons subdued him and he could shoot no more. And all the usual people—such as Lauren Boebert, the white supremacist and insurrectionist Republican representative of nearby Colorado district 3, and Tucker Carlson and Matt Walsh, and an endless parade of other power brokers and propagandists who had spent the preceding years vilifying and demonizing queer people and inciting violence against them—all acted temporarily shocked! shocked! that somebody had gotten some of the guns they made sure were easy to get and killed some of the people they had said didn't deserve to live. It was the whole usual thoughts and prayers thing.

And then came an interesting thing, by which I mean a horrifying thing. Within less than 24 hours, there was a noticeable pivot within the narrative, as many from the usual thoughts-and-prayers crowd started suggesting that the reason this man murdered queer people is that queer people insist on existing in our society, and that will naturally make normal people uncomfortable, and unless queer people become significantly less obtrusive, then the natural and expected and appropriate response will be more gun massacres in more gay clubs. It's not something anybody *condones*, you see—of course not!—but really, honestly... I mean *what do you expect?* These conservative fascists finally succumbed to the inevitable, and vocally took the side of the shooter in the matter of a hate crime massacre—which they have always done in all but word: by creating a regulatory environment ensuring that anyone who wants to kill a lot of people is easily able to do so; by creating a political-media atmosphere designed to radicalize people and give them an inexhaustible supply of ready targets; and thereby creating a world where massacres are not only likely but inevitable and plentiful and targeted. And there's a narrative bubbling up in the depths of social media right now, that the reason that Nazis rose to power in Weimar Germany was that Weimar Germany was so permissive of queer elements in its society, and so really what were good normal Germans supposed to do? *Not* support fascists with eliminationist intent?

Like I say, it's bubbling up right now in the rancid stew of far-right social media. It's not normalized yet. But then, any number of formerly shocking things that mainstream Republicans now say out loud on national television started the same way. So you could say that the idea that Nazism is a natural response to the existence of gay people is a notion that's in pilot season right now for Republicans, to see how it tests with their audiences. Look for it soon, maybe.

And now, as we're dipping our toes into 2023, Michael Knowles, who creates content for Ben Shapiro's far-right supremacist disinformation platform The Daily Wire, has in recent days turned his moist unblinking eyes and vapid fixed smile to the most recent target of harm and hate for Republicans, which is trans people. If you are a hate group like the Republican Party, trans people make a pretty good target, because there are so few of them (about 1.6 million in the U.S., or roughly 0.48% of the population), and also because general public acceptance of trans people is very recent and nowhere close to total, which means that their demonization and persecution can proceed far more directly. And direct it is! Knowles kicked off last week with a screed on his program, where he made a sort of anticipatory defense, insisting his ongoing invective about trans people can't possibly represent genocide because "transgender people is not a real ontological category.

It's not a legitimate category of being." A few days later, he put on what I assume was his uncle's suit and strode onto the stage of the annual conference of the Conservative Political Action Committee (CPAC) to proclaim that "transgenderism must be eradicated from public life."

It's all genocidal talk—quite literally. An intent to make 1.6 million people not be. There are many, many, many, many, many, many other stories like this as well. Many other deaths. Many other thefts. Endless suffering, as people who have been deemed to not matter are forced to pay the high cost of brokenness.

OK, but you all know this. So what's my point?

I guess it's this:

There comes a point when an accident isn't an accident anymore.

There comes a point when deniability isn't deniable.

There comes a point, I think, when people who have good qualities must stop being understood as "good" and start being understood as people who are lending their good qualities to monsters who have promised to use those good qualities to facilitate atrocities, who have promised to get their own monstrous hands bloody on behalf of the very fine people that support them, very good nice normal people who retain their reputational goodness while facilitating atrocity—a state which I have been calling "blameless supremacy." There comes a point when we have to recognize that the atrocity is already happening and has been for a long time, and those good qualities have been squandered, and are gone. There comes a point when everybody has had a chance to know better, and if they still don't know better, we have to assume they don't want better. There comes a point when you've joined what you've joined. There comes a point when fascism and supremacy is on the rise, when we have to choose sides.

I think we reached that point a very long time ago. I wonder if we ever left that point, honestly.

And there are a lot of people who will look at all these events, and their first question isn't "Oh my God, there is significant danger here to marginalized people! How do we stand with those who are threatened by this rising tide of fascist hate and violence, to surround and protect our friends and neighbors, our siblings and parents, our neighbors all around the world?" The first question asked—really the only question asked, usually—is "Oh my God, there is significant danger here that we would paint these aggressors with too broad a brush, and cast them as *irredeemably bad* by exposing the things they support and recognizing that they believe the things they say they believe! How do we appeal to their better angels, and establish a path for *redemption?*

How, indeed?

I wonder how many people who ask for redemption actually want it.

Here in my country, which is the United States, we greatly value redemption.

We don't talk as much about reparation, which is how you get redemption, unless it's to talk about why it's impractical or dangerous or impossible. But we love to talk about redemption.

OK. I'm game.

Let's talk about redemption.

◆ ◆ ◆

I've repeated myself in this book quite a bit. It's my fault. I warned you at the start that this is a fool's confession, and it takes a fool longer to get to conclusions than it might take others. We fools require regular reminders of basic truths, and so I find the almost liturgical repetition helpful to me.

Thank you for your patience.

Let's take one last look back at where we've been.

We've been looking at brokenness caused by injustice, abuse, and corruption. We've looked at the ways we yearn for repair, and yet repair never comes. We've been talking about reparation—literally, the progressive process of repair—which begins with an awakening to awareness of what is broken. And awareness moves us to conviction that what is broken can and should be fixed and that we share a responsibility to fix it. And conviction moves us to confession, an active proclamation bringing that awareness and conviction into the atmosphere of public consciousness and collective action. And confession leads to repentance—that is, realignment of our resources and intentions and systems and goals, away from managing |unsustainable brokenness and toward repair, maintenance, improvement, and payment of the attendant natural costs of disruption, money, time, and even the benefit and privilege many of us reap from brokenness.

We've also been talking about a supremacist spirit, which is committed to the foundational lie that some people do not matter, and which is opposed to any payment of cost, and which sabotages the process of repair by deliberately making repair more costly, first with suppression (ignorance that swallows our awareness, complacency that smothers our conviction, denial that refuses our confession), then with oppression that makes re-aligning with repentance a punishable crime, and which finally opposes the very act of repair itself with war.

And we've been talking about the luxurious enablements of each step of supremacist sabotage, each of which validates sabotage, creating a nurturing cradle for abuse and corruption and injustice, and allowing supremacist intention to become entrenched and empowered supremacy. We've contemplated an unprincipled neutrality that enables ignorance, an unstrategic compromise that enables complacency, an undeliberative exoneration that enables denial, a lazy reconciliation designed to accommodate oppression, and finally a pre-defeated surrender offered to avoid the cost of every necessary fight—a surrender which incentivizes and encourages aggressors to threaten endless war, and enables the inevitable violence of supremacist aggression and domination.

Last of all, we've been talking about the tools of reparation available to each of us if we wish to combat supremacist aggression and supremacy's enablers: of a simple witness to truth that observes what *is* without seeking permission from any authority to do so; of an uncompromising hope that rejects easy cynicism and cheap optimism to insist that unlikely but necessary change is not only possible but imperative; of a moral clarity that locates brokenness within itself first so that it can impeach all brokenness it sees with undeniable authority; of a solidarity that refuses to abandon to oppression any member of its human family and willingly meets the resultant strife; and of a defiance that seeks no fight but remains determined to engage any necessary fight that arises in order to hold to its commitment to repair broken things.

I think every act of repair—every step of repair, every use of every tool of reparation—is an act of defiance against supremacy and sabotage. And I think the work of reparation—including paying the costs of repair—is redeeming work.

Indeed, it's the only path to redemption I know.

So that's my answer to those whose first priority, in a time of rising atrocity, is establishing a path to redemption for those who enact and enable atrocities.

You want redemption? You truly want to redeem?

Then repair what is broken.

Fix abuse, corruption, and injustice, so we can engage in natural repair and maintenance.

Pay the cost of reparation: natural disruption and unearned wealth, comfort, and privilege.

You'll make the path to redemption you claim to want by walking it. I fear it'll be a rather fresh path you're making, but you'll make a trail for others to follow. If those who enact or support atrocities today want redemption, they can follow you.

If they don't, they won't.

And then you'll know.

So that's the path of redemption for you.

Yes, but again: redemption of what?

◆ ◆ ◆

My religious tradition is Christian, as I think I've mentioned. Specifically, I come from predominantly white sects of American Evangelical Christianity, though as a missionary kid growing up in what was then Zaire, I may have, through no effort of my own, received a bit less direct radiation from the "American" part of the whole thing than most . . . though on the other hand, perhaps I came a little nearer to direct white colonial privilege than most, too. I guess what I'm saying is I may be unusual but I don't think I'm particularly special.

We have a lot to say about redemption, we Christians. You might say it's our thing. As we have it, redemption is something that involves a cost paid, one that sets the person who had owed that cost free. Honestly, ask any Christian, and they'll be very happy to tell you this. So, I suppose, if I do the realigning and redeeming work of reparation, I should expect to find myself paying the cost of repair—whatever that cost might turn out to be—and I will find some measure of redemption for myself there, which will not only involve getting something but being freed from something.

In my tradition, the way we put this is to say "to live, you must first die."

I suppose the thing I'd be freed from is my blamelessness, along with my need to defend it with ignorance and complacency and denial and oppression and war. I suppose I'd also be freed from the compulsion to prove my exceptionalism—

with violence, if necessary—to anyone who won't recognize it. I suppose I'd also be freed from the compulsion to maintain a brokenness far more expensive than any cost of repair can ever be, and freed from the suppression and oppression I'd feel compelled to use to defend my reputation from the effects of my choice to enforce an unsustainable world upon everyone, including myself.

I suppose engaging in the redeeming work of repair will mean I'm somebody who works at constantly entering a deeper awareness, a greater conviction, a more complete confession, a more natural repentance, and a better and more lasting repair.

But . . . is that it?

Am I just doing this for the redemption of *myself*?

Christians actually believe in somebody who paid an impossibly high cost that he himself didn't owe, on behalf of everyone else, which set everyone free. Then they were told by that person to follow the example he set. That's the story, anyway.

Do we Christians believe that story? It's worth asking, that's for sure.

As I think I've mentioned at some point, predominantly white American Evangelical Christian churches have (institutionally speaking) served as the enthusiastic, joyful, energizing, sustaining, and organizing support system for the modern Republican Party. As for the Republican Party, I know I have mentioned it is observably a supremacist political operation—mostly white supremacist, to be sure, but you can find all the other supremacies in there as well, including Christian supremacy.

It's a hate group, in other words.

And I know a lot of white American Evangelical Christians. I think I've said it many times already: many are really nice good kind people, and many are much nicer than me in many ways, and a bunch of them really have given their entire lives and careers to impacting the world in meaningful ways that I have not, in ways that truly do honor the best of our shared religious tradition, and many of them mean a great deal to me, and some of them don't even support the hate group or the supremacist political movement the Republican Party represents, either with their votes or anything else, and many if they read these words would probably be genuinely sad that I'm saying these things that I find myself compelled to say because I believe they are true and important—and if these people are sad, part of me at least is sad that they're sad, because I don't want them sad, and at least a part of me still hates to think of myself as the cause of their sadness. And yet still, I must bear witness to the simple fact: The white American Evangelical Christian Church has become, institutionally speaking, the energizing, sustaining, organizing support system for a supremacist organization, a political party that functions as a hate group; which runs on every form of bigotry, and which is presently driving us toward downfall and destruction and unsustainability on several different levels.

And at a certain point, you've joined what you've joined.

It's a hell of thing.

What to do, what to do.

◆ ◆ ◆

I'm going pretty hard at white American Evangelical Christians specifically, I know. This is in part because they/we really have proved them/ourselves to be the sustaining lifeblood of this authoritarian supremacist movement, but also it's my act of moral clarity. They're where I'm situated, in ways I can't extricate myself. I am a Protestant-presenting suburban dad, you could say. I wear cargo shorts and button up short sleeved shirts with plaid patterns. Do you understand what I'm saying here? I'd have to do something dramatic to be seen as something else. But even if I did, I distrust the motives behind the impulse to separate myself. It feels self-defensive, self-aggrandizing, suggesting not a need to solve the problem but a need to be personally exonerated. It feels like the impulse to defend my own blamelessness, in other words. Moreover, white American Evangelical Christianity is the tradition that shaped me, and its members are the people who, to a great degree, shaped me. I am as I am in large part because of this. They are a part of me, and always will be, to such an extent that my using the word *they* to talk about them doesn't really seem as honest as *we*. But that's where the witness and moral clarity come in, you see—since they are where I come from, I can implicate *us* with significant authority. So let's say it: I am a Christian. I am a cisgendered heterosexual who is deemed "white" by society, and an employed able-bodied well-off Christian. I am indeed a Husband Father Christian®, and could put that without lying in my social media bio, right next to my pronouns (which are he/him).

So that's why I go so hard after my own religious tradition—because when we talk about our own failings we're not just talking about our individual failings, but about the failings of our groups. These days that's popularly understood to be the groups we vote with, but in truth the law doesn't treat me as a Democratic voter, it treats me as a white able-bodied employed cis straight married Christian guy; a guy who is preferred, a guy whose life matters even while other lives don't matter, a guy who checks the boxes, a *guy* who *fits*. I'm part of this; I don't get to choose about that. I just get to choose my alignment with it. For me, personally, choosing my alignment means I don't go to churches anymore; don't lend my support or my money or the tacit approval of my presence to any such institution. And that's cost me, in ways, and freed me in ways. But though I have separated myself physically, I won't separate myself in terms of culpability and blame, because here's the thing: In many practical ways, though they may try, *they* can't separate themselves from *me* either.

What reparation I do, I do on their behalf.

I am aware on their behalf.

I am convicted on their behalf.

I will confess the sins of white American Evangelical Christianity as a white American Evangelical Christian.

I will repent as one.

I will repair as one.

And then, maybe, I can help redeem something other than just myself.

To the best of my ability, I won't help the institution from which I sprung do the evil that it is doing in my country and the world, and I'll witness to that evil as I see it, but even as I remove my support, I intend to also lean into the moral complexity of finding myself there.

I won't add to the crime if I can help it, but I'll own the responsibility.

That strikes me as redemptive work.

◆ ◆ ◆

I go after white American Evangelical Christians specifically for other reasons, too. Ironically, most of them are principles I still believe, which I learned within that religious tradition. In my religious tradition (which again is Evangelical Christian), there is this fellow, a Jewish rabbi named Yeshua Ben Yosef (Mister Jesus if you're nasty), and he's sort of a big deal with my crowd. So I guess I'd like to share some stories about Yeshua Ben Yosef.

Don't worry. I'm *not* going to end this with a pulpit call (which, for those of you who don't know, is a traditional invitation at the end of the sermon to come up front and profess belief in Jesus and become a Christian), I *promise*. It's just that it helps me to use these stories to get at what I mean when I think about things like reparation and redemption. You may have your own tradition with similar notions. Please, use those instead. I wouldn't want to use them here. I'd probably screw them up in my well-meaning ignorance.

Anyway, there was this Yeshua fellow, who was a Jewish rabbi as I believe I mentioned, so I'm probably even screwing up my own tradition up in my well-meaning ignorance. (It's a fools' confession, you know.) We American Evangelical Christians are meant to listen to what he says, and we claim that we do what he tells us to do, but in my experience, this usually means we'll give you our interpretation of what we have decided he said, which just so happens to match what we already wanted to do.

Examples? Examples.

One thing he said is that the love of money is the root of all evil, and yikes most of us don't like that one. I'm not a massive fan of it either, if you want to be honest. Money really greases the skids in my experience. We have our interpretation of that one that lets us keep as much of our money as we can, and firmly control how the 10% we give away is spent so as to not disrupt our personal comfort and righteousness, to such a degree it's almost as if we're not so much giving freely as we are buying righteousness.

He also said that he came to set prisoners free, and we've got an interpretation of that one, too—one that lets us support a for-profit mass incarceration system, and the police and justice system that enforces and enacts it, and the lawmakers who set up laws to feed it, and even the most draconian punishments it can deliver, no matter how unjustly they are applied.

There's another thing Yeshua said that I don't think is very popular, at least in practice. It's about getting the log out of your own eye before worrying about the speck in someone else's eye. It's a metaphor. I take it to mean "worry about your own failings before you worry about somebody else's," and it's what I mean when I talk about moral clarity. We have an interpretation that takes it to operate on only an individual level, which is perhaps to be expected from a society that refuses to acknowledge anything collective. We also think it's something that is very good for other people to do before they criticize us, but we seem to believe we've already done it ourselves and therefore see ourselves perfectly clearly—after all, we're churchgoing Christians, the good people.

But never mind all that—these are all good teachings, and seem well-aligned with the work of reparation. I take no issue with them, other than that they are very difficult to actually do. I am nothing as good as the example Yeshua Ben Yosef sets, but I'd like to try to get near it, if I can.

It's good to have role models.

Later on this Jewish rabbi Yeshua (and trust me we've got a lot of stories about this guy) directly and materially challenged his own religious power structure, or so the larger story goes. And he also opposed the dominant economic, political, and military superpower of his day, too. And he managed to oppose both at the same time, by focusing on where the two intersected and supported one another. He did it pretty directly sometimes, and wickedly subversively other times, and frequently he used stories to totally reframe existing dominant ways of seeing things. He announced that he had come to repair what was broken and heal the sick and free those imprisoned, and at one point he said he intended to restore literally everything, so I'd say he had a pretty ambitious reparation program in mind. But then he said that the people who followed him would be known because they would do even greater things than him, and also by the way they loved one another, so he seemed to have big ambitions for his followers, too. And he was pretty big on loving people specifically by taking care of their material needs and healing their illnesses without worrying about whether or not they deserved it. It's noticeable, if you read the book. I mean, he does it a *lot*.

You'd think this would be unmissable to his followers today.

And they killed him—*they* being the dominant economic and military superpower of his day, which was the Roman Empire. It wasn't the *Holy* Roman Empire yet, because it hadn't yet made itself Holy, which is something it accomplished by making itself the power center of a religion dedicated to the Jewish rabbi they had murdered, and by revering him without ceasing in any way to be the thing that had killed him, which, again, was a dominant economic and military superpower.

This strikes me as a pretty good example of blameless supremacy, come to think of it.

Huh.

Anyway, before the Roman Empire decided Yeshua was their God, they murdered him. If you're a student of history you'll perhaps recognize that's how opposing the dominant economic and military superpower of your day often goes for people who do it, which makes it a pretty bad career move. And, if you're a student of history you'll perhaps recognize that Yeshua Ben Yosef's subsequent elevation to statist godhood is how power's appropriation of great moral leaders and prophetic voices often goes. And now Christians represent the dominant economic and military superpower of our day, and demand a position of privilege within that superpower, which is just something I thought I'd mention for no particular reason.

As our Christian tradition has it, in that moment of dying, Yeshua *redeemed* the entire world, specifically by paying a price that nobody else was willing or able to pay, and this actually allowed him to achieve a redemption that conquered death itself. Yeshua paid a cost that was intrinsic and inherited, automatic and inextricable—the exact type of burden I can't help but notice most conservatives, particularly most white conservative Christians, categorically refuse today when asked to shoulder it, because they insist that they are blameless, which is exactly what they also say Yeshua was when he shouldered a much larger burden.

So much for role models, I guess.

In the story, Yeshua predicts his death will happen, and that it will be a redemptive act; that it will, in fact, remake the world, by sending his spirit to anybody who followed the example he provided. From this I conclude it is fair to say Yeshua understood the idea that redemption involves paying costs, and that the thing that changes the world is an active spirit.

I think if white conservative Christians are truly interested in redemption, then the good news is, the path has been walked for them already.

If they want redemption they'll follow.

If they don't, they won't.

And then we'll know.

I am nowhere close to being as good as Yeshua Ben Yosef is in the stories, but I'd like to try to be like that a bit. I'd rather not be tortured to death, and I hope that's OK with you—but as I said, it's good to have role models. Anyway, that's why I oppose my own religious tradition, precisely where it intersects with the dominant political and military superpower of its day.

◆ ◆ ◆

Yeshua Ben Yosef was Jewish, as I believe I mentioned.

We follow Yeshua, we Christians. Yet most of us are not ethnically Jewish, and we do not consider ourselves members of the Jewish religion. There are dogmas that explain this, with scriptures to support it. Ask any Christian and they'll surely unpack it for you, but still sometimes that's weird to think about, that we all follow Yeshua but we don't belong to his religion. I also think it would be weird if all followers of Yeshua decided to become Jewish, and I have this instinct that such a mass conversion would probably not be the sort of thing that Jewish people would generally want or appreciate. However, we Christians worship a Jewish rabbi, but we aren't Jewish, and I think about that a lot.

I don't know of any explanatory Christian dogmas that don't either negotiate away or appropriate Judaism to some degree, and frankly I'm not very comfortable with those dogmas anymore, simply because I am not comfortable at all with any urge to negotiate Judaism away or appropriate it. Even if I wasn't a Christian, it would seem to me to traffic in antisemitism, but as somebody who claims to follow a Jewish rabbi, negotiating away that rabbi's religion seems bizarre. (I'm pretty sure this is all heresy to most conservative white Christians in a way that becoming a billionaire, or voting for a white supremacist fascist would-be dictator is not. Sorry for all the heresy, conservative white Christians. I'm just sort of thinking out loud here.) It makes me ask myself: Did this Jewish rabbi engage in this work of reparation, and this self-sacrifice, just to start another religion among religions, or even a religion to be supreme *over* other religions? To start a religion that is particularly self-aggrandizing and self-promoting, that apparently expects the whole world to not so much follow its example as bend to its will?

Did the man we call the Prince of Peace arrive to command his followers to *dominate?*

If not, why the hell is that what we're doing?

It seems more likely to me that what Yeshua was doing was something that transcends religion in a way; something that enters the world more like a new spirit moving people into an awareness of something that was always true. A new story that would change the atmosphere, in other words, not a new religion that would conquer the world. A story about a universe that reveals itself to the human awareness it has created and nurtured, not as power but as sacrifice, not as danger but as safety, not as complacency but as love, not as distant and remote but as present in every instant. A story about the universe providing an example to the human awareness it has created and nurtured: that those who have the least deserve the most consideration, that to live well in the world is to care for the needs of others, and that the best use of power is to give it away with no thought of whether it is deserved.

By the way, this seems the more likely motivation to me

because it's what Yeshua actually said he was doing. You know, in the book.

I mean honestly you'd *really* think we Christians would do the reading.

What to do, what to do.

Let's end with a few more stories.

Yeshua told another story once, about father who owned a vineyard and told both sons to work in it. One son said he would, but didn't. The other son said he wouldn't, but did. Then Yeshua told the gathered religious leaders that it was the son who refused the father's order but did the work anyway who had truly enacted the father's will, not the son who said he would do the work but didn't do it. And *then* he told them that the pagans and tax collectors and sex workers were entering the kingdom of heaven ahead of them.

Oh, man.

Try *that* one sometime on a Sunday.

He followed it up with a story about another father who owned a vineyard, who gave it to some tenants to take care of while he was away, but the tenants became murderers and thieves who refused to produce the fruit of the vineyard. Yeshua then announced that the father would return and take the vineyard away from the tenants it had been given to, and give it to others, who would produce its fruit. Fruit strikes me as a powerful metaphor, because fruit is observable, and undeniable, and nutritious and sustaining. People can taste it. People can live from it. Also, fruit happens naturally, but to reach the fullness of its potential, it requires cultivation, and so a vineyard is a *natural human system.*

Fruit also tells an undeniable story.

If people don't find sustenance from it, then it isn't fruit.

If it kills and harms, then it isn't fruit.

And Yeshua Ben Yosef said that if people don't do the work and pay the costs, then the means of producing fruit will at some point be taken away, and given to a people who will produce the fruit—and I remember that right before *that*, he had announced that the moment had already come; that the means of fruit had *already* been taken away from those who claimed to cultivate it but refused to do the work, even though they said the expected and proper things, and those means had been given to the people who were doing the work of cultivating it, even though they don't say the expected and proper things.

The purpose of a vineyard is to produce fruit.

So what's done with an unused vineyard? Yeshua's answer: It's taken away from those to whom it has been given, and given to the people who will produce the fruit.

Hm. Now, that's a good idea.

Go do that.

Take the vineyard away from Christians—from *us* Christians. Give it to people who will produce the fruit of reparation by doing the work of repair.

I'm serious.

I promise this isn't a pulpit call.

Do it *without* becoming Christians.

Take the vineyard of reparation and redemption that we white conservative Evangelical Christians claim as our exclusive property, which most of us aren't even using, and start producing its fruit. Or maybe it would be more accurate to say: Demonstrate the spirit by enacting the part of the church's story we white American Christians refuse to enact. Redeem the story we white American Christians have scorned even as we flatter ourselves in the telling of it. Redeem the spirit we white American Christians claim is for the world but which we hoard for ourselves.

I want to be very clear what I'm proposing here. I'm *not* asking you to become Christians. I'm *not* asking you to take on Christian doctrine or practices or beliefs. I'm *not* asking you to join a Christian church. In fact, if you don't belong to a Christian church, don't do that. If you are a Christian, stay with your church if it helps, but perhaps consider whether staying in such an organization would be the most effective way to cultivate reparation's fruit.

You may be an atheist. If you are, please *stay* an atheist—an atheist that does the realigning work of reparation and redemption. You know what that is? That's an unused spirit of redemption being taken away from a people that claim it as their sole property, and giving to the atheists, who will produce its fruit; and the same with the drag queens and the sex workers and the trans and non-binary people, who will produce its fruit, and the undocumented immigrants and political refugees, who will produce its fruit, and the prisoners, who will produce its fruit, and the Black Lives Matter activists, who will produce its fruit, and the local community organizers of mutual aid funds and bail bond funds, who will produce its fruit, whether they are Christian or not.

You may belong to other religions. Please, *stay* that way. As long as you are doing the realigning work of reparation and redemption which I am sure you can find within your tradition, you will be taking a spirit of redemption away from people who seek to possess the idea of redemption as their sole property—though they refuse to produce its fruit when it threatens their exceptionalism, their blamelessness, or their supremacy. Take it wherever you find it—even from the Christian tradition, if you happen to still find it there. Take redemption away from those who refuse to do redemption's work, which is reparation, and produce redemption's fruit.

We don't need to form some new institution to defend. Stay where you are. Enter the spirit of an expansive, open, diverse, and vital movement that was never the exclusive property of Christians anyway, a movement that would be worth joining, if only it existed, guided by a spirit that is worth celebrating and defending, everywhere it already exists.

If enough people do that, then before you know it, such a movement would exist, and we might not even need a religion we'd call *Christianity* anymore. For people who worship a man who died so that the world could live, letting Christianity die so that the world might have abundant life might seem like a very *Christian* goal. Paying natural costs of repair might actually redeem Christianity from what it's become—although, speaking as a Christian, I am not sure that "Christianity" is what we should be working for.

Changing the atmosphere is what we should want.

Entering the spirit of reparation is what we ought to be after.

The spirit is the thing.

◆ ◆ ◆

We've been talking about the redemption of Christianity, but again that's just because for me it's the nearest thing at hand. We could be talking about the redemption of many things. We could talk about redemption for the United States of America—a country that claims to be founded on principles of life, liberty, and the pursuit of happiness; a country that claims to provide liberty and justice for all; a country that actually was founded on supremacy and genocide and slavery. For such a country to become what it claims to be in its founding documents and its present-day propaganda, it would first have to become aware of what it is, then be convicted of the need to change, and willing to confess that need publicly, and able to realign itself away from what it is and toward its finest ideals, and then actually to do the work of the journey.

Let's talk about another prophet—an American one.

Martin Luther King Jr. comes up frequently these days. He was a Christian, which is something I think *we* Christians can be proud of, if *we* are willing to enter the same spirit he entered. King was very much in the tradition of Rabbi Yeshua Ben Yosef, in that he too opposed his own religious power structure, and the dominant economic, political, and military superpower of his day. And he managed to oppose both at the same time, by focusing on where the two intersected and supported one another. He did it pretty directly sometimes, and wickedly subversively other times, and frequently he used stories to totally reframe dominant existing patterns of belief. He gave a famous speech about a prophetic dream he had, of a country where those things had been made true—which is the popular and much-repeated part of the speech. The main theme of the speech was about all the ways the dream had *not* yet been made true, and the unsustainability of the injustice that still held sway in the country, and the inevitability of strife and unrest until justice arrived, and the need to do the work of repair—which is the less popular, and less-often repeated, part of the speech. King's speech ended like this:

> *And this will be the day—this will be the day when all*
> *of God's children will be able to sing with new meaning:*
> My country 'tis of thee, sweet land of liberty, of thee I sing.
> Land where my fathers died, land of the Pilgrim's pride,
> From every mountainside, let freedom ring!
> *And if America is to be a great nation, this must*
> *become true.*
> *And when this happens, and when we allow freedom to*
> *ring, when we let it ring from every village and every*
> *hamlet, from every state and every city, we will be able to*
> *speed up that day when all of God's children, black men*
> *and white men, Jews and Gentiles, Protestants and*
> *Catholics, will be able to join hands and sing in the*
> *words of the old Negro spiritual:*
> Free at last! Free at last!
> Thank God Almighty, we are free at last!

Wow. Coming from somebody who most of white America considered at the time to be a lawbreaking rabble-rousing anti-American socialist, that sounds downright patriotic.

Wait. Am I asking you to be *patriots?* Not exactly.

But . . . maybe?

Maybe let's be patriots of a country that doesn't exist yet; A country where all those fine aspirations have been cultivated until they are, at last, and for the first time, actually true, in a way that is undeniable because the fruit of it is all around, sustaining everyone without any question of *deserve*. And then let's enter a spirit that is willing to do the work to make it so, and not finish until that country is the country we see all around us. Maybe we can redeem our broken institutions and our broken nation, on behalf of everyone—even those blameless very fine people who are violently aligned against redemption and repair.

You know what that would be? That would be taking patriotism away from the white supremacists, and giving it to the people who will produce its fruit.

A lot of very fine people would have it that King only gave one popular part of one well-known speech, but he gave many others. The last of them is known as the Mountaintop Speech, and it was delivered in Memphis in solidarity with striking workers there. In it, King spoke of the work of repair that was needed and the unsustainability of any land that refused to do that work, and he spoke of the inevitable strife that would attend that unsustainability. He talked about going to the mountaintop, which evoked the Bible—a story from what Christians call the Old Testament and Jewish people call the Torah—of Moses, the leader of Israel, a nation of freed slaves, watching from the mountain at the end of his life as the people he had led entered their land, a land he had brought them to but which he himself would not live to see.

I like that; the idea of ending a speech about necessary work with a picture of arriving at the top of a mountain. Climbing a mountain certainly takes a lot of intentional work, and provides an amazing view that would be unavailable to anyone who didn't do that work.

Yes, I like that picture very much.

Less than 24 hours later, King was dead; as dead as the dominant economic and military superpower of his age had hoped he would become. If you recall, that is how opposing the dominant economic and military superpower of your age tends to go.

And many very fine people rejoiced on that day of mourning.

King may have climbed to the mountaintop, but "white" America hadn't.

Those deemed "white" in America had been offered the realigning work of redemption, and they had, by and large, declined. They still do.

They? We.

We? I.

What's being said isn't that "white" America is irredeemably bad. What's being stated is an old truth, which is that white America has proved remarkably unwilling to do any of the work of redemption, because it would cost us not only our money, but our exceptionalism, our blamelessness, our position as the chosen elect. The reaction of white America whenever this truth is spoken aloud suggests it is an ongoing unwillingness.

Or, let's put it this way: "White" America seems very happy to claim they live in Martin Luther King Jr.'s dream. It seems totally unwilling to climb his mountain.

But I think we can begin to enter King's spirit, if we set our compass for the mountaintop, and if we start to climb.

So let's take the United States away from those who scorn all its finest ambitions and ideals, and be the kind of people who will produce its fruit. In doing so, we'll redeem our broken natural human system, not just for those who deserve it, but for those who don't.

We're talking about white America. We could be talking about straight America, or cis-het America, or able-bodied America, male America, Christian America. We don't even have to be talking about *America*. We could be talking about many places, and many things.

Whose redemption did you think we were working for? Our own?

I don't know. Seems to me as if redemption isn't a prize to be won, but a gift that's given, carrying a price that needs to be paid, maybe a high one, by many of us, including ourselves.

I think we need to be willing to work in the vineyard. I think we need to climb the mountain. I think we need to do the work of redemption without expectation of receiving redemption in return, and let reparation's fruit be its own reward. We may as well. It's only once we've done so that we will truly be able to receive redemption anyway, even if somebody tried to give it to us, for the simple reason that blamelessness can't accept the premise that it needs redemption. Maybe if what we want is forgiveness, we need to stop forgiving ourselves and do something redemptive, so that other people who we have wronged can someday, and for the first time, have a bit of room to forgive us instead, should they choose to do so.

What do we do?

We do the work of redemption, so we have that gift to give.

We pay the price of redemption. If we do, we might even someday receive it ourselves.

All that's needed to start is willingness.

Go and find your willingness. I hope to go with you. If you don't see me, look behind you; I've always been a little slower than average. I may be lagging.

Do the realigning work of redemption. We'll know the cost when we start to pay. Set your compass and follow it to the top of mountain. I think we'll know when we've arrived.

◆ ◆ ◆

Imagine the view.

Tell stories that move the frame.
Align with new ideas and very old ones.
Change the atmosphere.
Release your blamelessness, embrace endless improvement.
Release supremacy, embrace solidarity.
Stop being Very Fine People.
Become what you are instead—which is art.
Redeem what brokenness you can, and receive
redemption as a gift.

Change your spirit, and change your alignment,
and then watch the atmosphere change

and then the world.

The compass shows the path.
The spirit is the thing.
May we fix every street.

ACKNOWLEDGEMENTS

THIS BOOK would not exist without the subscribers to my weekly newsletter, The Reframe; those who support my work by engaging with it—by writing words of challenge and encouragement, by sharing it, and most of all by reading it. I'd like to offer my particular thanks to the Founding Members, who keep the lights on and amaze me with their generosity:

A Lorelei Verthandi; Alan Jacobs; Ali Rayl; Allison Roberts (Upgrade); Alyssa Fechner; Amy Dee; Amy Hamilton; Amy Kelpe; Andrew Eastman; Andrew Hickey; Andrew Snelling; Andy Myers; Andy Oury; Andy Roth; Annie Mims; Annmarie Nye; Anup Patel; Becky; Ben Niemann; Bern Smith; Blake Turner; Bohdy Hedgcock; Brad and Susan Seaman; Brett Thomas; Brian and Donna Ackley; Bryan Ault; Cameron Booth; Carlos Ors; Carolyn Collins; Carolyn Corrigan; Chris D'Amore; Chris Godfrey; Chris Gumprich; Chris Slaughter; Christine M. Garretson-Persans; Christopher Harlow; chrome agnomen; Chuck Miller; Colleen Kennedy; Colm Buckley; Corin Buchanan-Howland; Cory Haggart; Cris Jones Linden; Dan Griffen; Dan Stoza; Dana Zipkin; Daniel Goldner; Darius Archer; Dave

Broske; David Bloom; David Brown; David Gerbosi; Debbie Goldsmith; Denise Loving; Desmond Daly; Dion McCarthy; Eileen Lindburg; Elaine Hines; Elaine Hines; Elizabeth Haste; Elizabeth Williamson; eMBlues; Emma Bartholomew; Eric Bolten; Eric Lanke; Eric Meling; Farah Houston; Franmina Nicollier; Friederike Wunschik; Glenn Raucher; Greg Mahaffey; Harold Smith; Heath McKenny; Howard A. Rodman; J. William Nicholson; Jackie Walton; James Hanford; Jana Branch; Jason and Rachel Aylsworth ; Jason Kohut; Jason Martens; Jeff Faucher; Jennifer Risty; Jim; Jim Kenny; Joe Callan; Joe Stapleton; Joe Walsh; John Berman; John Kerpan; John Manning; John Saunders; Jon Callas; Jon Miller; Josh Fraimow; Juli Bergman; Justin Kaufman; Jutta Topp; K Benavente; Karen Shaak; Kathryn Murphy; Kathy Schoback; Keith James; Kelly McGinnity; Ken Wheaton; Kenneth Maiuri; Kevin Leahy; Kevin Martin; Kevin O'Halloran; Kevin W. Harp; Kynan Barker; L Charap; Laura Maynard; Lauren Shepherd; Lisa Drewing; Mara Schmerfeld; Marc Arenberg; Maria Poulos; Mark Peterson; Mary Spock (who caught a typo just in time); Maryn Cobain; Matt A.; Matt Farrah; Matthew Goolsby; Matthew J Stollak; Meej Jupin; Melissa Morman; Michael Massaro; Michael Mock; Michael S. Dow; Michael Woehl; Michelle Carboneau; Miguel de Icaza; Mike Cabral; Mike Dalessio; Mike Tocci; Misha Ellison; Molly Mitchell; Monica McJunkin; Nate Dick; Nick Bauer; Noah Lang; Paul Belliveau; Pete Bledsoe; Peter Moore; Phil Ellis; Ramona Mirlea; Randall Bosetti; Ray Hatfield; Rebecca Tortell; Rena Brady; Rev. Dr. Ne0n Fleshbiscuit, CSG, ULC; Richard Jansen; Robert Ogner; Roderick Axley Jr.; Roni Sutton; Ross Clatterbuck; Roy Pardee; S.B. Yandel; Sandy Daigler; Sarah Parker; Scott Gordon; Steve Burns; Steve Lewis; Stone Jones; Stormy McKnight; Susan Milankov; Susan Tulino; Suzanne Offerman; Teresa Marx; The Honorable Simon T. Vesper, Esq.; Thomas J. Schlagel; Tina Hatch; Tom Brookes; Tom Chappell; Tom Marshall; Tony DeLano; Tony Ercolano; Tony Yannarell;

Trish Braidt; Troy and Beth Frizzell; Tucker Lieberman; Victoria Caplan; Vincent Catanzaro; W.P. Fleischmann; Wil Wheaton; Will Dollinger; Yani Yancey; Zul Jamal, and a handful of anonymous benefactors: This one's for all of you, and I owe you all a beverage of your choice when I see you out there in the world.

When I started writing the earliest versions of these essays I published them on the Google blogging platform Blogger, which would tell you how long I've been at it even if you didn't pay attention to the dates in the headers. Anyway, as soon as I started putting them up, there was this fellow who would come pester me about all the typos, except he managed to do it in a funny way, not a pester-y way. He's been copy editing all these essays since for free, allowing me to make the online versions considerably cleaner than the initial emails, and he did such a good job in my opinion that I thought it best for him to copy edit this book, which he did. Josh Fraimow, you're the (meticulous) man.

Marina Drukman designed *The Revisionaries* for Melville House, and she did such an amazing job that I couldn't think of a single reason to not keep a good thing going for this book. As you can see, I chose very wisely. Thank you Marina for your professionalism and your breathtaking skill.

For early and ongoing support, reactions, and creative advice, I thank Ben Colmery, Tom Marshall, Juanito & Karen Moore, Brad Willis, Emily Vietor, and dozens or hundreds or maybe even millions of people I fear I'm forgetting to whom I now give permission to hate me forever.

I'd like to thank the multiverse for being fun to think about, and for probably existing.

And to my wonderful family, you make it worth it all and you make it all possible.

I love you.

-A.R. MOXON, Grand Rapids, MI
-2024

www.ingramcontent.com/pod-product-compliance
Lightning Source LLC
Chambersburg PA
CBHW030349130626
46549CB00004B/1419